THEOLOGY IN EXODUS

THEOLOGY IN EXODUS

Biblical Theology in the Form of a Commentary

DONALD E. GOWAN

Westminster John Knox Press
Louisville, Kentucky

Book Design by Drew Stevens

Cover design by Bill Green

First edition

Published by Westminster John Knox Press
Louisville, Kentucky

This book is printed on acid-free paper that meets the American National Standards Institute Z39.48 standard. ♾

PRINTED IN THE UNITED STATES OF AMERICA

94 95 96 97 98 99 00 01 02 03 — 10 9 8 7 6 5 4 3 2 1

Library of Congress Cataloging-in-Publication Data

Gowan, Donald E., 1929– .
   Theology in Exodus : biblical theology in the form of a commentary
/ Donald E. Gowan. — 1st ed.
        p.   cm.
   Includes bibliographical references and index.
   ISBN 0-664-22057-6 (alk. paper)
   1. Bible. O.T. Exodus—Theology. 2. Bible. O.T. Exodus—
Commentaries. I. Title.
BS1245.2.G69   1994
222'.1207—dc20   94-8689

For Darlene
"Love never ends"
(1 Corinthians 13:8)

CONTENTS

BIBLICAL THEOLOGY IN THE FORM OF COMMENTARY

Although this book is organized like a commentary, following the text of Exodus from beginning to end, it is both more and less than what one would expect from a traditional commentary. On the one hand, it does not attempt to answer all the questions one usually expects to find discussed in a commentary, for its focus is sharply defined. It asks only one question of Exodus: What does this book say about God? On the other hand, it does far more than any other commentary on or exposition of Exodus has done. It takes each of the major affirmations about God found in Exodus and traces it through the rest of scripture and on into the theologies of Judaism and Christianity. Because this represents two new things, a new way of expounding a biblical book and a new way of writing theology, each term in the title of this introduction, "Biblical Theology in the Form of Commentary," needs to be explained more fully.

Theology

The word "theology" has been used in the title of this book in its most literal sense, that is, "discourse about God." Hence the title "Theology *in* Exodus," rather than "Theology *of* Exodus," for this is a study of what Exodus teaches about God, not an exposition of the whole message of the book. It intends to be a contribution to the presently burgeoning work in biblical theology by trying out a new way of approaching the subject.

It may be asked what remains to be said about God in the Old Testament that has not already been summarized in approximately the same way in a half-dozen or more recent theologies. Working through Exodus, asking the single question, "What does this book say about God?" has done two new things for me. First, it has revealed insights and emphases that the earlier theologies have tended to overlook, as the introductory remarks for many of the chapters of this book will note. Second, it has emphasized how different the Bible's language about God is from the language of a modern theology. Following the text of Exodus closely, as I have done, helps one escape the traditional Christian method of distilling the Bible's information into a list of "attributes," a kind of "essence of divinity," and keeps one nearer to Israel's sense of the presence of the one they called the Living God.

Biblical Theology

The present debate over biblical theology involves such fundamental questions as whether there is such a thing; if there is, how it is to be distinguished from the history of religion on the one hand, and from systematic theology on the other; and how it should be organized. Many methodological articles and monographs have been written on these questions, but it has been discouraging to observe that few of those who have argued for a method have actually produced a theology.[1] I have made no effort to produce a full-scale biblical theology here, and there is a real question as to whether that could be done, in this way. My undertaking is limited to those aspects of the Old Testament's teaching about God found in the book of Exodus.

This book claims to be theology-writing rather than exegesis, since the reflection that begins with texts in Exodus does not end there or satisfy itself with references to related passages (as standard commentaries do), but includes extended discussion of what all of scripture says on the subject, and then moves to consideration of its contemporary significance.[2] It attempts to take seriously the variety of voices in scripture, aiming not to harmonize by taking a synchronic approach. It intends to be different from the history-of-tradition method represented by Gerhard von Rad's theology, however, in that its aim is not to describe a series of different theologies but rather to trace the changes that have occurred within a line of continuity that extends through both Testaments, with emphasis on the continuity. The book claims to be "theology," then, in that it involves a critical evaluation of scripture and tradition in the light of contemporary needs, and it claims to be "biblical," in that it is the text of one book of scripture, rather than any philosophical or external theological system that provides its starting point and its structure.[3]

Theology in Exodus

Most readers will probably not be surprised at the choice of the book of Exodus as the basis for this kind of study, since it is the source of two of the most prominent themes of the Old Testament: the exodus from Egypt and the making of the covenant at Mount Sinai. For the aims of this book, however, more important than either exodus or covenant in themselves are a series of "classic texts" concerning the nature of God. The best known of these are the revelation of the divine name in 3:13–16 and 6:2–3, the first three of the Ten Commandments, and the divine self-affirmation in 34:6–7, but there are many others, as this book will demonstrate. Exodus contains a broad spectrum of texts concerning God, many of them formulated in striking ways, making this book superior to most other parts of the Old Testament for our purposes. Similar studies could be based on certain other books, such as the Psalter or Deuteronomy, because of the breadth of their language about God, but few other books will serve as an opening into the rest of the Old Testament as adequately as Exodus does.

Theology in the Form of Commentary

Recently several writers have advocated a return of some sort to the style of interpretation practiced in the precritical period, that is, a straightforward reading of the text as it is, on the assumption that it has something to say rather directly to the believing community. This does not represent a fundamentalist attempt to deny the validity of historical criticism, and the commentary that follows is very different from those written in the precritical period, but it is an effort to recover something of what earlier interpreters did in drawing theology from consideration of a consecutive sequence of texts. It will take what the present text says as the basis for reflection on that subject as it appears throughout scripture, and beyond. It will not attempt to be systematic, neither finding or introducing an organizing principle, nor claiming a unifying center. Perhaps a "biblical system" may be found some day, but this is preliminary to that, and it may be as far as one can go under the rubric "biblical theology." The search for unity will appear only in the effort to understand all of the theologies to be found in scripture as parts of the revelation of the one God.

The need to pay attention to context is one of the basic principles of exegetical method, and this book will broaden the sense of context in a way that has been suggested by several authors who have written on method, but which has not been put into practice to any extent. Brevard Childs's advocacy of theology in a canonical context insists that revelation in the Old Testament cannot be abstracted from the form of witness that the historical community of Israel gave it; that is, interpretation must take seriously the final form in which the biblical books appear.[4] My work with Exodus will follow Childs's approach more closely than I might be inclined to do in dealing with other books or other subjects, for although I believe the book is composed from earlier sources, I have not found that they represent significantly different views of God. On this topic the book may be read as a whole without paying much attention to sources.

There are larger contexts than the final form of the book, however. Harry Gamble has described the next level of context clearly: "In the nature of the case canonization entails a recontextualization of the documents incorporated into the canon. . . . Since the canon has such results, it cannot be regarded only as an anthology; in its actual effects the canon is a hermeneutical medium which by its very nature influences the understanding of its contents."[5] Because the sources in Exodus were compiled into a book that was accepted and continually reaffirmed as definitive for the life of the believing community, and because Exodus became a part of a collection of books that had the same force for them, the entire canon becomes a necessary part of the context in which Exodus must be interpreted. For each passage in Exodus, then, there may be relevant context in Psalms or Isaiah or Joshua. Their relative dates, to the extent we can determine them, may be important, as my comments on history of tradition later in this introduction will suggest. But as Hartmut Gese says of his history-of-tradition approach, "This later experience, . . . does not suppress and replace the earlier experience, and this is in accord with the growing structure of history in which the past affects the present and the future is embryonically existent in the present. . . . As little as history is a mere succession of incidents, so little is tradition a mere juxtaposition of materials. A totality must necessarily emerge."[6] Gese speaks of the canon of the Old and New Testaments only, however (advocating the inclusion of the Apocrypha in the canon), but the real context is larger than that. It must include the rest of the intertestamental literature, for that provides the actual historical connection between the Testaments. The believing community did not finally include those books in their canon, but the books reveal to us more of what was happening to the faith and life of the community that accepted the canon.[7]

Furthermore, the context must include (as far as is humanly possible) the continuation of the tradition through the history of the synagogue and the church. Contemporary Christians and Jews do not get their faith in a direct and unmediated fashion from scripture, but from the testimony of believing communities as to what scripture means (at least by means of translation, if nothing else, if we think of people in non-Christian environments who have been brought to faith simply by their individual reading of the Bible). So this "commentary" will attempt to put into practice hermeneutics as defined by Dietrich Ritschl:

> Hermeneutics—in the narrow sense—is the art of interpreting objects and above all texts from the recent and more distant past; here the centre of attention is the search for a meaning for the interpreter that comes down over time. Investigation of the formation of tradition is an important ingredient in this procedure, since it takes for granted that the significant content from the past has only been handed down because it has been able to establish itself in ever new traditions.[8]

Each section of the book will thus have three parts: (a) what the book of Exodus says about God, (b) what comparable materials elsewhere in scripture (and the Intertestamental literature) add to this aspect, and (c) a brief tracing of the theme through postbiblical history as a basis for reflections on the contemporary significance of this aspect of God (brief because of limitations of space and the author's expertise). This is an approach to the interpretation of scripture which I advocated earlier in *Reclaiming the Old Testament for the Christian Pulpit* and developed without much explanation for its rationale in *Eschatology in the Old Testament*. It is something that other authors seem to have called for, but have not done. Its rationale will be developed further in the next section.

Biblical Theology as History of Tradition

The "history of tradition" approach used here has some similarity to that advocated by Hartmut Gese but differs from it in significant ways.[9] I use the term not to refer to the efforts to discover the prebiblical traditions used by the authors of scripture, as in the works of Noth and von Rad (and partly in Gese), but to refer to the continuing influence of the Bible's major themes—the ways they were reaffirmed and modified by generation after generation of believers. Such a historical study may thus begin with any biblical book, and will look for predecessors to its thought in scripture, if any, and then will trace the reappearance of its ideas through the rest of the Bible. It is a fully historical treatment of the material, in contrast to the strictly canonical approach advocated by Brevard Childs,[10] in that it does not omit the history of the believing community's faith contained in the extracanonical Jewish literature produced during the Intertestamental period. But it does not seek to canonize some of that literature, as Gese does. Eventually the believing community recognized that these were not the documents that constituted them as the people of God, when the canonical principle developed, but the literature is evidence for us of the various ways the community responded to the testimony of scripture during a critical part of their history. The perennial problem of the relationship between the Testaments becomes far less severe when one recognizes that historically there is no gap to be bridged somehow.[11] There was continuity in the life of the believing community and continuity in the development of their faith, even though there was enough variety that some scholars now speak of "Judaisms" during this period.

What has been said so far about history of tradition may seem to make it a purely descriptive work, not "theology," and Gese's proposal has been criticized on those grounds. The continuation of the history from the New Testament period to the present represents my effort to bridge the "what it meant/what it means" dichotomy that has plagued the enterprise labeled biblical theology since that term began to be used.[12] I agree with other scholars who claim that carrying out the purely descriptive task of explaining what people of antiquity believed is actually history of religions or history of interpretation, and cannot appropriately be called theology.[13] The descriptive task must be done, with a critical evaluation of all the material available to us from the past, of course, but I maintain, with others, that the perspective from which the work is done and the aim for which it is done can make of it a theological enterprise, that is, one leading to conclusions the truth of which ought to be taken seriously by the believing community.[14]

"The Christian church is (among other things) a community which agrees to read certain writings on the assumption that the God of whom these speak is that same reality that it knows in the experience of its members."[15] This nicely expresses the position from which I begin to work. I do not claim some impossible objectivity; I acknowledge my bias. I work consciously as a Christian for whose life the Bible is definitive (using a more neutral word than the overworked terms "authoritative" or "normative"), and my work is addressed first to the church, although I hope to be fair enough in my treatment of the Old Testament that much of it can be meaningful to Jews as well, since we both worship the God of Abraham. This study thus begins with the recognition that the God I know is the God spoken of in the Old and New Testaments.[16] My life experiences correspond to the life experiences of those in scripture (in contrast, for example, to the life experiences of Gautama Buddha), so I begin with a hermeneutic of trust, not of suspicion.

> The Bible comes alive where authentic religious experience coincides with texts which are themselves testimony to an authentic religious experience: the past strikes a spark off the present or the present off the past, and both are illuminated. The chief reason why religious texts from the past are so difficult to understand is that modern man has become uncertain of his own religious experience. He mistrusts it, and expects his encounter with the past to supply information which he will obtain only if he is truly concerned with religious questions and experiences. Interpreters who lived before the modern age could still project their own experiences naively and unself-consciously on to texts from the past, in turn deriving such experiences from the texts. Modern interpreters, on the other hand, investigate the texts by means of historical criticism and then find that such interpretation does not lead to religious experience. The consequence is often trouble for their religious life in the present. They become technicians of tradition. Only one conclusion can be drawn from the problem as we have described it: it is important to be aware of one's present religious experiences and to articulate the degree of independence which they have from the past; or, to put it in academic terms, it is important to work out a theory of religion so that it then becomes possible to enter into a dialogue with the past which is no longer expected to meet the impossible demand that the present should be legitimated by the past. Such a dialogue would be open to the past. And again and again we shall have the pleasant surprise of finding unexpected allies there, indeed a better way of expressing things, which can give a new stimulus to religious life in the present.[17]

Having claimed for myself some such coincidence of religious experiences as Gerd Theissen speaks of, I must now try to show that I am doing something more than that naive projection onto the texts that was characteristic of precritical interpretation (although they were not all as naive as Theissen suggests).

As medieval art reminds us (depicting biblical characters dressed in contemporary fashion and living in European towns), precritical readings of the Bible typically modernized it, assuming the culture reflected in scripture was nearly identical to their own. Historical-critical scholarship recognized the difference, and we are still struggling to find an acceptable answer to the question whether that has made the words of scripture no longer meaningful for us.[18] What several scholars now speak of as a history-of-tradition approach offers a way, not of jumping the gulf, but of discovering that there has always been a way through. This approach acknowledges all the differences, but recognizes them as changes within the same world of discourse—that is, the continuing confession of faith of the people of God. It thus emphasizes the continuity within history itself, rather than discreteness. Medieval Europe, for example, was not a static world in and of itself, unconnected with the first century or with the twentieth century, and the strangeness to us of the language of the first century C.E. or the tenth century B.C.E. can largely be accounted for by tracing the history of how and why it has changed.

> [T]he distinction between what the text *meant* and what it *means* . . . quite arbitrarily concentrates on discontinuity in interpretation, without even considering the fact that when a text has been interpreted every day for over nineteen centuries, there will be important continuity of interpretation. It is not as though we have come upon the biblical texts as relics from an utterly alien culture, with no connection whatever to our lives.[19]

On these grounds, then, the "meaning" of Exodus for one who worships the God of Exodus cannot be fully discerned apart from what all those communities who believed in the God of Exodus have discerned in it. This includes the Jewish community, but some may be surprised to note that a biblical theology written from an acknowledged Christian point of view includes not only extracanonical material from the Intertestamental period (Pseudepigrapha and Qumran literature), but also traces the Old Testament themes into rabbinic Judaism. I include Judaism in this work, acknowledging that I have no expertise in rabbinics, for two reasons: Even a sketchy reading of the material shows that many Christian misunderstandings of Judaism need to be corrected, and whenever a Christian has an opportunity to do that, it should be done. But rabbinic Judaism, which developed in its own way the Old Testament themes developed sometimes differently and sometimes in much the same way in Christianity, has something valuable to contribute to Christian self-understanding. I see this not in the unfortunate ways of the past, when the self-understanding led to a sense of superiority, but as the taking on of a conversation partner who leads us to ever-new discoveries of the richness of the Old Testament sources on which we both depend.[20]

More must be said about scripture as testimony. Whose voice, or voices, do we hear? Various answers have been given. For precritical interpreters it was either the Holy Spirit alone, or the great, inspired leaders—prophets and apostles. For liberalism, the great leaders were retained but without divine inspiration; their voices were those of religious geniuses. Form-critical studies introduced the voice of the community, recognizing in scripture the evidence that much of the Bible was not the private production of individuals, but the reflection in writing of the experiences of groups. But the newer literary criticism has challenged that, claiming that we cannot get beyond the text either to a community or to the mind of a single author. The words themselves are the only voice we can hear, unless one accepts the views of reader-response criticism, in which one hears only one's own voice.

From what has already been said it will be clear that I agree with the insights of form-critical studies. One may attempt to take Exodus as a work of creative writing and read it as the voice of a single author, but there are good reasons to deny that is the single, correct reading, or even the best one. I understand the "author" of Exodus to be spokespersons for and to Israel, formulating one of its confessions of faith. So "voices" rather than a voice are to be heard. I speak of voices not to refer specifically to earlier sources, as in most of the discussions of the Pentateuch up until now, but with reference to the various contexts, mentioned earlier, within which Exodus took shape and to which it later gave words. There are various "contemporaneities": voices from the time prior to Israel's existence in Canaan (muffled for the most part), voices from other parts of the Old Testament which are probably earlier than the final form of Exodus, and voices influenced by and reaffirming the message of the book of Exodus as we now know it.

As to the pre-Canaan period, there is no way of getting at "what really happened" at Sinai—did Moses hear a humanlike voice or what? But this will not lead us to the premature conclusion that statements saying God spoke to Moses are "fiction," for we were not there and we do not really know. We cannot approach any of this directly, as if we had immediate access to the meaning of these words—the assumption shared by precritical and historical-critical interpreters. Our access is not only via Hebrew studies and via data concerning ancient customs, and so on, but via the communities that "authorized" speaking of God in this way. Gerhard Ebeling did not overstate it when he wrote: "Church history is that which lies between us and the revelation of God in Jesus Christ. . . . Through it alone has the witness of Jesus Christ come down to us."[21] The claim of the book of Exodus to know a great deal about God, even at times what God saw, heard, remembered, and knew, is more than the claim of a single individual or document; rather, it represents the chorus of voices of those who found that the claims of this document correspond to reality as they knew it, to their own experiences of who God is and what God does. We cannot know how the author came to these insights (apart from a theory of divine dictation), but we do know that these insights were validated by one generation after another—and that was certainly not because someone once said it, but because they discovered their truth for themselves. It is this ongoing testimony, then, of the many generations of believers who physically connect us with the time of the Bible's origin, that provides for me a basis for speaking of the truth of scripture, the basis for an understanding of what it may mean in our time to speak of the inspiration of scripture. And on these grounds, what I have called history of tradition is the method that must be used as one asks of any text, What should this mean to me?

After developing this approach I found an article by Wilfred Cantwell Smith (a historian of religion, not a biblical scholar) in which he describes the kind of course on the Bible he would like to see taught if he were chairman of a department of religion. His concluding remarks are of considerable interest, in the light of what has just been said:

> Most illuminating of all to elucidate, would be how the Bible has served, and for many still serves, spiritually: What is the meaning of the (historical) fact that through it men have found commitment, liberation, transcendence? . . . The final sector of our course would deal with the question, What does the Church, what does modern man, do with the Bible now? . . . This part of the course could be descriptive and analytic, a study of the process of what has recently been and is now happening. It could also, in the case of some scholars and teachers of a possibly creative quality, be constructive.[22]

Smith is aware of a problem, however, and his last sentence is, "Yet where could I find a man with doctoral training equipping him in this field?"

It is worse than that. Not only do doctoral programs not equip people to teach this way; the very magnitude of this project raises questions about whether one person can hope to be competent at it, since it includes studies of both Testaments, history of doctrine, rabbinic Judaism, and contemporary theology. I make no claim to equal competency in all these areas. In this book I have attempted to be thorough in my studies of Old Testament and Intertestamental material and to be intelligently selective in dealing with the New Testament. For the period beyond the New Testament, I have offered some examples of the persistence and development of each of the major themes, through the history of Judaism and Christianity. The aim has been not to offer an authoritative reading of these materials, but to stimulate thought about the continuing relevance of the themes, to make it clearer how the Old Testament has instructed believers throughout the centuries, and to encourage more thorough studies by others.

I am aware of the dangers that lie ahead of one who enters a field not his own. Yet I am convinced that excuse is no longer acceptable, if the present gulf that separates biblical scholarship from theology in general is to be bridged.[23] In the past, biblical scholars were content to do their exegetical work, leaving it to theologians and ethicists to decide how to use it. There is unanimous agreement that that has not worked, and the lack of communication between biblical scholarship and theology is being lamented in some cases, accepted in others. At present, some efforts are being made to bridge that gap, by initiating new conversations among the fields. This is another such effort. I believe the initial effort needs to be made by biblical scholars, acknowledging the risks involved in moving into other fields, but willing to undertake those risks with the conviction that only by broadening our spheres of interest in this way can we hope to see Bible and theology once again engaged in fruitful conversation.

When Exodus is read with the question of the role of God in mind, it is seen to have another plot, running beneath the surface story of Israel's bondage, deliverance, and journey through the wilderness to Sinai, and that is the "plot" of this book. God's story begins with the mystery of his absence (Exodus 1—2), as the author of the book tells how the king of Egypt put the Israelites to forced labor and attempted genocide, without telling us of any role God played in those events. Then, God introduces himself and his plans in such an impressive way that I must devote four chapters of this book to what is said about him in Exodus 3—4. After that extended introduction, God sets to work, and in Exodus 5—15 his work is entirely destructive, directed against the Egyptians. Once the Israelites are safe in the wilderness, however, beginning in Ex. 15:22, we see an entirely different side of God. He cares for all his people's needs and establishes an exclusive, intimate relationship with them at Mount Sinai. The people, who have been essentially passive throughout the story up to that point, are required to obey him, however, and they cannot do that (Exodus 32). The story of the golden calf and its aftermath bring Exodus to its theological conclusion and make possible the rest of the Old Testament, for chapters 32—34 take up the perennial question of how it can be possible for a relationship to continue between God and a rebellious people. Only the revelation that God is compassionate and gracious (34:6–7) enables the rest of Israel's story to happen.

CHAPTER 1

THE ABSENCE OF GOD

Exodus 1—2

Why, O Lord, do you stand far off?
Why do you hide yourself in times of trouble?
—Psalm 10:1

As the book of Exodus begins, the descendants of Jacob had been living in Egypt for almost four hundred years (Ex. 12:40). The great vizier Joseph, who had saved Egypt and his family from famine, had been dead a long time, and the present government had no memory of his accomplishments that might prompt them to look with favor on those members of his family who lived in their midst. They were just aliens with an alarmingly high birth rate. The pharaoh impressed them into labor in his building projects at Pithom and Rameses, but if we are to make sense of the first chapter of Exodus, it seems there were more Israelites than could be used, and the population continued to increase, leading Pharaoh to adopt some severe birth control measures. He attempted to enlist the midwives who served the Hebrew women, ordering them to kill the male children who were born, but they deceived him, and when it became evident that wasn't working, he ordered all Egyptians to take it upon themselves to kill male Hebrew children. In the midst of that suffering, the mother and sister of Moses hid him away in a basket floating on the river, and when the pharaoh's daughter found him and took him as an adopted son, it seemed possible that the Hebrews might have gained a champion in a position of power. Moses' first effort to do something on behalf of his people led to the loss of that power, however. He killed an Egyptian he found beating one of the Hebrews, but killing made him no hero in his people's eyes and put his own life in danger from Egyptian justice, so he fled into the desert, where he married into the family of Jethro, the priest of Midian.

In the midst of this suffering and missed opportunity, God has done nothing, as the story is told. In two chapters (prior to Ex. 2:23–25), God has been mentioned only once, and that is in connection with the piety of the midwives, who "feared

God" and let the male children live, so God rewarded them. The author acknowledges that popular piety had not died out, as it never does, and tells us that the activities of these good people helped the Israelites at that time, but in no way does the author claim God himself intervened in this time of suffering. The pharaoh, the midwives, Moses' mother and sister, the pharaoh's daughter, and Moses himself are living by their wits, as these stories are told. Is it coincidence that the author omitted telling us what God was doing in all this, or are we justified in thinking that the absence of God is in fact a part of the story?

THE ABSENCE OF GOD IN EXODUS 1—2

On Their Own: Exodus 1:1–2:22

Many commentators have noted that God is rather conspicuously absent from the first two chapters of Exodus, but no one has seen fit to make much of that. John Durham says of Ex. 2:1–10 that "The omission of any reference to God in these verses is surely intentional," and Terence Fretheim insists that "The nonmention of God must be given its full weight," but Durham does not pursue the subject at all, and it may be questioned whether Fretheim has followed his own advice.[1] Earlier in the same paragraph he has said, "the divine activity is unobtrusive," and this is really in keeping with traditional interpretations, which have deduced God's providential activity even where the authors of scripture have said nothing about it.[2] How much can legitimately be made of the silence concerning God in these two chapters? The answer takes two forms: evidence of contrast between the way these stories are told and the way the neighboring materials in the Pentateuch are written, and the author's explicit and powerful statement in 2:23–25 that now something different is about to happen.

Chapters 1—2 of Exodus are not the only place in the Pentateuch where the direct participation of God in human affairs is not described. The Joseph cycle in Genesis 37—50 has been contrasted with the earlier chapters of Genesis in this way, for throughout the life of Joseph no direct, divine intervention is recorded. The author of that cycle makes it very clear to the reader, however, that God has been at work behind the scenes, as he puts into Joseph's mouth the true interpretation of what has been happening: "God sent me before you to preserve for you a remnant on earth, and to keep alive for you many survivors. So it was not you who sent me here, but God" (Gen. 45:7–8a). And the characters in the story mention God frequently, in every chapter except 37 and 47. We have been aware, then, of their relationship with God throughout the story. Turning the page, to Exodus 1—2, we find nothing said by the author or the author's characters about what God is doing. That is in striking contrast to the rest of the book of Exodus, in which God is depicted as the dominant figure. God is mentioned in every chapter except 37—38 (which simply describe in detail the appurtenances of the tabernacle), and furthermore, God speaks in every other chapter except 18 and 35—39. This God who is so active and so vocal in the rest of the book is silent and is a nonparticipant in the events of chapters 1—2. Consider how these stories might have been told, if the usual style of Old Testament narrative had been followed. Pharaoh might have oppressed the Israelites because God hardened his heart, as he does later in Exodus. An angel of the Lord might have instructed the midwives, as the angel intervened in Hagar's distress in the wilderness (Gen. 21:17–19). We might have been given an annunciation of the birth of Moses, as was done for Samson (Judges 13) and Samuel (1 Samuel 1—2). God might have instructed Moses' mother and sister in a dream, as he told Jacob how to increase his flock in Gen. 31:10–16, and might even have appeared in the same way to Pharaoh's daughter, as he did to Abimelech, the Philistine king, in Gen. 20:3–7. We could have been told God's opinion of Moses' murder of the Egyptian, saving commentators much discussion of that ethical issue. Finally, Moses' sojourn in the desert might have been described in a way similiar to that used for Jacob's sojourn with Laban (Genesis 29—31) or David's flight from the wrath of Saul (1 Samuel 19—30: God is mentioned 107 times). But instead we hear only of human decisions and of their completely normal results.

This a rare piece of literature for the Old Testament, and as we shall see later, 2:23–25 show it is not coincidental. The absence of God here is deliberate, and thus it should be the object of some theological reflection, in the light of what is said elsewhere about God's "hiddenness." Exodus 1—2 are as "secular" as ancient literature could be. After the list of Jacob's twelve sons in 1:1–6, we could substitute for "Israel" the name of any of the peoples that sojourned in Egypt, and no other change would need to be made. This could be literature from any ancient Near Eastern culture. These are stories about human beings motivated by fear (Pharaoh, Moses' mother), affection for babies (the midwives, Moses' mother and sister, Pharaoh's daughter), and concern for the oppressed (Moses). In each case they do what they can, and whether there is any divine plan behind those human decisions remains unrevealed to us.

This is an accurate reflection of many occasions in human history when it is not clear, even to those most sensitive to God's work in our midst, what God may be doing, if anything. The author of Exodus does not reflect on that, as other authors do, he just portrays it, but when we reread these chapters in the light of the way he makes his transition to God's intervention in history (2:23–25), we see that reflection on our part is called for. Perhaps the book of Esther is the closest parallel in the Old Testament to these chapters, for in Esther God is never mentioned and people live by their wits and their courage. Deliverance for the Jews comes about because Esther is strong enough to follow her uncle Mordecai's instructions (chap. 4) and because of a couple of fortunate coincidences (chap. 7). The Esther-like form of storytelling is only preliminary to the main event in Exodus 1—2, however, for deliverance does not come ultimately from human efforts, but from divine intervention, as the next chapter will show.

What was God doing, during those years the Israelites suffered under the Egyptians? That is the question asked at every occasion when an individual or a community suffers without any good explanation for it, and unfortunately it is not a question we can answer. The remainder of this chapter will be concerned with the various ways people have found to deal with it. Here in Exodus the author offers no answer, but deals with it in the way typical of the Old Testament, speaking of the time when God's silence is broken, insisting the times of God's absence do not last forever. In the meantime, people do what they can, and in this story that is none too good. Moses, who might have helped, has failed and is out in the desert somewhere, a fugitive from justice. In the meantime, then, the people groan under their burdens, and cry out. But for Old Testament writers, "outcry" is not so negative as it would sound elsewhere. The only response to outcry may be silence for a time, as it is here, but these writers tell of a God who insists, "when they cry out to me, I will surely hear their cry" (Ex. 22:23).[3]

God Remembers: Exodus 2:23–25

The silence of God and about God is then deliberately and dramatically broken by 2:23–25, transitional verses, but profoundly important theologically, both in their choice of words and in their location.

> After a long time the king of Egypt died. The Israelites groaned under their slavery, and cried out. Out of the slavery their cry for help rose up to God. God heard their groaning, and God remembered his covenant with Abraham, Isaac, and Jacob. God looked upon the Israelites, and God took notice of them.

The transition from an account of purely human activities to a story dominated by the acts and words of God begins with the death of the king of Egypt under whom Moses had grown up. This is mentioned in order to suggest that now it might be safe for him to return to Egypt, as 4:19 confirms. The Hebrew expression introducing that sentence, "And it happened in those many days that the king of Egypt died . . . ," is unusual, but in the light of what follows we can see it intends to emphasize a long period of unmitigated suffering for the Israelite people. The New English Bible paraphrases it most effectively: "Years passed. . . ." During those years the Israelites groaned because of their bondage, and they cried out. Now, our author places what can be seen and heard on earth side by side with what is happening to God in heaven. There are key words here which will answer two essential questions, as we deal with this theologically: How could the author know what was happening to God? And, did the author really intend us to read what has preceded as a portrayal of a time when, to all human perceptions, God seemed to be absent?

James Plastaras was the first, and almost the only, commentator to notice the relationship between 2:23–25 and the psalms of lament,[4] but a good deal more can be made of that than he did, especially now, in the light of Samuel Balentine's work on the theme of the hiddenness of God.[5] The verbs that occur in these verses of Exodus frequently occur together in the psalms of lament and in conjunction with terms concerning the inaccessibility of God. In response to the Israelites' outcry (za'aq, shawa'), God is said to have *heard* their groaning, *remembered* his covenant, *seen* the Israelites, and *known* (without an object in the Hebrew text; RSV supplies "their condition"; NRSV uses "took notice of them"). Here the author makes the remarkable claim to know what is going on in heaven, to be able to tell us what is happening with God internally. The Old Testament uses a limited number of verbs of this type with God as subject, and we shall have to deal with most of them in studying the language about God that appears in Exodus. Old Testament authors were much more reticent than later theologians have been to claim they know something about "God in himself." But here we find a cluster of such words, and as Plastaras noted, they tell us that God responded to the laments of Israel in bondage as Israel at worship over the centuries found God responded to their prayers for help.

Examples from the Psalter will show how these words go together in the language of prayer. Psalm 31 is a lament of the individual which, in its concluding praise section, refers to the psalmist's outcry, which has been heard by the Lord, in the context of the sense of separation from God: "I had said in my alarm, 'I am driven from your sight.' But you heard my supplications when I cried out to you for help" (v. 22). In this one verse, the outcry (shawa'), the feeling of God's hiddenness, and God's hearing and seeing are all present. Earlier, "see" and "know" appear, also in an expression of praise: "you have seen my affliction; you have taken heed of (NRSV; Hebrew: "known") my adversities" (v. 7). Each of the key terms from Ex. 2:23–25, except "remember," occurs in this psalm, plus the idea of God's absence. A thanksgiving of the individual provides the missing term. Psalm 9 negates one of the most frequently used words for God's absence, "forsake" ('azav): "you, O LORD, have not forsaken those who trust in you" (v. 10). It brings together the cry and God's remembering: "For he who avenges blood is mindful of [NRSV; Hebrew: "remembers"] them; he does not forget the cry of the afflicted" (v. 12), Then it calls upon God to see the psalmist's continuing distress: "Be gracious to me, O Lord. See what I suffer from those who hate me" (v. 13). The same combinations of words may be found in Pss. 10:1, 11–12, 14, 17; 34:6, 15, 17f.

We can now see an answer to the question how the author of Exodus could dare to claim he knew what God heard, remembered, saw, and knew at this time in history. In their psalms the Israelites typically expressed their sense of a need for salvation (from enemies or illness) in terms of their being abandoned by God, of his hiding of himself, of not seeing or hearing them. When their prayers were answered, it was thus natural to say that God had heard them, had seen and known their distress, and had remembered. "Remember," when used with God as subject, typically means that God has determined to initiate action.[6] This is the language worshipers used to express their sense of the absence or presence of

God, and the author of Exodus has chosen that language to emphasize the emptiness of the lives of the Israelites before Moses' second effort to do something on their behalf.

We cannot know what sort of faith in God the actual slaves who escaped from Egypt, later to become Israel, may have had. The debates over their identity and number, and whether they knew the divine name Yahweh are inconclusive and will always remain so, barring some sensational manuscript discovery in Egypt. But if we read the story as it is told and compare it with other low points in Israel's history as the Old Testament tells it, we may conclude that this has been depicted as the darkest moment of all. Later they will find themselves in Canaan dominated by the Philistines (1 Sam. 4:1–7:2), with the ark of the covenant captured and the hereditary priesthood of the family of Eli brought to an end together with the destruction of the sanctuary at Shiloh (Jer. 7:12; Ps. 78:60). In spite of the efforts of Samuel and Saul their prospects for independence do not look good, but even then they have the memory of the exodus, of God's guidance through the terrors of the wilderness, and of their success in gaining access to the land to look back on. Much later everything will be lost with the fall of Jerusalem in 587 B.C.E.—land, king, temple, and hope (Psalm 137; Ezek. 37:11)—but they had at that time a long history and inspired persons in their midst to interpret their present disaster in terms of God's activity in their history (e.g., Ezek. 20:1–31), and to find in it a knowledge of the true nature of God which could lead to a new message of hope. At both of these low points a reason for their suffering is provided by scripture; it is the result of their abandonment of God, not his abandonment of them. But that is not true for Exodus 1—2.

These slaves have no history, and they are not accused of having done anything wrong.[7] As the story is told, they know about the God of Abraham, Isaac, and Jacob, and about his promises, but at this point there is nothing they could point to as evidence that God keeps his promises. Unlike all later occasions when God seems to be silent and doing nothing, on this occasion there was nothing to remember. They could not say, "But in the past God did help us, in spite of our dire distress." Neither would they have had any basis for saying, "Actually, we deserve this." These chapters thus represent the worst of those periods of suffering when even people of faith struggle to find any indication that there may be a God who actually does anything in the world, and so our reflections on them already call to mind various modern efforts at a "death-of-God" theology. Those who do not necessarily deny the existence of God, but claim we can think only of a God who does not do anything, are close to the problem as these parts of the Old Testament saw it. As the cartoonist Walt Kelley had Pogo say, "God is not dead; he is just unemployed."

These chapters are thus the first significant occurrence of the theme of the absence of God in the Bible, but it will reappear in various forms. We shall next trace it through the Old Testament, then more briefly look for evidence of its persistence (and modification) in the histories of Judaism and Christianity, and finally will return to Exodus 1—2 and the psalms of lament for a dialogue between them and contemporary theology.

THE ABSENCE OF GOD
ELSEWHERE IN THE OLD TESTAMENT

The theme of the presence of God has been a popular subject in Old Testament studies, but its opposite has been generally neglected. Samuel Terrien acknowledged it to be an essential part of a study of presence in his theology, *The Elusive Presence*,[8] but as James Crenshaw said of his book, "The adjective in the title hardly functions, so great is the sense of cultic presence."[9] A very useful recent study by Samuel Balentine supersedes earlier works, even though it focuses on one expression, the hiding of God's face, and treats other expressions for the motif of God's hiddenness more briefly.[10] Since about one-half of the occurrences of the hiding of God's face are found in the laments, and since we have found that the laments are the appropriate background to Exodus 1—2, it will be appropriate to begin with them and to use some of Balentine's conclusions.

The psalms of lament express the sense of God's absence more frequently and more bluntly than any other parts of the Old Testament. They use a wide range of vocabulary to express it, revealing how serious a problem it could be for the ancient Israelite. God is said to hide his face, or hide himself; he is accused of being distant, of forsaking his people, of sleeping, of forgetting, of remaining silent, of not hearing or seeing, and of having cast them off. Some of that vocabulary has already been apparent in the psalms quoted in the preceding section. In order now to take the laments in their own right, several other psalms will be cited, asking of them: What brought about such feelings? How did the psalmists account for God's apparent absence? And how did they deal with it?

The absence of God is expressed in powerful words at the beginning of Psalm 22:

> My God, my God, why have you forsaken ['*azav*] me?
>> Why are you so far [*rahoq*] from helping me,
>>> from the words of my groaning?
> O my God, I cry by day, but you do not answer;
>> and by night, but find no rest. (vv. 1–2)

The feeling that God is far away is expressed here and twice more in the psalm (vv. 11, 19); distant because he does not help, so he is accused of having forsaken the psalmist and of not listening to his prayers. Those feelings have been brought on by the mockery of people around him (vv. 6–8); that they are enemies who now gloat over him because of the serious illness that has befallen him is indicated by vv. 16–18. Not a friend is mentioned, and the loneliness he feels includes the sense of having been deserted by God as well. Furthermore, the symptoms of his illness have left him in the kind of severe pain that also produces extreme loneliness (vv. 14–15).[11] The two problems displayed in Psalm 22 reappear throughout the laments. Sickness and, to a much greater extent, the presence of enemies and the absence of friends have created intense feelings of loneliness which are not (in the complaint portions of the psalms) alleviated by any sense of a spiritual presence giving them strength to face their troubles.

Enemies are the problem throughout Psalms 35, 44, and 89, which speak of silence and distance (Ps. 35:22), of sleep (Pss. 35:23; 44:23), of rejection (Pss. 44:9; 89:38f.), of hiding (Ps. 44:24), and of forgetting (Ps. 44:24), with a plea for remembrance (Ps. 89:47, 50). Wrath occurs in parallel with hiding in Ps. 89:46, reminding us that the distance of which Israel complains is not spatial. The absence of God they are lamenting is neither nonexistence nor physical distance, but the absence of his blessings, and the absence of blessing is called his wrath. This helps to account for the apparent contradiction of language when God is sometimes asked to turn away, because the physical sense of his wrath has become too overpowering (e.g., Ps. 51:9; Job 7:19; 10:20). The "Where?" question also is concerned with effective power rather than spatial presence. Enemies use it in its mocking form, "Where is your God?" to ask why God isn't helping you (Pss. 42:3, 10; 79:10; 115:2; Joel 2:17; Micah 7:10). When asked by a believer, it may be a complaint over God's lack of activity (Judg. 6:13; Isa. 63:11, 15; Mal. 2:17) or may be a virtual demand that God act, as when Elisha strikes the water with Elijah's mantle, saying, "Where is the LORD, the God of Elijah?" (2 Kings 2:14).

The answer to our question as to how they accounted for God's apparent absence is that they did not. We have found no explanations in the psalms just surveyed, and an important contribution of Balentine's work on the hiddenness of God is the observation that there is a significant difference between the use of this concept in the Psalter and in the prophetic books.[12] The prophets have rationalized it and regularly associate it with judgment for Israel's sins. We shall look at one example of that shortly. But in the psalms of lament God's absence is not explained as the result of sin; rather the psalmists express their bewilderment at his silence, and in Psalm 44 the community protests that they have certainly done nothing to deserve this (vv. 17–21). This is another aspect of the continuity between Exodus 1—2 and the laments, for no attempt is ever made in Exodus to explain why God delayed doing anything about the sufferings of his people in Egypt.

How did they deal with such depressing feelings? The psalms make it clear that they didn't give up. This violent language is in fact evidence of the strength of faith of people who were convinced God had both the power and the will to help them, and who will not give that up in spite of evidence to the contrary. So they deal with it by crying out, even when it seems they are crying into emptiness. And they waited (Pss. 37:7; 39:7; 40:1). And the waiting was possible because of the hope engendered by remembering that God had graciously worked with power in the past (e.g., Pss. 22:3–5, 9–10; 44:1–8). We might sum it up by saying that insistence, persistence, and memory enabled them to prevail even without the answer to the question, Why?

It will suffice for our purposes to look at one example of the prophets' use of the theme of divine absence, for they are consistent in explaining it as a problem that can be dealt with by repenting and living in obedience to God. It is very likely true that the sense of God's absence may be the result of being conscious of one's sinfulness, but that is actually a quite different problem from the one we have begun to trace through the history of the Jewish and Christian faiths. In Isa. 63:7–65:16 there appears a kind of "prophetic liturgy," so called because various speakers appear and several genres are used, but there is a certain continuity suggesting the parts are to be read as a unit. This passage has been chosen because the lament genre is used and the vocabulary of absence appears in a significant way.

The liturgy begins with a hymn of praise (63:7–9), as is true of more than one lament in the Psalter (cf. Pss. 44, 89). God's "presence" (literally, "face"), which will play an important role later in this book (Exodus 32—34), is explicitly mentioned as that which saved them in the past (v. 9). Soon the complaints about God's absence in the present will be set over against that, but first something else from the past is introduced—Israel's penchant for rebellion against their God, and God's guidance for them in spite of that (vv. 10–14). Part of that memory is the lamenting question they had once asked, and which they will soon repeat,

> Where is the one who brought them up out of the sea with the shepherds of his
>   flock?
> Where is the one who put within them his holy spirit,
>   who caused his glorious arm to march at the right hand of Moses,
>   who divided the waters before them to make for himself an everlasting name,
>   who led them through the depths? (Isa. 63:11b–13)

The prayer that follows (63:15–64:12) is strongly reminiscent of the psalms of lament, but differs from them in one way by its strong awareness of their sinfulness. Let us note the references to God's absence:

> Look down from heaven and see,
>   from your holy and glorious habitation.
> Where are your zeal and your might?
>   The yearning of your heart and your compassion?
>   They are withheld from me. (63:15)
> We have long been like those whom you do not rule,
>   like those not called by your name. (63:19)
> . . . you have hidden your face from us,
>   and have delivered us into the hand of our iniquity. (64:7b)
>
> After all this, will you restrain yourself, O LORD?
>   Will you keep silent, and punish us so severely? (64:12)

At one point, or perhaps two,[13] they seem to blame their sinfulness on God, as if it was his absence that made them go astray:

> Why, O LORD, do you make us stray from your ways
>   and harden our heart, so that we do not fear you? (63:17)

But the final section of the liturgy is an oracle from God, setting things straight. He has been present all the time, and his apparent absence has been entirely the fault of the people:

> I was ready to be sought out by those who did not ask,
>   to be found by those who did not seek me.
> I said, "Here I am, here I am,"
>   to a nation that did not call on my name.
> I held out my hands all day long to a rebellious people,
>   who walk in a way that is not good,
>   following their own devices. (65:1–2)
> . . . when I called you did not answer,
>   when I spoke, you did not listen. (65:12b)

Third Isaiah here follows the lead of the earlier prophets, whose chief concern was to justify the approaching end of the relationship between Israel and Yahweh in terms of Israel's perennial failure to live up to the conditions of the covenant.[14] This postexilic passage differs from the earlier prophets, who condemned Israel wholesale, in that it now sorts out the righteous from the wicked in Judaism of the restoration period (vv. 13–15). Presumably, then, it ought to be only the wicked who would suffer from the absence of God, but by the time of Third Isaiah other authors had learned better.

Among the various theories as to the main theme that runs through Job is that of the presence—perhaps better, accessibility—of God. Martin Buber has titled a chapter on Job "A God Who Hides His Face."[15] Samuel Terrien claims it is the theology of presence, not the problem of suffering, which lies at the core of the book.[16] André Neher, in *The Exile of the Word,* speaks of the lengthy silence of God, from chapter 3 through chapter 37.[17] Job himself vacillates on this topic, as on every other except his own integrity. In chapter 7 he speaks of God's hostile presence, from which he longs to be freed: "Am I the Sea, or the Dragon, that you set a guard over me?" (v. 12). "Let me alone, for my days are a breath" (v. 16). "Will you not look away from me for a while, let me alone until I swallow my spittle?" (v. 19). These are examples of the intense language of pain that dominates the first cycle of speeches. They also come from the only part of the book in which Job addresses God directly (with a few exceptions), as Dale Patrick has shown.[18] In the first cycle Job is acutely aware of God's presence as an enemy, but he can pray to his enemy, addressing him fifty times as "you." After that, he speaks to God four times in the first speech of the second cycle (16:7, 8; 17:3, 4) and four times in his final speech (30:20–23). Otherwise he talks about God. So not only does God not speak throughout these many chapters, he is not even addressed from chapter 18 through chapter 29 (nor in Elihu's speeches, chaps. 32—37).

Although Job is in terror before the God who seems to be torturing him so, he knows he has no other hope but that same God, and so we find him longing to take the risk of a face-to-face confrontation. Chapters 13 and 23 express that most vigorously: "See, he will kill me; I have no hope; but I will defend my ways to his face" (13:15). But he knows he is not strong enough for that and must ask for mercy: "[W]ithdraw your hand far from me, and do not let dread of you terrify me. Then call, and I will answer; or let me speak, and you reply to me" (vv. 21–22). But there is no reply, and from this point on the question whether humans have any access to God remains in the air: "Why do you hide your face, and count me as your enemy?" (v. 24). And later, now in the third person: "Oh, that I knew where I might find him, that I might come even to his dwelling!" (23:3). If that could be possible, Job would lay his case before God, and he is sure he would be acquitted (23:4–7). But,

> [i]f I go forward, he is not there;
>   or backward, I cannot perceive him;
> on the left he hides, and I cannot behold him;
>   I turn to the right but I cannot see him.
> . . . he stands alone and who can dissuade him? (vv. 8–9, 13a)

At times Job seriously doubts whether God is tending to his business anymore: "Why are times not kept by the Almighty, and why do those who know him never see his days?" (24:1). "From the city the dying groan, and the throat of the wounded cries for help; yet God pays no attention to their prayer" (24:12). But with his last words he returns to his conviction that God is just; there is a hitch in the system somewhere so that Job cannot get access to the one who would surely vindicate him: "Oh, that I had one to hear me! (Here is my signature! let the Almighty answer me!) . . . I would give him an account of all my steps; like a prince I would approach him" (31:35a, 37).

Job's request is never granted; he cannot approach God, but God instead comes and speaks to him, with his own agenda (chapters 38—41). That seems to make all the difference to Job, according to the way most interpreters read his response: "I had heard of you by the hearing of the ear, but now my eye sees you" (42:5). One of the advantages of taking access to God as a major theme of the book is that this issue is resolved at the end; Job did not find God, but God found him. Two other much-discussed themes are not resolved; God refuses to discuss suffering or his justice, but that in fact leaves the book of Job in the same ballpark with Exodus 1—2 and the psalms of lament. No rationalization of the absence of God is ever attempted, but the issue is resolved by the coming of the God who saves. The same pattern of lament over suffering, which is not explained, but which is resolved in a more than satisfactory way by the coming of the saving God, may be found in Habakkuk, including a reference to hiddenness in 1:2: "[H]ow long shall I cry for help, and you will not listen?"

At first Ecclesiastes might seem to have developed this theme in another way,[19] but he does not in fact speak of an absent God, in the Old Testament sense of a God who does not act. The commonest verbs used with God as subject are *natan,* "give," and *'asah,* "do, make."[20] Koheleth speaks of a God who is active in the world (e.g., 2:24–26; 3:10, 13–15; 5:19–20); his problem is that he does not understand what it all means: "That which is, is far off, and deep, very deep; who can find it out?" (7:24; cf. 3:10–11; 7:14; 8:16–17; 11:5). He reveals no longing for God's nearer presence; unlike the typical Israelite, he does not see that as a solution to his problem. "Guard your steps when you go to the house of God; to draw near to listen is better than the sacrifice offered by fools; for they do not know how to keep from doing evil. Never be rash with your mouth, nor let your heart be quick to utter a word before God, for God is in heaven, and you upon earth; therefore let your words be few" (5:1–2).

A prophetic passage that does not lament the absence of God, but expresses wonder at it, seems an appropriate way to conclude our survey of this motif in the Old Testament. In Isa. 45:9–17 the God who hides himself is praised as the deliverer,[21] and this seems to involve the same line of thought we have found in those passages that struggled with the hiddenness of God and found a resolution to their problem only with the coming of the saving God. As God refused to subject himself to Job's inquisition, so also God here rebukes those who want to know too much: "Will you question me about my children, or command me concerning the work of my hands?" (v. 11b). Then comes the promise of restoration from exile; in Second Isaiah's time it had not yet been fulfilled, but for the prophet the promise is good enough. It leads to his marveling words of praise, which from this time on in Israel's history become possible because of trust that even while God remains hidden, his promise is reliable:

> Truly, you are a God who hides himself,
>   O God of Israel, the Savior.
> All of them are put to shame and confounded,
>   the makers of idols go in confusion together.
> But Israel is saved by the LORD with everlasting salvation;
>   you shall not be put to shame or confounded
>   to all eternity. (Isa. 45:15–17)

REPRESSION OF THE THEME OF ABSENCE
IN JUDAISM AND CHRISTIANITY

In the preceding section we considered some exemplary passages in which vocabulary dealing with God's inaccessibility appeared prominently. The motif is certainly most obvious in the Psalter, with some reference to it occurring in thirty-three psalms, but it also appears in twenty-two other books. Many of the references intend to negate the idea, for example, "I will not fail you or forsake you" (Josh. 1:5), but the idea has to be present before anyone thinks it necessary to negate it. Thus Balentine concludes *The Hidden God* with the assertion that the experience of God's hiddenness, like God's presence, "is an integral part of Israelite faith. Both experiences derive from the nature of God himself."[22] Our reflections on the nonappearance of God in Exodus 1—2 have led us to other parts of the Old Testament in which Israel has struggled to understand those times in life when God *does not* seem to be available with any help. That is the problem which Auschwitz has brought to the contemporary consciousness in the most painful way possible, but we are beginning to see that it is not a completely new problem. The concluding section of this chapter will attempt to suggest some possibilities for new dialogue between the Old Testament and post-Auschwitz humanity.

Judaism

During the Second Temple period the Jews continued to suffer as minority groups living within pagan cultures, and suffering as a part of daily life is reflected in the literature of the so-called Intertestamental period (the Apocrypha, Pseudepigrapha, and Qumran writings). It is almost certain that the psalms of lament were prayed with real feeling many times, but a survey of the materials written during this period shows that the Jews did not continue to produce literature like the laments or the book of Job.[23] They underwent the first attempt to wipe out the Jewish faith entirely, during the persecution ordered by Antiochus IV Epiphanes in 167–165 B.C.E., but that suffering is not described with language suggesting God's absence. Several laments over the desolation of Jerusalem are included in 1 Maccabees (1:24–28, 36–40; 2:7–13; 3:45, 50–53), but the vocabulary we have been studying is missing. The emphasis in 1 and 2 Maccabees is on the heroic acts of those Jews who remain constant in their faith, especially in the martyr stories of 2 Maccabees 6 and 7. Since these people were being held up as examples of faithfulness, it would have been inappropriate to suggest that God was not involved, even though they were in fact not being rescued. God is present in their testimony, and their faith in his eventual vindication of them is said to have kept them from wavering (2 Macc. 6:26–31; 7:6, 9, 14, 16, etc.).

Other books, of the "edifying story" type (Tobit, Judith, 3 and 4 Maccabees), hold up examples of faithful living amid tribulation and seem to find it inappropriate to suggest that those heroes might have been maintaining their integrity without the conscious sense of God's help (as Job did). Prayers for help continue to use the same appeals that appear in the Psalter (e.g., Bar. 2:16f.), but omit any strong expressions of the sense of God's absence. The *Psalms of Solomon,* written during the first century B.C.E., at about the time the Romans

occupied Palestine, use the language of the laments at times. "He hath turned
away his face from pitying them" (2:8) is used as the prophets used the
expression, since: "According to their sins hath He done unto them" (2:7).[24] The
appeal "Make not Thy dwelling afar from us, O God; Lest they assail us that hate
us without cause" (7:1) is not based on a sense of absence, for later the same psalm
says, "While Thy name dwelleth in our mist, we shall find mercy; and the nations
shall not prevail against us" (7:5).

Have the Jews lost the bold frankness of their ancestors? Is it too great a threat
to piety to admit that under certain circumstances they have no sense that God is
in their midst, doing anything? Or have they acquired some new insights into the
way God works, enabling them to speak of their troubles and the ways they deal
with them in different language? One of the common misevaluations of Second
Temple Judaism by Christian scholars is the claim that the sense of God's
presence was greatly diminished by the priestly-dominated, legalistic form of
their religion, and the claim that transcendence ruled their concept of God.
However, if the wisdom literature is at all representative of the thinking of
Judaism in general, there is evidence to the contrary. For the sages of this period,
all of God's attributes were present in divine wisdom, and wisdom was praised for
being immediately present to them in daily life. Before Antiochus's persecution,
Sirach (ca. 190 B.C.E.) has divine wisdom say that God instructed her (wisdom) to
make her dwelling in Jerusalem (Sirach 24:1–12), and then identifies wisdom
with "the book of the covenant of the Most High God, the law that Moses
commanded us as an inheritance for the congregations of Jacob" (24:23). Like the
other sages, Sirach is wise enough to acknowledge that some of what God does
remains a mystery to human beings, but that is no cause for anxiety (39:16–35),
and he assures his readers that help from the Lord is unfailing for those who wait
and trust (chapter 2).

After the anguish brought upon Judaism by the persecutions of Antiochus
Epiphanes, another sage, the author of Wisdom of Solomon, took suffering more
seriously than Sirach did, but did not lament over it the way earlier writers did.
Appealing to the belief in resurrection that had begun to prevail in Judaism, he
says:

> But the souls of the righteous are in the hand of God,
>   and no torment will ever touch them.
> In the eyes of the foolish they seemed to have died,
>   and their departure was thought to be a disaster,
>   and their going from us to be their destruction;
>   but they are at peace. (3:1–3)

Not even death can separate one from God, the witness of the martyrs has insisted,
and in life one has uninterrupted access to God through divine wisdom:

> In every generation she passes into holy souls
>   and makes them friends of God, and prophets;

for God loves nothing so much as the person
     who lives with wisdom. (7:27b–28; cf. 7:22–8:1)

It must be concluded that the literature produced by the Jews during these troubled
times shows a strong sense of the continual presence of God with the faithful.

The Jews faced another catastrophe with the fall of Jerusalem to the Romans in
70 C.E., followed by Hadrian's construction of a new city with a pagan temple
after 135 C.E. This time they heard no prophets declaring that this was God's
judgment upon them for their sins, so there is ambiguity in their reactions to it.
Two apocalyptic works written between the two wars with Rome (2 Esdras and *2
Baruch*) raised the question why God should have given victory to the more
wicked of the two, Israel and Rome. Each book purports to be dealing with the fall
of Jerusalem to the Babylonians in 587 B.C.E., but it is clear the real problem is 70
C.E. In the former book Ezra raises questions similar to those Habakkuk had asked
long ago: "Are the deeds of those who inhabit Babylon [i.e., Rome] any better? Is
that why it has gained dominion over Zion?" (2 Esd. 3:28–29). As he led up to this
challenge to God's justice, we encounter the one use of the Old Testament
language we have been tracing: "You made an everlasting covenant with him
[Abraham], and promised him that you would never forsake his descendants"
(3:15). The dialogue between Ezra and God leads to an eschatological solution of
the problem of justice, with the promise elaborated in detail that the day will come
when God will make it all right. In spite of the passion with which Ezra makes his
pleas, however, the vocabulary of forsakenness is not prominent, and it does not
appear at all in *2 Baruch.*

The ambiguity of the rabbis' response to the loss of the Temple, and even of
access to the city of Jerusalem, is revealed most clearly in the Talmud. Very
negative statements are countered by a lengthy section of affirmations:

> R. Eleazar also said: From the day on which the Temple was destroyed the gates of
> prayer have been closed, as it says, *Yea, when I cry and call for help He shutteth out
> my prayer.* [Lam. 3:8] But though the gates of prayer are closed, the gates of
> weeping are not closed, as it says, *Hear my prayer, O Lord, and give ear unto my
> cry; keep not silence at my tears.* [Ps. 39:12] . . . R. Eleazar also said: Since the day
> that the Temple was destroyed, a wall of iron has intervened between Israel and their
> Father in Heaven, as it says, *And take thou unto thee an iron griddle, and set it for a
> wall of iron between thee and the city.* [Ezek. 4:3][25]

Not since our work with the Old Testament have we found such extreme
statements about the absence of God. But the rabbis quickly set to work to
dismantle Eleazar's position, taking a truly challenging verse, Isa. 49:14, as their
text: "But Zion said, 'The LORD has forsaken me, my LORD has forgotten me.' "
They developed a parable based on the following verse, which concludes, "even
these may forget, yet I will not forget you." What does God forget, they asked?
Answer: the sin of the golden calf. What will not be forgotten is God's affirmation
at Sinai, "I am the LORD thy God."[26]

Similar exegetical work was done, in the Midrash to Lamentations, on a verse that expresses poignantly the sense of absence: "Why do you forget us for ever, why do you so long forsake us?" (Lam. 5:20). The section provides an example of the rabbinic technique for interpreting scripture:

> "Why do you forget us for ever, why do you so long forsake us:" Said R. Joshua b. Abin, "Four expressions were used by Jeremiah: rejecting, loathing, forgetting, forsaking. Rejecting and loathing: 'Have you utterly rejected Judah? Has your soul loathed Zion' (Jer. 14:19). And Moses answered, 'I will not reject them, or will I abhor them' (Lev. 26:44). Forgetting and forsaking: 'Why do you forget us for ever, why do you so long forsake us.' And Isaiah answered, 'Yes, these may forget, but I will not forget you' (Isa. 49:15)."[27]

It seems that in order for Judaism to survive amid all the sufferings inflicted upon it during the centuries following 70 C.E. some repression of the language of absence was necessary. For Jews as much as for Christians, affirmation of the saving presence of God was confirmed in experience often enough that it could be and must be reaffirmed in every generation, although they might use scripture's language of lamentation more readily than Christian worship did. The Passover Haggadah affirms the continuing presence in this way: "It was not one only who rose against us to annihilate us, but in every generation there are those who rise against us to annihilate us. But the Holy One, blessed be He, saves us from their hand."

The New Testament

The triumph of the resurrection of Christ and the continuing experience of his risen presence in the midst of the early Christian communities meant that language of forsakenness had no natural place in the New Testament. In the few places where words of this kind occur, they are always negated (John 8:29; 14:18; Rom. 11:1, 2; Heb. 6:10; 13:5). There is one occurrence that must be taken seriously, however, and that is Jesus' own use of the first words of Psalm 22: "My God, my God, why have you forsaken me?" (Matt. 27:46; Mark 15:34). It seems fair to say that for the writers of the New Testament, all the feelings of godforsakenness expressed by the writers of the Old Testament have been absorbed by Jesus on the cross. It is as if nothing more needs to be said about that, from their perspective. From our perspective, however, we must say more, for the Christian faith has not, in fact, completely done away with the sense of God's absence.

It has been hard for Christians to take literally those words from the cross. What could Jesus have meant by them? The temptation is to read the whole Passion story in terms of the resurrection and to claim Jesus knew in advance how it would all come out, so could calmly face the pain and humiliation and death. But he did not face it calmly. He went into Gethsemane "distressed and agitated"

(Mark 14:34, NRSV), saying, "I am deeply grieved, even to death." Some texts of Luke say, "In his anguish he prayed more earnestly, and his sweat became like great drops of blood falling down on the ground" (Luke 22:43–44; missing from codices Vaticanus and Alexandrinus). Matthew and Mark testify that he cried out with a loud voice as he died. As Jürgen Moltmann has emphasized, Jesus did not die "a fine death."[28] An even worse temptation, which must be quickly rejected, is to think that yes, Jesus went through all of this the way any human being would do, but that in his case, since he was divine, it was really a sort of demonstration— he could not really have felt abandoned by God. But that would be playing games with us. The church has rejected that as docetism.

The most frequently used way of alleviating the scandal of Jesus' apparent sense of having been rejected by God is to appeal to the fact that Psalm 22 ends with praise. It is said that Jesus may have recited the whole psalm on the cross and the evangelists cited only the first verse, or that even if Jesus said only that much, he knew it all, and those concluding verses would have been a comfort to him. But neither Matthew nor Mark offer any support for this. They leave us with the word "forsaken." And the saying was apparently too shocking for Luke and John to include in any form.

David H. C. Read has stated two other options in the form of a conundrum: "Was this Christ actually abandoned by God at this point?—a conception logically irreconcilable with the doctrine of the Trinity; or did He feel Himself to be so abandoned?—a conception scarcely less difficult to reconcile with orthodox Christianity?"[29] He reaches a conclusion close to the former statement, as do several contemporary theologians: "It would seem then that atonement could not be complete, the experience would be unfulfilled, unless He had also been where sin is 'when it is finished'—the death of the soul. This is hell—separation from God—and many have felt with Calvin that these words from the Cross are the best commentary on the profession of the Creed: 'He descended into hell.' "[30] Such a conclusion does affect our understanding of the doctrine of the Trinity. Karl Barth defined the deepest meaning of the incarnation with reference to the cry of dereliction:

> The incarnation, the taking of the *forma servi*, means not only God's becoming a creature, becoming a man—and how this is possible to God without an alteration of His being is not self-evident—but it means His giving Himself up to the contradiction of man against Him, His placing Himself under the judgment under which man has fallen in this contradiction, under the curse of death which rests upon Him. The meaning of the incarnation is plainly revealed in the question of Jesus on the cross: "My God, my God, why has thou forsaken me?"[31]

Moltmann's use of Jesus' cry from the cross shows how far a theologian may go in taking its implications seriously for a restatement of the doctrine of the Trinity, claiming that trinitarian language is necessary in order to deal with questions such as, "Who is God: the one who lets Jesus die or at the same time the

Jesus who dies?" His response: "The Son suffers and dies on the cross. The Father suffers with him, but not in the same way."[32] And later:

> [T]he doctrine of the Trinity is no longer an exorbitant and impractical speculation about God, but is nothing other than a shorter version of the passion narrative of Christ. . . . The form of the crucified Christ is the Trinity. In that case, what is salvation? Only if all disaster, forsakenness by God, absolute death, the infinite curse of damnation and sinking into nothingness is in God himself, is community with this God eternal salvation, infinite joy, indestructible election and divine life.[33]

This last sentence quoted from Moltmann points toward the conclusion that will be drawn here concerning Jesus' cry from the cross as the center of all our consideration of the absence of God. Let us return to a straightforward reading of the Passion narrative as the account of how a righteous man, Jesus, died with the feeling of being completely alone. The evangelists make it clear that was no fault of his, that he had done nothing to deserve it. Very early in Christian history those data from the Gospels led to the development of theories of atonement (which need not concern us here). Jesus' cry of dereliction was to be explained as the result of his assumption of the sins of all humanity, dying as an unforgiven sinner that others might be forgiven (cf. 2 Cor. 5:21 and Read's conclusion cited earlier). As if theories of atonement were not difficult enough, it then became necessary to struggle with the conviction that Jesus was fully divine, leading to the kinds of statements about incarnation and the Trinity quoted above. But these should not lead us to ignore the implications of Jesus' full identification of himself with other human beings (and not just with our sinfulness).

Martin Marty's book *A Cry of Absence* offers perhaps the best commentary of that sort on Ps. 22:1 as Jesus shouted it from the cross. We have been dealing all along with the truth that the absence of God may be felt for many reasons (or apparently none), and that sin is only one of them. Marty deals with pain, both physical and emotional, and that in fact brings us closest to Jesus' experience as the evangelists describe it. They talk about humiliation and bleeding and dying, not about atonement. Pain typically leads to outcry expressing one's intense feelings of loneliness—it did for Jesus. About this, Marty says:

> When I am henceforth lost in the wintry night, alone, I identify exactly with a cry already uttered: "O my god, I cry in the day-time but thou dost not answer, in the night I cry but get no respite" (22:2). The world in front of this text opens to me the possibility that by uttering the prayer, a prayer of aloneness, I am not only alone. Someone in whom I trust has shouted it out before, in worse circumstances. What is more, Jesus cried out because a pledge seemed to be broken, and that seemingly was turning to reality. *Because* it seemed so, it *was* being broken. He was not supposed to be abandoned, yet he was abandoned. "The cry of dereliction": under that term his shout enters the list of classic phrases. There are derelict ships and there was a derelict Son of God. . . . Those who trusted, even in abandonment, were not denied. The crucified victim was the *only* forsaken one, the true derelict. The rest of us die in

company, in *his* company. God certified his gift and his act and "raised him up." Never again is aloneness to be so stark for others.[34]

With those final words of Marty's we are getting a bit ahead of ourselves, to the promise "God is with us," but that will come soon, in Exodus 3. The church said that separation from God was finished, with the resurrection, for the risen Christ had promised, "And remember, I am with you always, to the end of the age" (Matt. 28:20). There seemed to be no place for "Why do you hide yourself?" in Christian worship, and it has not appeared. The Old Testament's language of absence has been repressed, but the experience did not disappear from the Christian life. In our sketchy survey of Christian history we shall shortly look at one place in which absence was acknowledged.

Christian Mysticism

It would be beyond my competence to attempt to trace all the occurrences of the motif of the absence of God in Christian writing throughout the centuries, but one striking form of that experience can and should be noted before turning to the modern era. It appears in the writings of the mystics and was given its classic description under the evocative title "The Dark Night of the Soul," by St. John of the Cross. Its unusual feature is that it is not the result of unwanted suffering inflicted by other human beings or by nature, nor does it just appear in the life of an ordinary person. The dark night of the soul is a regular part of the progress of those who undertake the discipline that they hope will lead them to ultimate unity with God. Evelyn Underhill explains it psychologically as an example of the law of reaction from stress.[35] The discipline accepted by those who have undertaken the life of a mystic is so intense and unremitting that eventually exhaustion sets in and the sense of the presence of God which had been cultivated is lost. It seems that "God, having shown Himself, has now deliberately withdrawn His Presence, never perhaps to manifest Himself again."[36]

St. John's treatise "The Dark Night" analyzes the experience in detail, speaking of two kinds of darkness, the sensory and the spiritual. Each of them eventually makes its contribution to the mystic's progress toward union with God, but they are terrible experiences to endure. The former purges the senses, the latter purges and denudes the spirit, for the aim of mysticism is the annihilation of selfhood, so as to do away with separation from God. So during the dark night, which for some has lasted months and years, God "leaves the intellect in darkness, the will in aridity, the memory in emptiness, and the affections in supreme affliction, bitterness, and anguish, by depriving the soul of the feeling and satisfaction it previously obtained from spiritual blessings. For this privation is one of the conditions required that the spiritual form, which is the union of love, may be introduced into the spirit and united with it."[37]

Underhill says, "only a blind reliance on past convictions saves them from unbelief."[38] In spite of the differences between this experience of absence and the others we have encountered, here is one element of continuity: the essential role played by memory during the times when there is no other support for faith. Nothing we have found before the literature of the mystics has spoken of the feeling of God's absence as anything of value; it has been something to endure, to triumph over, but as St. John described the dark night, and as others have chronicled their experiences, the way to mystical union with God must pass through that night. "And even though it humbles persons and reveals their miseries, it does so only to exalt them. And even though it impoverishes and empties them of all possessions and natural affection, it does so only that they may reach out divinely to the enjoyment of all earthly and heavenly things, with a general freedom of spirit in them all."[39]

Nietzsche's announcement of the death of God is generally noted as the marker that identifies the appearance of a new feeling of the absence of God, characteristic of secularism. We need not rehearse that whole story in this context, but in the next section we will consider some ways in which the old motif of absence is influencing contemporary theology.

SECULARISM AND THE ABSENCE OF GOD

When Nietzsche's madman announced in 1882 that "God is dead, we have killed him," Nietzsche provided for the twentieth century a slogan that has been variously used. For some theologians, the "death of God" is not used to refer to his absence (nonexistence) but is used instead to speak of the participation of God the Father in the death of Christ[40] and to mean that death was followed by resurrection. But others, both philosophers and theologians, mean that if there once was a God, there is no more—absence of the most thoroughgoing kind.

The rapid and revolutionary changes that occurred in scientific and historical research during the nineteenth and twentieth centuries have made radical changes in the thinking of not only philosophers and theologians but also ordinary people in the Western world. Efforts to explain everything past and present in rational ways led to the assumption that everything *could* be so explained, given time and cleverness enough. Thus miracles, long supposed to be clear evidence of God's activity in the world, came under the challenge of the theory that the laws of nature admit no exceptions. Once that was allowed, it did not take long to discover that God did not seem to be a necessary explanation for anything. For a time Deism provided a way to maintain belief in God as creator, but this was a God who had retired from involvement in the affairs of the world.

During the unparalleled advances in learning that took place in the nineteenth century, God seemed to fade away without a fight, as human beings took destiny into their own hands. Until World War I and the events that followed it, humans seemed at least potentially to be able to do a better job of it without the unnecessary, and indeed trammeling, belief in God. For those without faith, the absence of God seemed to be not a problem, as it had been in the past, but instead, freedom from the tyranny of dogma and hierarchy. Those who still believed were left on retreat, as they attempted to find persuasive evidence for the active presence of God in the world. They had to resort to the "God of the gaps," where science was concerned, or be satisfied with a solely personal God, the savior of their souls. Even that God was explained away as a "projection" by the positivists and psychologists.

This was a significantly new development in human history. Many people, since early history, had no doubt spent their entire lives without much concern whether there was a God or not, but now whole cultures took on that character. While for believers, the experience of God's apparent absence, inactivity, at times was still as distressing as ever, the move in the twentieth century has been toward a majority of the population for whom the reality of God's presence, activity, is not something ever to be taken seriously.[41] The apparent triumph of secularism in the Western world has had significant effects on what twentieth-century theologians have said about the absence of God.[42]

William Hamilton, one of the exponents of death-of-God theology, wrote, "It used to be possible to say: we cannot know God but He has made himself known to us, and at that point analogies from the world of personal relations would enter the scene and help us out." But he continued, "God is dead. We are not talking about the absence of the experience of God, but about the experience of the absence of God."[43] The "we" to whom Hamilton referred were theologians who intended somehow to continue to be Christians, with a "secular theology," for a world in which God did nothing but human beings could still do something. These were people who felt the absence of God, but who took it to be permanent, so that the problem and the possible solution became quite different from what we have been tracing through scripture and its consequent history. Death-of-God theology had a short history. For most who accepted its presuppositions, theology of any kind probably seemed dispensable, and its optimism about human potential was already out of date in the 1960s.

Theists in the Western world face the same evidence for absence that led to death-of-God language, and we shall consider briefly some of the responses that have appeared. The same periods of trouble that have afflicted people since the beginning still recur, and for those who still find the Bible to be a source of help, they are being dealt with in traditional ways. Karl Rahner, in a book of prayers he called *Encounters with Silence*, wrote of one kind of absence:

> When I pray, it's as if my words have disappeared down some deep, dark well, from which no echo ever comes back to reassure me that they have struck the ground of your heart. Lord, to pray my whole life long without hearing an answer, isn't that too

much to ask? You see how I run away from You time and time again, to speak with men who give me an answer, to busy myself with things that give me some kind of response. You see how much I *need* to be answered. And yet, my prayers never receive a word of reply.[44]

We are strongly reminded of the psalms of lament, when reading this prayer of Rahner's, for everything in the book is directed toward God, with faith insisting that God must be hearing even though life provides no evidence for it.

Peter Hodgson's study *Jesus—Word and Presence* speaks of two basic reasons for the experience of God's absence in contemporary society.[45] We have focused on secularism, but must now turn to the other, the heightened awareness of radical evil, especially as that has led to reflection on the Holocaust. For Jewish, and also Christian, theologians the question of what God was doing as that horror took place has raised in more critical ways than ever before issues of whether there is a God, if so what God's nature must be, and whether faith is any longer possible. The literature is extensive, but for our purposes I shall discuss only two works by Jewish scholars. The first, *The Exile of the Word: From the Silence of the Bible to the Silence of Auschwitz*, by André Neher, has been chosen because the author is a biblical scholar who has used his expertise to produce a meditation on "biblical silence" in dialogue with the "silence of Auschwitz."[46] His use of the theme of silence is more wide-ranging than our study of absence has been. He speaks of the absence of God from the stories of Esther and Ruth, of the eclipse in Genesis 22, of apparent "distractedness" in the Joseph cycle, and of silence of various kinds in Job 3—37, Psalm 22, 1 Samuel 28 (Saul's efforts to make contact), and 1 Kings 18—19, to mention only some of the major texts discussed. The title of the final section is significant, in the light of the effect the Holocaust has had on the Jewish community worldwide: "Silence and Perhaps."

Neher has found that he must deal with the possibility that the absence of God is permanent, but in his Jewish tradition he also finds the "perhaps," and he sees that that can be read in a major as well as a minor key. In traditional rabbinic fashion he takes two Hebrew words, each of which can be read in two different ways. One is *naham*, which will interest us when we come to Exodus 32. It is used of God's repentance, of regret, discouragement in the face of failure, but another form means consolation, pulling oneself together in the face of failure. The other is a word we have already dealt with, *'azav*, which means "abandon," but he also finds a meaning "gathering in." So abandonment and gathering in belong together, he concludes. But the best we can say about the future is "perhaps." He accepts the uncertainty that a better future may come but does not thereby deny that God is involved in it. God has given us something of value to do, and that must suffice.[47]

Emil Fackenheim has written extensively on the Holocaust, but his little book *God's Presence in History* speaks most directly to our present concerns. He packed a wealth of insights into the rabbinic tradition and contemporary philosophy and theology into just a hundred pages, but for our purposes his conclusions will be the most useful part. Some of the rabbinic material has been dealt with earlier, and this section has just surveyed the trends characteristic of secularism. Near the end of the book he sums up the resources from traditional Judaism that are inadequate in the face of Auschwitz: divine powerlessness, otherworldliness, the redeeming power of martyrdom, the idea it could have been just punishment for sin, the teaching that God shares Israel's exile, and the image of the eclipse of God.[48] The issue now is whether the divine eclipse in the present is total. "If *all present* access to the God of history is *wholly* lost, the God of history is Himself lost." Passover's reenactment of deliverance at the Sea has been a real event for the Jew because the God who had saved then was saving still. But can that any longer be so?

Fackenheim's response is that the Jews must endure, because if they do not, Hitler will have won after all.[49] "*The Jew after Auschwitz* is a witness to endurance. . . . He bears witness that without endurance we shall all perish. He bears witness that we *can* endure because we *must* endure; and that we must endure because we are *commanded* to endure." Thus Passover after Auschwitz mixes the longing that has always been there with defiance, and that has made endurance possible. Fackenheim's understanding of the Jew's relationship with God is thus similar to that of Neher, although his vocabulary is different. "We are here, exist, survive, endure, witnesses to God and man even if abandoned by God and man."[50] So the spirit of the laments of the Old Testament, with their blunt assessment of how bad it is and their insistence on not forsaking God even though God seems to have forsaken them, reappears in new forms in these Jewish interpretations of absence.

Can anything more be said to those who still believe in God in spite of his apparent absence from the world in which we live? I believe our consideration of the Old Testament suggests several points of dialogue. First, the sense that God was not active did not lead Old Testament writers to think a new theology was needed, as if they knew God's absence was permanent. Even today, the Western world is not as completely secular as we are tempted to think. Something other than a theology without God is called for, if we are to take the not-quite-despairing words of the Old Testament as a guide.

The Old Testament authors protest, and that is their most characteristic reaction to the sense of absence. In Exodus 1—2 the first explicit key that the author had been deliberately representing a time of absence was the reference to the outcry of the slaves, and it was outcry that first led us to the laments. Protest, complaint, challenges directed toward the absent God, the continued insistence that there is a God who intends it to be better than this—these are distinctive features of the faith of Israel. But moderns seem a bit timid by comparison. Except for some discussions of the Holocaust, either they give up and are left with little more than whimpering or they try not to think about it. "It's all right to yell at God" is not a message often heard in Christian circles, and that is because the Old Testament tradition of *faithful protest* has not been well preserved.

Faithful protest is accompanied by two features of better repute: waiting and hoping. Isaiah had done what he could, to no avail; what was left for him was waiting: "I will wait for the LORD, who is hiding his face from the house of Jacob, and I will hope in him" (Isa. 8:17; cf. Hab. 2:1). But how can the waiting be anything more than resignation, accepting the pain without expecting anything better? How can they speak of hope? The psalmist cried out, "And now, O LORD, what do I wait for? My hope is in you" (Ps. 39:7). As Martin Marty wisely observed about that statement, "Everything here turns, then, on the character of the living God. This Presence on the horizon differentiates wintry spirituality from mere wintriness."[51] What Israel knew about the character of God (after the exodus, so our author cannot write this way in chaps. 1–2) they got from their memory of what God had done, as Fackenheim has emphasized in his comments about Passover. The final point we can learn from the Old Testament is thus the critical importance of memory. I commented earlier on the fact that as the story is told, the slaves in Egypt had nothing to remember as they cried out to heaven, but we have seen that the outcries in Psalm 22 were interspersed with memories of what God had done for Israel and of the psalmist's previous nearness to God. That made it possible to go on crying out to "My God," even though that God did not answer.

And the authors of the Old Testament books did not finally give up waiting because they were convinced that in spite of those inexplicable times of suffering, when too many die while they wait, in God's good time he comes to save. That is the way the book of Job and the psalms of lament end, and that is the next act in the book of Exodus.

CHAPTER 2

THE NUMINOUS

Exodus 3—4

And Moses hid his face, for he was afraid to look at God.
—Exodus 3:6b

At the end of Exodus 2, God had just been introduced as an actor in the story, after the author had recounted a long series of disasters that befell the Israelites in Egypt without any significant participation on God's part. Once introduced, however, God will dominate the rest of the book. In this next section, usually designated the call of Moses, God speaks at length (about thirty-five verses) concerning what he intends to do in the near future. (Moses gets eight speeches, all of them short.) As for acts of God, he does not do much in these two chapters, and what he does is not very impressive. He teaches Moses a couple of "tricks" he can do to get the attention of the pharaoh, and then he tries to kill Moses. The "tricks" are just preliminary to the plagues, so can be ignored for our purposes. The attack on Moses, however, is something we shall take seriously, and rather than explaining it away, we will try to integrate it into our understanding of God as portrayed in Exodus.

God's lengthy speeches in chapters 3—4 provide for us in advance the theological interpretation of all the activity that will be reported in chapters 5—24. There is so much theology here that I have devoted four chapters of the book to this section. Another author might well develop other aspects of the passage that I have not chosen to emphasize. I have made these choices because they seem to me to be theologically important and because some of them have been overlooked by most authors. The subjects of these four chapters will be introduced as we now make a first reading of chapters 3—4.

This section stands in strong contrast to the first two chapters of Exodus. Previously, we have been in a world where people live by their wits without any direct interference from God. But now we enter a world most of us do not know, where strange events occur in nature, and where a man actually talks (debates!) with God. We shall not take up again the much-discussed historical question of what really happened at the burning bush, for the only answers that can be offered are those based solely on presuppositions.[1] We shall simply read it as Israel's testimony to what God once did for them, making use of Moses, and will approach the truth question by asking a historical question we can answer: whether subsequent experience has confirmed their testimony that it was God who did it.

Some commentators have seen Ex. 2:23–25 as a later insertion into the story of Moses, interrupting the context, but theologically the verses are in exactly the right place. We have seen how the choice of words calls attention to God's absence from the story up until that point. They also serve to introduce God as the main character from here on. As Moses is going about his day's work, he encounters a strange natural phenomenon, a bush that burns but is not consumed by the flames (3:2). Possible explanations of the phenomenon (such as Saint Elmo's fire) will not concern us, nor will the location of the mountain of God. The key elements in Moses' experience, because of the way they point us to the Bible's language about God, are the flame, the warning that this is "holy ground," and Moses' hiding of his face when he realizes he is in the presence of God (3:5–6). Fire is regularly associated with God, and we shall need to consider the value of that imagery. "Holiness" has been identified as the quality of divinity itself, as the term is used in scripture,[2] and so it seems that Exodus begins talking about God where we ought to begin. Moses first encounters holiness as fire and as a warning ("Come no closer!"), leading him to protect himself from it, but the one who speaks to him at that dangerous place is a God who is about to save his people. These few words (3:2–6) thus introduce us to the main features of the experience of the presence of God which Rudolf Otto described as the *numinous*.[3] Our task in this chapter, then, will be to show how Otto's work illuminates for us what the Old Testament says about God, and to trace the continuing evidence for the numinous qualities of human encounters with God, as the most elemental aspects of such experiences. God promises that when Moses and the people have come out of Egypt, they will worship him on that same mountain, and in chapters 19—20 that comes true, with even more impressive evidence of the presence of the holy God in their midst, so the appropriate parts of those chapters will also be discussed here.

THE NUMINOUS IN THE OLD TESTAMENT

Theology begins in Exodus as it begins in life, with the experience of something believed to be outside oneself, identified as "holy," and with the eventual identification of the holy as "God." This statement grows out of an acceptance of the accuracy of Rudolf Otto's classic description of the elemental religious experience in his book *The Idea of the Holy*.[4] His theories concerning the origins and nature of religion have been much debated, and as his critics have shown, there are philosophical weak points, but his phenomenology has been widely accepted and the few criticisms of that seem to be based largely on misunderstanding.[5] In history of religions studies, one of the most influential authors of this century, Mircea Eliade, acknowledged the ground-breaking value of Otto's analysis of the nonrational side of religious experience and undertook to move beyond that to deal with "the sacred in its entirety."[6] In Old Testament studies, Otto's influence can be seen in many works, often without acknowledgment. For example, among Old Testament theologians, Walther Eichrodt offers by far the most sensitive analysis of the suprarational aspects of the holiness of God, but he does not use the word "numinous" and does not refer to Otto, although it is obvious that he learned from *The Idea of the Holy*.[7] In other Old Testament studies Otto's name appears occasionally in footnotes, but I have concluded that because his influence on biblical studies has remained largely undiscussed, the potential value of his work for biblical theology remains to be used. This section will emphasize the pervasiveness of the experience of the numinous throughout scripture, and the synagogue and church subsequently, and this will become the foundation for conclusions that will be drawn in other chapters of this book.

Rather than beginning with a general description of Otto's analysis, let us proceed as biblical theology should, with a consideration of what is happening in chapters 3—4 and 19—20. These chapters claim that not only a great religious leader such as Moses, but that ordinary people, the Israelites, may be given access to a reality beyond anything we know in the everyday world. That is, they have had a personal encounter with God. Scripture has standard ways of describing such encounters, and we have already noted them in chapters 3—4: (1) Nature itself seems to be affected. In chapter 3 there is a bush burning without being consumed. In chapter 19 there is thunder, lightning, a thick cloud, a "trumpet blast," smoke, and a shaking of the whole mountain (vv. 16–18). (2) There is danger involved, and people need to take appropriate precautions because of it. Moses is warned to come no closer to the bush and to remove his sandals, for he is on holy ground. Later the people are told to "consecrate" themselves and are warned not to touch the mountain (19:10–13, 14b–15). It is important that they *can* take precautions, for this is not a danger to be escaped from, but to be approached as nearly as possible. Why, we shall see in a moment. (3) It is frightening, however. Moses hid his face, for he was afraid to look at God (3:6). The people are so alarmed at the thunder that even though God had instructed them to come up when the trumpet sounded a long blast (19:13b), they have an alternative suggestion: Let Moses do it (20:18–21). (4) But this is a good experience, not a bad one. From that eerily burning bush Moses hears these words, "I know their sufferings, and I have come down to deliver them." After he had brought the people to the mountain, Moses is instructed to tell the people that the God who will encounter them there is the one who bore them on eagles' wings and brought them to himself, and so on (19:4–6). Indeed, there is something about what is happening on the mountain that may draw them too close, so Moses is warned to fence it (19:12) and to warn the people "not to break through to the LORD to look" (19:21). And the result of the whole experience is the making of an exclusive covenant relationship between that daunting God and these people, with the gift of a law intended to be the source of life and blessing for them (cf. Deut. 30:15–20).

God's appearance on the mountain is thus described as both frightening and attractive, daunting and fascinating. We shall see that these apparent opposites seem to appear whenever a person senses the immediate presence of God, and we may find it convincing to conclude that they represent more than human psychology—that they but reveal something about the very nature of God.

The natural phenomena do not always appear in accounts of God's appearance to someone. For example, Jeremiah's call records only the hearing of a voice and the touching of his mouth by a hand (Jer. 1:4–10). The most impressive descriptions of God's appearance, however, are those designated as "theophanies," those in which awesome events in nature accompany his coming (using "epiphany" for other appearances). Sinai is the classic theophany in the Old Testament, and many pages of commentaries and articles have been dedicated to the effort to explain it in terms of natural events. Some attribute all the effects to a great thunderstorm, some to a volcanic eruption, and some divide chs. 19—20 into sources, one of which had the former and one the latter. Those who insist on a volcano as part or all of the explanation then set out to find one, and extinct volcanoes may indeed be found in northern Arabia (Midian), but not in Sinai or the Negev. But none of this is of any use to us, for both storm and volcano are inadequate to explain the imagery that occurs in other theophanies.[8]

Did the Israelites deduce from their observation of storms that God must have been present in their midst? Are these really descriptions of visionary experiences rather than natural phenomena? Or is it simply poetic imagery? Two of the most striking theophanies in the Bible, Psalm 18 and Habakkuk 3, may offer some insights into this question.

Psalm 18 is a psalm of thanksgiving, beginning with praise (vv. 1–2) and moving to a reference to past distress (vv. 4–5) and to the lament in which the psalmist had called for help (v. 6). His prayers had been answered by the direct intervention of God, the psalmist believes, and the appearance of God is described in a terrifying way. "Then the earth reeled and rocked; the foundations also of the mountains trembled and quaked because he was angry" (v. 7). Here is the earthquake, not of Mount Sinai specifically but of mountains in general, and it is accounted for by the anger of God, an element we did not see in Exodus 19—20. "Smoke went up from his nostrils, and devouring fire from his mouth; glowing coals flamed forth from him" (v. 8). Smoke and fire are also familiar from Exodus, but here they are connected in a much more personal way with God. Neither storm nor volcano quite accounts for such a picture.

> He bowed the heavens, and came down; thick darkness was under his feet. He rode on a cherub, and flew; he came swiftly upon the wings of the wind. He made darkness his covering around him, his canopy thick clouds dark with water. (Ps. 18:9–11)

The darkness appears in Ex. 20:21, but the rest of this goes beyond anything ever seen in nature. Elements from pictorial representations of enthroned deities of the ancient Near East have obviously been picked up by the poet here.[9]

> Out of the brightness before him there broke through his clouds hailstones and coals of fire. The LORD also thundered in the heavens, and the Most High uttered his voice. And he sent out his arrows, and scattered them; he flashed forth lightnings, and routed them. (vv. 12–14)

These are all elements similar to those recounted in Exodus 19—20, but the final verse of the theophany proper introduces some entirely new elements:

> Then the channels of the sea were seen, and the foundations of the world were laid bare at your rebuke, O LORD, at the blast of the breath of your nostrils. (v. 15)

Is this a recollection of the crossing of the Sea (Exodus 14—15), and if so, what does that have to do with the distress from which the psalmist had been saved? For this terrifying picture is intended to designate the gracious God who came to save the psalmist from distress that is alluded to figuratively ("he drew me out of many waters") and then literally ("he delivered me from my strong enemy"). The psalmist had been victorious over his enemies and gives God full credit for that, with language any of us might use: "This God—his way is perfect; the promise of the LORD proves true; he is a shield for all who take refuge in him" (v. 30). But what had really happened to lead him to use such extravagant language to describe God's help?

There is virtually universal agreement today that the psalms were used in the cult, and that a passage such as Psalm 18 could have been sung by or on behalf of any worshiper who had experienced deliverance from enemies. If so, it must then have made sense to the "average Israelite," and that is supported by the fact that theophanic language occurs in various parts of the Old Testament. The most significant passages are Pss. 50:2–3; 68:7–10; 77:16–19; 97:2a, 3–5; 144:5–7; Nahum 1:2–8; and Hab. 3:3–15.[10] The last of those will suffice as additional evidence for us. Once again we find references to bright light (Hab. 3:4), to earthquake (vv. 6, 10a), to victory over the sea (vv. 8, 15), and to God's anger (vv. 8, 12). But the picture is far more violent than that which we found in Exodus or Psalm 18. Associated with the coming of God are pestilence and plague (v. 5), of all things, and he is depicted as a furious warrior wreaking havoc with nature itself as he takes vengeance on historical enemies. But once again this is the God who has come to save his people (v. 13a, perhaps 14b, although the text is probably untranslatable). Can this be the same God of whom it is said, "The LORD is merciful and gracious, slow to anger and abounding in steadfast love" (Ps. 103:8)? The answer is that Habakkuk says something even more surprising than that.

This also is a psalm of thanksgiving, and at the end the poet records his reaction to the theophany he has been describing. It has the same two apparently contradictory features we identified in Exodus. First, "I hear, and I tremble within; my lips quiver at the sound. Rottenness enters into my bones, and my steps tremble beneath me" (Hab. 3:16). The effects of so terrifying an appearance are more than emotional; they have virtually demolished him physically. But the spiritual effect is expressed in one of the most striking statements of faith and confidence to be found anywhere in scripture:

> Though the fig tree does not blossom,
>   and no fruit is on the vines;
> though the produce of the olive fails
>   and the fields yield no food;
> though the flock is cut off from the fold
>   and there is no herd in the stalls,
> yet I will rejoice in the LORD;
>   I will exult in the God of my salvation. (Hab. 3:17–18)[11]

A study of Habakkuk 3 by J. H. Eaton argues that this was originally an oracle offered by a prophet as a part of the autumn festival in the temple at Jerusalem, following a rite of some sort that represented the theophany.[12] The proposed setting is hypothetical, of course, but Eaton's emphasis on the place of theophany in the cult and on the oracular character of a text such as Habakkuk 3 suggests a possible way of understanding all the theophanic language, and this will lead us back to Otto's description of the numinous. It may be that as Israelites such as Habbakuk, Isaiah, Ezekiel, and the authors of the psalms referred to earlier had visionary (or other) encounters with God and struggled to find language to describe the daunting aspects of what was essentially indescribable, they used the most awe-inspiring things found in nature: fire, earthquake, storm, and the like. What they actually saw and heard, we cannot reproduce, of course, but if we read their words with empathy, we may be able to sense what they felt, and the suggestion is that this was the true intention of those words.

Theophanies elsewhere in the Old Testament have thus offered this possible way of understanding the theophanies at Mount Sinai: Whatever Moses and the former slaves may have seen and heard (and that we can never determine), later Israel held the strong memory that God in all his power and graciousness had encountered them there, and the language of theophany was their natural way of talking about such an encounter.

But why did they insist on describing the power of God in such violent ways? Otto's description of the numinous aspects of the experience of the holy offers an explicit answer to that question. It is important to be clear about the difference between the two key words (numinous and holy) in the previous sentence, in order not to misunderstand Otto. In spite of his rather clear definitions, not everyone who has used his work, or criticized it, has taken adequate account of the differences. "Holiness" as the word is used in scripture includes nonrational, rational, and moral aspects. In postbiblical uses it has tended to become exclusively moral, equal to "goodness," and it was this attenuation of the word's significance that Otto set out to rectify. He never denied its rational and moral significance, and in fact, the latter parts of his book deal with them at some length, although not to the satisfaction of many critics. But his primary contribution was to elucidate the nonrational side of holiness, as a correction to the exclusively rational interpretations of religion that prevailed when the book was written (first edition: 1917).[13] So he invented the word *numinous* to denote what he called "this 'extra' in the meaning of holy above and beyond the meaning of goodness" (5–7). Despite its German and English titles, then, his book should not be read as if it intended to be a study of the Hebrew root *qdsh* or the Greek *hagios* or *hieros*. This section also will not take up holiness in general as its subject, but will focus on the nonrational side of the human experience of God's presence, and will move toward considering the relationship between the sense of the numinous and theology proper.

Otto was not always as careful in his choice of words as he might have been, and sometimes used "irrational," which is not what he really meant. He was not talking about a surrender of the mind, but of the fact that more than the mind is involved in religion. The "extra" that was his subject defies language, however, and one of Otto's major contributions was to show us how we have chosen terms drawn from everyday experience as analogies to the indescribable. Otto calls them "ideograms"(24). Such words will be noted in the examples I shall draw from the Old Testament to illustrate each of the aspects of the numinous he identified.

The organization of his book could have been better; he seems to have been more a poet than a logician, and so not all of his interpreters have related the three key terms, *mysterium, tremendum,* and *fascinans,* in the same way, but once he begins to describe them he is very persuasive. He found the Old Testament to be a rich source of material, although his evidence was drawn from various religions and periods. I intend to provide examples drawn only from the Old Testament, most of which Otto did not cite, and chosen with the specific intention of showing how the frightening and the attractive, Otto's *tremendum* and *fascinans*, belong together when God is spoken of.

Otto began by analyzing the adjective *tremendum* because he found it to be easier than the noun *mysterium*, and he discussed the former at some length, while its apparent opposite, *fascinans*, was given less attention. That, plus an unfortunate tendency to emphasis the cruder forms of the *tremendum*, the "gruesome" and the weird, has tended to repel some of Otto's readers and to lead others to follow his example too closely. The following choice of examples will attempt to provide a better balance, in keeping with Otto's own intentions (31). But we shall follow his order.

Tremendum: This is "a quite specific kind of emotional response, wholly distinct from that of being afraid, though it so far resembles it that the analogy of fear may be used to throw light upon its nature" (13). "The 'shudder' reappears in a form ennobled beyond measure where the soul, held speechless, trembles inwardly to the farthest fibre of its being" (17). So Moses covered his face, for he was afraid to look at God, and later the people were afraid and trembled and stood at a distance. Otto described three elements of the *tremendum*, that of "aweful-ness," that of "overpoweringness," and that of "energy" or urgency. By "aweful-ness" he meant those qualities of the experience that led to the analogies of fear, on the part of people, and of wrath and jealousy, ascribed to the numinous. But he emphasizes these are not the same qualities found in human beings; they are efforts to come as close as language can to convey the effects of an indescribable experience. Here are some biblical examples of those efforts:

> As the sun was going down, a deep sleep fell upon Abram, and a deep and terrifying darkness fell upon him. (Gen. 15:12)

> Then Jacob woke from his sleep and said, "Surely the LORD is in this place—and I did not know it." And he was afraid, and said, "How awesome is this place! This is none other than the house of God, and this is the gate of heaven." (Gen. 28:16–17)

> For the LORD your God is a devouring fire, a jealous God. (Deut. 4:24)

> The LORD is king; let the peoples tremble!
>   He sits enthroned upon the cherubim; let the earth quake!
> The LORD is great in Zion;
>   he is exalted over all the peoples.
> Let them praise your great and awesome name.
>   Holy is he! (Ps. 99:1–3)

These texts will not be explained at length; either the reader is sensitive enough to get the right feeling from them, or not. That a great darkness fell upon Abram is in itself enough to suggest a daunting experience, but added to it is the word *'eymah*, which at the purely human level means "terror." But the setting is one in which God makes a covenant with Abram and all that God says to him is filled with gracious promises. What is he to be "afraid" of? In the same way, Jacob's experience at Bethel leads to God's renewal of his promises, and Jacob recognizes that his dream has identified Bethel as a place where God can be found. In the effort to find a word to describe the awesomeness of that discovery, however, he uses *nora'*, which literally means "frightful." Older translations used "dreadful," and yet this is a good place, infinitely better than ordinary places. The same word is used of the name of God in Psalm 99:3, and because his name is "terrible," as the older translations rendered it, he is to be praised, not avoided.

The second element of the *tremendum* identified by Otto helps to account for the use of such words in Hebrew. It is in English the rather clumsy "overpoweringness" (a more acceptable formation in Otto's German). He also uses "majesty," saying there is at least "a last faint trace of the numinous still clinging to the word" (19). This denotes the feeling of infinite difference between the numinous and humanity, the consciousness of creaturehood over against one who is all-causing and all-conditioning. Psalm 68:32–35 selects language appropriate to evoke the feeling about the Holy One:

> Sing to God, O kingdoms of the earth;
>> sing praises to the LORD.
> O rider in the heavens, the ancient heavens;
>> listen, he sends out his voice, his mighty voice.
> Ascribe power to God,
>> whose majesty is over Israel;
>> and whose power is in the skies.
> Awesome is God in his sanctuary, the God of Israel;
>> he gives power and strength to his people.
> Blessed be God!

On the human side, we have already noted the effect God's appearance had on Habakkuk: "I hear, and I tremble within; my lips quiver at the sound. Rottenness enters my bones, and my steps tremble beneath me." But this is no devastating experience; it leads to hope: "I wait quietly for the day of calamity to come upon the people who attack us" (Hab. 3:16). Ezekiel's inaugural vision emphasizes at length the "awefulness," overpoweringness, and energy of the Holy One, leading to physical collapse on his part:

> Like the bow in a cloud on a rainy day, such was the appearance of the splendor all around. This was the appearance of the likeness of the glory of the LORD. When I saw it, I fell on my face, and I heard the voice of someone speaking. He said to me: O mortal, stand up on your feet, and I will speak with you. And when he spoke to me, a spirit entered into me and set me on my feet. (Ezek. 1:28–2:2)

Daniel reports a similar reaction to the near encounter with God:

> So I was left alone to see this great vision. My strength left me, and my complexion grew deathly pale, and I retained no strength. Then I heard the sound of his words; and when I heard the sound of his words, I fell into a trance, face to the ground. But then a hand touched me and roused me to my hands and knees. He said to me, "Daniel, greatly beloved, pay attention to the words that I am going to speak to you. Stand on your feet, for I have now been sent to you." So while he was speaking this word to me, I stood up trembling. (Dan. 10:8–11)

Note that is the "greatly beloved" one who is reduced to such a state by the nearness of God. The numinous experience shakes one, physically, mentally, and spiritually, but it is not a negative experience.

The third element of *tremendum*, energy and urgency, is represented in somewhat fantastic ways (for us) in Ezekiel's vision of the throne chariot. It contains the elements of the theophany in an original form—a stormy wind, cloud, and fire (1:4)—but emphasizes continual and untrammeled activity: "fire flashing forth continually." Of the four living creatures he says,

> Each moved straight ahead; wherever the spirit would go, they went, without turning as they went. In the middle of the living creatures there was something that looked like burning coals of fire, like torches moving to and fro among the living creatures; the fire was bright, and lightning issued from the fire. The living creatures darted to and fro, like a flash of lightning. (Ezek. 1:12–14)

In the presence of the Holy One we become aware of a vitality beyond our ability to perceive adequately, let alone think of controlling:

> The voice of the LORD breaks the cedars;
>   the LORD breaks the cedars of Lebanon.
> He makes Lebanon skip like a calf,
>   and Sirion like a young wild ox.
> The voice of the LORD flashes forth flames of fire.
> The voice of the LORD shakes the wilderness;
>   the LORD shakes the wilderness of Kadesh.
> The voice of the LORD causes the oaks to whirl,
>   and strips the forest bare;
>   and in his temple all say, "Glory!" (Ps. 29:5–9)

Surely no comment on that is needed except to emphasize that all this furious activity results not in dismay, but in "Glory!" For a similar expression of awe and praise at the power and vigor of God, compare Ex. 15:6–13.

Mysterium: Encounters with the numinous cannot really be described; they can only be alluded to by "ideograms," analogies drawn from ordinary human experiences, which are inadequate but at least point in the right direction (if not misunderstood and taken literally). That is because the numinous is something "wholly other," truly incomprehensible.[14] To denote the effects of becoming aware of so great a mystery, Otto uses words such as "stupor," "blank wonder and astonishment." The Old Testament asserts the wholly otherness of God in sentences such as "I am God and no mortal, the Holy One in your midst, and I will not come in wrath" (Hos. 11:9b), "I am God and also henceforth I am He" (Isa. 43:13a), and "I am the LORD, and there is no other" (Isa. 45:5a). Deuteronomy elaborates on the otherness of the Sinai experience in 4:9–36. Ezekiel was very careful to say that what he had experienced in his vision of the throne chariot was not something that could really be seen, let alone described or pictured. I have emphasized his qualifying words:

> And above the dome over their heads there was something *like* a throne, *in appearance like* sapphire; and seated above the *likeness* of a throne was something that *seemed like* a human form. Upward from what *appeared like* the loins I saw

something that *looked like* fire enclosed all around; and downward from what *looked like* the loins I saw something that *looked like* fire, and there was a splendor all around. *Like* the bow in a cloud on a rainy day, such was the *appearance* of the splendor all around. This was the *appearance* of the *likeness* of the glory of the LORD. (Ezek. 1:26–28)

It was not the Lord, nor the glory of the Lord, nor even the likeness of the glory of the Lord that Ezekiel saw, but he is willing to claim that he may have seen the appearance of the likeness of the glory of the Lord.

Elijah's experience of otherness is expressed in a very different way, although it begins with the familiar elements of theophany, and is located at Mount Horeb, the name used for the mountain of God in Exodus 3. There is a great wind, then an earthquake, then fire, but the Lord is said not to be in any of them (1 Kings 19:11–12). Theophanic language had never claimed the Lord was *in* those natural phenomena, anyway. Then comes the new and eerie element; not the "still, small voice" of traditional translations, but something almost untranslatable. Very literally, the Hebrew seems to say, "a thin sound of silence," whatever that may be, and I am sure we are not supposed to analyze it, but to pause in wonder before it. The NRSV has boldly departed from tradition in order to confront its readers with the true mystery: "a sound of sheer silence." God is not said to be *in* that either; it is part of the numinous experience, and then God speaks to recommission Elijah and encourage him (vv. 15–18).

Fascinans: The God of the Old Testament is thus not the God of the philosophers, whose existence and qualities can be deduced from observation and logical inference, nor is he quite the God of the rationalist theologians whose work Otto was trying to correct and supplement. But his corrections were not intended to produce a picture of a God like the terrifying Kali, in Hinduism, even though he did tend to overemphasize the *tremendum*.[15] Ordinary fear leads one to want to escape, but the "fear" produced by the presence of the numinous is always accompanied by an ineffable attraction, leading to the analogies of love, grace, mercy, forgiveness, pity, and comfort to be applied to the Holy One, and bliss, rapture, peace, and trust to the person involved in the numinous experience (31–40). The Old Testament examples chosen so far have all included elements of the *fascinans*; I have avoided expressions of the *mysterium tremendum* associated entirely with judgment, of which there are many. Those now to be presented have been selected because they are good examples of the vocabulary just mentioned. The combination of the feeling of otherness and of comfort is well-expressed in Isa. 57:15:

For thus says the high and lofty one
    who inhabits eternity, whose name is Holy:
I dwell in the high and holy place,
    and also with those who are contrite and humble in spirit,
to revive the spirit of the humble,
    and to revive the heart of the contrite.

The graciousness of God is praised throughout Psalm 111, and the psalmist does not find it at all inappropriate to put these lines together:

> He sent redemption to his people;
>> he has commanded his covenant forever.
>
> Holy and awesome (*nora'*—terrible) is his name. (Ps. 111:9)

"Fear of God" thus can appropriately be linked with love, once it is properly understood in the light of what we have found concerning the word "fear" as an ideogram pointing to something different from the things we normally are afraid of on earth: "So now, O Israel, what does the LORD your God require of you? Only to fear the LORD your God, to walk in all his ways, to love him, to serve the LORD your God with all your heart and with all your soul" (Deut. 10:12). Careful studies of the expression "fear of the LORD," which occurs so often in the Bible, have shown that it means something like "reverent obedience."[16] This explains how Moses can use the same word (*yare'*) in two apparently contradictory ways in the same sentence: "Do not be afraid; for God has come to test you and to put the fear of him upon you so that you do not sin" (Ex. 20:20). The former use speaks of true fear, which should lead one to want to escape; that is inappropriate at Sinai. The latter use speaks of numinous "fear," and Otto's observations need to be added to the word studies just alluded to, so that we do not misunderstand "reverent obedience" as a completely moral quality without anything of the daunting element that is present throughout scripture. In the prayers of the postexilic period the word remains as a standard part of the language: "O LORD God of heaven, the great and awesome [*nora'*] God who keeps covenant and steadfast love with those who love him and keep his commandments" (Neh. 1:5; cf. Neh. 9:32; Dan. 9:4).

Some of the most striking examples of the numinous experience have come from the unique event at Mount Sinai and from the visions of the prophets, but we have also found evidence that this is not something available only to visionaries and mystics. Otto developed a theory about the capacity of "divination," using a rather unfortunate word to denote the ability to be aware of the numinous, and a theory that there exists a religious *a priori* in human beings. These theories, which have led to most of the debate over his work, need not concern us much, for it is his phenomenology, and not hypotheses about the origins and nature of religion in general, that can be documented from the Old Testament evidence. Evidence that in Israel the numinous experience was sensed by ordinary people is to be found primarily in the psalms, some of which have already been quoted.

Now we are ready to think about that puzzling text, Ex. 4:24–26:

> On the way, at a place where they spent the night, the LORD met him and tried to kill him. But Zipporah took a flint and cut off her son's foreskin, and touched Moses' feet with it, and said, "Truly you are a bridegroom of blood to me!" So he let him alone. It was then she said, "A bridegroom of blood by circumcision."

The passage must be fragmentary, for it leaves so many things unsaid that we can never be certain exactly what it means. Martin Noth wisely observed, "in this brief form [it] is quite inexplicable,"[17] but other scholars have been less wise, and have explained it as if they really knew. Their theories will be of no value to us, so can remain undiscussed. The commentaries by Childs and Durham contain useful surveys of the research. The NRSV translation quoted above makes things appear to be a little clearer than they really are. The Hebrew text does not say "Moses' feet," but "his feet," so we cannot be certain whom the LORD tried to kill (Moses or the son), whose feet Zipporah touched with the foreskin (Moses', the son's, or God's [!]), or whom Zipporah was addressing with her mysterious saying. There is no parallel to "bridegroom of blood" anywhere in the Bible, and Arabic parallels are commonly resorted to, with various results. Childs has demonstrated fairly convincingly that the point of the story is circumcision,[18] but the only aspect of it that concerns us is the role of God.

The earliest interpreters already found this text completely unacceptable. The book of *Jubilees* retells the story, making the attacker Mastema (one of the devil's names), but the customary explanation of the rabbis was to identify some sin for which Moses was being justly punished.[19] Some contemporary scholars still rationalize and moralize it in one way or another; others take it more literally and reject it as a primitive remnant.[20] But the insights gained from applying Otto's work to the Old Testament may help us to see that although it takes an embarrassingly blunt form and remains in most respects unexplainable, it need not be bowdlerized or rejected as completely incompatible with the Old Testament concept of God. Let us consider the possibility that in Exodus 3—4 both the *fascinans*, God's gracious words promising salvation and all the assistance Moses will need to carry out the work, and the *tremendum* must be present, as we have seen them together in many other, less disturbing passages. The fact that Moses has been met by one who is wholly other is reinforced near the end of the passage by a shockingly brutal depiction of the *mysterium tremendum*. Some scholars who have recognized this possibility have spoken of the "demonic" in Yahweh, but that is an unfortunate choice of words, requiring still more explanation.[21] Their insights seem to be on the right track, however. Here we seem to have one of the few Old Testament expressions of the numinous in its most elemental form, uncontrollable power without any of the moral qualities that normally accompany it. Jacob's struggle with the mysterious stranger at night by the brook Jabbok (Gen. 32:24–32) is comparable. Others have suggested the puzzling encounter between Balaam and the angel in Num. 22:22–35 as a possible parallel.

Paul Volz emphasized that Israel is unique in the history of religion in that Yahweh comprehended everything, replacing the dualism of all other nations with monotheism, and that led to the dilemma of accounting for evil, with which we still struggle.[22] In his conclusion he pointed out that the "demonic" in the Old Testament faith in God was never repealed. The prophets did not overcome it, but renewed it, and here he alludes to Otto's book: "[A]nd so we must perceive God, the single cause, as a mystery, indeed as something uncanny. Also the cross on Golgotha can be accepted by faith only with trembling. . . . Only if this enormity is taken up into the concept of God and into piety—the uncanny power of God and anxious fear—if the righteous and gracious God is equally the frightful-terrible, do we stand before the depths of the Godhead and on the steps to the heights of faith."[23] Volz concluded that this Old Testament God is not one to be transcended; rather this trait is something we need to recover. Buber's use of "demonism" was influenced by Volz, but he could not resist the temptation to rationalize, as the rabbis before him had done.

Only Werner Schmidt, among the many writers who have dealt with this passage, has taken it in the straightforward way suggested by our work with Otto. Parts of the fairly lengthy conclusion to Schmidt's exegetical work are worth quoting:

> The Old Testament has not excised the tradition from an earlier time, Ex. 4:24ff., as an intractable statement of faith from a foreign, earlier epoch, but preserved it—perhaps one may dare to submit—because it did not contradict later experiences with the electing and judging God. In the present context the narrative gains an even sharper sense: the very one who is called is threatened—by the caller himself; the God who promised the liberation of the people falls upon his messenger. A reason why the irksome agent chosen after a hard struggle merits death even before the carrying out of his work is not provided. . . . The shadow side of human experience, the hard, dark, difficult, intolerable, and destructive, are not pushed aside or bracketed in the Old Testament. . . . The Old Testament knows of the distant, wrathful, "self-concealing" God (Isa. 8:17; 45:15; cf. Ps. 104:29, etc.), who withholds his presence, his nearness, his support. But this, like comparable narratives (Gen. 32:23ff., etc.), as well as the message of the so-called writing prophets (Amos 9:1ff.; Hos. 5:14, etc.), goes on to an even more difficult insight: He encounters the person overtly and immediately, and the near God is threatening, appears equally in the form of evil. The dangerous encounter results, however, in the salvation of the person—and therein the narrative agrees with the intention of the book of Exodus.[24]

The passage will always remain disturbing and poorly understood, but the above paragraphs have attempted to explain how it could have been accepted into the text of Exodus, and have remained there. How useful such an explanation may be will depend in part on our discovery of the ways later experiences of the presence of the loving, gracious God still include awestruck shuddering. Looking ahead, Otto's work will be appealed to again in the discussion of Exodus 5—15a, seeing these chapters as extended evidence of the *tremendum* in the form of divine judgment of oppressors. Chapters 15b—31 stand in contrast to the preceding as extended evidence of the *fascinans*, God's gracious act of covenant making. But chapters 32—34 take us more deeply into biblical theology, since they deal with the realities of how a relationship can be continued between a sinful people and the Holy God, in which judgment must occur but mercy enables life to go on.

Some critical reflections on Otto's theory in the light of the Old Testament evidence will conclude this part and point forward to a brief survey of the numinous in subsequent history: We have seen a range of evidence indicating that his phenomenology is accurate. The numinous experience appears throughout the Old Testament, from early to late materials and in various kinds of literature, with the characteristics he described. It takes its most striking forms in the experiences of visionaries but also becomes part of the standard language of prayer. Otto's work has helped us to recognize the abundant evidence in the Old Testament that its authors, as they expressed the faith of Israel, were not working merely with words and ideas, but were struggling to find words that would at least point toward something real that language is incapable of expressing. But what, if anything, does this tell us about God? Otto assumed these feelings were produced by something real outside the human person (thus not a purely psychological phenomenon) and that the real something was in fact God.[25] He has been challenged in this by those who claim that a purely natural explanation for these sensations may be posited,[26] and by neo-orthodox theologians, since the numinous has to do with "religion" rather than revelation.[27]

The Bible can offer little to help with debates of this kind. That Israel identified the numinous with Yahweh is indisputable, but that fact proves nothing about the general theory. What can biblical theology add to the discussion of whether it is legitimate to move from an analysis of the effects of the numinous experience to a claim that these tell us something about what God is really like? We are on the borderline between biblical theology and systematics, so we must be appropriately cautious, but four points may be gathered from the evidence:

1. The evidence shows consistency. Recall Volz's insistence that the more terrifying aspects of the deity remain a part of Israel's religion throughout history. The emphasis on God's grace is at least as strong in the earliest materials as in the latest parts (in fact, questions about graciousness are more likely to appear in late materials, such as Job and Ecclesiastes). This may be accounted for psychologically, of course, but it demolishes all developmental and evolutionary theories of Israel's concept of God.
2. The agreement on the part of many authors in choosing language in such a way as to insist there is no correspondence between this experience and any other shows that all naturalistic explanations are battling against the evidence. These are sophisticated authors, and we are not being confronted by a merely naive use of contradictions.
3. There is continuity over many generations in the association made between the numinous and the rational/moral qualities ascribed to God. This also proves nothing concerning the existence of God; they may simply be projections.

4. Finally, the rational and moral content of the religious experience in Israel differs from such experiences in other cultures, as they have been described by Otto, Eliade, and many others.[28] Here in Exodus 3 that difference is seen not only in the identification of the name of God—Yahweh—but in what is said about the specific activities of the Holy One. He promises to take a people who are no-people, wrest them from their present masters, bring them to the mountain where they may worship him, and give them a land. This takes us quite beyond the characteristics of the numinous experience. None of this can be deduced from those feelings, or projected from rational/moral associations. Our use of Otto's phenomenology does not then lead us down the road of natural theology, as Barth assumed it must. The religion of Israel, faith in Yahweh (not some anonymous "numinous" one), is defined by the Old Testament as being based on revelation, the words of that one who spoke at Sinai, but the nonrational accompaniment of that word of God is the *mysterium tremendum* and *fascinans*.

THE NUMINOUS IN JUDAISM AND CHRISTIANITY

Jews and Christians have affirmed the *fascinans* more readily than the *tremendum* in their literature (except where the latter is directed against the wicked). As we have seen in the case of Ex. 4:24–26, they have also sensed serious problems with what the Old Testament says about God in certain passages, and have rationalized and moralized these problems as best they could. No detached explanation of the passages as examples of the purely nonrational side of religious experience was accessible to them, and it is unlikely they would have appreciated it had it been offered, for both religions became fervently rational and moral.[29] But the literature shows that religion had not been dehydrated into philosophy, for the distinctive language used by the Old Testament to refer to God reappears, and it is unlikely that it represents only literary convention and does not also reflect the religious feelings of the time. The language is to be found primarily in two places (with a new use appearing in the New Testament): in the visionary language that the apocalyptic writers have inherited from the prophets, and in the language of praise.

Judaism

The physical effects produced by the word of God are recounted in 2 Esdras in terms that recall Ezekiel and Daniel. The angel Uriel, who is Esdras's interpreter, says:

> Rise to your feet and you will hear a full, resounding voice. And if the place where you are standing is greatly shaken while the voice is speaking, do not be terrified;

because the word concerns the end, and the foundations of the earth will understand that the speech concerns them. They will tremble and be shaken, for they know that their end must be changed. When I heard this, I got to my feet and listened; a voice was speaking, and its sound was like the sound of mighty waters. (2 Esd. 6:13–17)

The effects of the vision Esdras sees in 10:25–32 are so extreme that he falls over in a dead faint and has to be revived by the angel. Scholars debate whether this sort of thing is simply literary, modeled after Daniel 10, or whether it may reflect the actual experiences of the seers who wrote the apocalyptic books.[30] Studies of the reports of visions of mystics in later times have shown that physical effects of this kind are typical, so whether or not a given apocalypse from antiquity is a purely literary creation, such descriptions may be accepted as accurate reflections of the reality of the religious life of some people.[31]

An impressive theophany appears at the beginning of *1 Enoch*:

The Holy Great One will come forth from His dwelling,
And the eternal God will tread upon the earth, (even) on Mount Sinai,
[And appear from His camp]
And appear in the strength of His might from the heaven of heavens.
And all shall be smitten with fear,
And the Watchers shall quake,
And great fear and trembling shall seize them unto the ends of the earth.
And the high mountains shall be shaken,
And the high hills shall be made low,
And shall melt like wax before the flame.
And the earth shall be wholly rent in sunder,
And all that is upon the earth shall perish,
And there shall be a judgment upon all (men).
But with the righteous He will make peace,
And will protect the elect,
And mercy shall be upon them. (*1 Enoch* 1:3–8a)

As in the theophanies of the Old Testament, the tumult in nature is not found to be appalling by the believer, for it represents the coming of God to save, and the moral element is strong, for the "wrath" that is so represented is directed against the wicked (cf. *Assumption of Moses* 10). But these examples show that postexilic Judaism had not "domesticated" God so as to make of him either an impassive judge of the wicked or a gentle comforter of the righteous. They might speak of him in both ways, but they knew God was more than that, as the language of praise of ordinary people shows (cf. Judith 16:13–15).

Even the wisdom literature, which one might expect to have moved away from numinous feelings to a thoroughly rational interpretation of the religion, is so thoroughly infused with Jewish piety that strong religious feelings appear. As Wisdom of Solomon retells the story of the exodus, the plagues become even more awesome than in the original. In 16:15–29 a supernatural fire is described, an elaboration of the plague of hail and thunder and fire (Ex. 9:23–26):

> For—most incredible of all—in water, which quenches all things, the fire had still greater effect, for the universe defends the righteous. . . . Snow and ice withstood fire without melting, so that they might know that the crops of their enemies were being destroyed by the fire that blazed in the hail and flashed in the showers of rain; whereas the fire, in order that the righteous might be fed, even forgot its native power. (Wisd. Sol. 16:17, 22)

In the conclusion to the book, this and other cosmic reversals are cited: "For the elements changed places with one another, as on a harp the notes vary the nature of the rhythm, while each note remains the same" (19:18), and the point of all that is, "For in everything, O Lord, you have exalted and glorified your people, and you have not neglected to help them at all times and in all places" (19:22).

Sirach spoke not of the supernatural but of the natural in a lengthy hymn praising the Lord of creation (42:15–43:33). It concludes with words that convey the numinous feeling:

> We could say more but could never say enough;
>   let the final word be: "He is the all."
> Where can we find the strength to praise him?
>   For he is greater than all his works.
> Awesome is the Lord and very great,
>   and marvelous is his power.
> Glorify the Lord and exalt him as much as you can,
>   for he surpasses even that.
> When you exalt him, summon all your strength,
>   and do not grow weary, for you cannot praise him enough.
> Who has seen him and can describe him?
>   Or who can extol him as he is?
> Many things greater than these lie hidden,
>   for I have seen but few of his works.
> For the Lord has made all things,
>   and to the godly he has given wisdom. (Sirach 43:27–33)

Praise of God's incomprehensible goodness, less effective poetically but still conveying a sense of the numinous, may also be found in *2 Baruch* 75.

Forgiveness is one of those firmly held beliefs for which there is actually no fully logical explanation. How can a just God withhold what the sinner justly deserves? The answer, of course, appeals to the grace and mercy of God, but these are as much nonrational qualities as is the "wrath" of God, and so the passages that probe most deeply into the reality of forgiveness may appropriately take on a numinous aura. This is true of the first part of Prayer of Manasseh:

O Lord Almighty,
God of our ancestors,
of Abraham and Isaac and Jacob
and of their righteous offspring;
you who made heaven and earth
with all their order;
who shackled the sea by your word of command,
who confined the deep
and sealed it with your terrible and glorious name;
at whom all things shudder,
and tremble before your power,
for your glorious splendor cannot be borne,
and the wrath of your threat to sinners is unendurable;
yet immeasurable and unsearchable
is your promised mercy,
for you are the Lord Most High,
of great compassion, long-suffering, and very merciful,
and you relent at human suffering.
O Lord, according to your great goodness
you have promised repentance and forgiveness
to those who have sinned against you,
and in the multitude of your mercies
you have appointed repentance for sinners,
so that they may be saved. (Pr. Man. 1—7; cf. 2 Esd. 8:20–24)

These examples should suffice to show that the coexistence of shuddering and bliss when believers know themselves to be very near to God is not restricted to "primitive" religious experiences but remained an apparently essential part of the most highly developed religion of antiquity.

Is it possible, however, that rabbinic Judaism, with its strong emphasis on obedience to the divine law as definitive of religion, really lost the sense of the numinous that we have been tracing? A critique of Otto's work by Burton Leiser claimed that he had completely misunderstood "holiness" in the Old Testament.[32] He maintained first that Otto was wrong in saying that there was anything about dread or terror associated with the root *qdsh*, asserting that it meant only that certain obligations were required with respect to what was called holy. Such a position can be maintained only by ignoring texts such as Isa. 8:13: "But the LORD of hosts, him you shall regard as holy; let him be your fear [*mora'*], and let him be your dread [*ma'arits*]." His claim of error may be dismissed, then. His second criticism is that Otto's description of the numinous relationship between humans and God is nonsense; Leiser goes on to define a "Pharisaic" conception of holiness in completely rational terms focusing on duty. The remainder of the article is a study of many of the uses of *qdsh* in the Old Testament, uses of no interest to Otto because they are concerned with the ritual and ethical aspects of the term. The critique of Otto is beside the mark, then, but we must ask whether such a critique was possible because it accurately reflects the spirit of later Judaism.

Another Jewish scholar, Lawrence Hoffman, claims that what he calls "Ottonian numinosity" can be traced through Jewish worship from the second century through the ninteenth- and early twentieth-century Reform prayer-books.[33] He finds a shift away from the language of transcendence only in the twentieth century. Rather than citing the evidence he works with, from the liturgy, let us consider just a couple of midrashic texts in which *mysterium tremendum* and *fascinans* are powerfully expressed:

> When the Israelites heard at Sinai the word *I*, their souls left them, as it says, *If we hear the voice . . . any more, then we shall die* (Deut. v,22); and so it is written, *My soul failed me when he spoke* (S.S. v,6). The Word then returned to the Holy One, blessed be He, and said: "Sovereign of the Universe, Thou art full of life, and Thy law is full of life, and Thou hast sent me to the dead, for they are all dead." Thereupon the Holy One, blessed be He, sweetened [i.e. softened] the Word for them, as it says, *The voice of the Lord is powerful; the voice of the Lord is full of majesty* (Ps. xxix,4). . . . The Torah which God gave to Israel restored their souls to them, as it says, *The law of the Lord is perfect, restoring the soul* (*ib.* xix,8). (*Midrash Rabbah.* Song of Songs V.16,3)

The rabbis' exegesis of Ex. 20:19 shows they had not lost their sense of the daunting aspect of God's word, for they said that since the people at Sinai did hear it, they were killed by it. They must then add an interpretive story, supported by a proof text, to explain how it was possible for them to be restored to life.

An even more daunting passage has been discussed at some length by Jacob Neusner in his book *The Incarnation of God*. This incarnation of which Neusner speaks refers to the tendency in the Babylonian Talmud (especially) to depict God as a sage.[34] In many of the rabbinic stories God has been remarkably humanized, represented as involving himself in rather ordinary conversations with human beings. It might seem at first, then, that the suprarational really had disappeared from rabbinic Judaism, but Neusner finds the opposite to be true. There is a significant difference between the sage-stories and the God-stories. The point of sage-stories is to resolve tension of some kind, but the God-stories are open-ended, without resolution. Neusner concludes from this that "God is truly wholly other; alike but essentially unlike" (227). His classic example is the account of a conversation between God and Moses concerning Rabbi Akiba, who was martyred under Hadrian (ca. 132 C.E.). Moses visited Akiba's school and was so impressed that he returned to God and asked, "Lord of the universe, now if you have such a man available, how can you give the Torah through me?" God's answer was the blunt, "Be silent. That is how I have decided matters." Moses then asked to see Akiba's reward for his mastery of the Torah. He turned around and saw people weighing out his flesh in the butcher shop. (His actual death was through flaying alive by the Romans.) Moses said to God, "Lord of the universe, such is his mastery of Torah, and such is his reward?" God's answer was the same, "Be silent. That is how I have decided matters."[35] Neusner does not use the word numinous, but this is what he concludes about this disturbing story:

> It is to show that God, while like a sage, is more than a sage—much more. And, even in this deeply human context, that "more" is to be stated only in the submission expressed through silence. This I take to be the final statement of the incarnation of God of the Judaism of the dual Torah. God incarnate remains God ineffable. (230)

Evaluations of the feeling level of another religion must be made with considerable caution, and with dependence on the work of those who practice that religion, so no further effort will be made to trace the sense of the numinous through the history of Judaism. The few pieces of evidence cited above, however, suggest that it has not been lost.[36]

The New Testament

In the New Testament we find a continuation of the two types of numinous language found in the Apocrypha and Pseudepigrapha. The account of the transfiguration of Jesus is partly influenced by the theophanies of the Old Testament. As Peter, James, and John see Jesus' face shining and his clothes becoming dazzling white and Peter begins to babble (Mark explains, "for they were terrified") about building on the mountaintop three dwellings, for Jesus, Moses, and Elijah, "suddenly a bright cloud overshadowed them, and from the cloud a voice said, 'This is my Son, the Beloved; with him I am well pleased; listen to him!' (Matt. 17:5). Then comes the reaction we would expect, comparable to the effects of theophany in the Old Testament: "When the disciples heard this, they fell to the ground and were overcome by fear" (v. 6). The natural phenomena are much less extensive, but there are clear reflections of Sinai in the narrative. Peter's reference to Moses and Elijah reminds us that both of them encountered God on Sinai in the midst of awe-inspiring phenomena, and Moses' face shone as a result of his near contact with God on the mountain (Ex. 34:30). Jesus is the disciples' friend, and so it seems fair to understand the fear attributed to them as numinous awe rather than simple terror for their safety.

The physical, rather than emotional, effects of theophany appear in the account of the call of the apostle Paul (Acts 9:1–9). Once again, blinding light is the main feature, "suddenly a light from heaven flashed around him. He fell to the ground and heard a voice," which his companions also heard, although they did not see anyone. Paul was left sightless as a result of the experience, until a Christian, Ananias, came to befriend him.[37] Similar effects of a vision are recorded in Rev. 1:17: "When I saw him [the Son of man], I fell at his feet as though dead. But he placed his right hand on me, saying, "Do not be afraid; I am the first and the last, and the living one." Then one might expect Revelation to portray more elaborate theophanies, like the Jewish apocalypses, and that is true. Chapter 4 is a good example.

The book of Revelation also contains good examples of the language of praise, in the hymns it ascribes to those in heaven (e.g., 15:3b-4). An even more impressive outburst of wonder occurs at the end of Paul's lengthy effort to explain the continuing place of the Jews in God's economy, now that Christ has come (Rom. 11:33–36). It may not be unfair to him to say that in effect he finally admits he does not know, but instead of "Be silent. That is how I have decided matters," as the rabbis said later on, Paul bursts out in doxology:

O the depth of the riches and wisdom and knowledge of God! How unsearchable are his judgments and how inscrutable his ways!
"For who has known the mind of the Lord?
Or who has been his counselor?" [citing Isa. 41:11]
"Or who has given a gift to him,
to receive a gift in return?" [alluding to Job 41:11]
For from him and through him and to him are all things. To him be the glory forever. Amen.

Contemplation of the *mysterium* here leads only to the *fascinans*.

The most impressive example of numinous language in the New Testament occurs in Hebrews, and although it is fairly long, it needs to be quoted in full for that reason. The author brings together two mountains, Sinai and Zion, but Zion is for him the heavenly Jerusalem, not the city in Palestine. Furthermore, it is accessible now, not merely an eschatological hope, for the author of Hebrews is comparing Israel's worship at Mount Sinai with the customary worship of Christians in his (or her) time, since that brings them, through Christ, into the immediate presence of God. As is typical of the theology of Hebrews, the *tremendum* is associated with Sinai, and the *fascinans* with the Christian assembly, but it seems clear that the author can feel them both:

You have not come to something that can be touched, a blazing fire, and darkness, and gloom, and a tempest, and the sound of a trumpet, and a voice whose words made the hearers beg that not another word be spoken to them. (For they could not endure the order that was given, "If even an animal touches the mountain, it shall be stoned to death." Indeed, so terrifying was the sight that Moses said, "I tremble with fear.") But you have come to Mount Zion and to the city of the living God, the heavenly Jerusalem, and to innumerable angels in festal gathering, and to the assembly of the firstborn who are enrolled in heaven, and to God the judge of all, and to the spirits of the righteous made perfect, and to Jesus, the mediator of a new covenant, and to the sprinkled blood that speaks a better word than the blood of Abel. (Heb. 12:18–24)

Does the Lord's Prayer itself contain an element of the *tremendum*? The *mysterium* ("who art in heaven; hallowed be thy name") and the *fascinans* ("our Father," etc.) are clearly there, but what do we make of "Lead us not into temptation"? There is almost universal agreement that this has to be explained away somehow, and the voluminous literature on the subject contains a variety of efforts. The recent book by Jan Milic Lochman takes on the problem more directly than most, beginning with a quote from J. Carmignac's major study:

> For when we beseech God not to lead us into temptation, the only reason to do so is that there might be some danger that he would lead us into it. We thus run up against a final and incontestable dilemma. On the one hand, if God plays even the tiniest positive role in temptation to sin, he cannot be infinitely good, for he is helping to draw his earthly children into the greatest misery. On the other hand, if God plays no positive role, then we insult him by asking him not to do evil.[38]

Lochman cites J. Schniewind's commentary on Matthew, in which the petition is left as an irreconcilable contradiction, due to the mystery of evil,[39] but thinks more than respectful silence is possible, moving on to suggest it means something like, "Let us not be caught in the sphere of temptation," or "Do not let us correspond or conform to temptation." Apparently he and the others who take this route have not noticed that this does not solve the God problem at all.

May we dare to think Schniewind may have been closer to Jesus' meaning than the others? That is, remembering Jesus' prayer in Gethsemane, could it be that he also gave his disciples a model prayer in which terror must be present? I cannot answer that question, but our work thus far, plus some of what will appear in consideration of the *tremendum* in contemporary life, leads me to think we cannot reject the idea as completely out of the question.

The unprecedented form of numinous experience in the New Testament is the encounter with a human being that leads to worship, and of course Jesus is that human being. In Mark 4:35–41 we are reminded of the two different uses of "fear" by Moses in Ex. 20:20. Jesus and the disciples were in a boat crossing the Sea of Galilee when a great storm threatened to capsize them. The disciples awoke Jesus and he spoke to the wind, calming it, then tried to calm the disciples, saying, "Why are you afraid? Have you still no faith?" But the result of it all was that they "feared a great fear" (literally) and said to one another, "Who then is this, that even the wind and the sea obey him?" Echoes of the Old Testament theophanies may be present, but most important is the evangelist's evocation of something called "fear" which was the *result* of being saved from danger. It is the kind of reaction that up until now only the presence of God would produce in a Jew.

Immediately after this, in Mark, Jesus encounters a man with an unclean spirit (Mark 5:1–20). Some might disqualify him from this survey, but both he and the local populace are presented as witnesses to Jesus' supernatural power. The man in his madness is able to recognize the presence of God before him: "What have you to do with me, Jesus, Son of the Most High God?" The people who see the man clothed and in his right mind, who then beg Jesus to leave their neighborhood, are typically accused by preachers of wanting to get rid of him because of what he did to their pigs, but this overlooks one word (repeated in Luke 8:35–37, making it harder to overlook). "They came to Jesus and saw the demoniac sitting there, clothed and in his right mind, the very man who had had the legion; and *they were afraid*" (Mark 5:15). Mark does not suggest it was economic concerns that moved them, but claims they knew they were in the presence of an uncanny power.

The numinous language becomes stronger as we continue through Mark. When the disciples, who are struggling to row across the Sea of Galilee against a heavy wind, see Jesus walking toward them on the water, they are at first affected by the cruder form of numinous fear that Otto described at length. "But when they saw him walking on the sea, they thought it was a ghost and cried out; for they all saw him and were terrified" (Mark 6:49–50a). The result of Jesus' identification of himself, adding "Do not be afraid," was, according to Mark, that they were utterly astounded, but Matthew's version goes significantly further: "And those in the boat worshiped him, saying, "Truly you are the Son of God" (Matt. 14:33). The pattern in Matthew thus reminds us of Old Testament passages such as Jacob's dream at Bethel, where someone is given a sign that God is present, they are awed by it, and they know that the right thing to do is to worship. But here, these good Jews bow down to a man.

Luke claims that Jesus' healing of the paralytic whose friends let him down on a pallet through the roof of a house had a similar uncanny effect on people. His story concludes, "Amazement [*ekstasis*] seized all of them, and they glorified God and were filled with awe [literally, fear], saying, "We have seen strange things today" (Luke 5:26).

These passages, read in the light of our study of the numinous in the Old Testament, make Peter's reaction to so simple a thing as a great catch of fish understandable. In Luke 5:1–11, we are told the disciples had been fishing all night without success, but when Jesus tells them to let down their nets again they make a tremendous catch. Why not just say fisherman's luck? But Peter seems to overreact: " 'Go away from me, Lord, for I am a sinful man!' For he and all who were with him were amazed at the catch of fish that they had taken." Amazement can be connected with a feeling of sinfulness only if we accept that Peter felt a numinous presence there in the boat with him, without needing anything obviously miraculous, as in the previous stories, to convince him of that.

So also, we are told, with even less explanation, that as Jesus and the disciples made their way to Jerusalem for the Passover, presumably an event to which the disciples were looking forward, unable to grasp what Jesus had told them about it, suddenly "they were amazed, and those who followed them were afraid" (Mark 10:32b). We are told only that Jesus was walking ahead of them; our work so far may justify us in thinking that Mark is saying, suddenly they had an insight that this was more than a man.

John's theology virtually eliminates the *tremendum* from Jesus' presence on earth, so nothing is said of fear on the part of the man born blind. After he was healed we are told he worshiped Jesus, however (John 9:38). One further example of a numinous experience leading naturally to worship may be drawn from the materials dealing with the early church. Paul is recommending to the Corinthians prophecy (which probably means essentially preaching the Word) as superior to speaking in tongues. But he says, "But if all prophesy, an unbeliever or outsider who enters is reproved by all and called to account by all. After the secrets of the unbeliever's heart are disclosed, that person will bow down before God and worship him, declaring, 'God is really among you' " (1 Cor. 14:24–25). Paul believes that the power of the word of God as proclaimed by believers in worship can produce the same effect as the presence of Jesus had produced in his disciples. There will be more to say about the presence of Christ in the church in the next section of this chapter. At this point the principal thing to observe is that the New Testament has not only continued to use language conveying the sense of the numinous, but that it has done a completely new thing. It depicts good Jews being drawn into a numinous experience by the presence of the man Jesus, and even worshiping him as a result. We shall not take up here the question of whether all that may have been the creation of the writers of the Gospels; at any rate it became part of the evidence Christians used in their claims that Jesus was divine. For this writer, it seems most likely that it would have required actual experiences of this kind to lead any Jew to make such a claim.

Christianity

No adequate survey of the numinous in Christian experience can be provided, for that would require a history of "devotion," ranging over the whole of the Christian life. One would expect to find evidence of it appearing most prominently in prayers and hymns, and a few examples from the latter will be provided. The visions of the mystics can be left to one side, since their aim was to dissolve the difference between humanity and divinity, even though their language certainly reflects the three elements we have been tracing. We shall allude to only two theologians as evidence for the perseverance of numinous feelings among intellectuals whose environment was Western culture. Otto acknowledged that it was his early work on Luther that first made him aware of the nonrational element that distinguished religion from all other human experiences. "Indeed, I grew to understand the numinous and its difference from the rational in Luther's *De Servo Arbitrio* long before I identified it in the *qadosh* of the Old Testament and in the elements of 'religious awe' in the history of religion in general."[40]

It is often the case that Augustine had already written on something the Reformers take up with enthusiasm, and the same is true of this aspect of Christianity. In his *Confessions*[41] the three elements of the nonrational side of religion are expressed in striking language. The *mysterium* appears in statements such as these, following an impassioned doxology: "Yet, O my God, my life, my holy Joy, what is this that I have said? What can any man say when he speaks of thee? But woe to them that keep silence—since even those that say most are dumb" (Book 1, chap. 4). He holds the *tremendum* and the *fascinans* together, as one must, in "Even if I die, let me see thy face lest I die" (Book 1, chap. 5). And the three elements appear in a formulation so impressive that Otto and other writers on the subject quote it:

> Who shall comprehend such things and who shall tell of it? What is it that shineth through me and striketh my heart without injury, so that I both shudder and burn? I shudder because I am unlike it; I burn because I am like it. It is Wisdom itself that shineth through me, clearing away my fog, which so readily overwhelms me so that I faint in it, in the darkness and burden of my punishment. For my strength is brought down in neediness, so that I cannot endure even my blessings until thou, O Lord, who hast been gracious to all my iniquities, also healest all my infirmities. (Book 11, chap. 9)

Although narratives such as the Sinai materials in Exodus and the stories in the Gospels can tell of numinous experiences, it is hymnic language, such as Augustine employed, that conveys it best. As Otto considered "Means of Expression of the Numinous" (chapter 9, appendix 2), he discussed music as one of the most effective of those means, and it is the combination of words and music in hymns such as "Let All Mortal Flesh Keep Silent," "Ah, Dearest Jesus, How Hast Thou Offended?" "O Sacred Head Now Wounded," and "Were You There When They Crucified My Lord?" that may produce a strong awareness of the numinous in those who sing them.

LOSS AND RETENTION OF THE NUMINOUS IN THE MODERN WORLD

> If the literature of contemporary Christianity furnishes fewer expressions of numinous creature-feeling, it is not because the presence of God is now recognized by other criteria but rather because of the dominant humanistic character of modern life with its greatly attenuated God-consciousness. —Robert F. Davidson, *Rudolf Otto's Interpretation of Religion*[42]

> Whatever the situation may have been in the past, *today* the supernatural as a meaningful reality is absent or remote from the horizons of everyday life of large numbers, very probably of the majority, of people in modern societies, who seem to manage to get along without it quite well. —Peter L. Berger, *A Rumor of Angels*[43]

> First of all, the nonreligious man refuses transcendence, accepts the relativity of "reality," and may even come to doubt the meaning of existence. . . . Modern nonreligious man assumes a new existential situation; he regards himself solely as the subject and agent of history, and he refuses all appeal to transcendence. —Mircea Eliade, *The Sacred and the Profane*[44]

The unanimity expressed in these quotations suggests that the study of the numinous in human experience must be confined to the past and to what remains of premodern humanity, and yet the numinous has not completely disappeared from our secularized world. Eliade and Davidson talk of attenuated remnants of the sacred, experienced in degenerate forms in the rituals associated with death, war, radical political movements, esoteric cults, and in weakened forms in movies and novels (consider especially the science fiction and horror genres).[45] Berger, on the other hand, looks for possibilities of a recovery of the supernatural. He begins as Otto did, with an analysis of human experience, looking for signals of transcendence (which he calls "rumors") suggesting that there is a reality transcending that recognized by the secular world. The experiences he analyzes are "ordering" (the sense that it is possible for "everything to be all right"), play (which interrupts the normal course of time), hope, damnation (the sense of the total unacceptability of radical evil), and humor.[46] We can see from the list alone that he is considering a broader range of experiences than Otto did, but that some of them overlap. The language of theophany, however, is foreign to all except some mystics and charismatics who manage to perpetuate it. The traditional language we have been tracing has largely fallen out of use, so evidence for the persistence of such experiences must now be sought elsewhere. This section thus intends to point to some of the forms through which the numinous does still seem to express itself, even in this largely secularized world.

The loss of any awareness of transcendence appears to be so widespread in Western culture, even among people who faithfully practice their religion, that I would expect a fair number of the readers of this book to be puzzled by the whole effort to think seriously about the "nonrational." This is one of the reasons I have devoted so much space in this book to an exposition of the subject, with exclusive reference to its persistence throughout scripture and the history of Judaism and Christianity until recent times. It is certainly not because I am a mystic or charismatic and am seeking to justify my own religious experiences. I have never had a vision or audition and hope I never do. But I understand what Otto is talking about, and understanding of the numinous of course involves something other than the intellect. Because the "ideograms" by which some awareness of the numinous is expressed today are likely to be different from the past, and because the occasions for it may also be different (seldom in a "holy place"!), the scholar's final task is to try to identify some of the experiences that are in continuity with encounters with the numinous in the past.

Crises of various kinds are the most obvious and widespread occasions for awareness of the presence of the numinous. Those who have had dramatic conversion experiences may be able to interpret them and understand them better in the light of the material presented here. The same is likely to be true for those who have been healed in unexplainable ways, or who have been delivered from an apparently fatal situation. These are types of circumstances that have changed little if any from Old Testament times.

A completely new kind of apprehension of the numinous appears in the writings of a scientist, Harold Schilling, who finds that on the frontiers of science today one is confronted by true mystery. By "mystery," he is careful to explain, he does not mean an unsolved puzzle, or a gap in knowledge, that is, something we do not yet know but have the potential to understand eventually. When he says that reality as contemporary science reveals it is fundamentally mysterious, he means: (1) that reality "is not, and cannot be, known or understood or controlled fully," and (2) "that its character is such as to evoke a strong sense of wonder and awe, as well as a feeling of enchantment or fascination, and sometimes even of fear."[47] I have not traced the presumed abolition of mystery by modern science as a major contributor to the loss of the awareness of transcendence in our world, but Schilling has done that in order to move on to demonstrate how postmodern science has rediscovered mystery.[48] This strong numinous sense, which pervades Schilling's work, he ascribes to his contacts with the "depths" of reality revealed now by subatomic physics. Whether that "reality" has anything to do with the existence of a personal God can be questioned, of course, but for Schilling it undergirds his somewhat unorthodox form of Christian faith.

Gerd Theissen, who combines theology with psychoanalysis, has also defined a "critical faith," as over against ideological and empirical challenges, in terms of the human experience of the imponderables of "reality." His first definition of religion is "sensitivity towards the resonance and absurdity of reality," and he tells us that resonance and absurdity are his terms corresponding to *fascinans* and *tremendum*.[49] Whether these numinous experiences can really be claimed as contacts with God forms the subject of two volumes by John Bowker, who comes to no firm conclusions but provides an abundance of evidence, ancient and modern, to work with.[50]

Will the new science ever produce a truly postmodern world, as the old science produced the modern world, a new world in which the nonrational is no longer considered to be by definition unreal, or at least unimportant? There are few signs of movement in that direction so far, but it may be that in the distant future the twentieth century will be looked upon as the great transitional period between the eighteenth and nineteenth (rationalism) and the twenty-first (??). In the meantime, at the scholarly level, some openness has appeared, witnessed by work in various fields by scholars such as Otto, Eliade, Berger, and Schilling.

In chapter 6 of this book I shall ask whether the reality of our experience of *tremendum* in this life has led the writers of the Old Testament to speak of God, the creator, sustainer, and blesser of life, as a destroyer. To conclude this section, I call your attention to the frequency with which the experience of terrible trouble brings God to the minds even of those who never otherwise think of him. Is this a partial form of the numinous experience?[51] Reactions vary greatly. There may be anger at this unknown who has suddenly appeared in life as an enemy. There may be feelings of guilt, rationalizing the event as punishment. There may be resignation, accepting some mysterious wisdom as greater than ours. Or, for those who know the identity of this wholly other one, there may come "peace that passes understanding."

As a most remarkable example of that last experience, I quote from a pamphlet written by the Englishwoman Edith Barfoot, concerning the way her faith enabled her to deal with the suffering caused by rheumatoid arthritis over many years. It was written after twenty-one years with the disease, reprinted with an appendix after fifty years, and again with an epilogue after fifty-eight years of the pain and crippling caused by that affliction. Sir Basil Blackwell, who knew her, had her work and some tributes published after her death at age eighty-seven. She was a devout Catholic, and she had come to the conclusion, after some typical, early attempts to bargain with God over this, that suffering was the vocation given to her by a loving God. That is not a theology to be recommended by the healthy to others who suffer, and not a theology many are likely to accept, but one must respect her conclusion, for she lived with it for a long time. To use the terminology of this section, that was the *tremendum* in her life, the awe-ful conviction that God wanted her to suffer. But it was a true religious experience (and a remarkably long-lasting one), for it was never separated from the *fascinans*, that this was the call of a loving God who never deserted her. Her language does not resemble the theophanies or the magnificent poetry of scripture, nor is it analytical, like that of Schilling or Theissen, but in these simple words the reality of *mysterium tremendum* and *fascinans* is surely unmistakable:

> If in the course of human suffering the time comes for plunging into the depths of inexpressible pain, when the whole body is racked from head to foot with agony that nothing can alleviate, when the soul itself, the body's faithful ally, is numb because of the physical state which has overwhelmed it, so that it is incapable of conscious prayer for help, when human aid is of no avail, then, more than ever before, down below conscious understanding, there in the unplumbed depth he waits with open arms to receive the tortured being, while he infuses into the soul and mind of her the absolute trust which feeds the inmost consciousness with the knowledge that all is well; and with divine knowledge comes renewed strength to endure and lie still in the everlasting arms.[52]

CHAPTER 3

"I WILL BE WITH YOU"

Exodus 3—4
(Continued)

Even though I walk through the darkest valley,
   I fear no evil;
for you are with me.
                                                —Psalm 23:4

And remember, I am with you always, to the end of the age.
                                                —Matthew 28:20

God's response to Moses' first objection to his call has a potent ring to it: "But I will be with you." That promise seems especially important, since it is also God's first response to the objections of Gideon and Jeremiah when they are appointed to daunting tasks, but the commentaries typically do not devote much attention to it, and there have been only a few special studies of the expression, all of them recent. One of the reasons for that may be the prevalence of the word-study approach to exegesis, for this sentence contains no key words. Most concordances are of no help whatever in locating any form of this sentence, and even when one uses complete concordances, it is difficult to locate all the relevant passages, for the only word that must always appear is (in English) "with," and in Hebrew that may be *'eth*, *'im*, or the inseparable preposition *b^e*-. The Septuagint is consistent in using *meta* for this expression, but one must also allow for the possibility of *sun* or even *ev*. This means many hundreds of passages have to be examined, and it partly explains why each of the studies that has appeared so far has a slightly different list. My list will vary from each of the others, for reasons to be explained along the way.

The subject of the sentence may be "I," "he," "you," "God," or "Yahweh," and the object of the preposition may be "me," "us," "you (singular or plural)," "him," or "them."[1] The verb "to be" (*hayah*) may be omitted from a Hebrew sentence, at the discretion of the writer, so all that may appear are the subject and the prepositional phrase, forming a "noun clause," with the verb to be understood. Only a little over one-third of the sentences that interest us include the verb "to be."

Representative examples of the sentence are thus: "I am [will be] with you,"

"God [or the Lord] was with him," "The Lord [or God] is with us," and there are several other variations, but they are clearly just variants of an affirmation that is virtually formulaic, one that occurs about one hundred times in the Old Testament and reappears in highly significant ways in the New Testament.[2]

Since this is a virtual formula, occurring rather frequently and in passages of considerable importance, one may ask why the difficulty of gathering the relevant material had not been overcome long ago. One reason may be that in Christian worship the expression—lacking key theological terms as it does—has become melded into the language to such an extent that it has no longer been noticed as a distinctive promise. In the Old Testament it does have distinctiveness and a peculiar potency, as will be shown, but for Christians it has perhaps become a platitude. Those who participate in liturgical forms of worship have for centuries engaged in the dialogue:
"The Lord be with you."
"And with thy spirit."
They may be doing so without thinking much about what the liturgist has wished for them. Those who worship in nonliturgical ways are more likely to have sung the same formula in the hymn, "God be with you, till we meet again." The simplicity of the sentence and the frequency of its use in worship without explanation are additional reasons for its neglect by exegetes and theologians.[3] No Old Testament theology deals with it, not even Terrien's, which takes the presence of God as its unifying theme.[4] Special studies of the presence of the Lord focus on the materials dealing with the tabernacle and the temple, or on the term *liphne* ("before," "in the presence of"), rather than a sentence such as this one, which contains nothing more striking than a preposition.[5] But we shall see that the writers of the Old Testament used it in ways that are profoundly important theologically.

"I WILL BE WITH YOU" IN EXODUS

God's promise to be with Moses in the apparently impossible task he has assigned him forms a framework for the call story (cf. 3:12 with 4:12, 15). The dialogue begins with God's reference to seeing, hearing, and knowing his people's sufferings, making the connection with the author's introduction of God in 2:23–25, as we have already noted. Then God moves directly to business: "So come, I will send you to Pharaoh to bring my people, the Israelites, out of Egypt" (Ex. 3:10). Moses' response, "Who am I that I should go to Pharaoh, and bring the Israelites out of Egypt?" is a perfectly reasonable one. I think we shall conclude from the study in this chapter, however, that God's answer, *"But* I will be with you," should have been reassurance enough.[6] That Moses should not need anything more is also indicated by the "sign" that God immediately offers. It is not some additional, present-tense proof that God really means it, or of his ability to enable Moses to complete the task. Much of the scholarly discussion of the nature of the sign has resulted from questions of that type. But studies of the word *'oth* have shown that it is appropriate to understand it here as confirmatory:[7] After all has been accomplished in Egypt, Moses will find himself back at this same mountain with the liberated people, worshiping the same God who addresses him now. In the meantime, it should be enough to know that this God will be *with* him.

That should have been enough, but it is not, so the discussion will continue at some length, with God condescending to Moses' human weakness in several ways. The last of them is to allow Aaron to do the speaking for Moses, but even the speech itself will be possible for the same reason God gave at the beginning: "I will be with your mouth and teach you what you are to speak" (Ex. 4:12) and "I will be with your mouth and with his [Aaron's] mouth, and will teach you what you shall do" (4:15). With that, Moses is dismissed and the account of his call concludes.

This is the only passage in Exodus in which God speaks to offer the promise "I will be with you," but we have already seen some evidence that it is important to know exactly what that means. The sentence does occur twice more in the book, coming from human speakers. The first of them is unique in being the only ironic use of the formula. We are in the midst of the story of the plagues, and the pharaoh's advisers urge him to let the Israelites go before further disasters afflict the land. So the pharaoh offers to negotiate, asking exactly who is going to leave. When Moses answers, young and old, sons and daughters, flocks and herds, the pharaoh's reaction is nicely represented by the NRSV translation: "The LORD indeed will be with you, if ever I let your little ones go with you!" (Ex. 10:10). The other occurrence represents a more common use of the formula, to express a wish that God may help another person. Moses' distress in Exodus 18 is the result of the many disputes among the people that he is asked to adjudicate. His father-in-law Jethro's advice begins in a portentous way: "Now listen to me. I will give you counsel, and God be with you!" (Ex. 18:19). Having looked at the four chapters of Exodus in which the formula appears, we see that it is only in chapters 3—4 that it rightfully draws any particular interest, and since it is the setting in which this sentence occurs, rather than word or syntactical studies, that determines its significance, it will be necessary next to find the best way to evaluate its uses elsewhere in the Old Testament, in order to be sure we properly understand it in Exodus 3—4 and recognize how that use contributes to this aspect of Israel's concept of God.

THE OLD TESTAMENT

Here is an excellent example of the tendency for scholars' special interests to dictate what they find in the material they study. There have been three fairly thorough studies of "God with us." W. C. van Unnik's interest was in tracing the origins of the liturgical dialogue: "The Lord be with you." "And with thy spirit." "Let us pray."[8] The expression "and with thy spirit" does not occur anywhere in the Bible as a response to "The Lord be with you," so van Unnik looked for reasons why the church associated them in worship and was satisfied when he found texts referring to the spirit that were somehow associated with the "God-with" sentence. Horst Dietrich Preuss, on the other hand, had just published his dissertation on eschatology, and among other things he found a strong futuristic tone to the idea of "God with us," which no one else has observed.[9] Dieter Vetter had been studying with Claus Westermann at the time Westermann wrote his monograph on blessing, and for Vetter it is assumed from the beginning that this is a special form of blessing-statement.[10] In studies of other kinds, however, exegetes working with the calls of Gideon or Jeremiah have assumed the call story is the natural *Sitz-im-Leben* of the formula.[11] This variety shows us there is a need to take another look at it with an effort to avoid presuppositions that have hurt the earlier studies.[12]

One way to point out typical uses of the sentence is to begin with an exceptional case and then show why it is unusual. First, in Ruth 2:4, Boaz greets the reapers in the grainfield with "The Lord be with you," and they answer, "The Lord bless you." Their answer is a customary Israelite greeting; what Boaz says is not. There is only one other place where these words may have been used as a greeting (Judg. 6:12), but the angel's address to Gideon is more properly to be taken as a statement than a wish; thus, "The Lord is with you, you mighty man of valor." So we must be warned against thinking that our frequent liturgical use of "The Lord be with you" reflects a common usage in ancient Israel.

Second, the "you" in Boaz's address refers to a group of ordinary people at their daily work, and that occurs nowhere else. Two-thirds of the occurrences of this sentence refer to leaders of one kind or another; the others (with a few exceptions) are addressed by a leader to "Israel." Third, it is an ordinary day in Bethlehem and the reapers are experiencing no desperate needs to which Boaz's words come with a reassuring promise, and this is also the only case in the Old Testament where that is true. The evidence that will now be presented will show that "God is with you" and its parallels belong to a clearly defined set of circumstances; that is, when the addressee faces danger or a task where the risk of failure is very great.

Two of these unusual features of Boaz's greeting will provide for us an approach to the meaning and use of the formula which may be relatively free of presuppositions, since it is based on the frequency of occurrence of the phenomena. First, 68 of the 104 passages I have identified associate this promise with leaders, and that is important enough that the full list should be provided. It may be useful to classify them:

Leaders of clans: Ishmael, Abraham, Isaac, Jacob, Caleb, Job.[13]
Kings: Saul, David, Solomon, Jeroboam, Hezekiah, Abijah, Asa, Jehoshaphat, Amaziah, Necho (and add other governmental officials: Joseph, Zerubbabel, and the judges referred to in 2 Chron. 19:6).[14]

Military leaders: Joshua, the Judges in general (Judg. 2:18), Gideon, commanders of the army (2 Chron. 32:7–8). Later we will note that most of the promises to the kings are in military settings, which could expand this list greatly.[15]
Combined functions: Moses, Samuel.[16]
Priests: Phinehas (1 Chron. 9:20), Joshua (Hag. 2:4).
Prophets: Jeremiah (Jer. 1:8, 19; 15:20; 20:11).

It is evident at a glance that most of the famous characters of the Old Testament are included, except for the prophets. A reason for that will be suggested shortly. It is not surprising that only one ruler of the Northern Kingdom appears, since "God was with him" conveys such a favorable judgment. Given the Deuteronomistic Historian's highly negative opinion of Jeroboam, it is surprising that he does appear, and that may lead to the conjecture that 1 Kings 11:26–40 contains some old material of northern origin that has not been thoroughly edited by DtrH. One famous king of Judah—Josiah—is missing, in spite of his very high reputation (2 Kings 23:25), and that may very well be because of his military failure. It is characteristic of the postexilic period that priests tend to pick up attributes associated with kings before the exile, and that may account for the appearance of Phineas and Joshua in 1 Chronicles and Haggai.

It is a strikingly comprehensive list. Of the most important leaders in Old Testament history, only Josiah and two of the later postexilic leaders, Ezra and Nehemiah, are missing. Apparently the prophets were not the kind of people about whom it was natural to say, "God is [was] with him," since the phrase is associated only with Jeremiah. We are already led to a preliminary conclusion: that it was very important in ancient Israel to be able to affirm about one's leader (rather than about ordinary people), "God is with him." When the wish "God be with you" is expressed, nine of the eleven occurrences concern leaders. In another literary type, the narrator's summary "God was with him" is used in twenty passages to express the certainty that God was present to help a leader of one kind or another.[17] Only twice does it refers to tribes, to Judah as it goes up to possess the hill country in Judg. 1:19 and to the house of Joseph as it attacks Bethel in Judg. 1:22. When the phrase occurs as a promise addressed by a speaker to someone else (omitting for now divine oracles), the distribution is almost equally unbalanced. Seventeen passages refer to leaders,[18] four to the Israelite people (Num. 14:43—negative; Num. 23:21; Deut. 2:7; 20:1).

Another preliminary conclusion is that the remaining thirty-six occurrences of the formula may represent the democratizing of a statement that had its original setting in the divine confirmation of Israel's leaders. If so, the element of continuity between leader and people that made this possible is not hard to determine. It was danger, and that leads us to the other unusual feature of Boaz's greeting: It was given at a time when there was no danger or unusual stress for those to whom it was offered.

One of the most obvious pieces of evidence for the association of "God is with you" with danger is the fact that the words most often paired with it are "Fear not."[19] For example, Joshua's commission to lead the Israelites into the Promised Land is accompanied by, "It is the LORD who goes before you. He will be with you; he will not fail you or forsake you. Do not fear or be dismayed" (Deut. 31:8), and by, "I hereby command you: Be strong and courageous; do not be frightened or dismayed, for the LORD your God is with you wherever you go" (Josh. 1:9). Deuteronomy's prescription for the conduct of war in general includes the same two assurances: "When you go out to war against your enemies, and see horses and chariots, an army larger than your own, you shall not be afraid of them; for the LORD your God is with you, who brought you up from the land of Egypt" (Deut. 20:1; cf. vv. 3–4). The Chronicler, who has turned the old war ideology of Israel into a virtual liturgical event, uses "Fear not, the LORD is with you/us" in 2 Chron. 20:17 and 32:7–8.

The expressions are also used together in other precarious situations. The life of Hagar's child, Ishmael, was saved in the wilderness by divine intervention, as the angel addressed Hagar with, "Fear not!" The story concludes with the assurance that Ishmael was able to survive and thrive in that threatening place because "God was with the boy" (Gen. 21:17, 20). Amid Isaac's disputes over water with Abimelech of Gerar, God appeared to him with the message, "Do not be afraid, for I am with you" (Gen. 26:24). Jeremiah was reassured, despite intense opposition to his prophesying, including danger to his life: "Do not be afraid of them, for I am with you to deliver you" (Jer. 1:8; cf. 1:17–19). In his book, similar messages are addressed to the Judean exiles in the midst of their distress (Jer. 30:10–11; 42:11; 46:28). The pairing of these two expressions became so natural that Second Isaiah used them in a situation that was probably more discouraging than threatening:

Do not fear, for I am with you,
    do not be afraid, for I am your God. (41:10)
Do not fear, for I am with you,
    I will bring your offspring from the east,
    and from the west I will gather you. (43:5)

The need for assurance of divine help in precarious times was of course as real for ordinary people as for great leaders, and this provides a natural explanation for that "democratizing" tendency suggested earlier and illustrated by the Jeremiah and Isaiah passages just noted. We are beginning to see that in Israel no stronger promise of God's help could be offered than the one typically associated with his presence with a great man who had been called to carry out his work against all odds: "Fear not; I am with you."

We have seen how a narrator might affirm that God was with someone and how speakers within the narratives might make the same assertion concerning their own leaders. Less frequently, the speaker might express the wish that God would be with someone. There are two other forms in which the expression occurs: (1) when God's presence with the speaker himself is the subject, and (2) when the speaker is God. Form criticism has taught us to look for fixed genres of speech, and then to look for a possible setting in life in which that genre may have had its natural and original place, and that leads us to ask whether this formula has a relatively fixed use in any of the widely recognized genres of Old Testament speech. Unfortunately the evidence is not strong. Those who claimed an original cultic setting based their argument on passages such as Isa. 41:10 and 43:2, 5,[20] which have been explained as prophetic imitations of a priestly salvation oracle, but the priestly oracle is in itself hypothetical, and it seems unlikely that these relatively late passages addressed to the people as a whole are reflections of the earliest use of the formula. The "nomadic" origin proposed by Preuss and accepted by Vetter has neither literary nor sociological support. Although Preuss and Vetter rejected the conclusions of earlier studies that focused on the call stories, the approach we have been taking has now led us to consider how the call story fits with our general picture of "God with us" as an expression characteristically directed to leaders in times of distress or risk.

At this point our study supports the conclusions of Walter Grundmann, that the formula is "first a promise to the individual and only later is extended to the covenant people in its totality," and that it "makes the recipients strong and courageous to accept difficult and even hopeless undertakings."[21] Van Unnik also found that "it is often mentioned in connection with a special divine task, in which the particular man is assured of God's assistance."[22] The call stories are of course the most striking examples of God's choice of a particular man for a difficult or apparently hopeless undertaking.

There is debate over whether there existed a fixed genre, "call story," in ancient Israel. After all, that was not something that would occur in normal conversation, or presumably in any of the regular, institutional settings of daily life. Only a few people claimed to have experienced such calls. However, there is at least a clearly discernible pattern used by most of the authors who record call stories. Norman Habel's analysis of the pattern is widely accepted,[23] but for our purposes the more limited study by Ernst Kutsch provides a helpful guide.[24] Kutsch compares the calls of Gideon, Moses, Jeremiah, and Saul, finding four common elements in them:

Commission: Judg. 6:14; Ex. 3:10; Jer. 1:5; 1 Sam. 10:1
Objection: Judg. 6:15; Ex. 3:11; Jer. 1:6; 1 Sam. 9:21 (out of order, compared with the other stories)
Rejoinder: Judg. 6:16; Ex. 3:12; Jer. 1:7–8; 1 Sam. 10:7
Sign: Judg. 6:17–23; Ex. 3:12; Jer. 1:9; 1 Sam. 10:1b–7

This outline shows that in these stories the assurance "I will be with you" is not optional, nor is there any reason to think the authors would have been satisfied with any other promise at this point in their stories.

We do not have enough cases to be able to say it is certain that the formula originated in divine oracles addressed to leaders when they had call experiences, but it can at least be said that the formula finds a natural home in circumstances where someone is called by God to take on an overwhelming task, as God's response to their reasonable objections. Additional support for this conclusion may be found in the ways the appointments of certain other leaders are described, namely Joshua (Deut. 31:7–8, 23; Josh. 1:2–9), Jeroboam (1 Kings 11:29–38), and Zerubbabel, with the priest Joshua (Hag. 2:2–9). The most significant difference in their experiences is that they do not get to say anything, so the objection is always missing. Potential objections of Joshua, and Zerubbabel with the priest Joshua, are anticipated, however, in the admonitions to be strong and bold, to take courage. We have thus found three more examples, to add to the four discussed by Kutsch, in which two elements of the pattern by which God chooses a leader remain consistent: the commission itself and the promise "I will be with you."

Another point must be reinforced before we can begin to summarize. The setting of danger or risk that lies behind almost every occurrence of this sentence is very frequently one of armed combat, and it will be worthwhile to see just how often that is true. Of the 104 passages I have been working with, 64 are in contexts of violent conflict, with references to weapons, armies, or at least the threat of war. The danger or risk that motivates every occurrence of the sentence thus takes a specifically military form in about two-thirds of them. As noted above, this may account for the failure of the historian to say of Josiah that God was with him, for he died in battle. It may also help to explain why the term was not typically applied to prophets, for they were not military leaders as such, even though many of them were involved with war as oracle givers. Our penultimate conclusion, then, subject to testing against the passages that do not fit so well, is that when one of Israel's leaders faced a serious crisis in the life of his people, the most important thing that needed to be said about him, if there was to be any hope, was "God is with him," and some of those leaders claimed that God himself had said it to them. This is probably about as far as we can go in estimating what the original setting of the sentence was. What, exactly, it meant to say "God is with him" is something we still have to formulate.

Prior to that, it is necessary to see whether there are passages that raise serious questions about this conclusion. Some of the texts in which the speaker's words concern himself should be considered. In Gen. 28:20 Jacob uses the formula as part of his bargaining process with God: "If God will be with me, and will keep me in this way that I go, and will give me bread to eat and clothing to wear, so that I come again to my father's house in peace, then the Lord shall be my God." Jacob is no leader at this point, he is all alone, but readers know he will be the father of the twelve tribes. His words show that he does feel himself to be in danger, with a very uncertain future. The most unusual feature of this text is the occurrence of the formula in an "if clause," but Jacob actually uses that to begin his negotiations because God had already said "I am with you" in his dream (v. 15).

The democratizing of the formula discussed earlier will account for its appearance a few times in the psalms, but one might wonder why such a strong statement of assurance occurs so rarely in the language of the people's worship. It may be because of the sense that it more appropriately belongs with the trials of leadership than with the trials of ordinary people. The background of danger remains consistent. In Psalm 23, the individual is able to face evil and the "valley of the shadow of death" without fear because "you are with me" (v. 4). In Psalm 46 the people praise God, their refuge and strength, "who makes wars to cease to the end of the earth," and twice reassure themselves, "The LORD of hosts is with us" (vv. 7, 11). This fits the general pattern we have found, except that the whole populace is involved. Two other psalms (possibly three) are omitted from most other lists, but I think it is appropriate to include them. They say, "I am with God," rather than, "God is with me." Psalm 73 comes from one who felt that "All day long I have been plagued, and am punished every morning" and complained about enemies, but eventually came to the conviction "Nevertheless I am continually with you; you hold my right hand" (v. 23). Psalm 139 expresses the hope that "the bloodthirsty would depart from me," but it also says (in a passage that is somewhat difficult textually), "I awake, I am still with you" (v. 18b). The sense of danger is thus present in both psalms, and the affirmation of presence with God seems to express the same confidence in divine help that we have found in the "God with us" texts. One other psalm has an interesting variant on this, expressed as part of a lament rather than as a form of confidence: "For I am an alien with you; a sojourner like all my fathers" (Ps. 39:12, my translation). Here, unlike almost any other text using the Hebrew words meaning "with," a sense of the riskiness of utter dependence on the presence of one over whom the speaker has no control is clearly expressed.

Only three times does a speaker use the formula simply to describe someone. The young man who recommends David to Saul as a good musician adds, "and the LORD is with him," as if it were a permanent quality David possessed, and that is unusual (1 Sam. 16:18). It does also seem to be present in two late texts. I have found one case where the preposition b^e- is used instead of 'eth or 'im. In Isa. 45:14 the prophet promises that "the wealth of Egypt and the merchandise of Ethiopia, and the Sabeans, tall of stature, shall come over to you and be yours, they shall follow you; they shall come over in chains and bow down to you. They will make supplication to you, saying, 'God is with you alone, and there is no other; there is no god besides him.' " In Zech. 8:23, there appears the promise "In those days ten men from nations of every language shall take hold of a Jew, grasping his garment and saying, 'Let us go with you, for we have heard that God is with you.' " But these two are eschatological hopes, expressing the belief that the day will come when God will dwell without interruption in the midst of his people. This means that 1 Sam. 16:18 is one of the most unusual of all the uses of the formula, since it suggests that "the LORD is with him" is an attribute of David's. Elsewhere the almost "occasional" nature of the promise is evident; as van Unnik emphasizes, not "a permanent fact, but . . . a dynamic experience that acts in special cases."[25]

Finally, something must be said about the Immanuel passages in Isaiah, for they represent the most distinctive uses of this formula, and they provide one of the obvious links between Old and New Testaments. The promise never occurs in any form in Isaiah 1—39 except three times in chapters 7—8, where it takes the unique form *'immanu-el*. At least two of those occurrences are names; there is debate about the third. Isaiah 7 is no call story, but we do find the background of extreme danger—the threat that Judah may be invaded by Israel and Syria, the offer of a sign, an objection by the king to whom it is offered, and the formula, "God is with us," now expressed as the name that will be given to the child who is to be born to *ha'almah*, "the young woman" (7:1–14). Fortunately it will not be necessary for us to survey the immense literature on this chapter, for almost everything in it has been the subject of extensive debate. Consideration of the meaning of the name will suffice.

We find "May Yahweh our God be with us" in 1 Kings 8:57 and "Yahweh of hosts is with us" in Ps. 46:7, 11; these are the only other occurrences of the formula with the pronoun "us." Nowhere except here do we find "God [*'elohim*] is with us," so Isaiah has created a distinctive name.[26] The principal question about the name itself is, Threat or promise? The context calls for a threat, since Ahaz has refused to accept Isaiah's original oracle promising a quick end for Rezin and Pekah, and then has refused to ask for a confirmatory sign. Isaiah insists Ahaz will get a sign anyway, and the most convincing interpretation of that takes verses 15–16 to be the sign—a confirmatory one similar to the one God spoke to Moses about in Exodus 3: A child will (soon) be born and given a portentous name, "God is with us," in keeping with Isaiah's original oracle. "He shall eat curds and honey by the time he knows how to refuse the evil and choose the good. For before the child knows how to refuse the evil and choose the good, the land before whose two kings you are in dread will be descrted." That is, by the time this child knows the difference between good and evil, the danger that is leading you to take the disastrous course of seeking help from Assyria will have evaporated. There is thus a certain irony in the name Isaiah has created for this occasion. "God is with us," truly, but that will be of no avail, since Ahaz intends to do his will rather than God's. Under those circumstances, the best the prophet can do is assert that within a few years he will have been proved right.

This less than completely positive use of the formula by a prophet recalls what Amos had done with it shortly before the time of Isaiah. He cites it as something that has already, in the eighth century, been taken over by the people of the Northern Kingdom as words on which they can depend, come what may. In fact, seldom does it occur in a conditional form, although that may be found in Josh. 7:12; 1 Kings 11:38, and 2 Chron. 15:2. But Amos had evidently heard more than once the reassuring words "God is with us," and by his authority as a prophet he now attaches a condition to them:

> Seek good and not evil, that you may live;
>   and so the LORD, the God of hosts, will be with you,
> just as you have said. (Amos 5:14)

If we also take Isaiah's newly created name to be an ironic reflection of a popular assumption that God will be with them no matter what, it may help us to understand the puzzling occurrences of the same expression in chapter 8. The first of them concludes what is obviously an oracle of judgment, and should probably be taken as a vocative, "O Immanuel," so that now the invasion of the child's land by Assyria is threatened (8:5–8). The meaning of the name thus becomes far more obviously ironic than it was in chapter 7. If we are on the right track in understanding Isaiah's use of the formula in its first two occurrences, however, the third use, which is straightforward and traditional, becomes puzzling. It is an oracle of promise that Israel's enemies will be thwarted, and it concludes with *ki 'immanu 'el* (8:9–10). It would be very strange to introduce a proper name with *ki*—"for, because, that"—so it would appear that here we are intended to take the phrase simply as a promise, "for God is with us," and not as a name. Gilbert Brunet made the original suggestion that these verses are a quotation of an old, popular war song, earlier than Isaiah, and that they are quoted here in order to explain where the prophet got the words he used in his own way as a proper name, and this seems at least as likely as the more traditional interpretations to be found in the commentaries.[27]

Except for the continuity found in the dangerous setting of Isaiah 7—8, Isaiah's use of the formula thus appears to be very nontraditional. He has created a name from it, and uses that name, in 7:14 and 8:8, to raise questions about the overconfident use of the formula, as Amos also did in a more obvious way. The name itself did not become part of an ongoing tradition in Judaism. It is never used as a title for the Messiah in Jewish literature, and in fact Isa. 7:14 was not interpreted as a messianic prophecy until Matthew did so. We shall see, then, that Matthew also does something creative with the portentous but cryptic name *Immanuel.*

We conclude that "I will be with you" and its variants were not understood to be a general statement about the presence of God in the midst of his people. It is never, for example, associated with the ark, the tabernacle, or the temple, and only in Psalm 46 and two postexilic texts (Hag. 2:4–5; Zech. 8:23) is it connected specifically with Jerusalem. When later on we deal with the idea of God's presence with the tabernacle, we shall need to look at eschatological hopes for his permanent presence in the midst of his people, and Ezek. 34:30 is an example of the use of this formula in that way. But Ezekiel and Zechariah represent hopes for the more distant future, rather than affirmations about the present or immediate future, as the formula is normally used. We have just dealt with some prophetic criticisms of the temptation to make "God is with us" an unconditional assurance of the security of the status quo. Their insistence on the illegitimacy of that use adds support to our conclusion that the statement was not heard by Israelites as a platitude about general well-being. Rather, it was an affirmation of God's powerful presence in times of trouble; necessary, but not to be assumed. We have seen that its most likely original setting was in connection with a divine oracle calling an ordinary person to become Israel's leader, or with a leader's assumption of power in some other way. Any suggestion of a date for the appearance of the formula in Israel must be very tentative, but the evidence suggests the time of the settlement in Canaan and the early monarchy. That is, it seems likely to have been associated with the rise of the Judges and with Samuel, Saul, and David, then to have been projected back onto the patriarchs as those traditions were retold.

Since "I will be with you" is not a blessing in general, not simply reassurance that all is well, but is promise of help in times of great danger, or when setting out on an undertaking that seems very likely to fail, one would expect the results of the promise coming true to be success, and words of that sort do frequently accompany the formula. The verb *tsalaḥ*, "to succeed or prosper," occurs in Gen. 39:2, 3, 23; Josh. 1:8; 1 Chron. 22:1; 2 Chron. 13:12 and 20:17–20. A similar verb, *sakal*, "to prosper," appears in Josh. 1:7, 8; 1 Sam. 18:14–15; and 2 Kings 18:7. This helps us to add some content to "I will be with you," in answer to the question raised earlier as to what Israelites actually meant when they said it. Van Unnik came directly to the point when he said about the liturgical formula that interested him ("The Lord be with you") that the crucial question is, "What is contained in this 'to be with somebody,' when said of the Lord?" Our work requires some modification of his answer, but it is worth quoting for the purpose of comparison: "The term defines the dynamic activity of God's Spirit given to particular chosen individuals or the people of God, enabling them to do a work of God in word or deed by protecting, assisting and blessing them; this presence of the Spirit manifests itself in the individual and to the outside world."[28] We have not found support for his emphasis on the Spirit in the Old Testament, so would subtract that part, and our Old Testament materials would require us to add something about the element of risk, which is never missing. I began this chapter with the claim that God responded to Moses with a very potent promise, in spite of the fact that it contains no words that in themselves are even interesting: two pronouns (*I* and *you*), a preposition (*with*), and the verb *to be*, often not even said or written in Hebrew. But the contexts in which the promise occurs have revealed something to us of its distinctiveness as Israel used it, and something of its meaning and power. Was the Old Testament sense of what these words meant preserved and reaffirmed in appropriate settings later on, or was it lost or altered? We turn now to the literatures of Judaism and Christianity to seek the answers to those questions.

JUDAISM AND CHRISTIANITY

Although various forms of "God was with him" were favorite expressions of the Chronicler, appearing twenty times in his work, this does not indicate a trend toward a more frequent use of the sentence in postbiblical Judaism. It continues to appear in the literature, used in the same ways except for divine oracles, but surveys of the literature have so far located a relatively small number of occurrences. The lack of concordances to the Pseudepigrapha, the complete corpus of Qumran manuscripts, and the rabbinic literature means that some relevant passages may have been overlooked.

Judaism

In van Unnik's article on the origins of the liturgical use of *Dominus Vobiscum*, he reached the very dubious conclusion that in postbiblical Judaism the meaning of the phrase seemed to have been forgotten. Although he includes four Septuagint passages in his survey of the Old Testament, the basis for that statement is his reading of the ways Philo and Josephus dealt with some of the Old Testament texts we have considered. Since they paraphrased and did not retain the original wording, he concluded it was "probably unintelligible to their readers."[29] This, plus a few citations from rabbinic literature, led him to claim a marked difference between Judaism and the New Testament, where the phrase is freely used, expressing a self-evident truth. (281, 293). Philo and Josephus scarcely represent Palestinian Judaism, however, and it is unfortunate that van Unnik made so sweeping a statement based on such inadequate evidence. What we can find in the Apocrypha, Pseudepigrapha, and Qumran literature shows a continuity with the Old Testament that disproves completely his claim.

The earliest piece of extrabiblical evidence comes from the Aramaic papyri found at Elephantine (at the first cataract of the Nile). Among the records left behind by this community of Jewish settlers is a list of contributors, each of whom had given two shekels to the temple funds. This list is dated 419 B.C.E., perhaps roughly the time of Ezra (according to some chronologies), and one of the contributors is named Yahu'alai, daughter of Immanuiah.[30] Here we find a parallel to Isaiah's enigmatic Immanuel, but with the abbreviation of the divine name Yahweh: Immanuiah means "Yahweh is with us." And so far, this is the only person we know of from antiquity who bore such a name.

The apocryphal books contain a few uses of the formula, fitting the same patterns we found in the Old Testament, and introducing a new trend that will reappear elsewhere. In two passages one speaker refers to God's presence with another person. One of the additions to Esther (6:13) has Haman's wife and friends counseling him concerning his rivalry with Mordecai, and their concluding words are, "You will not be able to defend yourself, because the living God is with him [met' autou]." In Judith, as Holophernes prepares to invade Israel and seeks information about the people who are planning to resist him, Achior the Ammonite makes a lengthy speech recounting their history. He sums up the period of the monarchy as follows: "As long as they did not sin against their God they prospered, for the God who hates iniquity is with them [met' auton]" (Judith 5:17). It is easy to find parallels to both these speeches in the Hebrew Bible. Judith herself addresses a group with this formula as reassurance, comparable to several Old Testament speeches: "God, our God, is with us [meth' hemon], still showing his power in Israel" (Judith 13:11). And we find it also in a prayer. In 3 Maccabees, one Eleazar, who is a leader of the Jewish community in Egypt who are threatened with extinction by one of the Ptolemies, concludes a lengthy prayer with, "Let it be shown to all the Gentiles that you are with us [meth' hemon], O Lord, and have not turned your face from us" (6:15).

The variant form that appears in the Apocrypha represents a growing trend toward not speaking of God's presence without mediation of some sort. The promise in the Letter of Jeremiah 7 takes the form, "For my angel is with you [meth' humon], and he is watching over your lives." The presence of an angel of God with those at risk also appears in some texts of Tobit 12:13. At the end of the story, the angel Raphael, who had accompanied Tobias incognito on his journey, reveals his true identity to Tobias and his father Tobit. He says to Tobit, "When you did not hesitate to rise and leave your dinner in order to go and lay out the dead, your good deed was not hidden from me, but I was with you [sun soi emen]."[31] These are two examples of the well-known tendency to insert an angel between humans and God, a tendency already found in the Old Testament.

In the Pseudepigrapha, the book of *Jubilees* is of interest, since it retells Genesis through Exodus 14, so if it were really true, as van Unnik claimed, that the formula was no longer meaningful in postbiblical Judaism, we would expect to find it missing or paraphrased. The author quotes Gen. 21:20; 26:24; 28:15, 20; and 39:3, 23, however, and uses it three times in formulations of his own. He has created a farewell scene between Abram and his father, Terah, in which Terah blesses Abram as follows:

Go in peace.
May God eternal make straight your path
and the Lord be with you
and protect you from all evil. (*Jubilees* 12:29)

He then instructs Abram: "and take Lot, the son of Haran your brother with you [as] a son for yourself. The Lord be with you . . ." (12:30). Here are two expressions of a wish, similar to those we found in the Old Testament. The narrator's summary also appears in *Jubilees*: "And the land of Egypt was at peace before the Pharaoh on account of Joseph because the Lord was with him and gave him favor and mercy for all his family before all who knew him and those who heard witness of him" (40:9). This book in itself is evidence that the formula continued to be both repeated as the stories of scripture were retold, and used afresh.

One might expect the *Testament of Joseph* to reassure us that God was with him, since the expression occurs so prominently in Genesis 39, and two such passages do occur. In its greatly elaborated retelling of Joseph's temptations by Potiphar's wife, the author of the *Testament* does not quote any of the four occurrences in that chapter of Genesis, but does use it in his own way twice. The woman has brought him food mixed with enchantments, in an effort to subvert his will. To prove the power of God, Joseph prays, then eats it in her presence. His prayer is, "May the God of my fathers and the angel of Abraham be with me [*met' emou*]" (*T. Jos.* 6:7). Here the angel is added to the formula, rather than substituting for God. Near the end, Joseph's farewell includes these instructions: "You shall carry my bones along with you, for when you are taking my bones up there, the Lord will be with you [*meth' humon*] in the light, while Beliar will be with the Egyptians in the dark" (20:2). So in this testament the formula occurs in much the way it did in the Old Testament, within a prayer and a statement of assurance (cf. *T. Isaac* 4:37; 6:21, 32; *T. Abraham* 17:11; 18:7 Recension A).

Each of the authors noted so far clearly has been faithful to the special way the formula was used in the Old Testament. In every case except the references to the time of Joseph's death, the situation involves danger of some sort, and the tendency to restrict the promise to the lives of famous leaders continues (exceptions: Judith 5:17; 13:11; 3 Macc. 6:15). The single new feature is the tendency to say that it is an angel, or the power, or the right hand of God that is with the person.

The War scroll from Qumran contains some of the same uses. It may not be coincidental that among the scrolls from Cave I, this is the only one that uses *'eth* or *'im* in this way. War still seems to be the appropriate setting for such a statement. The occurrence that is closest to the Old Testament is in 1QM 19:1: *wmlk hkbwd 'tnw*, "and the king of glory is with us." Elsewhere, mediation appears: *wṣb' rwḥyw 'm ṣ'dynw*, "and the host of his spirits is with our steps" (12:8); *w'm 'bywnym yd gbwrtkh*, "and thy mighty hand is with the poor" (13:13). Although a verb that we excluded from consideration in the Old Testament is introduced in another place, it is worth noting for its preservation of the military aura: *'lwhykm hwlk 'mkm lhlḥm lkm*, "your God goes with you to do battle for you" (10:4).

It has not been possible to trace so elusive an expression through the literature of subsequent Judaism, but evidence that it was well understood by early rabbis is found in their comment on Ex. 3:12 in *Midrash Rabbah*: "an expression used only to one who is afraid," a point I have labored at some length.

The New Testament

New Testament authors speak of God with us, you, or them just as the Old Testament does, but they introduce something new when Jesus becomes either the object of the preposition or the subject of the sentence.[32] We may begin with two divine oracles, a type we did not find in the postbiblical Jewish literature. As Acts 18 recounts Paul's experiences in Corinth, between his expulsion from the synagogue and an incident when he was brought to trial before Gallio, the proconsul, the Lord said to Paul in a vision, "Do not be afraid, but speak and do not be silent; for I am with you, and no one will lay a hand on you to harm you, for there are many in this city who are my people" (Acts 18:9–10). It is brief, but we recognize significant elements of the Old Testament pattern: a risky situation, a divine commission, the admonition "Do not be afraid," and the assurance "I am with you," addressed to a man chosen by God to carry out his work no matter how difficult the circumstances might be.[33]

A call story of sorts appears at the beginning of the Gospel according to Luke. One of the new elements in the New Testament appears in Luke 1:26–28, for the recipient of the promise is a woman, and that never happened in the Old Testament. Judith did include herself when she affirmed "God, our God, is with us" (Judith 13:11), but that is as close as we get until we come to Mary. Danger or conflict cannot be said to form the background to the annunciation, although she certainly faced an uncertain future as a result of it, and her song contains definite overtones of the typical Old Testament setting (Luke 1:51–53).

Luke clearly understands how to describe such an event—God's choice of an unexpected person to carry out his will in spite of herself, with the divine gift of what she needs in order to accomplish his work. It has often been noted that the angel's address, "Greetings, favored one! The Lord is with you" (Luke 1:28), echoes the way the angel addressed Gideon: "The Lord is with you, you mighty warrior" (Judg. 6:12). Her reaction was typical, although not as extreme as some recorded in the Old Testament: "But she was much perplexed by his words and pondered what sort of greeting this might be" (v. 29). Recall that we have found "The Lord be with you" was not a standard greeting in Hebrew; customary would be "Peace be with you." So it is not at all surprising that the angel's next words are, "Do not be afraid, Mary, for you have found favor with God." These two visionary experiences thus use the formula with exactly the same implications it had in the Old Testament.

We find one example of a narrator's summary, and this also is Luke's work, although he is quoting the narrator, who is Stephen. Stephen's would-be defense of his work, which turns into an accusation of his accusers, takes the familiar form of a recital of Israel's history. When he comes to Joseph, he has not forgotten the prominence of "God was with him" in Genesis 39, for he includes it in his speech: "The patriarchs, jealous of Joseph, sold him into Egypt; but God was with him, and rescued him from all his afflictions" (Acts 7:9–10).

The promise had become an eschatological one in a few Old Testament passages. Zechariah looked forward to the day when God's presence in Jerusalem would be acknowledged by all people (8:23), and Ezekiel promised that when God made all things right, "they shall know that I, the Lord their God, am with them, and that they, the house of Israel, are my people" (34:30). Israel's hopes for

God's abiding presence with them are reaffirmed in Revelation's picture of the New Jerusalem:

> See, the home of God is among mortals.
> He will dwell with them as their God;
> they will be his peoples,
> and God himself will be with them. (Rev. 21:3)

The idea that God might abide among his people permanently (possible only when sin had been fully dealt with) and that the promise "I am with you" could be realized at all times, and not just in times of special need, is not prominent in the Old Testament. It appears appropriately in the few eschatological passages, and we found it also in expressions of strong personal faith in the Psalms (especially Ps. 73:23). But in the New Testament it will not be confined to the book of Revelation. We shall see that its association with Jesus will bring about a significant change.

An eschatological passage that introduces an intermediary appears in John 14:16. This is part of Jesus' farewell discourse to his disciples, and as a part of his reassurance that his death will not mean failure or even the complete loss of his presence with them, he offered this double promise:

> And I will ask the Father, and he will give you another Advocate, to be with you forever. This is the Spirit of truth, whom the world cannot receive, because it neither sees him nor knows him. You know him, because he abides with you, and he will be in you. I will not leave you orphaned; I am coming to you. (John 14:16–18)

This has an eschatological flavor because of the promise, "to be with you forever." Jesus' use of *parakletos,* "Advocate," who is also called the Holy Spirit sent by the Father in Jesus' name (14:26), reminds us somewhat of the tendency in postbiblical Jewish literature to introduce an angel, or the hand or power of God into the familiar formula, and we shall see next that this tendency continues in the language of the church.

The formula sometimes occurred as a wish in the Old Testament; in the church it became a standard benediction. Most of the New Testament letters conclude with some form of it. The least elaborated one is in 2 Thess. 3:16: "The Lord be with all of you." The one question to be raised about it is whether "Lord" refers specifically to God or to Christ, since two verses later another benediction appears: "The grace of our Lord Jesus Christ be with all of you." Here is another example of the addition of something to the "with you" formula. In the church the word to be added was "grace," and that became the most commonly used benediction. But there are four other occurrences of the unmediated form: Rom. 15:33 and Phil. 4:9 (God of peace); 2 Cor. 13:11 (God of love and peace); and 2 Tim. 4:22 (with your spirit). More common is the wish that grace be with the recipients of the letter: 1 Cor. 23; 2 Cor. 13:13 (with love and communion); Gal. 6:18; Eph. 6:24; Phil. 4:23; 1 Thess. 5:28; 2 Thess. 3:18; 1 Tim. 6:21; 2 Tim. 4:22;

Titus 3:15; Philemon 25; Heb. 13:25. It seems clear that the first-century church felt more comfortable expressing the wish that the grace of the Lord Jesus be with someone than with the wish that the Lord Jesus be with them, or that God be with them. Was the expression using "grace" a stronger one, or a weaker one? There is no suggestion of a chronological shift, since the form without "grace" appears in 2 Thessalonians and in 2 Timothy. The most important change, however, is the free interchange of God and of Jesus Christ in the traditional formula.

Before considering that change, the intermediate step is to be found in two authors' use of the formula with Jesus as the recipient of the promise. He fills the role of a Joseph or a David, appropriately enough, as one chosen by God to receive special power to carry out the divine will. Peter's summary of the gospel, in his speech to Cornelius and his household, says that the message was this: "How God anointed Jesus of Nazareth with the Holy Spirit and with power; how he went about doing good and healing all who were oppressed by the devil, for God was with him" (Acts 10:38). So far, that is something that could have been said about any of God's chosen leaders, but Peter of course has more to add, concerning death and resurrection, which now makes Jesus "the one ordained by God as judge of the living and the dead" (10:42). During Jesus' lifetime that could not be said, of course, and so when Nicodemus came to visit him at night, he remained with a traditional formulation: "Rabbi, we know that you are a teacher who has come from God; for no one can do these signs that you do, unless God is with him" (John 3:2, RSV; NRSV paraphrases: "apart from the presence of God"). John also has Jesus speak of himself in this way: "And the one who sent me is with me; he has not left me alone, for I always do what is pleasing to him" (John 8:29). And that reminds us that in the prologue to the Fourth Gospel, John makes the move from a perfectly acceptable statement about a great leader, from the Jewish perspective, as in the three examples just cited, to the radically new Christian statement that Jesus was divine. "The Word was with God, and the Word was God" (John 1:1b).

So the benedictions already noted could substitute Jesus for God, since for Christians the power of the blessing was the same. But for some reason, the only Gospel that uses the concept of Jesus being with his followers, as the Old Testament spoke of God being with his chosen ones, is not John, but Matthew. The first Gospel begins and ends that way. In the annunciation to Joseph, the angel quotes Isa. 7:14. Matthew could draw something very important theologically from the verse, from Isaiah's symbolic name: Immanuel. He translates it for his Greek-speaking readers, for they need to know that it means "God with us." Mary's child was not named Immanuel after all; Joseph is told to give him another symbolic name, Jesus, but that does not bother Matthew. He intends to show his readers that the old promise had come true in a new way with the birth of Jesus. He does not use the word *incarnation* as the church would later do, but that is his point. God was with them in Jesus.[34]

Matthew's work is framed by this promise. It concludes with Jesus commissioning his disciples to take on a daunting work: "Go therefore and make disciples of all nations, baptizing them in the name of the Father and of the Son and of the Holy Spirit, and teaching them to obey everything that I have commanded you. And remember, I am with you always, to the end of the age" (Matt. 28:19–20). Not "God will be with you" but "I am with you," and with you always. Here are the two radically new aspects of the Christian use of that portentous Old Testment promise. As Frankemölle observes, it must have been possible for Matthew to take over this formula "with you" only in the context of a relatively well-developed Christology that had no problem with the relation of Christ to Yahweh.[35] We have seen evidence for this in the interchange of God and Christ in the conclusions to the New Testament letters.[36]

Finally, there are two passages analogous to those psalms in which the person speaks of being with God, rather than of God being with them. Both introduce another new idea, however. It may be that Ps. 73:23 speaks of a hope for life after death, although the language is too vague for us to say anything very definite about that. In Luke 23:43 and John 17:24, however, presence with Christ after death is explicitly the subject. On the cross, Jesus promised the repentant criminal, "Truly I tell you, today you will be with me in Paradise." And in Jesus' prayer for his disciples, recorded by John, he says, "Father, I desire that those also, whom you have given me, may be with me where I am, to see my glory, which you have given me because you loved me before the foundation of the world." This reminds us of a different formulation, not using "with," in John 14:3b: "that where I am you may be also." The church thus spoke of Christ being with them in their earthly ministry, and of being with Christ after death. Paul had his own formulation of the latter belief, using the preposition *sun* rather than *meta*, which all other New Testament writers use.[37]

Although the formula was not used many times in the New Testament (apart from the benedictions), it was used in order to make some very significant claims about Jesus (especially in Matthew), and the reverse form, "with Christ," was used to speak of life after death. The benedictions show that it was democratized so as to include all believers at all times, and this was appropriate given the belief that every Christian received the gift of the Holy Spirit in order to be able carry out the ministry of Christ in spite of all obstacles.

Christianity

As with Judaism, only a few examples of the continuing use of forms of God's promise "I will be with you" can be cited. The dialogue between bishop and congregation—"The Lord be with you," "And with thy spirit"—had become a standard part of Christian worship by early in the second century C.E., as Hippolytus's *Treatise on the Apostolic Tradition* shows.[38] It was to precede the offertory prayer as follows:

The Lord be with you.
And the people shall say: And with thy spirit.
Lift up your hearts.
We lift them up unto the Lord.
Let us give thanks unto the Lord.
Meet and right.

Thus the entire congregation was offered this greeting by the bishop, a sentence that occurs in scripture in this exact form only in Ruth 2:4. Van Unnik's article discusses at considerable length the reason for the church's addition of the response "And with thy spirit," but perhaps 2 Tim. 4:22 is a near-enough parallel to account for it: "The Lord be with your spirit." A similar dialogue was to take place at the agape meal of the congregation. The same formula was used in a slightly different way, as a blessing upon those who had just been confirmed in the faith. After the bishop had prayed, anointed them with oil, and given them the kiss of peace, he said to each one, "The Lord be with you," and each one answered, "And with thy spirit."

By the second century this dialogue had thus come to play a rather prominent role in Christian worship, and it continues to be used to this day. It reflects biblical language, but as van Unnik emphasizes, its actual form is a creation of the church, not quoted from scripture or from synagogue worship.[39]

Two well-known hymns take up the formula in different ways. "God Be with You till We Meet Again" has already been mentioned. The poem itself has little content, and the melody is scarcely a catchy one, so its popularity during the past century should perhaps be attributed to the phrase that is repeated eight times in four verses: "God be with you." An eighteenth-century hymn, "God Himself Is with Us," contains a good deal more theology. The third verse contains echoes of both Testaments:

Lord, come dwell within us, while on earth we tarry,
Make us Thy blest sanctuary,
Grant us now Thy presence, unto us draw nearer,
And reveal Thyself still clearer.
Where we are, near or far, let us see Thy power,
Every day and hour.

Here is the eschatological hope for divine presence, as expressed in the Old Testament, made realized eschatology, in accordance with the New.

The presence of Christ with the worshiping congregation, which was expected by the faithful, as the liturgy and hymnody show, became a subject of hot controversy with respect to the sacrament of the Lord's Supper at the time of the Reformation, and among Protestants thereafter. The debate over the real presence of Christ in the elements is not a subject relevant to the present inquiry, except to note that our theological preposition "with" did appear in the claim that Christ was present "in, with, and under" the elements. Although the Reformed branch of

Protestantism denied that the body and blood of Christ were "corporally or carnally in, with, or under the bread and wine" (Westminster Confession of Faith XXIX.7), both Reformed and Lutheran churches insisted on union with Christ for faithful participants in the sacrament that went far beyond the concept "Christ with us." For example, the Scots Confession says that "Christ Jesus is so joined with us that he becomes the very nourishment and food of our souls," and "he remains in them and they in him" (XXI). Apart from the debate over the elements, then, the spiritual presence of Christ *in* the worshiper remained a part of Protestant teaching concerning the Lord's Supper.

We have seen that in the Old Testament, "I will be with you" was typically God's assurance to one called to do his work, even though inadequate for it, and it promised the power to accomplish God's will. We also found, however, that the promise could be misunderstood and could become the basis for complacency on the part of people as a whole who felt no sense of calling, as Amos 5:14 especially made clear. Is not "God with us" then a rather dangerous sentence? Van Unnik points out that Dutch silver coins contain the legend "God met ons," and what does that mean when a nation claims it? He also notes that German soldiers wore "Gott mit uns" on their belts even during the Nazi period.[40] The hymn "God Himself Is with Us" uses Old Testament material that conveys a strong sense of the numinous, and that, if recognized, will be cure enough for undue self-confidence, but it seems clear that a corrective is needed lest this sentence be taken to mean simply "God is on our side."

How can these ordinary words have such a powerful effect on those who believe them? A bit of phenomenology will quickly show us the answer. From infancy on to our death beds, what is the most reassuring promise we can ever hear from one we know, love, and trust? When we are afraid or uncertain, nothing can be more helpful than to hear, "But I will be with you." That means nothing coming from a stranger or someone we do not trust; it may then even be heard as a threat. But for the little child, afraid to try something or go somewhere for the first time, it is all right if a trusted parent says, "But I will be with you." And many who have gone through severe pain or grief have said afterward, "Thank you for being there," to someone who could show their love in no other way than just by being with them. So, for those who know and trust God, the Second Isaiah promise "Fear not, I am with thee, O be not dismayed, for I am thy God, I will still give thee aid; I'll strengthen thee, help thee, and cause thee to stand, upheld by my righteous, omnipotent hand"[41] will be taken personally, and will make a world of difference.

A recent book dealing with the presence of God claims, "The appropriate preposition to use for presence is *with*. . . . That represents a solidarity not found in God being present *to* the world as a subject of contemplation and worship only. He is certainly that, but the preposition 'with' conveys that he is on our side as we endeavour to make sense and value out of the world. . . . Yet the minimal distance preserved in presence *with*, which would be lost in presence *in*, is that distance which gives both God and us a measure of independence even in relationship."[42] I believe the distinction she has made among those three prepositions—to, with, in—is a valuable one, with which more should be done, in another context.

CHAPTER 4

THE NAME

Exodus 3—4
(Continued)

Our Redeemer—the LORD of hosts is his name—is the Holy One of Israel.
—Isaiah 47:4

> Therefore God also highly exalted him
> and gave him the name that is above every name,
> so that at the name of Jesus every knee should bend,
> in heaven and on earth and under the earth,
> and every tongue should confess that Jesus Christ is Lord,
> to the glory of God the Father.
> —Philippians 2:9–11

The fascinating and daunting elements of Moses' first meeting with God were immediately given rational content, when God spoke, with a promise ("I have come down to deliver them," Ex. 3:8) and an imperative ("So come, I will send you," 3:10). It is a savior who has appeared to Moses in so awesome a way, but he will not save without Moses' participation. Moses raised an incredulous question about his qualifications to undertake any such venture ("Who am I?"), but the savior had no comment to make about qualifications. Instead he assured Moses, "I will be with you." We have just seen that such a promise ought to be a fully sufficient answer, if it is given by one who is known and trusted. So Moses' second question is also a perfectly reasonable one: "Who are you?"

"I will be with you" is a weak promise unless we know who the promiser is. It might be a false assurance from the untrustworthy. It might be nice sentiment from one too weak to help. It might even be a threat rather than a promise.[1] Actually our work with Exodus so far has been in the realm of natural theology, as the book has led us to think about the human sense of the absence of God, about the human feelings aroused by the presence of the numinous, and about a promise, "I will be with you," that could come from anyone. The tracings we have made of each of these themes through scripture have led us to statements whose only basis is revelation, but in Exodus the question of revelation is first raised by Moses with his desire to know the name of the one who has spoken to him. In both Testaments, one of the most frequently used ways of emphasizing the uniqueness of the God revealed on Mount Sinai and of the salvation revealed in Jesus Christ involves the word "name."

This is my name forever, and thus I am to be remembered throughout all generations. (Ex. 3:15, RSV)
There is salvation in no one else, for there is no other name under heaven given among mortals by which we must be saved. (Acts 4:12)

As the ensuing study will show, when the Bible speaks of the name of God, it is referring to the fullest extent of the knowledge of God that is available to human beings.

Many authors have touched on this, as they have spoken of God's name as identical with his essence, as his way of manifesting himself in the world, as his action in the world, and the like. Some have become rather eloquent at this point, as quotations in the ensuing material will show, but they have not developed at any length the idea that the name of God is to be equated in biblical thought with his revelation of himself on earth. God gave to Moses a name, and the point of knowing that name was knowing *who* it was that was about to make possible the liberation of his people. Moses' question, "If I come to the Israelites and say to them, 'The God of your ancestors has sent me to you,' and they ask me, 'What is his name?' what shall I say to them?" (Ex. 3:12) was understood to be the most important question that could be asked, for the gist of it was, Who are you? And the answer, which became the basis for their existence and their way of life, the assurance of their future, was the self-introduction, "I am Yahweh."

"Name" is thus a very potent word, when it is used in expressions such as "the name of the LORD" or "the name of Jesus," but it is such a common word in itself (unlike "holiness," "spirit," "justice," "mercy," and the like) that there is a tendency to overlook the significance of the great frequency of its use in the Bible and in religious language in general. Biblical theologies discuss the names of God, but do not devote much space to the use of the word "name" in the Bible. Of course there are useful dictionary articles and a few special studies, and all scholars recognize the need to explain the meaning that names in general had for archaic cultures.[2] But few of them seem to have noticed that the power of personal names, at least, has not diminished all that much in contemporary societies, and it will be helpful for us to think about that before considering the meaning of the revelation of God's name in Exodus.

"As Americans, most of us are born nominalists," Carl Braaten has written. "We tend to think of names as mere labels. . . . Names do not really matter that much; we can exchange one set of labels for another, and the underlying reality remains the same."[3] That assumption has led to the explanations alluded to above, and of course it is true to a great extent. But elements of the power names exercised in archaic cultures remain in contemporary culture, and some of them are very significant. The contrast between the two understandings of names is usually described in terms of three features:

1. There is a transparency of meaning in most biblical names. Many of them are sentences, and it seems to have been important for one reason or another to know that *Isaac* means "he laughs" and that Jesus means "Yahweh

saves." On the other hand, the meaning of my name ("world ruler") has nothing to do with my life or anything else.

2. The name is said to have been thought identical with the thing itself, versus thinking of names as just more-or-less arbitrarily chosen labels. It is frequently said, for example, that Adam could give the animals their names (Gen. 2:19), not as an exercise of creative imagination—as a new product is named today—but because *he knew what they were.*

3. Since names were used in blessings and curses as sources of power, it was thought that to know the name of a deity was to have access to that deity's power, and to know a person's name gave one potential power over that person. As a result, deities and kings might have secret names, different from those by which they were usually called.

As just described, these do seem to represent a very different way of thinking from the way contemporary cultures use names. But let us look at each of these aspects again, with our own personal names in mind.

1. It is true that few of our given names have any transparent meaning. There are Joy, Christian, Daisy, and Ernest, to be sure, but who can tell us what Robert or Carolyn means, and what difference does it make? Surnames more often do not require translation. There are Smalls, and Whites, and Shoemakers, and Bowmans, but the meanings of those names are seldom noted, and in fact they tell us nothing about the individuals who bear them. Occasionally, however, children are still given portentous names. Readers will no doubt think of cases where parents have taken advantage of the archaic practice of making a personal name become a message, so we have not lost all touch with that.

2. There is far more continuity with the sense that the name equals the reality of the thing itself where personal names are concerned. The importance of Dale Carnegie's rule three, in his "Six Ways to Make People Like You," is emphasized by putting it under the title, "If You Don't Do This, You Are Headed for Trouble." Rule three is: *Remember that a man's name is to him the sweetest and most important sound in the English language.*[4] He recognized that our names are far more than labels. They have served from infancy to identify us as individuals distinct from everyone else, and have become not just our personal property; they are a part of us. Paul Tournier comments on how seldom people change their names, even though they may be ugly or embarrassing: "It seems, therefore, as if the usual name received from one's parents has a sacred character. It has some sort of magic power, so that one may fear or even hate it, but not dare to do anything about it."[5] Our very identity, our humanity, if you wish, is contained in our name. "What separates and distinguishes me from other people is the fact that I am called by my name; but what unites me with them is the very fact that they call me" (5). We are probably nominalists where other names are concerned, but not with respect to our own—or to the names of those closest to us. I need not provide examples of the power of the name of the beloved, which leads to poetry and song

and all sorts of nonsense. We still do not separate the name and the reality of the person.

Names still have power in another sense. There are attractive names and those that are unpleasant, and people identify the name and the reality of the person at that level, as well. Studies have shown that from school days on, a person named Mark, for example, will be treated differently from an Ethelbert. There are good names and bad names, just in terms of how they sound, and we make judgments about people equating name with reality.

> I have long had a suspicion that an entire generation of Americans grew up feeling inferior to just the *names* of the guys on the radio. Pierre André. Harlow Wilcox. Vincent Pelletier. Truman Bradley. Westbrook Van Voorhees. André Baruch. Norman Brokenshire. There wasn't a Charlie Shmidlap in the lot.[6]

Common expressions also show continuity with the way "name" is used in the Bible. "Name" still means reputation; we may have a good name or a bad name. "Name" can mean renown; we can "make a name for ourselves." Having done so, we will then *be* a famous name, so person and name are exactly identified. Name and possession are still associated, as in the Bible, for one may have nothing to one's name. We also mark possessions, not as animals do, thank goodness, but with our names—in books, on our doors or desks. Our name also has power to do things, as the name of God does in the Bible. When signed to a check or a contract, the piece of paper becomes more than paper; something happens as a result of the name.

3. The power of names in contemporary society has just been mentioned. We still use the names of God and of the devil in blessings and curses, although that kind of speech has become routine for most people, and it does not seem that many think of it as having the same kind of effectiveness that it had in antiquity. That is not to say people don't really mean something positive when they say "God bless you." But there is even a remnant of the old idea that to know a person's name gives one a certain power over that person. Alchoholics Anonymous and all the other "Anonymous" groups recognize that under certain circumstances it is best to be able to assure people that others need not know their name.

I hope that these fairly lengthy preliminary observations will help to eliminate some of the strangeness we feel when we see how strongly the Old Testament emphasizes the name of God. Looking ahead to our tracing of this subject through the history of belief, they will also help to explain why the word "name" is still so widely used in Christian language:

> "How sweet the name of Jesus sounds in a believer's ear"
> "Take the name of Jesus with you"
> "At the name of Jesus every knee shall bow"
> "All hail the power of Jesus' name"

"Ye servants of God, your Master proclaim, and publish abroad his wonderful
    name"
"The God of Abraham praise, all praised be his name"

I have never heard anyone explain what that word means as we use it in those
hymns and in our prayers, and that must be because we still have a fairly good
instinct, despite our nominalism, for the power of a name. That is what we shall
now trace, beginning with chapters 3 and 6 of Exodus.

THE NAME OF GOD IN EXODUS

Twice in Exodus God seems to reveal his name to Moses (3:14–15; 6:2–8), and
a third time God pronounces his name together with a description of his character
(34:6–7). The personal name of God, Yahweh, thus plays a very prominent role in
this book. God's self-introduction, in chapters 3 and 6, marks a major change in
the story of the descendants of Abraham, and his self-description, in chapter 34,
accounts for the possibility that their story may continue after the golden calf
incident, as we shall see later. In spite of all that has already been said about the
power of names, however, we must ask why the personal name of God is so
important to the Old Testament. That includes another question: Why does God
need a name at all? We shall need to study the words *YHWH* (Yahweh) and *shem*
(name) in the Old Testament, and *onoma* (name), *kurios* (lord), and *Jesus* in the
New Testament. We will not be able to reserve work on Ex. 6:2–8 until later, since
it is so closely related to Ex. 3:13–16.

Exodus 3:13–16

Moses' anticipation of the people's question, "What is his name?" leads to a
complex answer from God, which has led to an unending scholarly debate. If "I
will be with you" (3:12) has been somewhat overlooked, "I am who I am" (3:14)
has been far overworked. Fortunately, a theological discussion of the passage
does not have to get involved with all of the philological, historical, and literary
debates, most of which have led to no consensus as yet. Efforts to explain the
complexity of these verses led to a rather detailed separation into the Yahwistic
and Elohistic sources, but this requires making the kind of minute distinctions in
style that have rightly been questioned in recent years.[7] A major distinction
(perhaps the major distinction) between J (Yahwist source) and E (Elohist source)
is in their use of the divine name *YHWH*. E avoids it until Exodus 3, whereas J
says that at the time of Enosh "people began to call upon the name of Yahweh"
(Gen. 4:26), and the narrator uses it from the beginning (Gen. 2:4). It will never be
easy to explain how two such different points of view could have been combined
into a single account of Moses' call, so it seems safer not to try to distinguish two

sources in Exodus 3. We shall try instead to understand what it meant to Israel that the strata that very likely underlie this chapter have been combined in this way.

It is usually claimed that there is a threefold answer to Moses' question, What is (your) name? (1) "I am who I am. . . . Thus you shall say to the Israelites, 'I AM has sent me to you' " (v. 14). (2) "Thus you shall say to the Israelites, 'The LORD, the God of your ancestors, the God of Abraham, the God of Isaac, and the God of Jacob, has sent me to you' " (v. 15). (3) "Go and assemble the elders of Israel, and say to them, 'The LORD, the God of Abraham, of Isaac, and of Jacob, has appeared to me saying . . .' " (v. 16a). I shall suggest that the passage in its present form can be read as an answer (v. 15), supplied with an etymology (v. 14), and followed by further instructions (vv. 16–22).

Let me dispose of many of the questions that have led to extensive and inconclusive discussion but have no real theological significance by simply listing them, noting my own point of view as background to the material that follows:[8]

1. Was the name known prior to the time of Moses? There is some inscriptional evidence suggesting that it may have been, but it has been interpreted in different ways, and is far from conclusive.
2. Was the original form *YHWH,* or *YHW,* or *YH?* The strongest evidence points toward *YHWH.* Theories advocating the shorter forms as primary are more clever than convincing.
3. How was the name pronounced? Several lines of evidence point toward "Yahweh" as the ancient pronunciation.
4. Did the Old Testament authors think Moses and the slaves in Egypt knew the name before God spoke to Moses? Exodus 6 clearly says they did not (in spite of efforts to explain it differently). Exodus 3 can be read either way, but it makes no significant difference theologically.
5. Are chapters 3 and 6 parallel versions of the same event, or is chapter 6 a confirmation of Moses' call after his initial failure in Egypt? I believe that chapter 3 is the JE account of how Moses came to know the name YHWH, and chapter 6 is the roughly parallel P (Priestly source) account of the same revelation.
6. What does the name *YHWH* mean? Evidence that it was originally a verb form derived from the root meaning "to be" is very strong. But in spite of the lengthy discussions of its meaning beginning at least as early as Philo, the most important comment that the Old Testament itself has to make on this question is that the translation of the word is completely irrelevant to what it means as the proper name of God.

Now we can turn to the questions that will produce some theological results:

1. What did Moses really ask for? Did he require a name for the God of Abraham, Isaac, and Jacob, and if so, why? Or did he know the name *YHWH* already, and ask for its meaning? The rabbis pondered the "why" question, and that led them to opt for meaning as the nature of Moses' inquiry,[9] but in Exodus God responded with a name, not an interpretation. Let us say, then, that Moses is asking the deity who has identified himself as the God of Abraham, Isaac, and

Jacob for a personal name. The most likely answer to the rabbis' question why he
would do that seems to be that offered by Childs and Cazelles. Moses is being sent
to Egypt as a messenger, and every message must bear the name of its sender. The
typical message in the ancient Near East began, "Thus says N." If it was a royal
proclamation, it was likely to begin, "I am N," just as God's speech begins in Ex.
6:2. We cannot assume the people Moses was about to address in Egypt were
monotheists (Josh. 24:2, 23; Ezek. 20:7); if he was to speak in the name of the
God of their ancestors, he would need a name.

2. Moses is given a name: "Thus you shall say to the Israelites, 'Yahweh, the
God of your ancestors, the God of Abraham, the God of Isaac, and the God of
Jacob, has sent me to you': This is my name forever, and this my title for all
generations" (3:15, NRSV). That seems perfectly straightforward, and then the
instructions of what he is to say to the elders of Israel, in verses 16–22, which
begin with the same introduction, may be taken as the continuation of the
commission without any great difficulty. But what then do we make of verse 14,
which gives us the consonants *'HYH* instead of *YHWH* in a comparable sentence:
"Thus you shall say to the Israelites, ' *'HYH* has sent me to you.' " The usual
answer, since the development of source criticism, has been that this is a clear sign
of two different sources, with incompatible traditions about the divine name,
which have been rather loosely combined. There may very well be two sources
here, but it is not good to assume they have been carelessly combined. A rather
detailed examination of verse 14 is called for.

3. The mysterious words *'eheh 'asher 'ehyeh* have been interpreted in a great
variety of ways. Our approach will be to list them here, then to consider verse 14
with great care in order to reach a conclusion as to which is most likely to be
true:[10]

a. "Being": This first appears in the Septuagint, which translates the sentence *Ego eimi
ho on* as "I am the one who is." Philo and Maimonides, on the Jewish side, and most
of the church fathers, on the Christian side, assumed this was the correct
interpretation, and it has been defended by a few modern scholars.
b. "Active presence": This is the most popular modern reading, but it appears at least
as early as the Talmud and is quoted by Rashi: "*I am that I am.* The Holy One,
blessed be He, said to Moses: Go and say to Israel: I was with you in this servitude,
and I shall be with you in the servitude of the [other, i.e. Babylon and Rome]
kingdoms" (*b. Ber* 9b). In this way they accounted for the double occurrence of
'ehyeh "I am," making the first present tense and the second future. Among modern
scholars some emphasize God's activity, since the verb means not only "be," but
also "become," "happen." Others emphasize presence, presumably because of the
occurrence of the same verb just before, in "I will be with you" (v. 12), since there
is nothing in the verb itself to suggest presence.
c. "Causative activity": W. F. Albright and several who have followed his lead claim
the divine name itself and the explanation in v. 14 should be understood as
causatives, hence, "I cause to be what I cause to be." From this they deduce an

early creation theology in Israel. But we shall not pursue this theory further in what follows here, since it requires different vowels and one different consonant for the words in question, and introduces a causative stem for the verb *hayah,* which never occurs otherwise in the Old Testament.

d. Emphasis on certainty or emotional intensity, indicated by using the same word twice: So the sentence means something like "I am prepared and active."

e. Refusal to commit himself: Some take it as a rebuke of Moses and a refusal to answer him at all. This, of course, does not go well with the fact that what God does next is to give him a name. Others read it as something like "I will be whatever I mean to be." This kind of reading has also been challenged as not in accordance with the context, but I think I can provide a defense against that.

4. Should the verb *'ehyeh* be read as present or future tense? (Some even mix them.) The evidence points toward future, although it cannot be conclusive. The first-person singular of the verb "to be" is used in a rather restricted way in the Old Testament. It occurs without *waw*-consecutive forty-two times (counting the parallels 2 Sam. 7:14 and 1 Chron. 17:13 as one), and in twenty-nine of those God is the subject. All of the latter are future in meaning, and of those with other subjects, only Ruth 2:13, 2 Sam. 15:34, and some difficult and questionable passages in Job (3:16; 10:19; 12:4; 17:6) have anything other than a clearly future sense. With God as the subject, the verb form occurs nine times in the formula "I will be with you" and eleven times in the formula "I will be your God and you will be my people." This suggests very strongly that the form should be translated, not "I am," but "I will be."[11]

5. Does the root *hayah* ever mean "existence" in the Old Testament?[12] Certainly it is used many times simply to indicate that something "is" (e.g., "and the earth was a formless void," Gen. 1:2), but existence as over against nonexistence is not a subject Old Testament writers discuss, except perhaps in Second Isaiah: "I am Yahweh, and there is no other; besides me there is no god" (Isa. 45:5). But if the writer of Exodus had wanted to tell his readers that God said to Moses he is the only God who exists, or (worse yet) that he is "absolute existence" (Maimonides and others), there was a straightforward way to do it—exactly as Second Isaiah did.

As noted above, the verb is used frequently in the Old Testament to indicate some sort of becoming or happening, and that active sense appears to most scholars now to be more in keeping with the way Israel thought about God. But when the move is made to "active presence," that seems to go beyond anything supported by the verb or the sentence structure. As one of the eloquent representatives of that move, Georges Auzou says we can at least say the words are similar to "I will be with you," and that is as close to an argument for presence as anyone gets. Then he paraphrases, "It is I! I am who I am, that is, I am truly there, really present. Behold me; it is certain that I exist here and now for the one to whom I call."[13] But surely this pours far more content into *'ehyeh 'asher 'ehyeh* than it was intended to hold.

6. Studies of this *idem per idem* form can move us considerably closer to understanding why such a form might have been used here. Is it a refusal (like our vernacular, "That's for me to know and you to find out")? Does it represent emphasis, as double uses of words are used to make superlatives in Hebrew ("holy of holies" means "holiest")? Jack Lundbom's study concluded that the form serves a rhetorical function, to terminate debate, citing both ancient and modern examples.[14] For example, Pilate's last words about Jesus were, "What I have written, I have written" (John 19:22). No doubt the form does often function that way, but in Exodus 3—4 it by no means brings the discussion to an end.

As Childs has pointed out, there is no clear form-critical parallel to this passage, but there are six texts that are similar enough to be helpful:

> I will be gracious to whom [*'eth-*ᵃ*asher*] I will be gracious, and will show mercy on whom [*'eth-*ᵃ*asher*] I will show mercy. (Ex. 33:19)

> But I the LORD will speak the word that I speak [*'eth' *ᵃ*sher *'ᵃ*dabber*]. (Ezek. 12:25)

> They wandered wherever they could go [NRSV; lit., They went about where (*ba'*ᵃ*sher*) they went about]. (1 Sam. 23:13)

> And settle wherever you can [NRSV; lit., And sojourn where (*ba'*ᵃ*sher*) you sojourn]. (2 Kings 8:1)

> While I go wherever I can [NRSV; lit., And I am going where (*'al *'ᵃ*sher*) I am going]. (2 Sam. 15:20)

> Bake what you want to bake and boil what you want to boil [NRSV; lit., What (*'eth *'ᵃ*sher*) you bake, bake; and what (*w*ᵉ*'eth *'ᵃ*sher*) you boil, boil]. (Ex. 16:23)

The texts from 1 and 2 Samuel and 2 Kings suggest indeterminacy, but that can scarcely be true of the first two, in which God speaks about what he intends to do. I believe that those two, and also Ex. 16:23, denote the freedom of the subject to choose, and that idea can also apply to the other three.[15] With this we have almost reached an understanding of the cryptic sentence in its context. God will do as Moses asks. He intends to reveal his name, but first he reserves his freedom not in any sense to be defined by a name. Israel will be able to address him, but not possess him. I believe the best translation of the three words is, "I will be whoever I will be."[16]

7. If *'ehyeh '*ᵃ*sher 'ehyeh* is a comment on, explanation of, or qualification of the name *Yahweh,* how does one account for the difference in spelling, and for the fact that the former is a first-person verb form and the other is third person? I offer a relatively simple explanation, compared with those others have suggested. It is a play on words based on the etymology of *yahweh,* of a type much appreciated by Hebrew writers. "I am" (*'ehyeh*) is the first common singular imperfect of the root *hyh* ("to be"). "Yahweh" appears to be the third masculine singular imperfect of the same root, but with its archaic spelling *hwh.* As for the difference in subject, where wordplay is involved that does not matter. Isaac's name, which means "he laughs," is explained three times, twice in stories where it is Sarah who laughs

(Gen. 18:12–15; 21:3–6; Abraham in Gen. 17:17), but the difference in subject does not matter to the narrator.

I see Ex. 3:14–16 to be the same kind of etymologizing wordplay. The name of the God of Israel was Yahweh. It had no definition, as the names of other gods did (*Baal* means "master"; *Anu* means "sky," etc.).[17] But the relationship with the verb "to be" seemed evident, so in the account of God's revelation of his name to Moses a useful etymology of the name could be provided, in that special *idem per idem* form, a way of expressing the freedom of the subject, in order to emphasize the human inability to know God's "being." What Israel could know about God follows immediately in verses 16b–22.

I have reached a conclusion that is similar to, though varying somewhat from, those held by a good many other scholars. The method used has de-emphasized the making of hypotheses about historical developments and has emphasized a maximum use of the comparative material in the Old Testament. One summary that is in keeping with the conclusions reached here is worth quoting, even though it refers to Ex. 33:19 rather than the present text: "In this figure of speech resounds the sovereign freedom of Yahweh, who, even at the moment he reveals himself in his name, refuses simply to put himself at the disposal of humanity or to allow humanity to comprehend him."[18]

Exodus 6:2–8

This is a much simpler passage. There are no supernatural features accompanying the divine speech, there is no commissioning of Moses to do anything, and consequently no dialogue between him and God. The point of contact between Exodus 3 and 6:2–8 is that in both passages there seems to be something new about the announcement of God's name, even though he is associated with the past as the God of Abraham, Isaac, and Jacob. As the book of Exodus now reads, this scene takes place in Egypt, after Moses had obeyed God's instructions, with the result that his people are now suffering more than ever (chapter 5). There are some puzzling features in 6:2–7:7, however: the insertion of a genealogy (6:14–25), some necessary repetition in 6:26–27 to get the story under way again, and a doublet of 4:10–16 in 6:28–7:7. Some insist that a single author must have intentionally written it that way; their efforts to show that this is good Hebrew narrative style are far from convincing, however. It seems more likely that two sources have been combined on a very conservative principle (not wanting to leave anything out), and this led the author to fit in 6:2–8 the best way possible, now serving as a reiteration of God's insistence he would soon deliver his people from Egypt, in spite of Moses' initial failure.

Source analysis assigns the passage to the Priestly document, and the introduction of the divine name here takes a form that is a favorite among priestly writers: *'ani Yahweh,* "I [am] Yahweh." Walther Zimmerli's definitive study calls this a self-introduction formula.[19] It occurs at least fifty times in Leviticus and at least sixty-four times in Ezekiel, who came from a priestly family. The only other books where it appears often are Exodus (seventeen times) and Isaiah 40—66 (fifteen times). The related form "I am He" also appears five times in Second Isaiah. Outside the Old Testament it occurs frequently in the introductions to royal inscriptions and has also been found in oracles of other deities. For example, "I am Ishtar of Arbela" appears several times during the course of oracles that seers delivered to King Esarhaddon of Assyria.[20] Its provenance is thus relatively easy to determine.

In Exodus, Second Isaiah, and Ezekiel it introduces the God who acts to change the course of history, but since it is rare in most of the prophetic books (seven times elsewhere), it does not seem to be a typical prophetic form. In Leviticus it stands as a word of authority, indicating from whom the law comes, and of course its best-known occurrence is at the introduction to the Decalogue: "I am Yahweh, who brought you out of the land of Egypt." Zimmerli found two psalms that support his hypothesis that the original setting for the self-introduction "I am Yahweh" was Israel's worship, in which a speaker declared, as God's words, messages concerning his saving acts in history or commandments concerning how his people should live (Pss. 81:6–10; 50:7, 18–20).[21] Because of these associations with saving history and with law, Zimmerli says that the content of the formula "I am Yahweh" revealed more than the identity of the dialogue partner. It was the ultimate statement God could make about himself (20).

The claim that God appeared to Abraham, Isaac, and Jacob as El Shaddai, and not as Yahweh (6:3), is of considerable interest for the history of religion, but is not of much theological value, since we cannot be sure what El Shaddai means.[22] It is clear enough from Genesis that the religion of the patriarchs differed significantly from the religion that is about to be established in the book of Exodus. The Priestly writer acknowledges the difference, but has more interest in continuity, focusing on a theme that is completely missing from Exodus 3—4: God's intervention at this point is not motivated only by the sufferings of the slaves in Egypt. There are suffering slaves elsewhere, but he intends to take action only on behalf of these slaves, and that is because he had made a promise to their ancestors, sworn to them in a solemn covenant (Ex. 6:4, 8; cf. Gen. 15:18–21; 17:1–8).[23] This passage makes it a bit more explicit than in Exodus 3—4 that the new thing signified by the new divine name is that God now means to fulfill the promises of Genesis.[24] Promise will be the subject of the next chapter.

The term "name" occurs in several other significant passages in Exodus. Moses speaks in the name of God (5:23), and this is a common enough idiom for us, meaning that he represents God and speaks with authority granted by God. A more unusual expression that probably means the same thing is to be found in Ex. 23:20–21:

I am going to send an angel[25] in front of you, to guard you on the way and to bring you to the place that I have prepared. Be attentive to him and listen to his voice; do not rebel against him, for he will not pardon your transgression; for my name is in him.

Another use that continues to be familiar is the association of "name" with reputation or fame, as in Ex. 9:16, "so that my name may be declared throughout all the earth." "Taking the name of Yahweh in vain" (Ex. 20:7) will be discussed in the next section, along with the full breadth of uses of the name in the Old Testament, as will passages such as Ex. 20:24, "in every place where I cause my name to be remembered," where God's name is spoken of as the way God manifests himself on earth.

Preliminary conclusions, drawn from Exodus: Exodus 3 and 6 insist something radically new happened in the world at the time of the exodus event, so radical that the newness involved even God. His intervention in history "required" the revelation of his own name to the people he liberated, and to their oppressors, for of both it is said, "Then they will know that I am Yahweh" (6:7; 7:5; etc.). Much has been written about Israel's insistence on the reality and meaningfulness of historical change—revelation through history—in contrast to the strong tendency of other cultures to affirm constancy and deny the significance of change. In these passages we find the most extreme possible statement of that insistence. God's revelation of his name as the apparently necessary introduction to his intervention in history asserts that he is far different from "The One Who Is," ultimate reality, or absolute existence, for his most prominent characteristic at this point in the story is his involvement in change. As Auzou says, Yahweh is not a definition, but a designation; he is "the One who is intervening here."[26]

THE NAME OF GOD IN THE OLD TESTAMENT

Reflection on the continuing potency of personal names in contemporary society provides a helpful point of entry for understanding the ways the name of God is used throughout the rest of the Old Testament. The name *Yahweh* itself and the word *shem* used as a substitute for that name occur thousands of times, so some organizing principle has to be introduced in order to get at what is theologically significant. We shall begin with the uses most easy to understand, moving toward those that require more study, considering only a few representative examples of each.

Fundamentally, a name is something that is spoken, by which we call ourselves or others call us. The Hebrew verb used in naming formulas is, in fact, *qara'*, "to call" (see Gen. 1:5; 2:19). So it is appropriate to begin with the verbs of speaking, which are the verbs most frequently used with "the name of Yahweh." To "call upon the name of Yahweh" means to pray (Ps. 4:1, 3), and then more generally, to worship the Lord (Gen. 4:26; 12:8). Most of the other verbs are associated with worship: bless (Deut. 10:8), sing praises to (2 Sam. 22:50), boast of (Ps. 20:7), ascribe glory to (Ps. 29:2), give thanks to (Ps. 30:4), exalt (Ps. 34:3), declare (Ps. 102:21), acknowledge (Isa. 26:13), and magnify (2 Sam. 7:26). There are negative uses as well: some have blasphemed the name (Lev. 24:16), or reviled the name (Ps. 74:18). One might utter a curse in God's name that would be effective (2 Kings 2:24). Some who claimed to be prophets spoke falsely in God's name (Deut. 18:22). And the Decalogue forbids taking God's name in vain (Ex. 20:7).

These latter uses point to areas of life outside of worship. Prophetic speech was sometimes, but not always, to be found in a worship setting. The Decalogue's reference to taking God's name in vain probably referred originally to the practice of using the name of God in an oath, as in Isa. 48:1, "Hear this, O house of Jacob, . . . who swear by the name of the LORD, and confess the God of Israel, but not in truth or right" (cf. Lev. 19:12). It also would certainly have included blaspheming the name, mentioned above, and very likely the use of God's name in magical formulas.[27] Here we have moved from the purely human use of God's name as the way they identify or address him, to an appeal to God's authority and power. Returning to the cultic context, ministering in the name of the Lord would also denote the gift of some divine authority, in addition to service on God's behalf.

Since the name represents or actually conveys God's authority and power, it can also be associated with verbs denoting human action. This kind of speech is not so natural for us, although it may occur now and then, probably as a borrowing from the Old Testament. One may come in the name of the Lord, as David came against Goliath (1 Sam. 17:45), that is, filled with God's power; one enters the temple in the name of the Lord, presumably in obedience to God's will (Ps. 118:26), since recognizing one's sinfulness may lead one to seek the name of the Lord (Ps. 83:16). When we encounter the idea of seeking refuge in the name, we have moved in the direction of the concreteness of name as it will occur in other uses (Zeph. 3:12). Obviously the name of God is equivalent to the saving power of God. God's name may also be profaned by something other than the way one speaks it, for the sinful actions of Israelites are said somehow to profane it, which must mean that name is now equivalent to reputation (Lev. 18:21; Ezek. 36:22).

Remaining at the human level, verbs of emotion or intellect also occur. One may fear (Deut. 28:58), know (Ps. 9:10), remember (Ps. 119:55), and love (Isa. 56:6) God's name, and that obviously means name is being used to indicate the fullness of God's manifestation of himself in the world.

This identification of the name Yahweh with God's revelation of himself to humanity is emphasized in the formulas we have already noted in Exodus. "This is my name for ever, and thus I am to be remembered throughout all generations" (Ex. 3:15). "Yahweh is a man of war; Yahweh is his name" (Ex. 15:3). "I am Yahweh, that is my name; my glory I give to no other, nor my praise to graven images" (Isa. 42:8). "Our Redeemer—the LORD of hosts is his name—is the Holy One of Israel" (Isa. 47:4).

So when God's name becomes the subject of sentences, it seems that is just the appropriate way to describe what human beings can apprend of God as one who is active in the world. God's name protects (Ps. 20:1), helps (Ps. 124:8), is a strong tower (Prov. 18:10), comes from afar to judge the nations (Isa. 30:27–28), and endures for ever (Ps. 102:12). It is not quite exact, however, to say, "The nature of God is compressed in the name of God."[28] The verb seems too comprehensive, and more appropriate would be something like, "All that human beings can apprehend of the nature of God is found in his name."[29]

That God and his name were not understood to be completely identical is shown by our final group of uses, in which God does things with his name. There are some verbal uses comparable to those at the human level, but with different results. God proclaims his name over a place, and that makes it a holy place, where he can be met by his worshipers (Ex. 20:24; the ark is also said to be called by his name). He calls his name over a people, and they become his own special possession (Jer. 19:9; yes, even the nations: Amos 9:12). He swears by his own name, since there is nothing greater on which an oath could be based (Jer. 44:26).

Earlier suggestions that name is closely associated with character and reputation are strengthened by the sentences in which God is the subject. He made himself a name when he displayed his power over Egypt (Dan. 9:15). He is jealous for his holy name, which Israel profanes in the eyes of the nations by their behavior (Ezek. 39:25). When he makes known his holy name, the truth about it will be known among the nations (Ezek. 39:7). And, in one of the most important uses of all, in answer to the question whether there can be any future for perennially unfaithful Israel after the fall of Jerusalem, God's answer is, "It is not for your sake, O house of Israel, that I am about to act, but for the sake of my holy name, which you have profaned among the nations to which you came" (Ezek. 36:22). The sole basis on which a new life for Israel might be built is the character of God.

Finally, God's name seems to be an almost physical thing when he is said to put it (*sim*) or make it to dwell (*shikken*) in the place he chooses (Deut. 12:5, 11, etc.). This vocabulary, typical of Deuteronomy and the Deuteronomistic Historian (e.g., 1 Kings 9:3), may then be echoed on the human side by building a house for the name of the Lord (1 Kings 3:2). God had said of it, "My name shall be there" (2 Kings 23:27).[30] Since there was no image in the temple, this seems to be the way Israel expressed its conviction that God was really present there. Instead of his image, it was his name that dwelt there. Now, it is said that the more astute idol worshipers in antiquity knew the difference between the god and the statue. They believed the god was present in the statue, but did not completely identify one with the other. In a similar way, the Old Testament almost completely identifies God's name with the deity, but by making God the subject and name the object of many a sentence they preserved the distinction between what humans can know of God, the ways they can experience God, the sense of God's real presence in one place on earth, and the fullness of deity.

The Old Testament's use of "Yahweh" as the personal name of God thus falls between two extremes to be found in religion and philosophy. The one assumes the reality and power of the god are contained in the name itself, so that one can conjure with it. The opposite extreme claims God so far transcends all language that he cannot have a name.[31] For Israel the former extreme made God subject to human manipulation, and they understood that to be impossible, so the holiness of his name had to be protected. But they also seem to have recognized that to claim God could not be named would make him impersonal or pantheistic. In a polytheistic world, of course, it was necessary to be able to distinguish their God from those of other peoples. Once monotheism had triumphed within Judaism, it would seem that a proper name would no longer be necessary, and as we shall soon see, that did happen in a sense, as they no longer spoke the name "Yahweh." But there is more than that to a personal name. To "know that I am Yahweh" meant to encounter more than a force or a principle. Moses didn't go off to Egypt saying, "I have a strong moral conviction that drives me to do this." No one encouraged him saying, "May the force be with you." The operative words were, "I am Yahweh, and I will free you from the burdens of the Egyptians" (Ex. 6:6). Because he introduced himself by name, and one could then call upon him by name, it was known that this force now acting with such devastating effects on the Egyptians was a being with whom one could have a personal relationship.

"Name" begins as a word, part of some specific language, but immediately when applied to a person it takes on qualities different from other words. It is not merely a symbol for the person, as the Social Security number is; it absorbs that person's character and is assumed by the person as part of the self. And personhood seems to require a name. Paul Tournier's story to that effect may be taken a little further than he intended, and applied to our awareness of God.

He tells of a surgeon friend who was consulted by a woman about having an abortion. During the consultation she commented, "After all, doctor, it's not all that important. It's only a little bundle of cells!" But later in the discussion he asked her, "If you were to keep your baby, what name would you give it?" That produced a long silence. Finally she said, "Thank you, doctor, I'll keep it." Tournier comments, "When that mother gave a name in her mind to her child, she made him a person in her own eyes, a person whose life no longer belonged to her, whose life must be respected."[32] In a somewhat similar way, we may recognize that the invisible God—who is pure spirit, whom we can never truly comprehend, and who can certainly never adequately be denoted by some word in human speech—that God becomes a person to us, whom we can address and whom we feel we know to some extent, when he gives us a name by which we can call him.

THE NAME OF GOD IN
JUDAISM AND CHRISTIANITY

Judaism

Judaism continued to affirm the existence of a unique and personal God by recalling his name, but did that in a distinctive way, governed by a scrupulous concern to protect its holiness. At some time in the postexilic period Jews ceased pronouncing the name, and wrote it only in abbreviated form, except in copies of the scriptures. But in speech and in writing, substitutions such as *'adonai* (Lord), *hashshem* (the Name), and "The Holy One, blessed be He" became the rule. Only the priests who pronounced the benediction at the daily service in the Temple (Num. 6:24–26) and the high priest on the Day of Atonement continued to pronounce the name *YHWH,* and of course after the Temple was destroyed in 70 C.E. there was no reason for that practice to continue.[33] In discussion, the divine name came to be referred to as *shem ben d' 'othyoth,* "the name of four letters," or Tetragrammaton.

There is less use of the Tetragrammaton in the later books of the Old Testament than in the earlier parts—it does not appear in Ecclesiastes or Esther and appears only four times in Daniel, but there is no evidence beyond that as to when and why the name ceased to be pronounced. The only reason discussed in later rabbinic writing is the law in Lev. 24:16: "Anyone who blasphemes the name of the LORD shall be put to death; the whole congregation shall stone the blasphemer." The Septuagint interpreted the verse to mean mentioning (*onomazon*) the name, and later discussion found the meanings "point out" or "designate" and "pierce" for the verb *naqav.* From the former could be derived a prohibition against saying it at all; from the latter, uses for magic purposes were prohibited. No doubt the Third Commandment was a major factor, since conscientious Jews would want to be sure they had not taken God's name in vain even unintentionally. But it seems too much to say the Tetragrammaton had become a secret name, like the names of other deities, as Hans Bietenhard does,[34] for the four letters were known to all, and various kinds of legends grew up around them. The evidence for Jewish piety in the postexilic period indicates that the values of knowing God by a personal name noted earlier continued to be experienced.

The Apocrypha and Pseudepigrapha show no significant change in the meaning of the name of God for Jews, and Josephus has very little to say about it. In retelling the call of Moses he wrote, "And God declared to him His name which had not previously come to men, and about which it is not permissible to say anything" (*Antiquities of the Jews* 2:275f.). Philo, however, shows the influence of Greek thought, in that he has moved in the direction of asserting that

God transcends all names: "God indeed needs no name; yet, though He needed it not, He nevertheless vouchsafed to give to humankind a name of Himself suited to them, that so men might be able to take refuge in prayers and supplications and not be deprived of comforting hopes" (*On Abraham* 51). The Septuagint translation of Ex. 3:14 seems appealing to his philosophical mind, for he cites it, saying that God is called in scripture "He that is [*ho on*] as His proper name" (*On Abraham* 121). He is Jewish enough, however, to recognize the personal relationship that the name has established between God and his people, and does not speak of a secret name, as some non-Jewish writers of the time did. The name given for use in prayer is not, in fact, the Tetragrammaton, as the context of the first quotation above indicates, and as the following makes clear:

> God replied, "First tell them that I am He Who is, that they may learn the difference between what is and what is not, and also the further lesson that no name at all can properly be used of Me, to Whom alone existence belongs. And if, in their natural weakness, they seek some title to use, tell them not only that I am God, but also the God of the three men whose names express their virtue, each of them the exemplar of the wisdom they have gained—Abraham by teaching, Isaac by nature, Jacob by practice.[35]

Writing in Arabic, about a thousand years later, Maimonides shows the same influence of Greek philosophy in his interpretation of the name, but in other respects he reached conclusions similar to those we have found. He wrote, "It is possible that in the Hebrew language, of which we have now but a slight knowledge, the Tetragrammaton, in the way it was pronounced, conveyed the meaning of 'absolute existence.'" A bit later, explaining *'ehyeh 'ªsher 'ehyeh*, Maimonides wrote, "He is 'the existing Being which is the existing Being,' that is to say the Being whose existence is absolute."[36] But he will not draw any mystical conclusions from the four letters, as some other Jews of the Middle Ages were doing, and he warns against the use of God's names in amulets. He had observed the various senses in which the name of God is used in scripture, commenting that sometimes it means only the name (as in the Third Commandment), elsewhere means the essence and reality of God himself, and sometimes stands for God's word or command (95). But the Tetragrammaton is God's proper name, and he made a sharp distinction between God's true name and all the other names that speak of attributes. "Every other name of God is a derivative, only the Tetragrammaton is a real *nomen proprium,* and must not be considered from any other point of view" (91).

In spite of these sober teachings, the Kabbalistic strains of Judaism did engage in extensive mystic speculation, claiming that the whole Torah is composed of God's names, for example (*Zohar* III.73), and producing legends of gifted people who were able to pronounce the name without harm, and thereby to work miracles. For the nonmystical strands of Judaism, however, it may be fair to summarize their point of view by saying they rejoice in having a God who is known, because he has revealed his personal name to them, but consider that name to be so much a repository of his holiness that it should be treated with the greatest possible respect. So it is not pronounced and documents containing the name are treated with special care as a way of honoring the God who bears that name.

The New Testament

In the first century C.E., when the Jews honored the name of God by refraining from pronouncing it and by protecting its written form in various ways, the first Christians, on the other hand, gloried in using a new name as much as possible. The New Testament shows no interest in the Tetragrammaton but uses the word "name" as frequently as the Old Testament does. Usually the New Testament writers are speaking of the name of Jesus.

"Name" and "name of the Lord" are not used very often of God the Father, except in quotations from the Old Testament (e.g., Matt. 21:9 par.; Acts 2:21). Passages such as Luke 1:49 and Rev. 15:4, which are not quotations, are obviously strongly influenced by Old Testament language. The New Testament ordinarily speaks of *theos* (God), *kurios* (Lord), *pater*—or the Aramaic *'abba*— (Father), or substitutes "Heaven," especially in Matthew (e.g., Matt. 13:11, etc.). A few texts where God's name is used in a prominent way are thus the first evidence that needs to be discussed. The first petition of the Lord's Prayer is "Hallowed be your name" (Matt. 6:9; Luke 11:2). We have become familiar enough with the ways in which "name" stands for the character and reputation of God in the Old Testament, that Jesus' use of the word in the prayer needs little more explanation. Sanctifying God's name is also a familiar theme, especially as it appears in Ezekiel (36:22–23), so the prayer clearly stands in continuity with Old Testament thought.[37]

The most prominent use of the name of God appears in the Gospel according to John, where it plays an important role in John's explanation of Jesus' relationship with God. The first uses are reminiscent of Old Testament language, except for their use of "my Father." Jesus says, "I have come in my Father's name, and you do not accept me; if another comes in his own name, you will accept him" (John 5:49), using "name" to refer to a commission, the source of one's authority. Later, he uses name to refer to the source of power, also familiar to us from the Old Testament: "I have told you, and you do not believe. The works that I do in my Father's name testify to me" (10:25). For God's name to be glorified in or because of a human being, as Jesus asks in John 12:28, is also not radically different from something the Old Testament might say. A new claim is made, however, when Jesus says he has been given God's name—not only God's power but also God's character are to be found in him: "Holy Father, protect them in your name that you have given me, that they may be one, as we are one. While I was with them, I protected them in your name that you have given me"

(17:11b–12a). Not only did Jesus' possession of the name of God give him the power to protect his disciples, it also made him the manifestation of God in their midst: "I made your name known to them, and I will make it known, so that the love with which you have loved me may be in them, and I in them" (17:26). The name of God is thus one of several ways John found to speak of the relationship between Jesus and the Father. There will be more to say of this at the end of the section.

As the New Testament authors speak of the name of Jesus, some of what they say is in direct continuity with the way the name of God is used in the Old Testment, but they found new uses. We shall separate them as much as possible. The name of Jesus was extolled (Acts 19:17), glorified (2 Thess. 1:12), called upon (1 Cor. 1:2), and thanks was given in his name (Eph. 5:20). It was also blasphemed (James 2:7). One might bear the name of Christ (Mark 9:41), which reminds us of being called by the name of the Lord in the Old Testament. Paul cited the name of the Lord Jesus as the source of his authority, in 1 Cor. 1:10; 5:4; 2 Thess. 3:6. As prophets in Israel spoke in the name of the Lord, so prophesying (Matt. 7:22), preaching (Luke 24:47), and speaking and teaching (Acts 4:17f.; 5:28, 40) in the name of Jesus are characteristic activities of the early Christians. Jesus has taken the place of God in each of these formulations.

The potency of the word "name" (or perhaps more accurately, of the name "Jesus") is extended in the New Testament, however, as it is used in new ways. Wherever two or three gather in the name of Jesus (presumably meaning that they call upon his name in prayer), he has promised to be present in their midst (Matt. 18:20). Prayer "in Jesus' name" is explicitly referred to in John 14:13f.; 15:16; 16:23f.; and elsewhere; thus the power of Jesus was called upon as Israel called upon the power of God. His power, manifested through his name, also brought about exorcisms (Luke 9:49; 10:17) and healings (Acts 3:6, 16; 4:7, 10; James 5:14). And his name was the source of salvation (Acts 4:12), forgiveness (Acts 10:43), and sanctification and justification (1 Cor. 6:11). So, baptism was performed in the name of Jesus (Acts 2:38; 8:16; in the name of Father, Son, and Holy Spirit in Matt. 28:19). For John, it was thus something to be "believed in" (John 1:12; 2:23; 20:31; 1 John 3:23; 5:13). As the name of God in the Old Testament was God at work in the world, now the name of Jesus is God at work in the world.

In spite of all the good things brought about by belief in his name, the first Christians found that life could be much harder because of their loyalty to Jesus, and so they also spoke of suffering for the name (Acts 5:41; 9:16; 1 Peter 4:14, 16) and even of dying for it (Acts 21:13). Now, it no longer denotes power so much as the character and reputation of the Lord, and it seems that when it is used in this way the person of the Lord and his name have become virtually identical.

"Lord" is thus applied both to God the Father and to Jesus without qualification or explanation. There has been a long debate over the origins of the use of *kurios* to refer to God, in Hellenistic Judaism, and to Jesus in Christianity.

Fortunately, that can be summarized briefly here, because of recent publications.[38] There is evidence now that prior to the rise of the church, Jews had begun to substitute *'adonai* or the Aramaic *mara'* or Greek *kurios* for the Tetragrammaton. Thus, when Christians began to speak of Jesus as *ho kurios,* they were making a striking claim concerning his relationship with God. The association of the words "name," "Jesus," and "Lord" appears in the most impressive way in a passage that is now considered to be a quotation by Paul of an early Christian hymn, which concludes:

> Therefore God also highly exalted him
>   and gave him the name that is above every name,
> so that at the name of Jesus every knee should bend,
>   in heaven and on earth and under the earth,
> and every tongue should confess that Jesus Christ is Lord,
>   to the glory of God the Father. (Phil. 2:9–11)

John carried the identification of Jesus with God the Father one step further, in his uses of *ego eimi,* "I am," in ways that clearly echo the explanation of the divine name in Ex. 3:14 and Second Isaiah's uses of "I am Yahweh."[39] Certain passages do not mean much unless they are understood in this way. Jesus says, "I told you that you would die in your sins, for you will die in your sins unless you believe that I am" (John 8:24; cf. v. 28). When he made the mysterious claim, "Before Abraham was, I am" (8:58), his audience threatened to stone him, so it was apparently no mystery to them, but an expression too close to the divine name to be tolerated. The encounter with Jesus of those who came to arrest him in the garden became a numinous experience when he asked them, "Whom are you looking for?" They answer, "Jesus of Nazareth," and he responds, "I am." John tells us that that apparently straightforward answer led them to step back and fall to the ground (18:4–6). So, although no reflection of the Tetragrammaton itself appears in the New Testament, and that name seems to have been of no interest to the early Christians, the explanation of the divine name in Exodus 3 with the first-person verb "to be" was used as one of several ways Christians tried to express their conviction that Jesus had been more than a prophet, teacher, or martyr, and had to be in some way identified with the presence of God on earth.

This need created a serious problem for Jewish followers of Jesus, who were good monotheists. They could not say Jesus was another god, and it is clear they knew enough theology to understand it was inappropriate to claim the Creator and Sustainer of heaven and earth had been walking around in Palestine. The way the Old Testament speaks of divine Wisdom (esp. Prov. 8:22–31; and cf. Wisd. Sol. 7:22–30) provided one way to begin to reflect on the divinity of Christ (1 Cor. 1:24; Col. 1:15–20; John 1:1–18). Eventually the doctrine of the Trinity would focus on the terms "Father," "Son," and "Holy Spirit" as the most useful words for talking about what could and could not be said of that relationship. One may also think that since the name of God had a certain identity of its own in the Old

Testament, but was more than a mere attribute, this may account for the prominence of its use in the New Testament, as the name of Jesus takes on the fullness of the character of the God of Abraham, Isaac, and Jacob. Karl Barth suggested as much when he asked if decision is not called for when "in place of the invisible form of the name of the manifest God which is primarily real only in the region of human conception—the unique contingent, somatic, human existence of Jesus has entered?"[40]

Christianity

The instinctive sense for the power of personal names has remained strong enough to this day that most of the time the terms "name of the Lord" or "name of Jesus" continue to be used without any need for explanation.[41] Ernst Lohmeyer devoted an unusual amount of attention to the question, "What is meant by the name of God?" in his book on the Lord's Prayer, however, and his summaries correspond very well with the way I concluded the Old Testament part of this chapter:

> Among the functions exercised by the concept of the name of God, the first is that name characterizes God as person, as an immeasurable and infinite 'I'; it keeps him from floating off into the lofty heights of the 'Godhead' or from dissolving into the incomprehensible expanses of pantheism. . . . For the name is on the one hand God himself in all the incomprehensibility of his majesty and his presence, while on the other hand it is still a name, and that means it can be grasped by human thought, uttered by human speech, assigned a place in human ideas and accepted or rejected, affirmed or denied by human hearts.[42]

In an interesting sermon on the Third Commandment, Paul Tillich spoke of the numinous quality of the name of God, beginning with the embarrassment that we may feel about speaking of God in contemporary society. There is a certain appropriateness in that, he claimed, "For the presence of the divine in the name demands a shy and trembling heart." His conclusion made a distinction between the name, which to a real extent is accessible to us, and God himself, comparable to the distinctions made above by Lohmeyer and in my conclusion to the Old Testament section: "I tried to make of it not only a sermon about the divine name, but also about God himself. I was thoroughly defeated in this attempt, and I had to learn that no one can give a sermon about God himself."[43]

Karl Barth discussed the name of God in his section on the root of the doctrine of the Trinity. He moves from the name to the Second Person of the Trinity in a way similar to that which I suggested the early church may have done. "In His name is concentrated everything in His relationship to His people, i.e., to the pious, and from the name of *Yahweh* somehow proceeds everything the people or the pious who stand in this relationship with Him, have to expect from Him." In the Old Testament, "the hidden *Yahweh* Himself is present in His name and all predicates of His name are those of the hidden *Yahweh* himself." Then he notes that in the New Testament, into the place of the name of Yahweh there comes the existence of the man Jesus of Nazareth.[44]

Moses' apparently simple question, asking for a name, was thus a very profound one, for it led to the insistence that God is no "oblong blur," as someone claimed, but is a being with whom it is possible for humans to have a personal relationship, knowable enough that we can call him by name.

The Old Testament has little comfort to offer to contemporary advocates of religious pluralism. Its insistence that God has a name is bound up with its insistence that Yahweh is the only God—in early times the only God Israel has anything to do with, and eventually the only God there is. All that it has to say about other deities is to deny first their legitimacy as objects of worship and finally to deny their existence. Christianity stands in the same tradition, although it has complicated matters with its doctrines of incarnation and the Trinity. It intends to remain faithful to the Old Testament, however, in its refusal to call Christ "another god" and in its efforts to define the Trinity as one God in three persons. One may hope that in the future useful discussions might begin between Christians and Jews, on the one hand, and Muslims, on the other, since Mohammed was thoroughly monotheistic, and understood Allah to be the God of Abraham. But beyond these three historically related religions, with their similar understandings of the deity, the challenges scripture presents to other religions can by no means be resolved so easily as the declaration "God has many names"[45] would suggest.

CHAPTER 5

PROMISE

Exodus 3—4
(Concluded)

I, the LORD, have spoken, and I have done it, says the LORD.
—Ezekiel 37:14

Let us hold fast the confession of our hope without wavering, for he who promised is faithful.
—Hebrew 10:23

At last we come to the heart of God's conversation with Moses. In Ex. 3:8 God makes an oblique reference to what he had promised Abraham in Gen. 15:18–21. The form of the sentence is not promise, but a declaration that he is now underway to deliver his people from oppression and to give them the land of the Canaanites: "I have come down to deliver them from the Egyptians, and to bring them up out of that land to a good and broad land." The same intention is expressed a bit later in the form of a promise in verse 17: "I will bring you up out of the misery of Egypt, to the land of the Canaanites." Two of the Old Testament's major themes have been introduced here, the exodus and the settlement in the Promised Land. Both have been extensively discussed, concerning their historicity and their meaning for the faith of Israel, but our focus on God in the book of Exodus will lead us in some slightly different directions from the previous studies and will not require us to review all the research and hypotheses associated with them.

"Promise" is a good word. As properly used, it means someone offers to do something that the intended recipient would like to have done.[1] But there is tension in the word. Usually it implies an interval of time, for if the person intends to do the good deed immediately, no promise will be necessary; the person will just do it. So a promise says, "Sometime, but not now." Promises usually require us to wait. Waiting involves tension enough in itself, but that introduces a second kind of tension, involving what we know of the character of the promiser. Did the promiser mean it? Is the promiser able to do what she or he promised? If a promise is to mean anything to us, it also calls for trust.

With these general reflections in mind, it already begins to seem rather strange that scripture has taught Judaism and Christianity to claim that one of the most distinctive characteristics of God is that he makes promises. Admittedly, that is not ordinarily seen as something problematic, since "promise" is a good word. Usually we think we are saying something good about God when we speak of his promises. On our side of the relationship, "trust" is also a good word. But what about waiting? Why should God say, "Sometime, but not now," if what he offers to do for us is something good for us? Surely, opponents of our religions might attack that as one of the greatest weaknesses in our beliefs about God. But that is the kind of God scripture offers us, from his promise to Abraham in Gen. 12:1–3 to "Surely, I am coming soon," in the next-to-last verse of Revelation. And so, in much of Christianity, at least, patience has also been upheld as a necessary, though perhaps less desirable, virtue.

The promises to Abraham, Isaac, and Jacob have been the subject of considerable scholarly literature in recent years, but most of that discussion can be bypassed in this chapter, since it is indirectly related to the concept of God.[2] Most of the interest has focused on the promises as a historical and literary issue. Can solid evidence be found to justify dating the promises in the pre-Mosaic period? At what point did the promises in Genesis become the basis for the structure of the whole Pentateuch (or Hexateuch)?[3] Answers to such questions might be of considerable theological importance if they could be agreed upon, but at present they remain open questions.

"Promise," in a broader sense, has been the subject of other studies that will also be touched on only peripherally in this chapter. For the writers of the New Testament books, the Old Testament promises were understood to be prophecies that had been fulfilled in their time, and "promise" sometimes continues to be used almost as a synonym for "prophecy."[4] Related to this is the proposal to identify the Old Testament with promise and the New Testament with fulfillment, as a way of explaining the relationship between the Testaments.[5] This is far too simplistic a solution, however, since the Old Testament already speaks of fulfillments (e.g., Josh. 21:45) and the New Testament offers unprecedented promises (e.g., 1 Thess. 4:15–17). Since the subject of this book is God, every effort will be made to restrict the use of these studies to what they may contribute to the answers to a single question: "What does it mean to have a God who is a promise maker?"

Some of the difficulties that complicate a theological treatment of this subject have already been alluded to. Terminology is another one. No Hebrew word corresponds to the English word "promise." The word "promise" does appear in English translations of the Old Testament, but the underlying Hebrew is usually one of the ordinary roots for speaking, *'amar* or *dibber*. This is not a mistranslation, for the contexts show that those words were indeed what we call promises. Here is another example of the truth that the word-study approach may miss some of the important ideas of scripture, for there is no word one can trace throughout the Old Testament in order to study the concept of promise.[6] The technical term that comes closest to the sense of promise in Hebrew is the word for "swearing," "taking an oath" (*nishba'*). It is frequently used with reference to the promises made to Abraham (as in Gen. 22:16–18), and we find it in Ex. 13:5, 11; 32:13; and

33:1. The same covenant-making oath is referred to by the Priestly writer in Ex.
6:8 with a different expression that means essentially the same thing: "to lift the
hand" (cf. Num 14:30; Neh. 9:15; Ezek. 20:5–6; 47:14). Since a promise is a
personal commitment to do something, oath taking was the most impressive way
of emphasizing the commitment it involved.

In the New Testament, *epangello* and related forms are a good equivalent to
our word "promise." But the English term itself is not without problems. The
Oxford English Dictionary definition indicates the word usually implies "something to the advantage or pleasure of the person concerned," but does admit that
the verb is sometimes used in a negative sense. For exactness in this chapter, we
must disallow the loose usage of "promise" that would enable it to include its
opposite, "threat."[7]

Promise also differs from prediction, it should be noted, a term we may use
generally for other kinds of sentences referring to the future. When we turn to
Genesis, we shall also find that Westermann has emphasized the difference
between promise and blessing, since blessing is normally present tense. But in
Genesis 12:1–3, blessing is *promised,* so the two kinds of speech will have to be
considered together.

Westermann has described three types of promise:[8] (1) *assurance,* which is a
statement such as "I have given [them] into your hand" (Josh. 8:1), or "I am with
you" (Jer. 1:8); (2) *announcement,* which uses an imperfect verb, such as "I will
bring you up from the land of Egypt" (Ex. 3:17); and (3) *portrayal,* which
describes a scene in the future, such as Isa. 11:1–10. In order to accomplish our
purpose it will be necessary to limit the material to be discussed, and a different
way of classifying the promises will serve the purpose. Let us call them short-term
and long-term. All of Westermann's "assurances" would be short-term, for their
fulfillment is imminent. Short-term promises from a deity are a commonplace in
religion.[9] They are associated with the "holy war" in the Old Testament and in
other cultures, and also with other oracles containing commands that will be
rewarded if obeyed. They sometimes are used as motive clauses connected with
law: ". . . that all may go well with you and with your children after you" (Deut.
12:25). They may be offered as God's answer to a petition: "I will do the very
thing that you have asked; for you have found favor in my sight, and I know you
by name" (Ex. 33:17). They typically refer to the future of individuals.

Long-term promises seem to be a distinctive characteristic of the Bible, and
they necessarily speak of the future of a people. Our emphasis in this chapter will
be on the major examples of this type. We shall have to deal briefly with Old
Testament eschatology, in which all of Westermann's "portrayals" are found, and
prior to that will work with the promise that Israel would always have a son of
David to sit on the throne in Jerusalem, and with the promise to Abraham, Isaac,
and Jacob. Exodus begins to describe God's saving activity with a reference to
Genesis (Ex. 2:24), and so that is where we must begin.

THE PROMISES TO THE ANCESTORS IN GENESIS

Since we have begun with Exodus 3—4 (and the parallel in Ex. 6:2–8), it is the wording of Gen. 12:1–3, 7; 15:18–21; and 17:1–8 that will be of the greatest importance to us.

Genesis 12:7 adds the promise of the land of Canaan to God's initial words to Abram:

> Go from your country and your kindred and your father's house to the land that I will show you. And I will make of you a great nation, and I will bless you, and make your name great, so that you will be a blessing. I will bless those who bless you, and him who curses you I will curse; and by you all the families of the earth will bless themselves. (Gen. 12:1b–3)

From that point on, living with as yet unfulfilled promises that are frequently in great jeopardy runs as a major theme through the rest of the book. Having been promised blessing, Abram's family immediately faces the curse of famine (Gen. 12:10–20). He leaves the Promised Land, for no one could live there, and instead of becoming a great nation must live as a sojourner in a truly great nation, Egypt. His efforts to stay alive lead him to make it impossible that he will ever become a nation of any kind, for his wife ends up in the pharaoh's harem. And the point of the whole bizarre story is that God will find a way to keep human mistakes from making it impossible for the promise to be fulfilled.

The difficulty of waiting forms a part of two of the subsequent stories. When God offers another promise in Gen. 15:1, Abram may have been justified in asking when something was going to happen. "O LORD God, what will you give me, for I continue childless, and the heir of my house is Eliezer of Damascus? . . . You have given me no offspring, and so a slave born in my house is to be my heir." God elaborates the promise; Abram's decendants will be as the stars of heaven, and we are told Abram "believed the LORD; and the LORD reckoned it to him as righteousness" (15:6). That God expects people to believe he will keep his promises is the occasion in scripture for introducing the necessity of faith. As von Rad points out, that occurs only once in Genesis, but it is the problem of faith that lies behind the whole Abraham cycle.[10]

That the promise was made equally to Abraham and Sarah becomes clear when she tries an expedient, giving him her slave girl Hagar, so that he might have a child somehow. And a son is born, but he is not the child of the promise (Gen. 16; 17:17–21). Sarah finds belief as difficult as her husband did, so that when the promise is repeated yet again she could not help laughing (Gen. 18:9–15). But at last a son is born, and it looks as though God is trustworthy, after all (Gen. 21:1–7). In the next chapter, God says to Abraham, "Take your son, your only son

Isaac, whom you love, and go to the land of Moriah, and offer him there as a burnt offering on one of the mountains that I shall show you" (Gen. 22:2). This awful story is Israel's reflection on those times when God seems not just inactive, but actually working against what he has promised. But the end of the story contains Israel's insistence that God does remain faithful, no matter how impossible the circumstances seem to be.

By the end of Genesis, however, only one part of the promise shows any sign of being fulfilled. Abraham's family has grown to significant numbers, and the book of Exodus begins with that fact (Exod. 1:7, 20). It is no great cause for rejoicing, however, since their numbers seem a threat to Pharaoh, and that means any chance of the rest of the promise being fulfilled is being jeopardized anew. Genesis 12 through Exodus 2 thus forms a lengthy introduction to the call of Moses, with Ex. 2:24 signaling a radically new development in the story: "God remembered his covenant with Abraham, Isaac, and Jacob." The need for faith, trust, and patience will not have disappeared, however, as Moses soon learns.

PROMISE IN EXODUS

The plot of Exodus and the rest of the Pentateuch, continuing through 2 Samuel, is how God went about fulfilling the rest of his promise to Abraham. The JE source does not cite the promise explicitly, but chapter 3 makes sense only if the reader's awareness of it is assumed. Twice the identification of the deity as the God of Abraham, Isaac, and Jacob leads into his declaration that he is about to give his people the land of the Canaanites (v. 6 and vv. 7–10; vv. 15–16 and v. 17). We cannot be sure whether 2:24 was originally a part of JE, but if it was, then the mention of covenant makes it all explicit. Before the old promise can be fulfilled, a new one must be made, however, for God's people are the slaves of a great nation, and so deliverance (the exodus theme) is introduced as the essential first step (vv. 8–9, 17, 20). Of the old promise, only the gift of the land is mentioned. Verses 8 and 17, with their lists of the inhabitants, may be compared with Gen. 12:7; 15:18–21 (which has a somewhat different list), and 17:8. It is certainly the heart of the conversation between God and Moses, but as JE has elaborated the story of his call, relatively few verses are dedicated to the promise.

In the parallel passage in Ex. 6:2–8, however, the Priestly writer makes the promise dominate the whole text. There are clear references back to the Priestly account of the covenant with Abraham in Genesis 17. Here, unlike Exodus 3—4, God refers back to the promise made to the ancestors, with reference to his intent to give them the land, mentioning the covenant in verse 4 and his oath in verse 8. The new promise of deliverance must also appear, as it did in the JE version (vv. 5–6). And the relationship of God and people, of which Gen. 17:7 speaks, is reaffirmed in Ex. 6:7. In a much clearer way than Exodus 3—4, this short passage outlines what is about to happen in the ensuing chapters.

The fulfillment of the promise of deliverance will be undertaken immediately, in Exodus 7—14. It would seem to have been finished once the Israelites had escaped from Egypt, but one of the most important things about a religion of promise is that divine promises never seem to be exhausted. So Ezekiel (20:33–44) and Second Isaiah (Isaiah 43, etc.) will look forward to a second exodus.

The promise "I will take you as my people, and I will be your God" (Ex. 6:7) will be fulfilled at Sinai (Exodus 19—31). But Sinai will not be the end of that story, either, for two reasons. God added a new promise when he offered the covenant to Israel:

> Now therefore, if you obey my voice and keep my covenant, you shall be my treasured possession out of all the peoples. Indeed, the whole earth is mine, but you shall be for me a priestly kingdom and a holy nation. (Ex. 19:5–6)

What it would mean to become a priestly kingdom and a holy nation is never worked out at any length in the Old Testament, but it will be taken up in the New Testament. Should it be associated with Gen. 12:3b, "by you all the families of the earth will bless themselves," and Gen. 22:18, "and by your descendants shall all the nations of the earth bless themselves"[11] (RSV)?

This covenant, unlike those with Noah and Abraham, is conditional, and so it is not final because it will depend on human obedience in the future. The tensions within that promise come to the surface immediately, with the story of the golden calf and its aftermath in Exodus 32—34. How God can fulfill his promise that he intends to have an intimate relationship with his people when the people refuse to uphold their side of the relationship is given a preliminary answer in Exodus 34, as we shall see, but of course that will not be the end of the story.

The promise of the land is elaborated with details about the forthcoming occupation in Exodus (13:5, 11; 23:27–31; 33:1–3; 34:10f.), but it was not fulfilled within the Pentateuch, and that is the primary reason scholars such as von Rad claim the books were once grouped as a hexateuch. At one point the book of Joshua claimed it was done: "not one thing has failed of all the good things that the LORD your God promised concerning you; all have come to pass for you, not one of them has failed" (Josh. 23:14b). But it is more accurate to say the occupation of the land became complete only in the time of David (2 Samuel 8). Once again, a twofold modification of the promise appears. It is expanded from the simple "kings will come from you" in Gen. 17:6 to "Your house and your kingdom shall be made sure forever before me; your throne shall be established forever" (2 Sam. 7:16). But both the monarchy and possession of the land will be jeopardized again and again after the time of Solomon, so these promises, like all the others, never become past tense. They are partly present, but always partly future. Now let us see how Israel maintained the conviction that their God really did intend all these good things for them, when they were never more than partly so, and eventually, with the fall of Jerusalem in 587 B.C.E., were completely gone.

The issue appeared very early in Moses' career as a divine mediator. He and Aaron went to Pharaoh, as instructed, with the demand, "Thus says the LORD God, the God of Israel, 'Let my people go, so that they may celebrate a festival to me in the wilderness' " (Ex. 5:1). The result was the imposition of heavier labor on the slaves, forcing them to gather their own straw for brick making without decreasing the number required per day (5:6–21). Moses felt betrayed. "O LORD, why have you mistreated this people? Why did you ever send me? Since I first came to Pharaoh to speak in your name, he has mistreated this people, and you have done nothing at all to deliver your people" (5:22–23). All God does is repeat his assurance that he is about to do something to Pharoah, reminding us of the ways he responded to Abraham in Genesis.

Instant satisfaction is sometimes offered, however. As the pharoah's army approached the people, trapped on the shore of the Reed Sea, and they complained to Moses, "What have you done to us, bringing us out of Egypt?" (Ex. 14:11b), Moses reassured them, "The Egyptians whom you see today you shall never see again. The LORD will fight for you, and you have only to keep still" (14:13b–14). And it happened.

These first two crises led to questions whether God was willing or able to deal with Israel's enemies. The final one in Exodus raised the question whether God was obligated to keep the covenant promises when Israel had already violated its part. Chapters 32—34 of Exodus take us deeply into Israel's reflections on how there can be any kind of beneficial, ongoing relationship between God and a sinful people, and we shall deal with that at length in chapter 8 of this book. For now, note that as Moses reasons with God, he appeals to the unconditional covenant made with the ancestors: "Remember Abraham, Isaac, and Israel, your servants, how you swore to them by your own self, saying to them, 'I will multiply your descendants like the stars of heaven, and all this land that I have promised I will give to your descendants, and they shall inherit it forever' " (Ex. 32:13). Similar appeals to what they believed to be God's sincere intent form one of Israel's ways of dealing with the apparent failure of God's promises, as we shall see in our survey of the rest of the Old Testament.

PROMISE IN THE OLD TESTAMENT

With the fall of Jerusalem in 587, the end of the monarchy, and the loss of the land, it appeared that Israel had finally forfeited all its rights under the Sinai covenant. Some exilic authors were able to maintain hope that God had not completely and finally given up on Israel by appealing to the unconditional covenant and its promises, the one made with Abraham, Isaac, and Jacob. The conditional blessings and curses in Leviticus 26 were evidently formulated at a time when the curses, including exile, had already come true, for the chapter concludes with an offer of a way to reverse Israel's punishment. "But if they confess their iniquity and the iniquity of their ancestors, in that they committed treachery against me and, moreover, that they continued hostile to me . . . then will I remember my covenant with Jacob; I will remember also my covenant with Isaac and also my covenant with Abraham, and I will remember the land" (Lev. 26:40–42). And without explaining how it could be, there may even be some hope for the Sinai covenant, for the passage continues, "but I will remember in their favor the covenant with their ancestors whom I brought out of the land of Egypt in the sight of the nations, to be their God: I am the LORD" (v. 45).

Some exilic authors maintained the continuing validity of the promises, all evidence to the contrary. Second Isaiah says nothing about Sinai, but makes new divine promises with reference to the three unconditional covenants.

> Look to Abraham your father
> and to Sarah who bore you;
> for he was but one when I called him,
> but I blessed him and made him many.
> For the LORD will comfort Zion;
> he will comfort all her waste places. (Isa. 51:3)

Abraham and Jacob are referred to in a new promise of divine help (Isa. 41:8–10), God's oath to Noah is compared with a new divine oath, "that I will not be angry with you and will not rebuke you" (Isa. 54:9–10), and finally God says, "I will make with you an everlasting covenant, my steadfast, sure love for David" (Isa. 55:3b). How could such claims—that the old promises that had failed would soon be renewed—meet with anything but an incredulous reaction? As with other subjects, we may find in the Old Testament's language of worship some clues concerning the way Israel dealt with the problem of a God who says, "Wait."

The Psalter takes up the problem in both the laments of the individual and the laments of the community. Psalm 77 takes the failure of promise as its principal subject. The psalm begins with a call for help (v. 1) and a complaint (vv. 2–10), as laments usually do, but it is unusual in not having a clear-cut petition. The complaint emphasizes first the psalmist's persistence (v. 2), then raises the question of God's apparent failure any longer to keep his promises (vv. 7–10):

> Will the LORD spurn forever, and never again be favorable?
> Has his steadfast love ceased forever?
> Are his promises [lit., "word"] at an end for all time?
> Has God forgotten to be gracious?
> Has he in anger shut up his compassion?
> And I say, "It is my grief
> that the right hand of the Most High has changed."

The resolution that this psalmist finds is in remembering that in the past God did fulfill his promises: "I will call to mind the deeds of the LORD; I will remember your wonders of old" (v. 11). He praises God for redeeming the descendants of Jacob and Joseph (vv. 12–15), and that leads us to expect a recollection of the exodus, which he gives us by writing his own theophanic description of the parting of the Sea (vv. 16–19), leading to the conclusion, "You led your people like a flock by the hand of Moses and Aaron."

This appeal to memory, Israel's and God's, appears frequently in the laments. In Psalm 77 it is Israel's memory, used as reassurance that in times of past distress God did not fail them, so there is hope also for the present. Sometimes God's memory is appealed to, as if to remind him of his expressed good intentions for Israel, as in Ps. 80:8–11, 14–19. In times such as these the faithful in Israel did not take history to be revelation, but instead revelation—in this case Israel's conviction that those promises had really come from God—was thrown up against history.

In one case, however, the problem was left without resolution. Psalm 89 tackles the promise to David of an eternal dynasty at a time when that dynasty either had come to an end (after 587) or was in dire straits (some date it earlier). The psalmist will not search for a loophole in order to find a way out for God, but expresses the promise even more strongly than it is stated in 2 Samuel 7 or Psalm 132: "Once and for all I have sworn by my holiness; I will not lie to David. His line shall continue forever" (Ps. 89:35–36a). Then comes the complaint:

But now you have spurned and rejected him;
    you are full of wrath against your anointed.
You have renounced the covenant with your servant;
    you have defiled his crown in the dust. (vv. 38–39)

We have thought about the issue on the human side, involving the need for faith, trust, and patience. This psalm makes clear that the issue on God's side is faithfulness (*'emeth* or *'emunah*). His faithfulness is praised in the first part of the psalm (vv. 14, 33), but that only sets up the question in the second part: "LORD, where is your steadfast love of old, which by your faithfulness you swore to David?" (v. 49). This psalm has no answer to the question. Dare we say it remained in the psalter as Israel's continuing faithful question to God about the reason why they had to wait?

Lamentations, written as an early reaction to the fall of Jerusalem, has something positive to say about waiting, amid its expressions of deep distress at having lost everything:

The LORD is good to those who wait for him,
    to the soul that seeks him.
It is good that one should wait quietly
    for the salvation of the LORD.
    . . . .
For the LORD will not reject forever.
Although he causes grief, he will have compassion
    according to the abundance of his steadfast love;
for he does not willingly afflict or grieve anyone. (Lam. 3:25–26, 31–32)

Other ancient Near Eastern cultures explained disasters as the interventions of their deities in history, as Israel did, but here is something distinctive.[12] Scholars who have written on promise have emphasized that promise made history meaningful to Israel in ways not found in other cultures, for it left them open to a future that was expected to be different from (better than) the present. The texts I have chosen show that it gave them the possibility of openness to a better future even when present conditions seemed to deny all possibility of hope. For belief in the promises of God to survive the fall of Jerusalem and the exile, they must have been a part of Israel's faith for so long that Israel had no other way to think of Yahweh than as a promise maker, a God moving toward a different future, and a God who had shown enough evidence of his faithfulness in the past that some basis for trust could still survive.[13]

As the prophet we call Second Isaiah sought ways to convince the discouraged exiles in Babylonia that the time was at hand when God was about to restore them to the Promised Land, he appealed to fulfilled promises of the past as evidence of God's beneficent will toward them and of his power to accomplish it. Promise is already beginning to be used as "proof from the fulfillment of prophecy," as the Old Testament was regularly used in later times (cf. Isa. 43:9).

> The former things I declared long ago,
>> they went out from my mouth and I made them known;
>> then suddenly I did them and they came to pass.
> Because I know that you are obstinate,
>> and your neck is an iron sinew and your forehead brass,
> I declared them to you from long ago,
>> before they came to pass I announced them to you,
> so that you would not say, "My idol did them,
>> my carved image and my cast image commanded them." (Isa. 48:3–5)

Having alluded to this evidence from the past that God had the will and the ability to accomplish what he declared in advance, the prophet announces new promises: "From this time forward I make you hear new things, hidden things that you have not known" (48:6b), and the ensuing verses rebuke the exiles for their inability to believe the promises that are forthcoming (48:8–21).

It was not enough to remind this discouraged audience of good things that had happened in the past, for the present seemed ample evidence that God had forsaken them (cf. Isa. 49:14–21). Earlier prophets had explained the fall of Jerusalem and the exile in terms of Israel's perennial rebelliousness and God's justice; what reason could be given for saying that God was now making new promises? The prophet compares their time to another time of judgment and promise, that of the great Flood:

> For a brief moment I abandoned you,
>> but with great compassion I will gather you.

In overflowing wrath for a moment I hid my face from you,
　　but with everlasting love I will have compassion on you,
　　　　says the LORD, your Redeemer.
This is like the days of Noah to me:
　　Just as I swore that the waters of Noah
　　would never again go over the earth,
so I have sworn that I will not be angry with you
　　and will not rebuke you. (Isa. 54:7–9)

Judgment had been followed by promise in the past, and the prophet insists that the promises now coming from his lips are as valid as those God had given and upheld in the past. God insists:

For as the rain and the snow come down from heaven,
　　and do not return there until they have watered the earth,
making it bring forth and sprout,
　　giving seed to the sower and bread to the eater,
so shall my word be that goes out from my mouth;
　　it shall not return to me empty,
but it shall accomplish that which I purpose. (Isa. 55:10–11)

Those words are followed immediately by another promise of restoration, to be accompanied by the celebration of nature itself.

The exilic period was thus a time for the offering of new divine promises, often referring back to the classic promises associated with the covenants with Noah, Abraham, and David, and sometimes to Sinai as well. There was a new element in the prophetic promises, however, that leads most scholars to find it necessary to use the word "eschatology," in spite of the debates over how that word should be defined. I have dealt at length with the eschatology of the Old Testament in another book, but space in that book did not permit a full discussion of the definition I used.[14] A more complete explanation seems to be needed here, in order to distinguish the promises of the prophets from the others in the Old Testament.

The promise to Noah affirmed that the good earth would continue to be a good earth (Gen. 9:8–17), and the promise to David insisted his dynasty would continue forever (2 Sam. 7:16). What is now good will remain good. As for Abraham, it would get better. He was promised greatness and blessing (Gen. 12:1–3). Israel at Sinai also could expect something even better than their freedom from slavery, for God promised, "you shall be my treasured possession out of all the peoples" (Ex. 19:5). The promise given to Moses early in the book of Exodus was of a different type, however: "I declare that I will bring you up out of the misery of Egypt" (Ex. 3:17). This promise of deliverance or salvation took the evil in the world seriously, in a way that could somehow be overlooked in the promises associated with all four covenants. At the time of the fall of Jerusalem, when Israel was losing everything and all the world seemed to have gone wrong, it was that kind of promise the prophets eventually found themselves compelled to utter. Let us look at a series of examples in order to clarify what is distinctive about these promises:

> In that day the branch of the LORD shall be beautiful and glorious, and the fruit of the land shall be the pride and glory of the survivors of Israel. And he who is left in Zion and remains in Jerusalem will be called holy, every one who has been recorded for life in Jerusalem, when the LORD shall have washed away the filth of the daughters of Zion and cleansed the bloodstains of Jerusalem from its midst by a spirit of judgment and by a spirit of burning. (Isa. 4:2–4)

This picture of the glorious future calls for the washing away of filth and the cleansing of bloodstains.

> He shall judge between many peoples, and shall decide for strong nations afar off; and they shall beat their swords into plowshares, and their spears into pruning hooks; nation shall not lift up sword against nation, neither shall they learn war any more. (Micah 4:3)

This one calls for an end to war.

> Then the eyes of the blind shall be opened, and the ears of the deaf unstopped; then shall the lame man leap like a hart, and the tongue of the dumb sing for joy. (Isa. 35:5–6a)

Human infirmity will be no more.

> I will make the fruit of the tree and the increase of the field abundant, that you may never again suffer the disgrace of famine among the nations. (Ezek. 36:30)

No more hunger.

> I will cleanse them from all the guilt of their sin against me, and I will forgive all the guilt of their sin and rebellion against me. (Jer. 33:8)

Sin and guilt will be erased.

> They shall not hurt or destroy in all my holy mountain. (Isa. 11:9a)

No more killing or harming of any living thing.

These passages are in continuity with the Exodus promises, in that they speak of God's intention to deal with what is wrong with the world and with humanity, but they have moved beyond anything in Exodus in that they convey a sense of *radical wrongness.* They confront the evil in this world without the optimism of law or wisdom, traditions that sought to make humanity and the world better by educating and by regulating behavior. They differ from cultic texts, which provide "religious" ways of dealing with sin: means of cleansing and assurances of forgiveness. They struggle with evil in a way that does not appear in the promises of the Abrahamic or Sinai or Davidic covenants, for those were promises that did not confront an insoluble problem; they assume that God can work with what presently exists to make it better. They differ also from descriptions of institutional prophecy that appear occasionally in the Old Testament, for those prophets dealt with sin and the possibility of a better future by exhorting and warning and calling to repentance (e.g., 2 Kings 17:13; Jer. 26:4–6).

These texts spring from the conviction that something is radically wrong in this world, so that only radical change can make it right. To this extent they have something in common with later apocalyptic thought, but they do not yet personalize evil, give to evil a cosmic dimension, or systematize and periodize their picture of the triumph over evil. Their vision of the future still deals with this world, with the nation of Israel, the city Jerusalem, other nations, farmers and children and old people. The radical victory over evil that is hoped for does not call for "going to heaven" or the complete abolishment of the world we know. The prophets shared Israel's basic world-affirming spirit. Everything was made by God, so nothing is bad in itself—but sin has by now left it hopelessly corrupted. These texts promise *transformation* as the radical victory over evil.

These promises do not address the comfortable, those who are essentially satisfied with life as it is. Indeed, the comfortable also have hopes for the future, but for a future in essential continuity with the present; for more of the same, with improvements. That is not eschatology. The prophets found the predicament of their time to be so bad that they could not conceive of God's future developing in any natural way out of what presently exists. Transformation meant bringing the old order to an end and replacing it with something new. And so, if we consider the literal meaning of the word "eschatology," which is "the doctrine of the end," and ask, "End of what?" the Old Testment's answer is "The End of Evil."[15]

For the history of the eschatological tradition, the reader is referred to my other book on Old Testament eschatology. All that can be done in this context is note some of the Old Testament promises that were later held to with special fervency in Judaism and those that meant the most to the early Christians. I have shown that the restoration of Zion became a virtual center for the hopes expressed in the prophetic books, and Jerusalem has remained to this day a focus for Jewish hope. The other promise that has been most important to them is that of return to the land. Christians, on the other hand, have shown little interest in those two promises, but have taken the new covenant passage in Jer. 31:31–34 and promises of eschatological forgiveness to be keys to their existence. In addition, the Messiah and resurrection have been so important to them that they have diligently found more promises of that kind than some of us think really exist in the Old Testament. As to what eschatology meant for the relationship of Jews and Christians to God, the story will be slightly different for the two. For Jews the promises of the ingathering of the exiles and the glorification of Zion remain unfulfilled, and the nonfulfillment has now extended a long time. Christians claim fulfillment of many of the Old Testament promises in Jesus Christ, but the fulfillment is incomplete, and in some cases the incompleteness is troublesome. Their relationship to the future is thus somewhat more complex than it is for the Jews.

Israel's belief that Yahweh is a maker of long-term promises, the fulfillment of which was partly affected by their own behavior, and partly by the imperfectly understood will of God, made their religion distinctive in several ways. (1) Meaning was not to be determined from myths about the beginning, as in other religions, but from the future, from what they were told God intended to do to change things. (2) But the promise of change did not involve rejection of the world, as in Eastern religions or later gnosticism, for even the eschatological promises spoke of continuity with the present order, transforming it rather than abolishing it. (3) Promise afforded one way of acknowledging the reality of evil in the world—although it could not be explained—for by offering something better it affirmed that God is at work against evil. (4) It provided for human responsibility, even though it spoke of the future as being in God's hands, for along with the promise of a new life and a new world came the insistence that the recipients would have to live in that new way. (5) It dealt with failure, in that human sin, which might thwart one promise, did not stop God from making new promises. (6) It required faith, for no promise was ever completely fulfilled to everyone's satisfaction. (7) It called for trust in another, not in oneself, for the promises were not human plans; they were offered by another. (8) It required an eschatology, for a promise *never* completely fulfilled is not a trustworthy promise. (9) And it involved Israel with a personal God, for no force or ideal can encounter us with an offer to do something we want and need, nor can it respond to new needs with new promises.

History shows different emphases on the promise-making character of God. During relatively stable periods, such as the time of the Israelite monarchy and the hegemony of European Christendom, religion tends to claim it has the answers to individual needs and hopes in the present, and hopes for the coming of a different community are not encouraged. It is during unstable periods, when the promises of the past do not seem to be fulfilled in the present, that hope is maintained by emphasizing the future, since the present has little to offer. There have been long periods like this, especially in Jewish history. Why go on thinking God will do anything about those old promises? We have found in the Old Testament evidence for the power of memory to keep promises alive, and shall attempt to trace that in subsequent history. Having looked briefly at the special character of Old Testament eschatology, however, most of which still remains entirely future, we shall also need to acknowledge that the future itself can take hold of the imagination so as to produce hope, and action based on that hope.[16]

PROMISE IN JUDAISM AND CHRISTIANITY

Our study would become much too diffuse if we tried to trace every kind of promise in the literature subsequent to the Old Testament. There is little to be gained from the general references to promises, fulfilled in the past or hoped for.

The special form of apocalyptic promise is a study in itself. We shall be guided by the concerns expressed earlier, and shall try to trace the tensions created by living with promises. We shall find that Abraham was so closely associated with promise in both religions that many of the passages in which he is mentioned provide valuable insights into the subject. For both religions, the first century C.E. was critical. For Christianity, the coming of Jesus led to the claim that eschatological promises had been fulfilled. For Judaism, the fall of Jerusalem in 70 C.E. meant that the faithfulness of God had to be justified once again.

Judaism

In the Apocrypha, Baruch deals with the fall of Jerusalem in 587 B.C.E. in a rather puzzling way, since it rewrites some of the history in ways that contradict the Old Testament. Its reiteration of the Old Testament promises is the only thing that needs to concern us, however. The first part takes the form of a message sent from the exiles in Babylonia to the people remaining in Jerusalem (1:14), in which the reasons for the fall of the city are discussed. The words of God to Moses are quoted, in this conflation of Old Testament texts:

> I will bring them again into the land that I swore to give to their ancestors, to Abraham, Isaac, and Jacob, and they will rule over it; and I will increase them, and they will not be diminished. I will make an everlasting covenant with them to be their God and they shall be my people; and I will never again remove my people Israel from the land that I have given them. (Bar. 2:34–35)

The promise of the land is obviously the main emphasis, but we also notice the Sinai covenant formula—"I will be your God and you shall be my people"—and the promise of increase. Some scholars date Baruch after the fall of Jerusalem in 70 C.E., which would make this entirely a reference to the future, but it is more often dated around 100 B.C.E., at a time when the Second Temple stood in Jerusalem. If that is correct, then this book was written when the promise of restoration had been partly fulfilled, so that the first readers might have been encouraged by their memory that this had already partly come true. The point of view of the book does not acknowledge that, however, and the attitude that overlooks the Second Temple as fulfillment and considers the true fulfillment to lie entirely in the future reappears several times in apocalyptic surveys of past and future history.[17]

God's faithfulness to his promises in the past is recalled as the basis for appealing for his help in the present in some passages, however. This is in continuity with Old Testament prayers. One of the prayers in the Additions to the Book of Esther includes, "Ever since I was born I have heard in the tribe of my family that you, O Lord, took Israel out of all the nations, and our ancestors from among all their forebears, for an everlasting inheritance, and that you did for them all that you promised" (*laleo*; Add. Esth. 14:5). Later she says, "Remember, O

Lord; make yourself known in this time of our affliction" (Add. Esth. 14:12). A prayer in 3 Maccabees puts it more directly:

> And because you love the house of Israel, you promised [*epangellomai*] that if we should have reverses, and tribulation should overtake us, you would listen to our petition when we come to this place and pray. And indeed you are faithful and true. And because oftentimes when our fathers were oppressed you helped them in their humiliation, and rescued them from great evils, see now. . . . (3 Macc. 2:10–13a)

The reference to promise may take the form of a blessing, instead of a petition, as in 2 Macc. 1:2: "May God do good to you, and may he remember his covenant with Abraham and Isaac and Jacob, his faithful servants." These recollections of past fulfillments as the basis for hope, and appeals to God to remember his promises are continuations of the prayer language of the Old Testament, but in the Intertestamental literature a new emphasis appears, and that is the claim that God has promised to be merciful.[18]

Forgiveness is not a significant theme in Genesis. It appears only at the end, when Joseph's brothers ask it of him after Jacob's death (Gen. 50:17). It becomes a major theme in Israel's story only with the incident of the golden calf, as we shall see later. But in the Intertestamental literature forgiveness and more general appeals to the mercy of God have been associated with Abraham and with the promise of God. This seems to be a new trend, and it will help to explain an important emphasis in the New Testament. There is some basis for it in the Old Testament, and the most significant passage is Micah 7:18–20:

> Who is a God like you, pardoning iniquity
>   and passing over the transgression
>   of the remnant of your possession?
> He does not retain his anger forever,
>   because he delights in showing clemency.
> He will again have compassion upon us;
>   he will tread our iniquities under foot.
> You will cast all our sins into the depths of the sea.
> You will show faithfulness to Jacob
>   and unswerving loyalty to Abraham,·
> as you have sworn to our ancestors from the days of old.

Here God's promise of compassion, which first appears in Ex. 34:6–7, has been projected back onto the covenant with Abraham, and that idea appears more prominently in postbiblical Judaism than in the Old Testament (e.g., Wisd. Sol. 12:21f.; Pr. Azar. 11f.; 2 Macc. 2:17f.; *Psalms of Solomon* 7:8–10; 9:8–11).

The Prayer of Manasseh is a penitential prayer that directly associates forgiveness with promise:

> Yet immeasurable and unsearchable is your promised [*epangelia*] mercy,
>   for you are the Lord Most High,

of great compassion, long-suffering and very merciful,
and you relent at human suffering.
O Lord, according to your great goodness
you have promised [*epangellomai*] repentance and forgiveness
to those who have sinned against you,
and in the multitude of your mercies
you have appointed repentance for sinners,
so that they may be saved. (vv. 6–7)

This text makes an unusual use of Abraham, however, by explicitly disassociating him (and Isaac and Jacob) from the promise of repentance and forgiveness, since they never sinned (v. 8). We are likely to read Genesis differently, but the author may have deduced their sinlessness from the absence of any reference to repentance or forgiveness in the stories of the patriarchs. As the religion of the Torah had developed in the postexilic period, the need for repentance and forgiveness had been recognized (as the later rabbinic literature makes even more clear[19]), and suitable texts were found in the Old Testament to enable writers to claim this also was one of the old promises of God. The primary connection of the idea of promise with Abraham, in their thinking, then led them to associate God's mercy with him, even without any specific texts they could cite.

All the texts cited so far in this section were probably written before the fall of Jerusalem in 70 C.E. Although the Jews suffered repeatedly during those years, the authors quoted could refer with great confidence to God's faithfulness and mercy, as demonstrated in the past and in their own experience. The disastrous and long-lasting consequences of the war of 66–70 brought into Judaism the necessity of accounting for an apparent reversal of God's ways with them, however. We shall focus on two early reactions to the catastrophe, with only brief reference to some later rabbinic statements. Second Esdras was written late in the first century, ostensibly by Ezra, who is misdated as contemporary with the fall of Jerusalem in 587 B.C.E. He raises a long series of theological questions about that event, but we know that the real author of the book is actually struggling with his own immediate problem, the fall of Jerusalem in 70 C.E. He begins by retelling history, the standard way for a Jew to work through a theological issue. The sin of Adam is more important to him than to any other Jewish author, but when he gets to Abraham he states one of the basic beliefs that creates his problem: "You made an everlasting covenant with him, and promised him that you would never forsake his descendants" (2 Esd. 3:15). In one of his laments that soon follow, however, he asks "why Israel has been given over to the Gentiles in disgrace; why the people whom you loved has been given over to godless tribes, and the law of our ancestors has been brought to destruction and the written covenants no longer exist" (4:23). Most of the answers given in this book are eschatological, that is, there is no present explanation that human beings can understand (e.g., 4:1–11; 5:40), and no present solution, but in the near future all will be made right (e.g., 7:14–16). So God says, "this age is hurrying swiftly to its end. It will not be able to bring the things that have been promised to the righteous in their appointed times, because this age is full of sadness and infirmities" (4:26b–27). And this is followed by the admonition, "Do not be in a greater hurry than the Most High" (4:34), a new way to speak of the theme of waiting.

Ezra is deeply troubled by the injustice of what he and his people have experienced, however, for "those who opposed your promises have trampled on those who believed your covenants" (5:29). "But we, your people, whom you have called your firstborn, only begotten, zealous for you, and most dear, have been given into their hands. If the world has indeed been created for us, why do we not possess our world as an inheritance? How long will this be so?" (6:58–59). He also is troubled by the message he gets that in the end only a few will be saved. The best answer offered to him is, "I saw and spared some with great difficulty, and saved for myself one grape out of a cluster, and one plant out of a great forest" (9:21). It is a deeply pessimistic book, for in spite of God's assurances that Ezra and others will be saved, the author says, "What good is it that immortal time has been promised to us, but we have done deeds that bring death? And what good is it that an everlasting hope has been promised to us, but we have miserably failed?" (7:119–120). The answer is a challenge not to accept defeat, quoting Deut. 30:19: "Choose life for yourself, so that you may live" (2 Esd. 7:129).

The shock of 70 C.E. has been so great for the author of this book that even the offer of new promises, as in 7:119–120, is not much help. The promise of a better future, to come soon, in which all will be made right, is the only answer he can find to his questions about God's justice and faithfulness, and for him God's mercy is a rather dubious subject. The best he can do is go on questioning.

Second Esdras is not typical of the Jewish response to the fall of Jerusalem, however. A few years later, 2 Baruch took up the same problems, but the atmosphere of the book is quite different. Once again the subject is supposedly the fall of Jerusalem in 587 B.C.E., and this time Baruch is the questioner (2 Apoc. Bar. 3:5b–9).

[H]ow will the name of Israel be remembered again? Or how shall we speak again about your glorious deeds? Or to whom again will that which is in your Law be explained? . . . and where is all that which you said to Moses about us?

The answer is eschatological, again; all this will be only for a time (4:1). But the discussion continues, and later Baruch brings up the point we shall see Moses making in Ex. 32:11–13:

Therefore command mercifully and confirm all that you have said that you would do so that your power will be recognized by those who believe that your long-suffering means weakness. . . . For as many years have passed as those which passed since the days of Abraham, Isaac, and Jacob and all those who were like them, who sleep in the earth—those on whose account you have said you have created the world. And now, show your glory soon and do not postpone that which was promised by you. (21:20, 24)

Waiting is part of the bargain, however, for a bit later God affirms his long-suffering nature, which Baruch finds to be a problem: "And it will happen at that time that you shall see, and many with you, the long-suffering of the Most High, which lasts from generation to generation, who has been long-suffering toward all who are born, both those who sinned and those who proved themselves to be righteous" (24:2). Baruch does not have the deep pessimism concerning the possibility of salvation that appears in Esdras, however, and he presents the picture of the ideal future in very positive ways (see 44:11b-15). He even expands the promise to Abraham to include the full eschatological hope:

> For at that time . . . the belief in the coming judgment was brought about, and the hope of the world which will be renewed was built at that time, and the promise for the life that will come later was planted. (57:2)

Later the rabbis took different routes from these apocalyptic books in an effort to account for the apparently complete failure of the promise. The Talmud does express their hope for restoration in a thoroughly eschatological way; that is, they believed it would be entirely an act of God: "Whoever goes up from Babylon to the Land of Israel transgresses a positive commandment, for it is said in Scripture, They shall be carried to Babylon, and there they shall be, until the day that I remember them, saith the Lord" (citing Jer. 27:22; *b. Ketub.* 110b–111a). The saying reaffirms their belief in the promise in a rather extreme way.

In the Aramaic of the rabbinic literature a technical term meaning "promise" has finally appeared. Unlike the root meaning of the English and Greek words, which have the idea of saying something in advance, the root of *b^eṭaḥah* means "trust," so the word itself is a rabbinic contribution to the concern we have been tracing. A promise is something in which one trusts.

The Passover Haggadah contains the traditional mixture of praise to God for fulfilling his promises and hope for fulfillment in the future. The midrash on Deut. 27:5–8 begins:

> Blessed be He who keeps his promise [*b^eṭaḥah*] to Israel, blessed be he. For the Holy One, blessed be he, premeditated the end of the bondage, thus doing that which he said to Abraham in the Covenant between the Sections, as it is said:
>
> [then quoting Gen. 15:13–14]
>
> (The participants lift up their cups of wine and say:)
>
> And it is this promise which has stood by our fathers and by us. For it was not one man only who stood up against us to destroy us; in every generation they stand up against us to destroy us, and the Holy One, blessed be he, saves us from their hand.[20]

All that sounds very good, but the service began on a different tone: "This year we are here; next year may we be in the Land of Israel. This year we are slaves; next year may we be free men" (21). It is clear that both aspects of the promise are essential. Before the Hallel, the prayer praises God who "has brought us forth from slavery to freedom, from sorrow to joy" but the Grace after the meal includes a prayer for God to remember, "for rescue, goodness, grace, mercy, and compassion" (51, 63). And the service ends, "Next year in Jerusalem," still hoping for restoration to the Promised Land.

This partial survey of the way Judaism dealt with the promises of God after the fall of Jerusalem provides some of the evidence leading to the conclusion that although it became a religion of the Torah, which might have emphasized the present over the future, entirely replacing hope based on trust in God with assurances based on keeping the law, that did not happen. When the eschatology of Judaism, which will not be dealt with here,[21] is added to the kinds of materials just cited, it becomes clear that the stable, rabbinically governed system was always modified by the expectation that their hopes for a very different world would one day be fulfilled by the God who had promised it long ago.

The New Testament

For the first Christians the tension seemed to have been released. With the resurrection of Christ, the promises of God seemed to have been fulfilled, or to be in the last stages of their consummation. Even after Paul had struggled with the obvious, continuing imperfections of Christianity as it was practiced at Corinth, he could write:

> As surely as God is faithful, our word to you has not been "Yes and No." For the Son of God, Jesus Christ, whom we proclaimed among you, Silvanus and Timothy and I, was not "Yes and No"; but in him it is always "Yes." For in him every one of God's promises is a "Yes." For this reason it is through him that we say the "Amen," to the glory of God. (2 Cor. 1:18–20)

For Christian writers, the Promised Land and the glorification of Zion were of little interest, and they used them in distinctly nontraditional ways, but they found in the covenants with Abraham, with David, and with Israel at Sinai promises they believed had been fulfilled in their time with the coming of Jesus. Among the Gospel writers, it is Luke alone who puts a strong emphasis on promise, so we shall begin by following his references to the three covenants, noting what other authors have done with them along the way.[22]

When the angel Gabriel announced to Mary that she would bear a son, he declared that her son would be the fulfillment (or the reestablishment) of God's promise made to David in 2 Samuel 7:

> He will be great, and will be called the Son of the Most High [cf. 2 Sam. 7:14; Ps. 89:26–27], and the Lord God will give to him the throne of his ancestor David. He will reign over the house of Jacob forever, and of his kingdom there will be no end [cf. 2 Sam. 7:16; Ps. 89:29, 36–37]. (Luke 1:32–33)

Evidently Luke was not bothered by the fact that Jesus never became a king. After the resurrection, Christians must have begun to think rather soon of a heavenly enthronement of Christ, at the right hand of the Father, for Luke's version of Peter's Pentecost sermon also includes a reference to 2 Samuel 7: "Since he [David] was a prophet, he knew that God had sworn with an oath to him that he would put one of his descendants on his throne" (Acts 2:30), and shortly after, speaks of his being "exalted at the right hand of God" (2:33). When the promises to David are referred to, it seems that the resurrection of Jesus was seen as a kind of enthronement, validating this member of David's family as the one who would inherit an eternal kingdom. This may be the reasoning that lies behind Paul's introduction to his letter to the Romans:

> . . . set apart for the gospel of God, which he promised beforehand through his prophets in the holy scriptures, the gospel concerning his Son, who was descended from David according to the flesh and was declared to be Son of God with power according to the spirit of holiness by resurrection from the dead, Jesus Christ our Lord. (Rom. 1:1b–4)[23]

The author of the letter to the Hebrews also cites 2 Sam. 7:14, as well as Ps. 2:7, as having been fulfilled in Jesus, who alone can be called Son of God. The promise to David was thus completely spiritualized by the New Testament writers, in order to uphold their claim that Jesus was the Messiah, who was in Jewish expectation to be an earthly king, the son of David.[24] There was nothing in his life on earth they could cite, apart from his genealogy, that would lead one to think of Jesus as the fulfillment of this promise, so there must have been other Old Testament promises that took precedence over the Davidic material.

Mary's song concluded with an allusion to the promise to Abraham, associating it with the mercy of God, a development we found in the Intertestamental literature, but she has nothing more specific to say about it. The rest of her song is closely related to the song of Hannah (1 Sam. 2:1–10), as has often been noted, but oddly enough, she does not allude to Hannah's conclusion, which contains a reference to the coming annointed king, as one might expect after what Gabriel had told her. Instead, she says:

> He has helped his servant Israel,
>   in remembrance of his mercy,
> according to the promise he made [lit., "as he spoke"] to
>   our ancestors,
> to Abraham and to his descendants forever. (Luke 1:54–55)

Her words seem to point forward to Luke's next song, the prophecy of Zechariah. He also associates mercy with the covenant made with Abraham, and connects mercy with deliverance from the enemy, another theme we found in the Intertestamental literature:

> Thus he has shown the mercy promised [no word for "promise"
>   in the Greek] to our ancestors,
>   and has remembered his holy covenant,

the oath that he swore to our ancestor Abraham,
   to grant us that we, being rescued from the hands of
      our enemies,
might serve him without fear, in holiness and righteousness
   before him all our days. (Luke 1:72–73)

Earlier Zechariah had referred to the promised child as a mighty savior from the house of David, so his song was able to combine the two covenants because deliverance from the enemy had already been associated with Abraham. Later, the covenant with Abraham will be used as the primary evidence for the inclusion of the Gentiles in the church, and that is already anticipated in Luke's prologue, when Simeon partially quotes Isa. 42:6 or 49:6: "a light for revelation to the Gentiles" (Luke 2:32).

Paul made a brief reference to Christ as fulfillment of the promise to Abraham, that "by your offspring shall all the nations of the earth gain blessing for themselves" (Gen. 22:18), when he wrote, "For I tell you that Christ has become a servant of the circumcised on behalf of the truth of God in order that he might confirm the promises given to the patriarchs, and in order that the Gentiles might glorify God for his mercy" (Rom. 15:8–9). Note that mercy is mentioned again. The promise to Abraham is such a major element in Paul's argument for salvation by faith apart from works of the law, that we shall have to devote a separate paragraph to that, a bit later.

Jesus was connected with the Sinai covenant via Jeremiah's prophecy of a new covenant (Jer. 31:31–34), to which Jesus alluded at the Last Supper (Luke 22:20; also Matt. 26:28; Mark 14:24). That Jeremiah associated his new covenant with the one made at Sinai is clear from his reference to "the covenant that I made with their ancestors when I took them by the hand to bring them out of the land of Egypt" (Jer. 31:32). That Jesus' reference to new covenant was intended to recall Sinai is indicated in two ways. The Gospels call the Last Supper a Passover meal (Luke 22:8, 15), thus connecting God's redeeming act at the exodus with his redeeming act on the cross. And Jesus says it is the new covenant "in my blood" (Luke 22:20), which must be a reference backward to the sealing of the Sinai covenant with blood in Ex. 24:8 and forward to his death on the cross. Although we have seen some evidence in the Intertestamental literature for an association of forgiveness with the Abrahamic covenant, Jesus' claim that he was the fulfillment of Jeremiah's new covenant provides a better explanation of the church's claim that his death and resurrection made possible the forgiveness of sins. Jeremiah's promise concluded, "for I will forgive their iniquity, and remember their sin no more" (Jer. 31:34). This must be the basis for the unexplained conclusions drawn in two of the sermons in Acts. On Pentecost, Peter's sermon reached its climax with "Repent, and be baptized every one of you in the name of Jesus Christ so that your sins may be forgiven; and you will receive the gift of the Holy Spirit. For the promise is for you, for your children, and for all who are far away, everyone whom the Lord God calls to him" (Acts 2:38–39). And Paul's sermon in the synagogue at Antioch of Pisidia made the move from promise to resurrection to forgiveness:

> And we bring you the good news that what God promised to our ancestors he has fulfilled for us, their children, by raising Jesus. . . . Let it be known to you therefore, my brothers, that through this man forgiveness of sins is proclaimed to you; by this Jesus everyone who believes is set free from all those sins from which you could not be freed by the law of Moses. (Acts 13:32–33, 38–39)

Here Luke brings in Paul's contrast between the law of Moses and faith in Christ as the means of obtaining forgiveness.

Hebrews also quotes Jeremiah 31:33–34 as part of its argument that Jesus' sacrifice was a perfect atonement for sins (Heb. 10:14–18), and cites the new covenant passage in full as a part of its claim that the covenant established by Jesus is superior to those in the Old Testament (Heb. 8:8–13; cf. 7:22). A different reference to Sinai appears in 1 Peter 2:9–10, but like all the others cited so far, it claims that the Old Testament promises have now been fulfilled in Jesus. In God's introduction to the covenant-making process, in Ex. 19:4–6, he had promised that if the people would obey him and keep his covenant they would become "my treasured possession out of all the peoples . . . a priestly kingdom and a holy nation." In 1 Peter that has become present tense, for the church. "But you are a chosen race, a royal priesthood, a holy nation, God's own people."

Luke and other authors make it clear what evidence they have to justify their claims. The Messiah was not supposed to die and be raised from the dead, according to Jewish beliefs, so those events were not proof without some new interpretation of scripture. But something happened to the followers of Jesus at Pentecost and thereafter that made changed people of them, and they cite this as the evidence that first convinced them the resurrection had initiated a new age. It was the gift of the Holy Spirit. It is "the promise" for Luke. His Gospel concludes with Jesus' words: "And see, I am sending upon you what my Father promised; so stay here in the city until you have been clothed with power from on high" (24:49). Acts refers back to this saying: "While staying with them, he ordered them not to leave Jerusalem, but to wait there for the promise of the Father" (1:4). On the day of Pentecost, Peter interpreted the ability of Jesus' followers to speak so that all could understand as the gift of the Holy Spirit, which had come to them through the risen Christ: "Being therefore exalted at the right hand of God, and having received from the Father the promise of the Holy Spirit, he has poured out this that you both see and hear" (Acts 2:33), and Peter says repentance and baptism will bring the same gift to his hearers (2:38). This is not exclusively Luke's theology, for Paul connects the fulfillment of the covenant with Abraham in Jesus Christ with receiving "the promise of the Spirit through faith" (Gal. 3:14). He probably means that the Spirit is the content of the promise.[25] Ephesians also makes the gift of the Spirit the experiential evidence that God's promises have been fulfilled in Christ: "In him you also, when you had heard the word of truth, the gospel of your salvation, and had believed in him, were marked with the seal of the promised Holy Spirit; this is the pledge of our inheritance toward redemption as God's own people, to the praise of his glory" (Eph. 1:13–14). Note the echo of Old Testament covenantal language, in "God's own people."

Paul began with the gift of the Spirit when he used the promise to Abraham as his scriptural evidence of the primacy of faith over law, in Galatians 3 and 4.[26] He began where the Galatians were, conscious of having received that gift, and asked, "Did you receive the Spirit by doing the works of the law or by believing what you heard?" (Gal. 3:2). He assumed the answer was the latter, and thus compared the Galatians' experience with the classic case, that of Abraham: "Just as Abraham 'believed God, and it was reckoned to him as righteousness,' so, you see, those who believe are the descendants of Abraham" (3:6–7). Having then used Deut. 27:26 as evidence that law puts one under a curse (3:10–12), he made a key statement: "Christ redeemed us from the curse of the law . . . in order that in Christ Jesus the blessing of Abraham might come to the Gentiles, so that we might receive the promise of the Spirit by faith" (vv. 13–14). We can easily connect blessing, promise, and Gentiles with Abraham, and Paul used typical rabbinic exegesis in the next section to bring in Christ, insisting that since "offspring" is singular in Gen. 22:18 (which speaks also of blessing and nations/Gentiles), it refers to only one descendant, namely Jesus. That leaves the key element, Spirit, unaccounted for in the Abraham tradition. The way Paul introduced Abraham into his argument may provide the explanation for that. In 3:6–7 he quoted Gen. 15:6, which stands in the context of Abraham's question about whether he will ever have descendants (Gen. 15:2–3), then wrote, "so you see, those who believe are the descendants of Abraham" (Gal. 3:7). As Paul saw it, then, these spiritual descendants of Abraham in Galatia were the fulfillment of the promise made in Genesis.[27] He had to develop further the argument for the superiority of the promise (which requires faith) to law, because of the problem in Galatia (3:19–5:1). For our purposes, however, it will suffice to note his explicit repetition of his point that those who have faith in Christ are the ultimate fulfillment of the promise to Abraham: "And if you belong to Christ, then you are Abraham's offspring, heirs according to the promise" (3:29).

Of course Abraham is the key Old Testament figure for Paul in his debates over the law because of a single verse, Gen. 15:6, and that means his use of the Abraham material and his numerous references to promise along the way have a different emphasis from the allusions to the promise to Abraham we have encountered earlier. Paul speaks of promise in these passages the same way as the other New Testament authors cited thus far, as something brought to completion in Jesus. He took up essentially the same problem in Romans 4 as he had worked through in Galatians 3—4, but in a somewhat more ordered and theoretical way, in that the personal appeal to the readers' possession of the Spirit is not used. Once again he used promise in his own way, linking it with faith: "For this reason it depends on faith, in order that the promise may rest on grace and be guaranteed to all his descendants, not only to the adherents of the law but also to those who share the faith of Abraham" (Rom. 4:16; cf. vv. 22–24).

At the conclusion of Romans 4, Paul is still speaking of fulfilled promises, but justification and peace with God is not the end of the story after all, for in the verses that follow he moves to hope (Rom. 5:1–5). The New Testament contains both realized and futuristic eschatology, and that seems to be widely enough recognized at this time that the earlier debates over the subject need not be rehearsed.[28] So the tension had not been fully released by the resurrection of Christ and the gift of the Spirit, after all. Paul's discussion of whether his message of justification by faith alone logically meant Christians ought to "continue in sin in order that grace may abound" (Rom. 6:1) holds the insistence that the eschaton has come firmly together with hope for a different future. He first argues that sin is impossible for Christians. "How can we who died to sin go on living in it? . . . For whoever has died is freed from sin" (6:2, 7). But soon it becomes clear that that is a moral, not an ontological, impossibility, for soon he pleads, "Therefore, do not let sin exercise dominion in your mortal bodies, to make you obey their passions" (6:12). Christ's death and resurrection are declared to be their death to sin and resurrection to a new life (6:4), but he speaks of that latter resurrection also in the future tense: "we believe that we will also live with him" (6:8). So Paul and other early Christian authors acknowledged the realities of the Christian life: Something had happened to change them so radically that it seemed fully appropriate to say God's best and most final promises were coming true. They believed they were living in the last days. But not all their human imperfections had been overcome, and the world around them so far showed no evidence that Jesus had brought "peace on earth." To acknowledge both realities, Paul could write that the Lord Jesus Christ "gave himself for our sins to set us free from the present evil age, according to the will of our God and Father" (Gal. 1:4), and on another occasion, "But our citizenship is in heaven, and it is from there that we are expecting a Savior, the Lord Jesus Christ. He will transform the body of our humiliation that it may be conformed to the body of his glory, by the power that also enables him to make all things subject to himself" (Phil. 3:20f.). As Werner Georg Kümmel writes, "He always held fast both to the conviction that the eschatological fulfillment had already begun and to the hope that salvation would be fully completed."[29]

The letter to the Hebrews also claims that the Old Testament promises were not fulfilled until the coming of Christ (11:39–40) and seems to insist that truly eschatological forgiveness (which would mean one would never sin again; Jer. 50:20) had become a reality (10:18). At any rate the letter contains dire threats against anyone who "willfully persists in sin" after becoming a Christian (10:19–31). It uses "promise" in a thoroughly futuristic way, however, for in chapter 6 the theme is patience and hope (6:9–20) and in chapter 11 promise is associated with faith, and for Hebrews faith means looking forward to a promise not yet fulfilled (11:8–18). These are examples of the insistence that can be found throughout the New Testament: A new age truly began with the resurrection of Christ, but it is in process, and we have not yet seen all of the radical changes God has begun to bring about.

In some of the later works of the New Testament the word "promise" tends to be used mostly for what is still entirely future: eternal life (Titus 1:2; 1 John 2:25), the crown of life (James 1:12), the kingdom (James 2:5; cf. Heb. 12:26), and the second coming of Christ (2 Peter 3:4, 9, 13). By the time 2 Peter was written, the delay in the final fulfillment of these hopes had already become a problem for some Christians, so that the major theme of the letter is the issue we have been tracing throughout this chapter: the necessity for those who believe in a God who makes promises to wait for them to be fulfilled. The writer of the letter understands the nature of the problem, for he asks his readers, "What sort of persons ought you to be?" (2 Peter 3:11; cf. Heb. 10:35–39).

The New Testament witness thus left the Christian church with tensions unlike anything found in Judaism, for it insisted that somehow God's redemptive work had been completed in Jesus Christ, that the eschaton was present in him. This has led some to emphasize sanctification in this life, insisting that perfection is achievable, as in some of the "holiness" movements. On the other hand, the New Testament speaks of a continuing evil age, and looks forward to the second coming of Christ as the time when all will be made right. This has led to opposite extremes, sometimes to antinomianism, more often to rejection of this world and concentration either on heaven or on the expectation of the imminent return of Christ. The wisest of Christians, however, have found that these "logical" extremes are distortions, not only of what the New Testament authors wrote, but of the realities of Christian experience. In the next section we shall trace a few aspects of the theme of promise as it has appeared in the Christian tradition.

Promise in Christian History

"Promise" has been used in such a wide variety of ways in Christianity that it cannot really be traced as a theme the way some of the other subjects introduced by Exodus have been. If it is taken to refer to the fulfillment of prophecy, then the whole history of the relation between Old and New Testaments will be introduced.[30] If it is thought to be essentially equivalent to eschatology, then that major branch of theology, including all the varieties of apocalyptic thought, would have to be surveyed.[31] But for theologians as influential as Luther and Calvin, promise is practically synonymous with "the gospel,"[32] leaving us with a virtually unmanageable subject.

The "promise of God" means something to Christians who are sure they know the imminent date of Christ's return, to mystics who seek to become one with God even in this life, to sacramentalists for whom the sacrament is in itself "capable of conveying the grace of which it is the sign," to social activists seeking to change the laws of the land, to evangelists as they strive to save souls, and to liberation theologians. They may agree to a certain extent on what the promise of God is, but the contents and the role of promise in their lives will not be identical, and in some cases will serve to divide them sharply from one another. It is a bit ironic that the concept of promise can be traced in the Old Testament, which has no word for it, whereas in Christendom, which has an explicit, readily understandable term, a whole series of separate, and in some cases complex, histories is called for.

Two recent works have provided helpful introductions to aspects of two of those histories. James Preus's study of the relation of the young Luther's thought to medieval exegesis takes promise as its unifying theme, but its focus on hermeneutics already narrows what might be said about promise in the Middle Ages, since sacramentalism, teachings about life after death, and apocalypticism are properly ruled out.[33] Christopher Morse has examined the role of promise in Jürgen Moltmann's theology, setting it against the background of the debate over eschatology in twentieth-century theology, and evaluating the adequacy of Moltmann's use of it as a ruling concept in his *Theology of Hope*.[34] Two other twentieth-century developments have potential for similar studies. Pannenberg's theology is often compared with Moltmann's, because both have so much to say about the future, but the former's acceptance of a certain understanding of apocalyptic as the basis for his work seems to make promise much less significant than it is for Moltmann.[35] Liberation theology looks for real change in history, comparable to the deliverance of the Hebrews from Egyptian slavery, to be brought about by the action of the faithful in accord with God's will for justice.[36] Its use of the promises in scripture might be studied with profit, but unfortunately liberation theologians up until now seem to have made a rather superficial use of Exodus, one of their favorite texts.[37]

The biblical concept of God as one who makes long-term promises concerning his intentions for the eventual salvation of the world has had the positive effect of assuring believers that God has the power to do what he promised and that he is faithful to his intention, in spite of human opposition or failings.[38] In its biblical form, it also insists that believers take history with the utmost seriousness, as the realm of God's saving work. But it also calls for patience, on the human side, and leads inevitably to efforts to understand why fulfillment is often so long delayed. Sometimes that results in a redefinition of promise so as to assure the faithful that they are really being fulfilled in the present, and accounting for absence of blessing by ascribing them to human failures, either ritual or moral. In the twentieth century that was done in a new way, by defining eschatology in existential terms and denying its temporal sense, but that has already been shown to be inadequate.[39] On the other hand, the Christian faith has always remained to some extent in the tension between the present and the promised future, acknowledging that God, for reasons mostly known only to God, has not yet fully carried out his intentions, so that a major program must be the upholding of patience and hope over against the temptations of discouragement or cynicism.

EPILOGUE TO EXODUS 3–4:
THE KINDNESS AND SEVERITY OF GOD

Throughout the book of Exodus there lies just under the surface the question, "Who is God and what is he doing?" The chapters we have been studying at some length began with the affirmation that humans sometimes encounter in this world something that is "wholly other," which they call "God." "Wholly other" means that this is no philosophical construct, no psychological projection, but a true encounter with something completely outside of oneself, which first dismays, then delights. This "wholly other" impresses us as being infinitely powerful, but we respond not to a force, but to a being who speaks to humans and who may be addressed, for he has a name, and it is Yahweh.

According to Genesis, Yahweh established a personal relationship with a couple in the distant past, Abraham and Sarah, the ancestors of the people who are now in slavery in Egypt. That relationship seemed to have been in abeyance for a time, but Exodus 3—4 emphasizes that God takes it with the utmost seriousness. God had felt the suffering of his people. God had made a promise to their ancestors, and he is a God who keeps his promises; he will not let them suffer any longer. With Exodus 3 begins the story of Israel's salvation, liberation from slavery, the classic, mighty redeeming act of God. At the mountain Moses met God the Savior.

But Moses was warned not to get too close. It was dangerous to be near God. Moses discovered that if God had commissioned him to do something, he really had no choice in the matter. (But God did promise "I will be with you.") He found that although God gave him a name by which God could be addressed, it was also clear that the name provided no inside information as to who he was. And if God's willingness to discuss matters with Moses, and to reassure him, giving him power to perform signs, had any initial effect of diminishing the terror that inevitably accompanies the presence of this Savior of theirs, the Savior settled that matter by attacking him on his way back to Egypt.

And God revealed from the first that to relieve his people's suffering he would have to inflict suffering on the Egyptians. He did not speak of judgment, or of sin and punishment; early in Exodus he will speak only of getting glory for himself (14:4, 17; cf. 9:15). Neither is there any reference to a need for obedience or the acceptance of a unique way of life on the part of those he was about to save. That would come later. Is this liberation theology's "preferential option for the poor"? It is certainly a preferential option for Israel, at this point, as 3:9, 16–17, 21–22 and 4:22 indicate, with Egypt as the obverse in 3:20–22 and 4:23. But we shall see that that is too simplistic a view, when we consider more broadly what scripture has to say about the nature of God.

I have called this epilogue "the kindness and severity of God," and that phrase is not taken from the Old Testament, which is popularly thought to emphasize God's wrath, but from the New Testament, famous for its message about the God of love. One of Paul's reactions to his discovery that "God has imprisoned all in disobedience so that he may be merciful to all" (Rom. 11:32) is "Note then the kindness and severity of God" (Rom. 11:22). It would be an apt title, not only for the book of Exodus, but for the Bible. My choice of the New Testament text here is another way of insisting that we find the same God in both Testaments. In Exodus 3—4, as throughout the Bible, we have encountered a God who offers himself graciously to humans, but also withholds himself, partly in his otherness, partly in what humans inadequately call "wrath." He is a God whose will may not be resisted, but who condescends to human weakness. He feels Israel's suffering, and yet he proposes to kill the pharaoh's firstborn son (Ex. 4:23).

I believe that Otto's emphasis that the numinous is both *tremendum* and *fascinans* offers a sound beginning point from which to work on the Exodus texts concerning the kindness and severity of God, and therefrom, to trace the believing community's continuing encounters with that *mysterium*. What comes next is predominantly the *tremendum*. For the kind of activity attributed to God in almost all of chapters 5—15 is destructive.

CHAPTER 6

THE DIVINE DESTROYER

Exodus 5:1–15:21

In wrath may you remember mercy.
—Habakkuk 3:2

Our God is a consuming fire.
—Hebrews 12:29

God has identified himself to Moses and has announced his intention and motives. He intends to set free a specific group of Egyptian slaves and to lead them to the land of the Canaanites (Ex. 3:8, 17; 6:6, 8). His motives for intervening in Egyptian affairs are twofold: (1) He knows their sufferings; he has heard their cries because of the way the Egyptians have oppressed them (3:7, 9, 16; 6:5). But there are other suffering people on earth who will not be part of this story, so there must be a second motive. (2) He had made a commitment to their ancestors, and it will remain unfulfilled no longer (6:2, 8; only implicit in 3:6, 16).

God had alluded to the methods he will use in 3:19–20 and 4:21–23, and in chapters 5—15 we see them worked out in full. In 3:19–20 he warned Moses:

I know, however, that the king of Egypt will not let you go unless compelled by a mighty hand. So I will stretch out my hand and strike Egypt with all my wonders that I will perform in it; after that he will let you go.

The matter is taken up again in 4:21–23, where it becomes more puzzling, because of the reference to the hardening of Pharaoh's heart:

When you go back to Egypt, see that you perform before Pharaoh all the wonders that I have put in your power; but I will harden his heart, so that he will not let the people go. Then you shall say to Pharaoh. "Thus says the LORD: Israel is my firstborn son. I said to you, 'Let my son go that he may worship me.' But you refused to let him go; now I will kill your firstborn son."

God knows that he will have to take destructive action against Pharaoh. The Egyptian king must be forced to give up these people, who are valuable possessions, part of his work force. There is no thought here of appealing to principles of freedom or equality or fairness, ideas that do appear with reference to slavery in Israelite law (Deut. 15:12–18). The Israelites, after all, had not been purchased by Pharaoh, nor were they captives of war; they were immigrants who had lived in his country for a long time who had lately been impressed into forced labor. But the king of Egypt is an absolute monarch, and it does not surprise us that no time is wasted with appeals of that sort. Neither does the idea that Pharaoh might be compensated for his loss ever appear; presumably he had forfeited that right because of his cruelty. Indeed, the Egyptians shall pay extra because of that (Ex. 3:21f.; 12:35f.).

God tells Moses in advance that he intends to make sure Pharaoh (and the Egyptians) will suffer because Pharoah has made the Hebrews suffer, will make sure of it by hardening Pharaoh's heart so that finally he must lose his firstborn son. God does not look for an easy way to free his people from slavery. This is no "just war," in which victory is sought with the fewest possible casualties. On the contrary: God intends to "make an example" of Pharaoh and Egypt, by multiplying their sufferings at length. That calls for some explanation, and God will offer it, during the course of the plagues, as we shall see (Ex. 9:14–16; 10:1f.; 14:4). We shall look with care at these passages later, and shall in fact take them more seriously than the commentators in general have done. They have all struggled with the problem of God's hardening of Pharaoh's heart, but few have thought to discuss at all God's choice of death and destruction as his means of getting glory over Pharaoh (14:4). They just accept it, as the author of Exodus accepts it, but in our day we cannot avoid asking how this fits with the whole of scripture's picture of God.

Certainly, theological questions raised by Israel's affirmation that "Yahweh is a warrior" (Ex. 15:3) have been taken seriously in recent scholarship.[1] Scripture's insistence that God has intervened in history in violent ways has regularly been discussed in studies of the term "the wrath of God."[2] And God's association with wholesale death and destruction sometimes becomes a part of the debates over theodicy, although for many authors if that can be called a just punishment for sin there seems to be no problem with it. These remarks will already have alerted the reader to the fact that the whole problem of evil in biblical theology that lies behind the accounts of the plagues and the Wonder at the Sea, lies there virtually untouched by previous studies of the book of Exodus. If that is not yet completely evident, let us ask this question: If God could harden Pharaoh's heart, why did he not instead soften his heart, and thus avoid all that suffering and death? Christians believe that by the working of the Holy Spirit, God can and does bring about radical changes in human personalities; would it not have been far better to treat Pharaoh as he treated another persecuter of his people, the apostle Paul (Acts 9:1–22)?

The fact is, of course, that Israel remembered its earliest history as involving widespread destruction and death, not the conversion of the Egyptians, and Israel believed God was involved in—no, responsible for—it. Have we thus asked an unfair question, a strictly "New Testament question," in the preceding paragraph? Is it really true that the violent God of the Old Testament has been replaced somehow by a loving, gracious God in the New Testament revelation, as some have claimed, from Marcion to the present? I shall claim that this question about God's chosen ways of working in the world is not one peculiar to the New Testament, but is already raised by the Old Testament. For example, alongside the Old Testament's assumption that it was perfectly just for God to wipe out the entire population of the earth, in the Flood, stands God's insistence that this will not be his way of dealing with sin in the future (cf. Gen. 6:5–7, 11–13, with 8:21f. and 9:8–17). We have no clue as to what God's alternate way may be until near the end of Exodus. Forgiveness will be introduced in Exodus 32—34, as a way of dealing with sin that really has nothing to do with justice, since human ideas of justice usually expect suffering to be the appropriate recompense for sin.

There is thus a tension running through the Old Testament, from God's nonexecution of the death penalty in Genesis 3 and 4, alongside his destruction of almost all that lives in Genesis 6—8, to Ezekiel's promise that God will one day give humans a new heart and a new spirit, alongside his terrible messages of doom for his perennially rebellious people. Amid the Old Testament's frequent depictions of God as the Divine Destroyer, there runs a continuing line of thought that this is not what God really wants. Although the violence of nature is usually accepted without question (cf. Job 38—41) and is sometimes seen to be used by God as a manifestation of his justice (Exodus 14—15; Psalm 18; Habakkuk 3; etc.), a world without violence is also dreamed of (especially Isa. 11:6–9), as if the present ecology is not what God really intended at all (Gen. 3:14–19). God's saving acts are often depicted as involving terrifying violence, as in Isaiah 34 or 63:1–6, but there is also a mysterious servant of the Lord, who suffers violence rather than inflicting it, so as to make others whole (Isa. 52:13–53:12). Which is truly God's way? Must one be rejected in favor of the other, or can we possibly understand both to be aspects of the divine will and character?

Others have dealt with the plagues and Wonder at the Sea in terms of whether they happened at all, and if so what really happened; when they should be dated; and whether the narrative is a unity or must be analyzed into prior sources. If nothing happened at all, that raises a serious theological question about the basis for the Israelite faith, so that must be discussed in due time, but the other issues have little theological significance. Israel's belief that God's true nature was revealed by the fact that he saved them from oppression in Egypt and gave them a good land in which to live became the most prevalent theme in their theology (cf. Deut. 26:5–9; Josh. 24:2–13; Psalm 105; Micah 6:4–5). We must give that due attention in this chapter, for it is central to Israel's testimony to who God is, but this subject has been so widely discussed that it does not need to be repeated at length here. Israel's testimony to what God did for them is well-known; their testimony as to *how* he did it raises many questions that previous studies have only touched on.

Exodus 5:1–15:21 forms a coherent unit of material for our purposes, because it is dominated by a single theme concerning God. In the account of the plagues and the Wonder at the Sea, God is engaged in one kind of action throughout, and that is to bring destruction and death to the Egyptians via a lengthy series of natural disasters. This introduces us to another prominent theme in scripture as a whole: God as a destroyer, and God's use of the forces of nature for that purpose. There are many themes in the Bible related to this, and in order to keep the subject from getting out of hand, we shall restrict this chapter to the kinds of destruction depicted in Exodus. This will allow us to keep other, related subjects on the periphery, alluding to them where necessary:

1. These acts can be taken as examples of the wrath of God, but that subject will not be studied as a whole, although what will be said here contributes to it.[3]
2. "Vengeance" as used in the Old Testament has been shown by G. E. Mendenhall to be "exercise of force in contexts the normal legal institutions of society cannot handle,"[4] hence the Old Testament word *naqam* does not really mean "revenge." It is not used of God's action in Exodus, so no further study of the word is called for here.
3. Elements of the "holy war" or "Yahweh war" ideology have been found here, but they do not contribute enough to require attention in this chapter. The subject of war in general would draw us away from the distinctive problem raised by Exodus, since Israel does not fight the Egyptians; Yahweh alone is the warrior.[5]
4. Egypt is the archetypal "enemy nation" until Babylon comes along, and that might tempt us to move from Yahweh's treatment of Egypt in Exodus to his judgment of the nations in the prophets. That would be a book in itself, and we shall restrict ourselves to the appearance of destructive natural forces in the oracles against the nations.
5. Human violence in general, thought to be condoned or commanded by God, must also remain peripheral, since, as we shall see, violent action on the part of the Hebrews plays a very small role in Exodus.[6]
6. Aspects of creation-theology must be dealt with as carefully as possible, since theologians have seldom said much about violence in nature,[7] and that is the only kind of nature to be encountered here. But we would distort the present subject if we were enticed into discussing broader aspects of creation-theology.
7. The theological and philosophical problem of evil lurks just behind all of this. We shall avoid strictly philosophical questions that are in no way alluded to in scripture (such as whether God is "Absolute Being"), and shall attempt to let the Bible's approach to what we call "evil" help us focus on a relatively manageable part of the unsolvable problem. Scripture is more modest than the philosophers or systematic theologians. It makes no claim to know what is going on in the Godhead, "God in Himself," or even to know why the world is made this way. But the writers of scripture did claim they knew there is a God in charge of nature and history, and claimed they understood what God was doing in certain situations. As a preliminary statement of the limited approach to be taken in this chapter, then, let us say that instead of taking up "the problem of evil," the Bible deals with "the meaning of certain harmful events."

THE DIVINE DESTROYER IN EXODUS

The contents of Ex. 5:1–15:21 set it apart from the rest of Exodus, in that the section deals throughout with the contest between Yahweh and the pharaoh. The prevalence of violence in this section, compared with the rest of Exodus, is revealed by a quick survey of the kinds of violence reported elsewhere in the book, and by noting the verbs used here with Yahweh as subject. Human violence is reported in chapters 1, 2, and 5 (the pharaoh's mistreatment of the Hebrew slaves), in 2:12 (when Moses killed the Egyptian), in 17:8–13 (when the Amalekites attacked the Israelites), and in 32:25–29 (when the Levites killed three thousand of those who had worshiped the golden calf). Divine violence is intended but thwarted twice, by Zipporah in 4:24–26, and by Moses in 32:7–14. From the first of the plagues (7:14ff.) through the Wonder at the Sea (chapters 14—15), all the destructive activity that is reported has God as the subject.

An impressive assortment of verbs is used to describe this activity. Moses first attempted to convince Pharaoh that Yahweh might fall upon (*pg'*) the Hebrews with pestilence or sword, if they did not go into the wilderness to sacrifice (5:3). That, of course, did not happen. Two verbs meaning "strike" are used in connection with the first two plagues. The Lord struck (*nkh*) the Nile, turning it to blood (7:25), then struck (*ngp*) the whole country with frogs (8:2). The former verb is also used of killing the firstborn in 12:12, 29, and the latter is used in the same context of striking the Egyptians in general (12:23, 27). For the fourth plague God sent (*shlḥ*) swarms of flies (8:21). "Send" is also used of all the plagues in 9:14. The author does not ascribe the gnats, in the third plague, to direct divine action, but the magicians of Egypt do, saying, "This is the finger of God!" (8:19). The "hand of the LORD" caused a pestilence that killed all the livestock of the Egyptians (9:3). In one of the severest of the plagues, God caused hail to fall (*himṭir*, 9:18, 23), which struck down (*nkh*) everything in the open field, human, animal, and plant. The innocent-sounding verb "bring" (*hebi'*) is used of the locust plague, but they devoured (*'kl*) the last remnant left after the hail (10:4f.). In Moses' instructions for the observance of the Passover he tells the Hebrews to remember that the Lord killed (*hrg*) all the firstborn in the land of Egypt (13:15). He sent his "destroyer" (or destruction, *mashḥith*) among them (12:13, 23). At the Sea, the Lord fought against the Egyptian army (*lḥm*, 14:14, 25), confused them (*hmm*, 14:24), and shook them off into the returning sea (*n'r*, 14:27). Then, the Song of the Sea abounds with violent language. God threw (*rmh*) horse and rider into the sea (15:1); he cast (*yrh*) Pharaoh's chariots and army into the sea (15:4). He shattered (*r'ts*) the enemy (15:6), he overthrew them (*hrs*), and his fury consumed them (*'kl*, 15:7). When he blew (*nshp*) with his wind, the sea covered them (15:10).

These chapters are thus filled with destruction and death, all of it the work of Yahweh. But from this point on we shall not speak of Yahweh's action as "violence," in order to stay in accordance with the traditions of English translators. The English word "violence" (or "violent") is never used of God in the RSV, and that corresponds to the fact that the Hebrew word *hamas*, which is usually translated "violence," is never used of God. The Hebrew term always refers to human action that is condemned by God, so even though God has been said to be involved with violent action in the first part of this chapter, from now on, that word will be reserved for human behavior. It is a different matter when we look for "destroy," "destroyer," and "destruction" in the RSV concordance, however. Those three English words are used to represent forty-three different Hebrew words, and at least thirty-six of them are associated with God's activities, hence the title of this chapter, "The Divine Destroyer."

It is not too strong a term to use for God as he appears in these chapters. They describe an appalling environmental disaster. Not only do Pharaoh and his officials, the responsible parties, suffer, but also the peasants who had nothing to say about the system in which they lived. The country as a whole is left desolate. In the first plague, the Nile grew foul and the fish died (7:21). In the second, all those frogs died, and the land stank (8:13f.). In the fourth, the land was ruined (*shahat*) because of the flies (8:24). In the fifth, the livestock died (9:6). In the seventh, people, animals, and vegetation were struck down, shattered (9:25). In the eighth, the locusts stripped any vegetation that was left and the pharaoh calls them "this death" (10:17). Then, in the tenth plague, the firstborn of every family died (12:29). After all this, the report of the drowning of the army seems rather anticlimactic, although the Old Testament never tells it that way. Wasn't this overkill, when the aim of it all was presumably just to make it possible for a group of immigrants to leave the country?

God does explain why he did it that way, and when we consider those explanations against the background of tradition that lies behind this section and against the theological background of the concept of a divine destroyer, we may be able to understand better how the plagues and God's action at the Sea fit into biblical theology as a whole. In looking at God's explanations, notice what is not stressed, since that may show that many familiar expositions of the exodus have emphasized what the author of the book of Exodus did not.

God immediately warned Moses that he would not be able to bring the Hebrews out of Egypt by persuasion or by any nonviolent means. It would take force, and God would provide it (3:19f.). But that first warning did not suggest the length or magnitude of the process. The next advance message does so, explaining it as a result of God's hardening Pharaoh's heart and leading to the necessity of killing Pharaoh's firstborn son (4:21f.). This answers none of our questions; it only deepens them. Why would God choose either of these? The familiar interpretation appeals to the next significant text as the answer: "I am the LORD, and I will bring you out from under the burdens of the Egyptians, and I will deliver you from their bondage, and I will redeem you with an outstretched arm and with great acts of judgment" (6:6). Here the sins of the Egyptians are cited, noting "burdens" and "bondage," and God is the Redeemer carrying out great judgments against them. Terence Fretheim, for example, claims that the key word for understanding the plagues is *shephet,* "judgment," which occurs in 6:6; 7:4; and 12:12. That God stands in judgment of the way the Egyptians treated the Hebrews is not to be questioned, but it is interesting to note that the author never emphasizes that the plagues are punishments for the pharaoh's sins. Even these three occurrences of *shephet* may be speaking more of God's power and righteousness than of the Egyptians' sins. Words for sin are strangely missing from Exodus 1—15. Only one root occurs, and it is used by Pharaoh himself. The plague of hail convinced him, temporarily: "This time I have sinned; the LORD is in the right, and I and my people are in the wrong" (9:27). The author then echoes his words, "But when Pharaoh saw that the rain and the hail and the thunder had ceased, he sinned once more and hardened his heart, he and his officials" (9:34). The locust plague led him to admit he had sinned against Yahweh, Moses, and Aaron, and this time he asked forgiveness (10:16f.), but in none of God's speeches or Moses' speeches is it ever said explicitly (apart from *shephet*) that the plagues are punishment.

God's explicit explanation comes in 9:14–16:

> For this time I will send all my plagues upon your heart, and upon your servants and your people, that you may know that there is none like me in all the earth. For by now I could have put forth my hand and struck you and your people with pestilence, and you would have been cut off from the earth; but for this purpose have I let you live, to show you my power, so that my name may be declared throughout all the earth.

After six plagues the author feels that a comment on this lengthy process is needed, and three positive things are offered: "that you may know that there is none like me in all the earth," "to show you my power," and "so that my name may be declared throughout all the earth." This is a contest. God needs to make a point ("to show you my power"; "there is none like me in all the earth"), and he needs to prove it not just to Pharaoh, or even to Israel, but to all the earth.

These points are reinforced in two other passages. Between the plagues of hail and locusts, God says to Moses, "Go in to Pharaoh; for I have hardened his heart and the heart of his servants, that I may show these signs of mine among them, and that you may tell in the hearing of your son and of your son's son how I have made sport of the Egyptians and what signs I have done among them; that you may know that I am the LORD" (10:1f.). Here a reason for the hardening of Pharaoh's heart is offered; it is to provide the opportunity for God to reveal himself by *signs.* The plagues are referred to as "wonders" (*mopheth*), mighty and awe-inspiring acts ("miracles" to us), and as "signs" (*'oth*), events that are intended to convey information of some kind about God.[8] Associated with that is the word "know," which appeared with Pharaoh as its subject in 9:14 and with Israel as its subject in 10:2. Yes, all of this seems to have been initiated because of Israel's sufferings in Egypt, but once we read beyond chapter 6, they fall into the background, and something else is going on. That is confirmed by the destruction of the Egyptian army in the Sea. Israel was safe on the other side, but the army had to die:

> And I will harden Pharaoh's heart, and he will pursue them and I will get glory over Pharaoh and all his host; and the Egyptians shall know that I am the LORD. (14:4)
> And I will harden the hearts of the Egyptians so that they shall go in after them, and I will get glory over Pharaoh and all his host, his chariots, and his horsemen. (14:17)

Missing from chapters 5—15, then, are words for oppression and suffering. Judgment occurs three times, as we have noted; redemption (*g'l*) twice (6:6; 15:13); and deliverance (*ntsl*) twice (6:6; 12:27). But "know," with either the Egyptians or the Israelites as its subject, runs through the whole account, like the thread that holds it all together (6:7; 7:5, 17; 8:10, 22; 9:14, 29; 10:2; 11:7; 14:4, 18). And that takes us back to its first occurrence in this section, which may thus be the theme verse. When Moses and Aaron first encounter the pharaoh with their request that the Hebrews be permitted to go into the wilderness to sacrifice, the king's scornful answer is, "Who is Yahweh, that I should heed his voice and let Israel go? *I do not know Yahweh,* and moreover I will not let Israel go" (5:2). The rest of the story, through 14:18, tells how God remedied that deficiency.

Knowledge is the expressed aim of the plagues. This conclusion is reinforced by the designation of them as "signs" four times (7:3; 8:19; 10:1, 2), and some content of the intended knowledge is provided by the reference to God's getting glory over Pharaoh in 14:4, 17. There seem to be two underlying traditions that add additional content, once we recognize them. The author has not been dependent on either of them, reworking both of them extensively, but once we recognize the relationships between the plague story and these two aspects of ancient Near Eastern tradition, the point of all this destruction begins to become much clearer.[9]

First, we can recognize allusions to the mythological battles for supremacy among the gods, known especially from the Babylonian Creation Story (*Enuma Elish*) and the Ugaritic texts. This whole section of Exodus is a personal contest between Yahweh and the pharaoh, and the issue is one of sovereignty, as Pharaoh indicates by his scornful question, "Who is Yahweh, that I should heed his voice and let Israel go?" The reason for the extended battle between them, even though Pharaoh loses every engagement, is that Yahweh will be satisfied with nothing less than being acknowledged as the sole power. This is why he needs to "get glory" over Pharaoh by destroying his army. Yahweh's people were already free, but the contest among the "gods" was not yet over. We know, and very likely it was common knowledge in Israel also, that Pharaoh was considered to be a god by the Egyptians. The author of Exodus will not so dignify him, however, and this is the first and most important way he has modified the old tradition. Pharaoh is just a king, whom Yahweh could have annihilated with one stroke (9:15), but the Egyptian belief that he was divine is denied here not with sarcasm, as in Ezek. 29:1–9 and 32:1–16, but with an extended story, some of which echoes the way battles for supremacy among the gods were told elsewhere.

Like the myths of cosmic battles, nature was used in terrifying ways in Exodus 5—15. In *Enuma Elish,* Marduk uses lightning, winds, and flood as his weapons against Tiamat.[10] In order to show how serious the issue is, more than one contest is also required before victory is won. None of the myths extends the suspense as much as the ten plagues do, but in *Enuma Elish,* first Anu is sent to deal with Tiamat and he cannot face her (III.80–85, 111), so Marduk is appealed to. Marduk has to provide some evidence of his power before the assembly of the gods before they will commission him, however, and he does that in a way that reminds us of Moses' staff changing to a serpent. Both perform a "trick" before the court. Marduk is able to make a cloth vanish, then reappear (IV.19–26). The continuity of the Ugaritic texts is very difficult to establish, but at least one example of the extending of a contest is clear. Baal attacks his rival Yamm with his club, Yagrush ("Chaser"), but "Yamm is firm, he is not bowed; His joints bend not, nor breaks his frame." A second club, Ayamur ("Driver"), enables Baal to vanquish his enemy (131). Terrifying natural phenomena are not described as they are in Exodus and *Enuma Elish,* but the name "Yamm" is the word for "sea," and Baal, as Rider on the Clouds, is known to be the storm god. Both Marduk and Baal are claiming kingship of the gods, against powerful rivals, and once we see that the claim of sovereignty runs throughout the plague story, then these old traditions may be recognized as lying behind Exodus, though at a considerable distance.[11] Pharaoh is a purely historical figure, with no weapons except political power, but the true God's sovereignty has not yet been acknowledged, and like the gods of myth, he takes nature's most awesome forces into battle with him.

Since the story takes place on earth, mostly in the vicinity of the court of the king of Egypt, the author can make use of another form, with extensive modifications of it. This is the story of a contest between a king's royal advisers—the court wise men—and an upstart rival. We have forms of this in Genesis 41, where Joseph is the new, successful wise man, and in Daniel 2, 4, and 5. The most extended version of it is the story of Ahikar, which is known to us in at least eight versions, ranging from perhaps seventh century B.C.E. Aramaic to the Arabic of the *Arabian Nights.*[12] There are other examples, but we need no more than these for our purposes, since the pattern is so regular.[13] The story always involves a king and an apparently impossible dilemma of some sort. In Genesis and Daniel it is the interpretation of dreams, and of the handwriting on the wall; in Ahikar it is the king of Egypt's request for a castle in the air! The king's own wise men are always baffled by the dilemma, but the hero of the story resolves it by using his superior gifts. These are always contests of wits, with no significant action expected in their resolution. So Ahikar puts two boys into a big basket hitched to some eagles, lets them be carried into the air, and has them call down to the expectant king of

Egypt, "More bricks, more bricks!" According to the rules of the game, if you are left openmouthed for fifteen seconds, you have lost, and the Egyptian king does have to acknowledge that Ahikar is indeed the wisest man on earth. But in the more extended versions of the story, he also had to pass a series of tests posed by the royal wise men, which provides a certain parallel to the series of plagues, some of which the pharaoh's magicians could reproduce.

There are many points of contact that show the court wise man story is one of the traditions underlying the account of the plagues, especially at the beginning and through 8:18f., where the magicians admit they are defeated. The dilemma is Moses' rather than the king's, and it does not involve a trick question such as building a castle in the air, but there is a certain pretext, a similar agreement to take something at face value, even though both sides know that isn't the case, which reminds us of the trick questions. Moses asks leave to take his people into the wilderness for three days to worship. We know they don't intend to come back, and so does the pharaoh, but he plays by the rules until he begins to lose his grip, after the plague of hail, and accuses Moses of having some evil purpose in mind (10:10). The early encounters between Moses and the magicians are close parallels to the way court wise man stories are told, with the newcomer succeeding where the incumbents fail. But the most significant difference is that this is no contest of wits; it is a contest of real power, and that is where the old mythological material is needed. And the story ends differently, for this king is never convinced. His momentary confessions of sin in 9:27 and 10:16–17 fit the pattern, but they don't last. Note that both of these old traditions are contests to determine supremacy: who is wisest, in the latter; who has power to rule, in the former. So it is not surprising that as the author of Exodus formulated Israel's traditions that Yahweh had demonstrated his supremacy over the pharaoh, he would have been influenced by these two familiar genres. With the evidence of the key texts in mind and the support of this study of tradition, we may now begin to develop some conclusions about the theology of Exodus 5—15.

First, note two features that are *not* emphasized in these chapters. Human action plays a minor role, compared to the activity of Yahweh. Pharaoh adds to the suspense at the beginning, forcing the Hebrews to make bricks without straw (5:6–21), so that Yahweh's plan at first seems to have made things worse rather than better (5:22–23). His other major move is to send the army after the people (chapter 14), but both of these violent acts are doomed to failure. Moses, Aaron, and the magicians are the other actors, but they are merely the functionaries of the two main characters. The "despoiling of the Egyptians" (12:35–36) is an embellishment of Yahweh's victory over Egypt. So Yahweh dominates the flow of the story, with human free will having the capacity only to delay and distort what must happen.

Justice and human freedom are not the central issues.[14] We have noted the relatively rare occurrence of key words pointing to these subjects. Only the pharaoh speaks of sin, and his words cannot be taken very seriously. Moses does not confront him, as the later prophets confronted the kings of Israel and Judah, with the message that the king stands under divine judgment for injustice and oppression (cf. 2 Sam. 12:1–15; Jer. 22:18–30; Amos 7:10–12). Moses' message is not condemnation for the pharaoh's mistreatment of his slaves, but a demand sent by an authority who claims to be superior to the king: "Thus says Yahweh, the God of Israel, 'Let my people go.' "

The major theme of the section is thus the question of sovereignty, as we have seen first from the reasons Yahweh gives for the succession of plagues (9:14–16; 10:1f.; 14:4, 17), supported by the vocabulary that recurs most frequently. The section begins with the demand "Let my people go" (5:1) and that sentence introduces six of the ten plagues (7:16; 8:1, 20; 9:1, 13; 10:3). The problem as it is presented here is not human suffering in general, but that Pharaoh has been mistreating *Yahweh's* property, and now refuses to let them leave the country in order to *serve* Yahweh (7:16, 26; 8:16; 9:1, 13; 10:3).[15] "Whose people are these?" is the question, and the real meaning of that question, as Israel understood it, and so told this story, is "Who is our God?" The way the true answer will be demonstrated is laid out in three verses that contain most of the key terms:

> But I will *harden Pharaoh's heart,* and I will multiply my *signs and wonders* in the land of Egypt. When Pharaoh does not listen to you, I will lay my hand upon Egypt and bring *my people* the Israelites, company by company, out of the land of Egypt by great acts of judgment. The Egyptians shall *know that I am the Lord,* when I stretch out my hand against Egypt and bring the Israelites out from among them. (7:3–5)

These signs are intended to be revelation to the Egyptians. Five times the basic formula "know that I am Yahweh" appears (7:5, 17; 8:22; 14:4, 18). Elsewhere, they are to know that there is no one like Yahweh (8:10; 9:14), to know that the earth is Yahweh's (9:29), and to know that Yahweh makes a distinction between the Egyptians and Israel (11:7). This knowledge is more than just intellectual apprehension of some fact, as Zimmerli has shown in his detailed study of the formula.[16] He concluded that the results of coming to "know that I am Yahweh" were "adoration that kneels because of divinely inspired recognition, an orientation toward the one who himself says, 'I am Yahweh.' " (88). God thus intends to accomplish something with Pharaoh and the Egyptians, and not just something for the Israelites. (They also are to come to know that he is Yahweh; 6:7; 10:2). Our term "conversion" is probably too strong a word to use here, as the text never speaks of Egyptians becoming worshipers of Yahweh, but the choice of words does show Israel believed this great show of power was intended to force Egypt to acknowledge that Yahweh, and Yahweh alone, is God. In striking contrast to Pharaoh's derisive reaction, at the beginning, "Who is Yahweh, that I should heed him and let Israel go? I do not know Yahweh, and I will not let Israel go" (5:2) stands God's question, near the end of the contest, "How long will you refuse to humble yourself before me?" (10:3). In answer to one of our early questions, as to why God did not change Pharaoh to make him a person who would let the slaves go willingly, we find that the Old Testament speaks of God overriding human freedom only when he calls someone to do his special work, such as Moses or Jeremiah.

These observations may provide for us a helpful way to approach the perennial problem of the hardening of Pharaoh's heart. We shall not try to soften the problem, by claiming that when God is said to harden the king's heart he is merely confirming what Pharaoh had freely chosen, or by saying it is a way of speaking of the truth that there comes a point when freely chosen acts of sin become a pattern of behavior from which we cannot escape.[17] Comparing the different ways the sources (J, E, and P) speak of the hardening of heart has not solved the problem, so we shall not repeat any of that information here.[18] The most important observation to be drawn from the source-critical analysis of the section (about which there are many uncertainties) is that the sovereignty of Yahweh is emphasized most strongly in the later materials. As the story is now told, Yahweh warned Moses before he ever met Pharaoh that he would harden his heart (4:21), and after the people have gained their freedom, he finishes the job by hardening the hearts of Pharaoah and the Egyptians one last time (14:4, 8, 17), so the whole story is introduced and concluded with this theme. Childs has issued an appropriate warning, however, with his insistence that these texts have been overinterpreted by trying to make of them basic source material for the discussion of free will and determinism. That remains a paradox for systematic theology, but the way the theme of hardening the heart functions theologically in this passage can be understood without psychologizing or simply calling it paradox.

If freeing the Hebrews from slavery had been God's main intention, as Israel told the story of the plagues and the Sea, then for God to harden Pharaoh's heart so as to extend the agonies of the process would be indefensible on any grounds. But Israel did not tell the story that way. For them the intent of the plagues was to make a convincing demonstration that Yahweh alone is God, and that would require unconditional surrender by the pharaoh. There could be no negotiating, no compromises, no easy way so that Egypt's king could save face. "Let my people go" was a nonnegotiable demand. It was not even something to take seriously at first, for Pharaoh, this absolute monarch, god incarnate, and for that reason it is said that he hardened his own heart (8:15, 32; 9:34) or simply that his heart was hard (7:13, 14, 22; 8:19; 9:7, 35; not hard*ened,* as in NRSV). But the exercise of awesome force finally begins to have some effect on him when the plague of hail comes, and he tries some apparently serious negotiating (10:8–11; again after the darkness, 10:24–27). I believe it is with reference to this that Israel believed it necessary to speak of Yahweh's hardening of the heart of Pharaoh. Why would not any sensible person, even an absolute ruler, be willing to compromise a bit in order to bring this to an end? The king of Egypt, after pretending to bend a little, will not do so. The reason must be that God will accept no negotiated settlement. Nothing less than the pharaoh humbling himself before Yahweh will do (10:3).

And so, Israel claimed, God did not permit him to enter into any honest bargaining, for compromise would in fact defeat God's purpose.

The hardening of Pharaoh's heart is thus not to be taken as an example of how God normally deals with human beings, even with the greatest of sinners. It is a concept chosen by Israel for this specific purpose, to emphasize the thorough-going claim their God makes. Let us remind ourselves again of his aims: "That you may know that there is none like me in all the earth" (9:14); "That you may know that the earth is the LORD's" (9:29); "That my name may be declared throughout all the earth" (9:16). This material took its final shape during the exile, when explicitly monotheistic claims were being made by Israel, and those claims have influenced the way they finally told the story of the plagues and the Sea (cf. Deut. 4:35, 39; Isa. 44:6–8, etc.).

All this had no effect on Egypt, however, either as we now reconstruct ancient history, in which there is no evidence for any such extensive natural disasters as having devastated the land, nor in the ways Israel told of Egypt in its own history writing. No conversions are recorded, and in Israel's memories of the exodus the only result they could claim was freedom from slavery, after all, in spite of the way they formulated Exodus 5—15. All this destructive activity seems to have failed to accomplish the purpose that is emphasized so strongly throughout the passage, except that Israel was persuaded. "Israel saw the great work that the LORD did against the Egyptians. So the people feared the LORD and believed in the LORD and in his servant Moses" (Ex. 15:31). But not for long. Thus we see that the question with which this chapter began, about the Bible's reports of God's use of destructive activity, and whether that is really God's chosen way to accomplish his purpose with humanity, is present—implicitly—in Exodus 5—15.

Before we pursue that further, note that what we make of the reality of the plagues and the Wonder at the Sea will determine the nature of our questions. If we believe every detail happened exactly as recorded, then God himself is responsible for all that destruction and it has only been reported by humans. The issue is a single one: Why does God work that way? On the other hand, if we take seriously the fact that there is no evidence from historical records or archaeology for a destruction of the entire environment of Egypt (fish, cattle, vegetation all gone, thus wholesale starvation), then we may conclude that a series of less sweeping natural disasters occurred at the time the ancestors of Israel escaped from Egypt, which were then magnified in accordance with their importance to Israel and interpreted as acts of God. Then we have more than one possible question. Was this interpretation due entirely to the human propensity to see violence as the best or only way to solve the world's problems (thus in need of correction)? Or was their interpretation at least partially correct, for God is a divine destroyer? There is a third possibility. The absence of confirming records might lead to the conclusion the whole thing is fiction, in which case it tells us nothing about God, but tells only about the human love for violence. The reader has no doubt already concluded that my approach is the second of these three, but we should not forget that we cannot prove that any of the three is *the* correct approach.

In order that the centrality of God's claim to absolute sovereignty in Exodus 5—15 not be overlooked, the powers of nature are said to be the sole means he uses to accomplish his purpose. Usually, according to scripture, God works through human beings, and this leaves us with the need to try to discern how much of what happens is his will, and how much is due to human freedom. But nature has no will of its own and is solely God's instrument. Fretheim's commentary takes one approach to this, in terms of his conviction that creation-theology is a major formative element in the book of Exodus. He sees the plagues as "ecological signs of historical judgment"[19] and takes the reference in Ex. 1:7 to Israel's "filling the land (or earth)" to be an indication the author wants to tell us Israel was carrying out God's intention in creation ("Be fruitful and multiply and fill the earth," Gen. 1:28), which the king of Egypt attempts to thwart. He thus makes Pharaoh responsible for the anti-creational aspects of the plagues, and says when God removes them, the appropriate language is that of re-creation.[20] We do not find any such language in Exodus, however, and it is God who initiates and ends the plagues at will. God's action, in the plagues and Wonder at the Sea, sets creation against creation, producing devastation that can scarcely be explained as "correspondence between deed and consequence," as Fretheim does.

Water, the essential environment for fish, becomes blood by an act of God, and the fish all die. The frogs, which have multiplied uncontrollably, all die, and the result of the removal of the plague is that the land stinks with them (scarcely re-creation language). Not much is said about the effects of the gnats, but we know they can torment humans and animals. The swarms of flies are said to "ruin" the land (the same root, *shahat,* used of the destruction of the firstborn in 12:13, 23). A pestilence kills the livestock of the Egyptians, and after the boils (minor, compared to the others), the plagues of hail and locusts are said to have left Egypt a wasteland. What point was God really trying to make, with all that pain and all that death, with the reduction of that land to chaos? The book of Exodus does not explain why God treated nature that way, so once again it will be necessary to trace how this material fits into the whole of scripture's concept of God; in this case, tracing the appearances of the Divine Destroyer.

THE DIVINE DESTROYER
IN THE OLD TESTAMENT

This theme first appears early in the Bible, in the Flood story, which thus stands in tension with the materials around it. The stories of the Garden of Eden, of Cain and Abel, and of the Tower of Babel depict a God who stands in judgment of human sin, but who protects the wrongdoers from the worst that might befall them. Adam and Eve do not die immediately because of their disobedience, and God even provides them with clothes, now that their self-consciousness has made nakedness a problem. Cain is not executed for his crime of murder and is actually provided with protection by God from any who might kill him. The builders of Babel are scattered before their ability to concentrate power in one place could cause the excessive harm that too much human power always causes. There is an interesting and subtle balance between justice and mercy, described in a different way in each account.[21]

But in contrast to these stories, the Flood narrative tells us that because of the unspecified wickedness, corruption, and violence of humanity as a whole, God decided to wipe out everything that lived, except for the one righteous man, Noah, and his family (Gen. 6:5–8, 11–13). This is the archetypal cosmic disaster, of which the plague narrative is a more modest example. In the Flood, God used nature against itself in order to destroy all flesh along with the earth (Gen. 6:13). "All the fountains of the great deep burst forth, and the windows of the heavens were opened. . . . He blotted out every living thing that was on the face of the ground, human beings and animals and creeping things and birds of the air; they were blotted out from the earth" (Gen. 7:11b, 23). So destruction as the cure for sin is introduced very early in Israel's canon of scripture. Of course, the Flood story was not originally theirs. It had circulated throughout the ancient Near East since long before Israel existed, and it is known to us now in enough forms that we understand it was just something everyone knew about. Since it was common knowledge, when Israelite authors compiled the traditions of how things began on earth, they included the Flood story, even though it did not fit very well with the other narratives we have in Genesis 1—11, and they modified it to correspond with Yahwistic theology as best they could. No longer was it the result of the irritation of the gods at human clangor, a cataclysm so violent it alarmed even them, as in the version contained in the Gilgamesh Epic.[22] It is depicted as the just punishment of world-corrupting sin.

The Israelites had some problems with the story, even though they made it conform to their monotheism and their understanding of the justice of God. That is shown by the conclusions to be found in both the Yahwist and Priestly sources. In the Yahwistic source (J) God says, "I will never again curse the ground because of humankind, for the inclination of the human heart is evil from youth; nor will I ever again destroy every living creature as I have done" (Gen. 8:21). The Priestly source speaks of the covenant made by God with "every living creature," with the rainbow as its sign, and containing the promise, "never again shall all flesh be cut off by the waters of a flood, and never again shall there be a flood to destroy the earth" (Gen. 9:11). The two sources agree that the pattern of the Flood will not be the dominant theme of scripture. God does not intend the destruction of the wicked to be his way of restoring the goodness of creation. Yet, stories of the sweeping destruction of life—human, animal, and vegetable— continue to appear in the Bible, and so, from Genesis 8 on we encounter tension between the concept of a God who corrects, punishes, and purges by means of death, and the concept of a God who has chosen another way of dealing with sin. In Genesis 1—11, however, we are not given a hint of what that will be, and in fact God's other way begins to be clearly revealed only in Exodus 32—34.

There is another great natural disaster in Genesis, the destruction of Sodom and Gomorrah. Once again the destruction is almost complete; only Lot and his family escape. The means of destruction is cosmic: "Then the LORD rained on Sodom and Gomorrah sulfur and fire from the LORD out of heaven; and he overthrew those cities, and all the Plain, and all the inhabitants of the cities, and what grew on the ground" (Gen. 19:24–25). But here also there appears a question about these methods. It takes the form of Abraham's reasoning with God over the justice of destroying a whole city, when there might be some righteous people in it (Gen. 18:23–33). The passage cannot be discussed in full here, but it clearly introduces a radically disturbing element into the notion of strict justice, when God agrees that ten righteous people in a city could save the lives of all their wicked neighbors.[23] The dialogue between Abraham and God assumes that God is one in whom mercy triumphs over justice, but Sodom and Gomorrah are destroyed anyway, with only the righteous remnant (Lot and his daughters) being saved, so the tension continues.

Wickedness was emphasized as the reason for the destruction in the Flood story and in the account of the fall of Sodom and Gomorrah, and we have seen that it introduced the narrative of the plagues and Wonder at the Sea, although it was not emphasized as strongly. The theme of wholesale destruction appears once more in Exodus, in a passage to be dealt with at length later, since it is so important to the theology of Exodus. The sin of the golden calf led God to decide (subject to Moses' approval!) to do with Israel what he had done in the Flood: wipe out the whole lot of them and start over with one righteous man; this time, with Moses (Ex. 32:7–10). But now the Flood pattern is averted, thanks to Moses' intercession, as he cites good reasons for forbearance in the divine economy, as he understood it (vv. 11–14). And as we shall see later, Exodus 32—34 works out the basis for a continuing life of God's people, even though they continue to be sinners. The alternate way seems to have triumphed already.

In the prophetic books we see that the theme of the divine destroyer had not been completely repudiated by their understanding of Yahweh's long-suffering and forgiving nature, however. Eventually the prophets learn that something more than forgiveness will be required, in order for Yahweh's will to be done on earth. The prophets reuse both the Flood pattern (universal destruction) and the Sodom pattern (destruction of non-Israelites) in speaking of God's use of the forces of nature against the wicked. In order to follow the kind of divine activity that is distinctive in Exodus 5—15 through scripture, we shall put to one side all that is said about God's use of human forces, such as the armies of Assyria and Babylonia, as agents of judgment. We look now at some of the most striking examples in the prophets of direct, divine action, destroying human life and the vitality of the world as God's means of dealing with sin.

Two examples of the divine use of nature against itself as judgment of the sins of non-Israelites (i.e., Israel's enemies) will suffice to show that the theme of divine destroyer not only survived in the prophets but was elaborated. In Isaiah 34, the nation to be judged is Edom, but the introduction to the passage has a universal scope (v. 2):

> For the LORD is enraged against all the nations,
>   and furious against all their hoards;
>   he has doomed them, has given them over for slaughter.

The kind of cosmic judgment that is characteristic of later apocalyptic makes an early appearance here, with the announcement that "All the host of heaven shall rot away, and the skies roll up like a scroll" (v. 4a). The next section mixes the imagery of the divine warrior with that of a great sacrifice, as the Lord depicts his slaughter of the Edomites with the imagery of the slaughter of lambs, goats, rams, oxen, steers, and bulls, soaking the land with their blood (vv. 5–7). Then comes the destruction of the land itself:

> And the streams of Edom shall be turned into pitch,
>   and her soil into sulfur;
>   her land shall become burning pitch.
> Night and day it shall not be quenched;
>   its smoke shall go up forever.
> From generation to generation it shall lie waste;
>   no one shall pass through it forever and ever. (vv. 9–10)

The future desolation of the land is then described at some length in terms of its possession by the animals: hawk and hedgehog, owl and raven, jackals, ostriches, wildcats, hyenas, and buzzards, plus the wild spirits thought to inhabit the wilderness (vv. 11–17). This is no "wildlife sanctuary." The "endangered species" in those times was humanity, and the prophets frequently spoke of the occupation of a formerly habitable land or city by wild beasts as a kind of return to chaos (cf. Isa. 13:21; 23:13; Jer. 50:39; Ezek. 5:17; Hos. 2:12; Zeph. 2:14f.). What was a show of divine power in Egypt, with the temporary occupation of the land by frogs, gnats, and flies, has become a permanent reversal of creation here, for Edom, "the people I have doomed to judgment" (v. 5b).

A different use of the destructive powers of nature appears in Ezekiel's account of how Gog and his forces will be destroyed by direct, divine action. This occurs within the Holy Land, after the restoration of the Jewish exiles, and so creation itself is only temporarily disrupted and the destruction is confined to the enemy. But it is a terrifying description of the wrath of God:

> For in my jealousy and in my blazing wrath I declare: On that day there shall be a
> great shaking in the land of Israel; the fish of the sea, and the birds of the air, and the

animals of the field, and all creeping things that creep on the ground, and all human beings that are on the face of the earth, shall quake at my presence, and the mountains shall be thrown down, and the cliffs shall fall, and every wall shall tumble to the ground. I will summon the sword against Gog in all my mountains, says the LORD God; the swords of all will be against their comrades. With pestilence and bloodshed I will enter into judgment with him; and I will pour down torrential rains and hailstones, fire and sulfur, upon him and his troops and the many peoples that are with him. So I will display my greatness and my holiness and make myself known in the eyes of many nations. Then they shall know that I am the LORD. (Ezek. 38:19–23)

In Isaiah 34, all that seemed to be accomplished by the cosmic upheaval was the destruction of Edom, but Ezekiel says the destruction of Gog is for the same ultimate purpose as the plagues in Egypt: They are intended to demonstrate to the nations who is God. There remains a hope, in the minds of the prophets, that the exercise of overpowering force in the world will convince those who see it, but that stands alongside a conviction that another kind of divine action is needed, as we shall see shortly.

The earliest of the canonical prophets, Amos, turned the plague theme to a new use, claiming God had turned nature against itself in the effort to make a point with Israel, but with no better effect than the plagues had in Egypt. In Amos 4:6–13 the prophet recites a litany of seven disasters that had befallen Israel (six of them by forces of nature): famine, drought, blight, locust, pestilence (in the manner of Egypt), sword, and "overthrow" (earthquake?). After each comes the refrain, "Yet you did not return to me, says the LORD." The doxology in verse 13, with its creation-theology, seems an appropriate conclusion to the passage, as a reminder that all of nature is Yahweh's, to do with as he pleases.[24] Amos seems to be referring to the tradition of the plagues, which had been intended to bring Pharaoh to "know that I am Yahweh," but which had failed. And in his day, since instances of divine destruction had accomplished nothing, Amos came to the conviction that only the death of Israel could lie ahead (Amos 5:1–2, 16–20; 6:9–10; 8:1–3; 9:1–4, 9f.). A later prophet would not deny that death is the way God works in the world, but would speak of death and resurrection (Ezek. 37:1–14).

More thoroughgoing environmental disasters appeared in the visions of other prophets, as the form taken by God's direct action against sin. In Isa. 2:6–22, the "terror of the LORD" and the "glory of his majesty" come to level the earth. No natural forces are described this time, but people are depicted hiding in caves of the rocks and holes in the ground (vv. 10, 19, 21) to escape some overpowering force that will bring low everything that is proud and lofty: the cedars of Lebanon, the oaks of Bashan, the mountains and hills, every high tower and fortified wall, even the ships of Tarshish (vv. 12–16). It is an oracle against pride, one of the sins that concerned Isaiah most, and since the various Hebrew roots that were used metaphorically to mean pride all literally had to do with height (like our use of "haughty"), in this vision pride is brought low by leveling out the surface of the

earth. The aim of this cataclysmic divine appearance on earth is essentially the
same as that of the plagues in Egypt: "The LORD alone will be exalted on that day"
(vv. 11b, 17b).[25] The people who survive the disaster will finally give up their
idols because they have been overpowered.

A more detailed picture of the desolation of the earth as the final demonstration
of divine power is provided in the so-called Isaiah Apocalypse, probably one of
the latest parts of the Old Testament.[26] Chapter 24 begins:

> Now the LORD is about to lay waste the earth and make it desolate,
>   and he will twist its surface and scatter its inhabitants.

Rather than quoting at length from the chapter, a list of words from the NRSV
translation should reproduce its effect: despoil, dry up, languish, wither, pollute,
desolation, ruins, terror, tremble, utterly broken, torn asunder, violently shaken,
stagger, sway, fall. No other agent but God is alluded to as the source of this return
of the earth to chaos, but the reason is emphasized:

> The earth lies polluted under its inhabitants;
>   for they have transgressed laws,
>   violated the statutes,
>   broken the everlasting covenant. (Isa. 24:5)

This is probably a reference to the covenant made with all flesh at the time of
Noah, for it was called an everlasting covenant (Gen. 9:16), and it explicitly
forbade bloodshed (Gen. 9:5), which is said to pollute the earth in Num. 35:33.[27]
What is to be accomplished by all this terror is in continuity with what we found
in the story of the plagues, in Ezek. 38:19–23, and in Isa. 2:6–22. It is the final
demonstration of the absolute sovereignty of Yahweh: "for the LORD of hosts will
reign on Mount Zion and in Jerusalem, and before his elders he will manifest his
glory" (Isa. 24:23b).

We shall look at two more examples of divine destruction in the prophets,
because they introduce two elements not seen in those we have already considered. The most striking of them all is Jer. 4:23–28, a vision in which creation itself
seems to be completely undone. It is so powerful that it must be quoted in full,
including the apparent insertion, which includes the new element, the preservation of a remnant:

> I looked on the earth, and lo, it was waste and void;
>   and to the heavens, and they had no light.
> I looked on the mountains, and lo, they were quaking,
>   and all the hills moved to and fro.
> I looked, and lo, there was no one at all,
>   and all the birds of the air had fled.
> I looked, and lo, the fruitful land was a desert,
>   and all its cities were laid in ruins
>   before the LORD, before his fierce anger.

For thus says the LORD: The whole land shall be a desolation; yet I will not make a
    full end.
Because of this the earth shall mourn,
    and the heavens above grow black;
for I have spoken, I have purposed;
    I have not relented nor will I turn back.

This is a version of the Flood theme, in which God goes right back to the
beginning, wiping out all of creation because it is irredeemable, but preserving a
remnant with which to start over. We need not worry about whether "yet I will not
make a full end" was originally part of the poem, for it became an essential part of
the prophetic message concerning the fall of Jerusalem and the exile. They
understood that disaster to be like the Flood, and their only basis for hope in the
future was that God would bring a righteous people out of the death of exile.

The date of the book of Joel is debated, and cannot be fixed with any certainty,
but this prophet's relative optimism concerning the possibility of repentance and
his ability to link an interpretation of natural disaster as divine judgment with a
promise of the restoration of nature because of divine mercy strongly suggests
that he had experienced the truth of the restoration from exile. He speaks of a
single plague, but a most terrifying one, that of locusts. This may not be a
prediction of the future, or a vision, but may refer to a present-tense experience,
for in the midst of the description of terror comes a call for repentance (Joel 1:14;
2:12–14; cf. 2:15–17). After the lengthy description of the destruction brought by
the locusts, as the agents of God's wrath (1:15; 2:11), at the turning point in Joel's
message there appears a quotation from Ex. 34:6–7 as the basis for hope in a
different future: "Return to the LORD, your God, for he is gracious and merciful,
slow to anger, and abounding in steadfast love, and relents from punishing"
(2:13). God's two ways of dealing with sin now appear in chronological order,
with repentance intervening, for Joel 2:18–32 speaks of the restoration of nature
and of human society.

This is good postexilic Jewish theology, where repentance is possible,
necessary, and effective. Natural disasters may still be used by God as means of
judgment, but the Flood pattern had already been endured in the exile (Isa. 54:9f.).
The preexilic prophets, however, faced a grimmer future, and that was expressed
unequivocally by Ezekiel, who picked up the exiles' complaint that Israel was
dead, and added divine confirmation of it, through his vision of the valley of dry
bones (Ezek. 37:1–14). The death foreseen by Amos had occurred; now the only
question was whether God had any intention of raising the dead, and this key
passage for Old Testament theology affirms that he does. "I am going to open
your graves, and bring you up from your graves, O my people; and I will bring
you back to the land of Israel. And you will know that I am the LORD" (Ezek.
37:21b–13a). But Ezekiel's truly new insight (shared by Jeremiah in 31:31–34) is
that the knowledge of God intended to be brought about by the plagues inflicted
(futilely) on Egypt and the plagues inflicted (futilely) upon Israel would become

reality only through a truly new creation. It would not replace destruction and death, but after death would come resurrection. So Ezekiel promised the gift of a new heart and new spirit for humans (36:25–27), which would make repentance possible (36:31), and which would be accompanied by the restoration of nature to its proper functions (36:29–36).

Does this continuing insistence that in order to deal with evil, God kills—and not only the wicked, but the innocent (as in Ezek. 21:3f.), and fish and birds and trees—mean that René Girard is correct in seeing the Old Testament as a "long and laborious exodus out of the world of violence," which does not reach its goal except in the New Testament?[28] Or could Walter Stuermann, in his book that carries the same title as this chapter, be correct in developing a thoroughgoing natural theology, concluding that since science has shown nature to be a mixture of chaos and order, the nature of God must also be Chaos-Order?[29] More must be said about this after we have traced the theme of divine destruction into our own time, but at this point some preliminary conclusions concerning the Old Testament itself should be offered, suggesting that it is more realistic about the nature of the world we live in than Girard asserts, but is not so totally dependent on what we can learn from nature as Stuermann held it to be.

In thinking about the tension between God's wrath and mercy that runs through all the strata of the Old Testament, I was helped initially by Rudolf Otto's discovery that terms such as "wrath" and "mercy" are rationalizations of elemental, nonrational experiences of the presence of the numinous. This helps us to appreciate why in all religions the terrifying in nature has been associated with the gods, and it is clear that Israel was no different from others in that respect. It also should protect us from taking those concepts to be more than imperfect analogies drawn from human experience in an attempt to speak about the Wholly Other. But it leaves some very large questions unanswered. Otto assumed there really is a God who produces those numinous experiences, but his critics have found his work inadequate at that point. Has he really done anything more than describe an aspect of human psychology? From the point of view of Jewish or Christian theology, for example, should the association of wrath with God be dismissed as "anthropopathy,"[30] and the attribution of natural disasters to the will of God be considered "mythology"?

The idea that God destroys his enemies using the powers of nature is a part of the common theology of the ancient Near East that Israel shared with its neighbors.[31] The Flood story is the classic example of the universality of such a concept of God. We have seen that Israel both affirmed it and had some problems with it, and that tension will be traced into the New Testament, with startling results, for destruction is prominent there also, but it is the Son of God who is destroyed. Israel and its neighbors all spoke of divine destruction because it corresponded to the reality they had to cope with. Let us use the word "violence" for the time being, in thinking about how Israel shared in the common theology. Most deities in all religions are associated with violence, in some way. This is only natural, since daily life confronts one with various kinds of violence, in nature, in society, and in one's own body. A "nonviolent god" would be divorced from the reality all archaic peoples experienced, and the same is true of all but the most protected inhabitants of "civilized cultures."[32] Such a God would be largely irrelevant to the needs of people, at their most elementary level.[33] So people have instinctively associated the violence of nature with deities. The association of gods with the state involves them in the establishment and maintenance of power, and that also includes killing or other violence so as to preserve order, and killing as a means of conquest.

We have seen that most of the Old Testament accepts without question the common idea that God's work must involve setting nature against nature at times, destroying the life-giving ability of creation, since wicked humanity must also be destroyed. The Flood theme continued to be used, in spite of the reservations concerning its validity already recorded by the Yahwistic and Priestly sources. This is part of Israel's acceptance of the common theology of the ancient Near East. It is understandable that they accepted it, because it was coherent with the nature of the world in which they lived, where violence ruled. Looking ahead, we might as well agree it is also coherent with the world in which we live, as natural science describes it, and as the news reports it, suggesting a way for us to approach the concept of God as destroyer, once that has surfaced as a problem, to the extent that it did not surface for Israel.

Israel's "alternate theology,"[34] as expressed first in Ex. 34:6–7, and as cited in Joel 2:13, did raise questions for them about God's *ultimate* intentions, beyond judgment by destruction and death, and in their eschatology a new creation was hoped for. The foremost challenge to the common theology appears in Isa. 11:6–9, which seems to propose for the future a wholly new ecology, so different from the way nature works now that we can scarcely imagine whether it could work. The challenge to all violence in nature is made explicit in the last verse: "They shall not hurt or destroy in all my holy mountain" (Isa. 11:9a), because the earth will be full of the knowledge of God. And we remember that that was the aim of the plagues: knowledge of God. Israel's correction of the common theology was also projected back to the beginning, since the Priestly creation story accounts only for the eating of plants (Gen. 1:29f.), and killing for food is presented as an accommodation for an imperfect world, after the Flood (Gen. 9:3). This has led some theologians (using also Gen. 3:14–19) to attribute all the destruction and death caused by the animals to the effects of human sin on the natural world.[35] Blaming sin for the violence of the present environment, as well as for social and political violence, made it possible for many believers to this day to see much of God's use of death and destruction as no problem. Only the pain and death of the innocent raised questions about the character of God.

This "common theology" has thus provided a good fit for the way every society has maintained relative order and stability throughout history, using violence, sometimes cautiously, often arbitrarily, and justifying that by appeals to a theology that spoke of a god who behaved in the same way. And since violence is not confined to human actions, but seems built in the working of the natural world, acceptance of such a theology has ordinarily been widespread, even among those who have suffered under it. Yet, alongside the Old Testament's impressive descriptions of God's awesome power are to be found these minority reports, which have been appearing "in the margins" of this chapter, and which will become the focus of our work on Exodus 32—34. This God who will turn creation back to chaos in order to punish sinners is also a God who grieves over human wickedness (Gen. 6:6), who will change his mind rather than administer just punishment (Ex. 32:14; Hos. 11:8f.), who protects sinners from the worst consequences of their acts (Gen. 4:15), and who "delights in showing clemency" (Micah 7:18). So, the same psalm can praise God because he "works vindication and justice for all who are oppressed" (and with the ensuing reference to Moses, there is no doubt about how he does that, Ps. 103:6f.), and praise him because "the LORD has compassion for those who fear him. For he knows how we were made; he remembers that we are dust" (Ps. 103:13b–14). The Suffering Servant passage in Isa. 52:13–53:12 also suggests God himself experiences the violence justly inflicted on sinners, a theme that appears in only a few places in the Old Testament but becomes a major part of New Testament theology. Never does the New Testament, or subsequent Jewish and Christian theology, eliminate completely the divine destroyer, however, so the issues we have been tracing thus far remain alive. The destruction of evil continues to be a part of God's work for good, leaving us with the question whether we can conceive of his work in any other way.

JUDAISM AND CHRISTIANITY

Tracing all the theological issues raised by Exodus 5—15 in detail could produce several volumes. Taking the plagues and the crossing of the Sea as manifestations of the wrath of God, for example, would lead to the problems created for Judaism and Christianity by the insistence of much of Greek philosophy that God must be free of all passions and emotions. We shall leave that large subject to one side until the last section of this chapter, since it appears in some useful forms in recent works. The fact that only Yahweh takes violent action against the enemy in Exodus 5—15 has been used as an argument for pacifism, but since we have not encountered war between two armies yet, we need not let "Yahweh is a warrior" lead us into the debate over God's relationship with war. Some of the material in the direct line of tradition we are tracing will be useful in considering modern discussions of the problem of evil, and its contributions will be noted where appropriate, without trying to take up all aspects of the problem.

In order to keep within a carefully defined line of tradition, the following points will be taken up, in each of the three parts of this section: First we shall note authors who have made some use of the plague and Sea narratives, other than just retelling them. Then we shall look for good examples of the continuing insistence that the justice of God requires the destruction of the wicked, focusing on those in which God is said to act directly, using the forces of nature. We shall have a special interest in what is said about how his destructive activity affects God.

Judaism

It is not until we come to the sayings of the rabbis that we find in Jewish literature any strong sense of incongruity between the two firmly held beliefs, that God is slow to anger and abundant in mercy, and that he also is certain to destroy the wicked, often by turning parts of his good creation into agents of ruin and death. Prior to the rabbinic literature, the two beliefs are simply affirmed, as they are in the Old Testament, as essential aspects of God's nature. The destruction of the wicked is assumed to be the essential means of administering justice and is often cited as proof that God is just. Mercy means essentially God's willingness to accept repentance. Some authors use the plagues as classic examples of how God deals justly with the wicked.

Philo retold the story at length in *De Vita Mosis I*. He thought the fact that there were ten plagues was "a perfect number for the chastisement of those who brought sin to perfection."[36] Even though we found that sin was not emphasized in the biblical account, and that the emphasis was on bringing Pharaoh to acknowledge the superiority of Yahweh, Philo says little about Moses' confrontations with the king and speaks frequently instead of the Egyptians' cruelty and lawlessness. He notes something that has been a major theme of this chapter: "The chastisement was different from the usual kind, for the elements of the universe—earth, fire, air, water—carried out the assault. God's judgment was that the materials which had served to produce the world should serve also to destroy the land of the impious; and to show the mightiness of the sovereignty which He holds, what He shaped in His saving goodness to create the universe He turned into instruments for the perdition of the impious whenever He would."

The fact that the Hebrews in Goshen suffered none of the plagues provides the perfect conclusion for Philo's account, with his strong emphasis on punishment, "For never was judgment so clearly passed on good and bad, a judgment which brought perdition to the latter and salvation to the former" (146).

Jubilees condenses the plague material into four verses, but also interprets it as God's punishment of Egypt for enslaving Israel: "Ten great and cruel judgments came on the land of Egypt so that you might execute vengeance upon it for Israel" (*Jubilees* 48:7). Wisdom of Solomon 16—19 has a lengthy but still incomplete version of the plagues, with a great deal of rambling commentary, and the gist of it is like Philo's conclusion. Descriptions of locusts and flies (16:9), hail and fire (16:16–19), and darkness (17:1–21) are followed by contrasting pictures of God's care for the Israelites. Then the killing of the firstborn is recorded (18:5–25), and the miracle at the Sea (19:1–9). Among his concluding remarks is, "They justly suffered because of their wicked acts; for they practiced a more bitter hatred of strangers" (19:13b). The plagues could thus serve as a pattern for pictures of the last judgment, as in the Apocalypse of Abraham. Near the end, God grants Abraham's request to know the ten plagues he has prepared against the heathen, and he lists them: sorrow from much need, fire, pestilence among the cattle, famine, earthquake and sword, hail and snow, wild beasts, pestilence and hunger, sword and flight in distress, and thunder, voices, and destroying earthquakes. A later rabbinic comment added something new to the prevailing emphasis on punishment: "All the punishments for rebellion which God brought upon the Egyptians had the object of purifying them from evil, as it says, 'Wounds cleanse away evil' (Prov. 20:30)" (*Pesiqta Rabbati,* 196a).

These examples, referring explicitly to the plagues, obviously make an emphasis that overlaps the next group, a series of passages in which the idea that justice requires the destruction of the wicked is expressed in striking ways. The idea that the Egyptians' punishment fit their crimes is expressed in *Jubilees* and reappears in other ways elsewhere. This book has added detail about the pharaoh's order to kill the newborn males of the Hebrews, saying that for seven months these children had been thrown into the river (47:2f.). The drowning of his army in the sea was thus an appropriate punishment: "Just as the men of Egypt cast their sons into the river he avenged one million. And one thousand strong and ardent men perished on account of one infant whom they threw into the midst of the river from the sons of your people" (48:13f.). A similar comparison of sin and punishment appears in an eschatological section of the book. The land will be corrupted because of the deeds of the faithless, and then, "All of them will be destroyed together: beast, cattle, birds, and all of the fish of the sea on account of the sons of men" (23:18).

Such sweeping destruction is stated as a general principle by Sirach. God destroys the proud completely (10:13); "the Lord lays waste the lands of the nations, and destroys them to the foundations of the earth" (10:16). The powers of nature are his agents:

> There are winds created for vengeance,
> and in their anger they can dislodge mountains;
> on the day of reckoning they will pour out their strength
> and calm the anger of their Maker.
> Fire and hail and famine and pestilence,
> all these have been created for vengeance;
> the fangs of wild animals and scorpions and vipers,
> and the sword that punishes the ungodly with destruction.
> They take delight in doing his bidding,
> always ready for his service on earth;
> and when their time comes they never disobey his command.
> (Sirach 39:28–31; cf. *Psalms of Solomon* 15:7f., 12a; *2 Apoc. Bar.* 70:8, 10)

That God's punishment fits the crime is also the theme of a series of citations of scripture in the *Mekilta* on Ex. 15:1, concluding, "By means of the very things with which the nations of the world act proudly before Him, God punishes them."[37] One of the rabbis hastened to explain one of the most ferocious pictures of God in the Bible (Deut. 32:39–43), commenting on "When I whet my flashing sword, and my hand takes hold on judgment" (v. 41b), by emphasizing this is not random violence: "Punishments go forth from God swift as lightning, *but* his hand has hold of justice" (*Sifre on Deuteronomy*). But no explanation or qualification of the destruction itself seems to be called for. Even the traditional Passover Haggadah contains a prayer for the manifestation of God's wrath on the wicked:

> "Pour out thy wrath upon the nations that know Thee not, and upon the kingdoms that call not upon Thy name. For they have devoured Jacob, And laid waste his habitation" (Ps. 79:6–7). "Pour out Thine indignation upon them, and let the fierceness of Thine anger overtake them" (Ps. 69:25). "Thou wilt pursue them in anger, and destroy them from under the heavens of the Lord" (Lam. 3:66).[38]

Doing justice seems to require divine destruction, but God takes no pleasure in it. Commenting on the curses in Deuteronomy 28, the Talmud says:

> Now does the Holy One, blessed be He, rejoice in the downfall of the wicked? Is it not written, *as they went out before the army, and say, Give thanks unto the Lord, for his mercy endureth for ever* (2 Chron. 20:21), and R. Johanan said, Why are the words "for he is good" omitted from this thanksgiving? Because the Holy One, blessed be He, does not rejoice in the downfall of the wicked?[39] And R. Johanan further said, What is the meaning of the verse, *And one came not near the other all the night?* (Ex. 14:20)—The ministering angels wanted to chant their hymns, but the Holy One, blessed be He, said, The work of my hands is being drowned in the sea, and shall you chant hymns? (*b. Megillah* 10b)

The Exodus material that has introduced these questions to us had raised similar questions for the rabbis long ago, although they did not seem to pursue them as far as we will have to. The Song of the Sea (Exodus 15) led to a comment in the *Mekilta* similar to the one found in the Talmud. "There was no rejoicing over the destruction of the wicked before Him on high. Now, if there is no joy before Him on high at the destruction of the wicked, how much the more is there no joy at the destruction of the righteous, of whom one is as important as the whole world."[40] That God takes no pleasure in the death of the wicked was also understood to be the meaning of the reference to his grief before he destroyed the world in the Flood: "Before He brought on the flood, God himself kept seven days of mourning, for He was grieved at heart" (*Tanhuma B., Shemini,* 11a).

God is pained at the necessity of punishing those he has created who have rebelled against him, bringing suffering to the innocent, but mercy for the innocent seems to require the destruction of those who are guilty.

The New Testament

The early church's overarching interest in the redemption of sinners led to some significant changes from the language of the Old Testament and Judaism to that of the New Testament, concerning God's direct action for the maintenance of justice. That the changes did not endure as Christianity developed makes it the more important not to overlook their presence in the New Testament. It has little to say about God taking action against evildoers in this life. Interventions in history such as the exodus, the defeat of the Philistines (2 Sam. 5:17–25), the routing of Sennacherib's army (2 Kings 19:35–37), the appointment of the Assyrians and Babylonians to carry out God's judgments against Israel (2 Kings 17; Isa. 10:5f.) and Judah (Jer. 34:1–5), and restoring the exiles to Jerusalem play no part in the New Testament except in memory. There is a single, divine intervention: the appearance of Jesus. Matthew's carefully constructed genealogy makes the point that Jesus' appearance on earth was the culmination of forty-two generations of history (Matt. 1:1–17). Elsewhere, his coming is said to mark "the fullness of time" (Eph. 1:10). That one event marked God's decisive action in history for both judgment and salvation:

> Indeed, God did not send the Son into the world to condemn the world, but in order that the world might be saved through him. Those who believe in him are not condemned; but those who do not believe are condemned already, because they have not believed in the name of the only Son of God. (John 3:17–18)

God the destroyer remains in the background throughout, to the extent that some claim the Old Testament image has been eliminated entirely from the New.[41] It seems more faithful to the material, however, to say that the image has been expressed in different ways, rather than to claim it has been completely superseded.

The New Testament has little to say about God taking direct action against evildoers in this life. Jesus, for example, denied that one can deduce from sickness or accident that the victim has been punished by God for some sin, in the case of the man born blind (John 9:3) and the people who had been killed by the collapse of a tower in Siloam (Luke 13:1–5). In at least two passages a New Testament author did make such a deduction, but it surely is significant that the direct activity of God most often reported is that leading to conversion of sinners (the work of the Holy Spirit) and not to their destruction. The two relatively unusual cases appear in Acts. In 5:1–11 the deception of Ananias and Sapphira led immediately to their deaths, and the reader is surely intended to understand that as divine punishment for their sin, although that is not explicitly said. Herod Agrippa's miserable death, recorded in Acts 12:20–23, is said to have immediately followed his acceptance of popular acclaim as a god and is attributed to an angel of the Lord who struck him down. This is the kind of conclusion that has been drawn from misfortunes of various kinds by some Christians from that day to this, and so it should be emphasized that there is little of it in the New Testament.

The book of Job had long ago challenged the belief that sin can be deduced from suffering, and the persecutions that Jews had experienced since the second century B.C.E., in which it was precisely the most faithful people who suffered the most, may very well have contributed to the hesitation New Testament writers had about attributing misfortune to a divine act of judgment. But they were no less emphatic than Judaism about the certainty of divine judgment at some point in the future. It was typically projected into the last days or, at other times, into the experience of individuals after death. It is present throughout the New Testament, but usually as background, for the dominant message is the redemption of sinners, not their destruction, redemption via the destruction of the Son of God.

That background shows up more clearly in Matthew than in the other Gospels, and it is developed most thoroughly in the Pauline writings and in Revelation, so most of our examples will be taken from those three sources. There is a tendency for New Testament writers to separate God from this kind of activity, by using passives, for which the agent is not stated, and abstractions, such as "wrath" and "destruction." But occasionally they will make God the subject of such a verb. Jesus' ministry is introduced by Matthew, as by the other evangelists, with the preaching of John the Baptist, and John's preaching includes such an abstraction, "the wrath to come," one of several New Testament ways of referring to the last judgment (Matt. 3:7; Luke 3:7). It is the wrath of God that is coming, however, as Eph. 5:6; Col. 3:6; and Rev. 11:18 say explicitly. Jesus presumably speaks of God in the harsh saying, "And do not fear those who kill the body but cannot kill the soul; rather fear him who can destroy both soul and body in hell" (Matt. 10:28).[42] Matthew has quite a collection of sayings of Jesus concerning destruction in hell, such as, "And if your eye causes you to sin, pluck it out and throw it away; it is better for you to enter life with one eye than with two eyes to be thrown into the hell of fire" (Matt. 18:9; cf. 5:22, 29, 30; 23:33). And as in that saying, fire has become the means of destruction most often mentioned by Jesus:

> Just as the weeds are collected and burned up with fire, so will it be at the end of the age. The Son of Man will send his angels, and they will collect out of his kingdom all causes of sin and all evildoers, and they will throw them into the furnace of fire, where there will be weeping and gnashing of teeth. (Matt. 13:40–42; cf. 13:50; 18:8; 25:41)

Fire is a highly effective means of destruction, so the Divine Destroyer has by no means disappeared from the Gospels, but the theme appears in a radically different form from the way we found it in the Old Testament. It is virtually confined to the end, either of the life of an individual or of history (see 1 Thess. 1:4–12). The present manifestations of God's power in the ministry of Jesus took the forms of healing and forgiveness, rather than judgment.

Only in the apocalyptic parts of the New Testament do we find strong continuity with ways the destructive activity of God is described in the Old Testament (e.g., 2 Thess. 1:4–12; 2:8). Revelation picks up the theme of plagues, and for that reason is the only book that says anything significant about God setting nature against nature. It will be taken as the New Testament example, then, of the first three points discussed under Judaism: reuse of the plagues and Sea traditions, God's upholding of justice by destroying the wicked, and the participation of the nonhuman world in that activity. Then two passages from the Pauline letters will be considered for their profound influence on the Christian understanding of justice and mercy.

Revelation describes the coming annihilation of this present, evil order in more terrifying detail than any of the earlier Jewish apocalypses did. Since one scholar has claimed that there are more allusions to the Old Testament in Revelation than there are verses, it is not surprising that the plague tradition is reused here. The book is filled with warfare, but at three points, lengthy series of largely natural disasters are inflicted on the earth, and in these we see the reappearance of the theme of direct divine activity, without human involvement. When the Lamb opens the sixth seal (Rev. 6:12–7:3), there is an earthquake, the sun becomes black and the moon like blood, stars fall, the sky vanishes, and everyone hides in caves and among the rocks of the mountains (an obvious reference to Isa. 2:10, 19, 21). They know the day of the wrath of the Lamb has come (6:16f.). For some reason the winds are stilled, and the order comes not to damage the earth, the sea, or the trees until the servants of God have been marked with a seal on their foreheads (7:1–3). In this first sequence, it is the sky that is most affected, and there is to be an interval before the earth itself begins to suffer, but that comes with the book's next series of sevens (Rev. 8:7–9:21).

The blowing of the first trumpet brings hail, fire, and blood; a third of the earth, trees, and grass are burned. With the second trumpet a third of the sea becomes blood. The third trumpet causes a star to fall from heaven, turning a third of the waters on earth to wormwood. With the fourth, a third of the light is darkened; with the fifth, smoke and locusts come up from the bottomless pit, to attack those who do not have the seal of the Lamb on their foreheads, but to leave trees and grass untouched. The sixth trumpet calls forth an angelic army whose weapons are fire, smoke, and sulfur, and one-third of humankind is killed in this way. Note that the author has no intention of simply projecting the Egyptian plagues into the future. He creates his own sequence of natural disasters, amplifying them to make them far more terrible than those in Exodus, but finding blood, locusts, hail, and darkness to be very suitable for his purposes.

Finally, "the seven bowls of the wrath of God" are poured out upon the earth (Rev. 16:2–21). Another feature from Exodus appears; the first plague is a "foul and painful sore" on those who had the mark of the beast. The second bowl makes the sea like blood and everything in it dies. The third turns the rivers and springs to blood, and we see in these plagues two additional, close references to Exodus. The fourth is original; the sun is allowed to scorch the earth with fire. The fifth once again produces darkness over the kingdom of the beast, and the sixth reminds us of Exodus, since with the drying up of the Euphrates there appear "three foul spirits like frogs coming from the mouth of the dragon, from the mouth of the beast, and from the mouth of the false prophet." With the pouring out of the seventh bowl, a loud voice comes from the throne saying, "It is done!" That brings lightning, earthquake, and hail. "God remembered great Babylon and gave her the wine-cup of the fury of his wrath" (16:19b).

After all that terror, Revelation promises God will create a new heaven and a new earth (21:1):

> God himself will be with them;
> he will wipe every tear from their eyes.
> Death will be no more;
> mourning and crying and pain will be no more,

because "the first things have passed away" (21:3b–4). The need for God to destroy evil in this very physical way held its place in Christian thought in spite of the relatively minor role it plays in the New Testament, and alongside the very different picture of God's victory over evil contained in the theology of the cross.

We find in three classic texts from the writings of Paul the beginnings of the Christian working out of the Old Testament's intimations that God is somehow both the subject and the object of the destruction that is necessary for the overcoming of evil. The Christian understanding of the meaning of the cross will lead to the theology of incarnation. That is not developed in the passages we shall consider, but the new way of dealing with evil is clearly present. These texts have produced a tremendous volume of scholarly literature, and no attempt will be made here to deal with all that they contain. They shall be read only for what they contribute to our study of the theme of divine destruction, and that means most of the traditional interests discussed in the literature will be left aside.

The theme of the wrath of God plays an important role in Romans, and its appearance in two passages points to material of interest to us. Paul begins the argument of the book with a twofold statement of the meaning of the gospel. The positive side is this: "For in it the righteousness of God is revealed through faith for faith; as it is written, 'The one who is righteous will live by faith' " (Rom. 1:17). But the negative side will be developed first: "For the wrath of God is revealed from heaven against all ungodliness and wickedness of those who by their wickedness suppress the truth" (1:18). We need not get into the debate over natural theology, which has made much use of Rom. 1:19f., nor does Paul's selection of sins contribute anything useful. When we ask about the concept of God that lies behind verses 18–32, some interesting parallels with Exodus 5—15 begin to appear. The sovereignty of God is the issue in both passages, in the sense of God's insistence on being acknowledged as the only God. Paul says pagans are to be judged because "they did not honor him as God or give thanks to him" (v. 21b), and they "exchanged the glory of the immortal God for images" (v. 23a). Knowledge of God, which we found to be a major theme running through Exodus 5—15, is also important here, although Paul uses it somewhat differently. Pagans need no "signs and wonders" in order to bring them to a knowledge of the true God, Paul claims, for enough evidence of his power and divine nature is visible in creation that they have no excuse for not recognizing what the true divine nature is (vv. 19–21a).[43] Their refusal to acknowledge God is thus comparable to Pharaoh's refusals in spite of the repeated demonstrations of God's power that he witnessed. The result is that God once again allows nature to turn against itself, to destroy itself. The fact that in Paul's reasoning, sin is described as God's punishment of idolators, which has caused a great deal of discussion among commentators,[44] appears in an interesting light when looked at in this way. Cosmology has been replaced to a great extent by anthropology in the New Testament, and so it is human nature alone that is described as turning against itself in self-destructive ways.

Much has been made of the threefold statement, "God gave them up" to lusts, degrading passions, and debased minds (vv. 24, 26, 28).[45] This is a strange analogy to the mystery of God's hardening the heart of Pharaoh. Now, however, God is not said to inflict pain directly, in order to prove his sovereignty, as in Exodus, but is said to allow pain as a result of the sins that are produced by unbelief. Paul uses "wrath" here in a sense closer to that of the Old Testament, for unlike its usual New Testament reference to the last days, he finds evidence of the working out of God's wrath in present history, in perversions of human nature that he believes to be the result of failure to believe in the one true God. The gospel, however, is the good news that the wrath to come need be feared no longer by those who have faith in Jesus Christ.

Romans 5:1–11 is a kind of summary passage, making the transition between major sections of the letter, and as such it presents in a few words Paul's message that God has in Jesus Christ made an entirely new response to sin. For our purposes, we need to begin reading in the middle of the text, with sinners: "For while we were still weak, at the right time Christ died for the ungodly. . . . But God proves his love for us in that while we still were sinners Christ died for us" (Rom. 5:6, 8). We hear nothing now of destruction of the sinner; rather it is Christ who has been destroyed, in order to show God's love for the sinner. Destruction still occurs, but it is suffered by the maintainer of justice, and this frees sinners from the judgment they deserve: "the wrath" (v. 9). Love and wrath appear side by side, in verses 8–9, and there is no suggestion of any conflict within God, and certainly not a hint of setting the love and mercy of Christ over against the justice and wrath of God the Father.[46] The death of Christ is the proof of God's love (v. 8a), and in the light of the tradition we have been tracing, it does not seem inappropriate to say that God's love for sinners has the effect of "reversing" his wrath upon himself.

This does not mean that those with faith in Christ have been freed from all the destructive forces in this world, however. Paul knew from experience that suffering still occurs. Some of that, of course, is certainly still the result of sin, but here, as in 2 Thessalonians 1, he thinks of the suffering that is the result of being a Christian. He has found that suffering need not be destructive, and so destruction itself has been transformed by Christ's acceptance of it for himself. Suffering as a

Christian may be joyfully accepted (vv. 3–5), for the love of God can transform it from a destructive to a constructive experience. What God has done about evil in the world has been to take it upon himself. That has not yet abolished it, so it is still necessary at times to think about the wrath to come. But the New Testament writers do not feel the need to say very much about that, for they already sense themselves participating in God's new creation, which is coming into being after the destruction of the old, on the cross.

So Paul affirms, in 2 Cor. 5:17–21, "If anyone is in Christ, there is a new creation: everything old has passed away; see, everything has become new." Something had to be destroyed, but that has already happened. Our focus on this aspect of the message means that here, as in Romans 5, it helps to read the passage backward, for it is at the end that we encounter sin. The passage ends where the gospel begins, with the sinless one becoming "sin" (v. 21). All interpreters agree that this does not say Christ somehow became a sinner. Rather he accepted the burden of human guilt for himself; "he came to stand in that relation with God which normally is the result of sin, estranged from God and the object of his wrath."[47] That is not to say, however, as some have insisted on doing, that the will of Christ was somehow different from the will of God the Father, for it was God who was doing the reconciling in Christ, as verse 19 says. For our sake the effects of sin were born by Christ—"not counting their trespasses against them"—but there is no distinction between the work of Christ and the work of God, as verses 18–19 show.

If the death of Christ meant that God himself had somehow become the object of divine destruction, this meant that Christ and God must somehow be one. This is a part of the data that went into the development of the theology of incarnation, and then into the doctrine of the Trinity. That may not have been predictable, from where we began, in this chapter, but aspects of Trinitarian theology will in fact be the major emphasis as this chapter reaches its conclusion.

Christianity

The biblical witness to God's exercise of destructive power in the world has produced several lines of tradition in Christian history, and has led to a series of ongoing debates concerning the nature of God. On the one hand, most Christians probably agree with the need for something like the second-century author Lactantius's defense of the attribution of anger to God:

> For it is not right that, when He sees such things [slaughter, fraud, plunder, etc.], He should not be moved, and arise to take vengeance upon the wicked, and destroy the pestilent and guilty, so as to promote the interests of all good men. Thus even in anger itself there is also contained a showing of kindness.[48]

On the other hand, many Christians have instinctively reacted against the idea of a destructive God, so that there has been a continuing willingness to agree with statements such as this:

And the defect of the Jewish presentation of God in much of the Old Testament is the imputation to him of strong vindictiveness with liability to such passing human emotions as rage, fury and jealousy, hence the thoughtful and refined heretic Marcion pronounced the God of the Jews just, but not wholly good. And Christianity to our own day has been in its doctrine of judgment in bondage to the Judaic spirit, of which it inherited a large measure from the beginning.[49]

Each of the related themes has produced such an extensive literature in the history of Christianity that for this section it will have to suffice to list them with some description and a minimum of exemplification. Since contemporary thought now suggests a certain coincidence between what natural science understands about destruction and death in the world and what scripture says about God's activity, most of the section will be devoted to a development of those ideas.

Six related themes can be classified under two headings: one concerning "destructions" of various kinds, and the second concerning questions about the nature of God.

"Destructions"

1. Like Job's friends, many Christians have believed the orthodox understanding of the justice of God permitted them to deduce sin from suffering. Calamities of every kind, from individual illness to natural disasters such as earthquakes, to the fall of the Roman Empire, have been thus interpreted as sure signs of God's intervention in the world to punish sin. But, apart from direct divine inspiration, God's moral judgments cannot be read off from historical events in that way, as experience and good theology have taught.[50] Many, Christian and otherwise, still cannot resist the temptation, however, and so this effort to understand God must still be dealt with in theology.
2. After the New Testament period, the concept of hell, which is described in the briefest terms in early Jewish and Christian literature, was greatly elaborated. By the Middle Ages, the tendency for European Christianity to focus on the afterlife included what we can only call a surrender to the human fascination with violence, projecting tortures even worse than those used in daily life into eternity. They believed it to be the will of God that sinners should suffer so, as a much later author, Jonathan Edwards, made plain in his well-known sermon, "Sinners in the Hands of an Angry God."[51] But we have seen that hell is background to the New Testament message, and it is certainly true that on this subject Christians have said a great deal on a subject about which they really know nothing.
3. From time to time expectations that God will soon intervene to bring a complete end to history have flourished, and these, of course, have produced elaborations of the ideas in Old Testament eschatology and in the book of Revelation concerning the destruction of the old world, so that a new creation may take its place. Liberal scholarship sought to dismiss all that as "myth," but current cosmology, which suggests the present expansion of the universe will one day reverse itself, leading to the end of the cosmos, has been called "far more bizarre and dramatic than anything that the Hebrew imagination conceived."[52] Thus we may not be able to escape

thinking about how our understanding of God can account for the potential destruction of all creation.

Questions about the Nature of God

1. Is the "wrath of God" to be understood as personal or impersonal? Scripture clearly speaks of a personal God, but the influence of Greek philosophy on Christianity has been so profound that the notion of God as "pure Being," not subject to any needs, emotions, or changes, tended to be taken by most theologians as if it were revealed truth. The willingness of twentieth-century thinkers to take a new look at everything has led several to conclude that the biblical picture of a personal God has philosophical validity, as well as corresponding to the way believers have experienced God all along.[53]

2. Can wrath, which includes the destruction of his creation, be rightly attributed to a loving God? The quotation from Lactantius, above, shows that this had already become an issue in the second century C.E., for his main concern in his treatise on the anger of God is to combat the influence of Epicureanism, which led some Christian writers to claim God could experience love but not wrath. C. H. Dodd, in his commentary on Romans, upheld essentially the position Lactantius was attacking, but he maintained that "wrath" in the New Testament is impersonal on the basis of his understanding of scripture, not because of Epicurean philosophy.[54] Other contemporary writers, however, argue that wrath, properly understood, is an essential part of divine love, properly understood, but their work contributes little that is explicit for our concern about God's destructive activity in nature.[55]

3. If Jesus experienced the effects of the divine destruction of sin on the cross, did God the Father participate in any way in that suffering? Early in the history of the church, "patripassionism," the belief that God the Father suffered on the cross, was declared to be an error, and discussions of the doctrine of the Trinity have frequently struggled to separate God the Father from God the Son, with reference to suffering. It seemed to solve the problem to say the God the Son suffered and died on the cross, while God the Father remained untouched and unmoved by it. This complicated the understanding of incarnation, however; for some, who were determined to protect God from suffering of any kind, claimed that it was only Christ's human nature that suffered, while his divine nature was somehow isolated from what happened on the cross.

Contemporary theology, while usually not becoming completely patripassionist, tends to take the suffering of God with great seriousness, and is approaching it from several directions.[56] This is not a subject that can appropriately be developed here, but it is one of the related themes, because of the New Testament's claim that the remedy for evil is to be found in the death of the Son of God on the Cross. The approach to be suggested next will have to make some use of it, however.

What do we make of Heb. 10:21: "It is a fearful thing to fall into the hands of the living God," or of Heb. 12:29: "for indeed our God is a consuming fire"? Note that this is the *New* Testament, and that I am quoting from the book that emphasizes as strongly as possible Christ's once-for-all sacrifice for sins, which means we can "approach with a true heart in full assurance of faith, with our hearts sprinkled clean" (Heb. 10:22). We have just noted that some distort the God of the Bible by emphasizing only the fearful side, by explaining all disasters as "acts of God," or by making more of the threat of hell than scripture does. Others move toward dualism, in order to protect the idea of a loving God, and blame all the destructive activity in the world on the devil. To them, the title of this chapter will sound shocking, if not blasphemous. Most Christians seem to assume that evil has to be *destroyed* somehow, and during these first two millennia a violent destruction of some sort has almost always been in the picture. But now and then the idea of universal salvation appears, and that presumably would call for the eventual revoking of free will and some sort of "smothering" of evil with love. And of course we were reminded by the materials in chapter 1 that others will question whether God does anything, beneficial or destructive, in the world.

Must we who live late in the twentieth century, sensitized to pain perhaps more than any who have lived before us, now set about to correct the biblical picture of God on the assumption that all of the destruction in scripture is entirely due to the human fixation on violence? At the beginning of this chapter I pointed out that the subject would impinge on creation-theology, and I believe that approaching the question via what natural science teaches us about the way the world works will be helpful.

Was the world created without pain, violence, or death, as Genesis 1 suggests, and as many have affirmed more explicitly than the Bible does? If so, it was a very different world from anything we have known or can really imagine, from its simplest biological processes to its major geological movements. George Williams points out that two points of view have been represented by Christian writers.[57] The one explains all the suffering in nature as the result of human sin, drawing its reasons largely from Gen. 3:14–19. The other implicates only humans and the angels in the effects of sin, which means nature today is as God made it. The former seems virtually impossible, now, in spite of its rather widespread use in the past, for our improved understanding of the physical and biological processes that make life itself possible has revealed that destruction, pain, and death are essential to them. They had to be present long before human life, and human sin, appeared on earth.

> The death of old organisms is a prerequisite for the appearance of new ones. For the death of individuals is essential for release of food resources for new arrivals and the death of species for creating biological 'niches' for new species. . . . But in biological evolution the creation of the new does not happen without pain and suffering and both seem unavoidable.[58]

We begin, then, by taking seriously the essential roles of destruction, pain, and death in the way the world functions, accepting as God's creative work all those features of the nonhuman world that cannot be explained as the result of human tampering. They include the geophysical forces: volcanoes, earthquakes, storms, floods, meteors, drought, glaciers, and the movement of the sea. These forces destroy and rebuild landforms, and as a result the life that depends on those landforms either changes or dies. The human experience of such events as earthquakes and volcanic eruptions has led philosophers to call them "natural evils," but we shall avoid as much as possible the term "evil," since it is so tricky. A short excursus will be necessary here, in order to explain why this section is not a treatise on the problem of evil.

There is, in fact, no "problem of evil" in the Bible, as philosophers and theologians have debated it. That is, the writers of scripture never ask about the origin of evil (the snake in Genesis 3 explains nothing about origins), never try to explain how there can be evil in a world created and ruled by a good God (not even in Job). They all assume God is good and God is sovereign, and they know evil is real, but they do not try to resolve the paradox. The Bible deals with existential rather than logical questions, and so the scriptural subject is not the "problem of evil," but the "problem of pain." That requires no definition, as evil does.[59] We know what pain is, but what is or is not evil is a moral judgment, made by human beings (often with a claim of divine validation). And so the philosophers and theologians define evil as they please, which makes defining it away one of the routes to theodicy. So-called natural evil is one of the regular problems in the debate over how evil should be defined, and that is why this excursus is necessary here. Is a volcanic eruption evil if no humans are in the way, to get hurt? Then it depends on one's concern for the chipmunks and the trees. But no such judgments are necessary when we focus, as scripture does, on pain. We know what that is, and the existential questions are straightforward: How to avoid it? How to get rid of it? How to bear it?[60]

We shall not try to define "natural evil," then, but shall only observe that these geophysical forces kill great amounts of animate and inanimate life, causing extensive pain in the process, and as far as we can tell now, this is the way God created the world. In the realm of biological processes the situation seems to be the same. Even lay people are coming to understand what biologists have known for a long time: Within the world's ecosystems, normal life cycles depend on the destruction and death of other living things. Even if all the animals on earth were to become vegetarians, they would be destroying the life of plants, and the plants get their life from the decay of other plants and animal matter in the soil. We don't know whether inanimate forms of life experience pain, as some process theologians suggest, but their death and decay is evident, and its necessity is evident.

Then come violent disruptions of ecosystems, such as drought, plagues of insects, and disease, wiping out some species entirely. These had been happening long before human beings began to speed up that process, so it must have been the way the world was created. Too much emphasis on this side of nature can lead to serious doubts about the character of God, so we must remind ourselves that one of the traditional proofs of the existence of God pointed to the order and beauty in the world, and we must not forget that is also part of what God has done. It is not our present subject, however.

All of life, as we know it, involves pain and requires death. (Having reached the age where something hurts every day, I am not talking abstractions.) Could this mean that, if there is a Creator at all, he is either a sadist or totally inept?[61] I do not believe that, since what I know of the world, its horrors and its blessings, corresponds to scripture's testimony to a righteous Creator. But we must examine this further. Exodus 5—15 tells us that God killed a great many fish, frogs, cattle, trees, horses, and human beings. Presumably all of the animals and many of the human beings could be called "innocent," so all of that dying cannot be accounted for by saying it was punishment for sin. It was the people left alive who were "punished" by all this. And the others would all have died eventually, anyway. Yet, death is regularly identified as one of the great evils, even though it is inevitable and necessary. Everything dies, except amoebas, and their lifestyle is scarcely to be coveted. If we all lived forever, the world could not support us, so what's the problem?

There is a problem, of course. We grieve the loss of loved ones, especially when they seem to die too young, and grief is one of the parts of life we would like to do without.[62] But if death is necessary, could we then be truly human and be free from the experience of grief?[63] Furthermore, we cannot really conceive of our own death. Arnold Toynbee commented on the fact that we call ourselves "mortals," when in fact everything is mortal. He said we must distinguish ourselves from other dying things in that way because it doesn't seem right that we should be mortal.[64] The truism that everyone has to die, sooner or later, doesn't solve that problem, but Christians have found another solution, the promise of eternal life with Christ, which means that Paul's "last enemy to be destroyed," death (1 Cor. 15:26), has already been destroyed, as they face their own deaths. From the Christian perspective, then, instructed by a realistic understanding of how our world works, death in itself need not be labeled "evil."

> We really cannot envision a world, on any Earth more or less like our own, which can give birth to the myriad forms of life that have been generated here, without some things eating other things. Life preys on life. . . . Here again, biologist and theologian need not quarrel that nature is perpetually renewed in the midst of its perishing. That is a fact of the matter. Indeed, biologist and theologian may agree that the logic of creation requires destruction as well as construction, on scales both large and small, both before humans arrive and after as well. . . . The question is not whether the world is, or ever was, a happy place. Rather the question is whether it is a place of significant suffering through to something higher.[65]

As Israel told the story of the exodus, the God who "kills and brings to life" (1 Sam. 2:6) chose to kill all those animals and people, at that time, for a necessary purpose. Death remains a problem for us, of course, when it seems untimely, and most of all, when it is extremely painful. Pain also seems a necessary part of our world, but excessive pain cannot be explained away by any means. That problem is the true issue of theodicy, and to deal with it in full would take us beyond the subject of this chapter, and in fact beyond what the materials of the Bible can contribute. But since destruction and death involve pain, we must go as far as our materials allow us to do.

All of life, as we know it, involves pain. The newborn's first act is to cry. A world without pain would presumably be inanimate. Paul Brand's work with those afflicted by leprosy, who have lost the sense of pain in the affected parts of their bodies, has given him insights into this subject most of the rest of us lack. He realizes that pain is essential for *healthy* life, since it protects us from doing severe harm to our bodies. He even experimented with trying to provide artificial pain for leprosy patients, but found he could not replace what God had once given. He concluded, "Pain exists not as a proof of God's lack of concern, but because it has a place in creation significant enough that it cannot be removed without great loss."[66]

Suppose we consider the potential of thinking about the nature of God not in the philosophers' terms—absolute Being—but the way scripture speaks of him: "the Living God." The term is not used with great frequency in the Bible, but it is well distributed, occurring thirteen times in the Old Testament (excluding two parallels), and fourteen times in the New Testament, and in a variety of literary types. The various writers used the term most often to speak of the intense vitality, the active presence of God:

> For who is there of all flesh that has heard the voice of the living God speaking out of fire, as we have, and remained alive? (Deut. 5:26)

> My soul thirsts for God, for the living God. When shall I come and behold the face of God? (Ps. 42:2)

> We are mortals just like you, and we bring you good news, that you should turn from these worthless things to the living God, who made the heaven and the earth and the sea and all that is in them. (Acts 14:15)

> For to this end we toil and struggle, because we have our hope set on the living God, who is the Savior of all people, especially of those who believe. (1 Tim. 4:10)

All of our language about God is only analogy, and must be used with the greatest caution,[67] but this term, "living God," suggests it may not be inappropriate to consider what our knowledge of life on earth may teach us about the nature of God, insofar as those conclusions correspond with what scripture says. If God is the Living God, what does it mean that all life as we know it involves pain?

Are we justified in thinking there may be correspondences between life as God knows it and life as we know it? Contemporary theology is much bolder in drawing such conclusions than traditional theology could allow, for tradition was dominated by the philosophical concept of the impassive God, unmoved and existing in pure bliss. Scripture speaks of God as Creator. All creative activity, as we know it, involves struggle, frustration, pain of one kind or another—always mental and spiritual and often physical as well. Could God's activity in creating the world have been completely different? Certainly, we must admit Genesis 1 suggests it, since there he simply speaks and it happens, but Genesis 2 describes it as happening in stages, with God considering what is needed next, and the poets of Israel even dared to borrow the mythological themes of combat as they spoke of creation as a victory (Ps. 74:12–17; Isa. 51:9–11). Could it be that God did not create life on this earth to be any different from what it is now—for example, he did not make it blissful—because there is no such life, not even the life of God himself?

The Bible depicts God not only as a Creator, who is not a part of the world he has made, but also as one who desires, establishes, and maintains a relationship with his world, and most closely with human beings. So he is called husband (Hos. 2:16) and father (Isa. 63:16; Matt. 6:9), and both Testaments insist he has made a covenant with humankind. The doctrine of the Trinity even insists that relationship is inherent in the nature of God himself. But all relationships, as we know them, involve pain of various kinds. Much of the pain in human relationships is clearly due to sin, but it is doubtful that can account for all of it. Human freedom, even in the most loving relationships, leads to tension, misunderstanding, and frustration, and not all of that can be blamed on sin. It is in part the inevitable result of our uniqueness as individuals. In nature, relationships are even more uncompromising, for in addition to a lot of cooperation in ecological systems, life is ultimately based on the consumption of one life form by another. We find no evidence in this world for the possibility of relationships based on freedom that do not involve some of this harshness. A. R. Peacocke's considerations of the place of death and pain in the structuring of the universe led him to this conclusion: "So the very order and impersonality of the physical cosmos which makes pain and suffering inevitable for conscious and self-conscious creatures is, at the same time, also the prerequisite of their exercise of freedom as persons."[68] Can we comprehend a world of living, interrelated creatures without pain of any kind? Having already thought about our grief at the loss of loved ones, it would seem that love will always lead to pain, whether or not sin is involved.

Scripture speaks of God as Creator, as Love, as one who intimately involves himself in a relationship with the people he has made. Recent theology is bold enough to assert that this life, as we know it on earth, is a reflection (greatly distorted, of course) of the life of God, and this must mean that the life of God also involves pain.

> Christianity seeks to draw the harshness of nature into the concept of God, as it seeks by a doctrine of providence to draw all affliction into the divine will. . . . God is not in a simple way the Benevolent Architect, but is rather the Suffering Redeemer. . . . God rescues from suffering, but the Judeo-Christian faith never teaches that God eschews suffering in the achievement of the divine purposes. To the contrary, seen in the paradigm of the cross, God too suffers, not less than his creatures, in order to gain for his creatures a more abundant life.[69]

Of God's work as Creator, Peacocke has written, "There is always *pathos* in persons creating something which then has independent, if derived, existence and such *pathos* can be properly predicated of God as Creator."[70] Of God as Love, Paul Fiddes writes, "Christian theologians have been required to reflect upon the meaning of God's love for the world in the light of a modern psychological understanding of what it means to be personal. Truly personal love, it has been emphasized, will involve the suffering of the one who loves; the world being what it is, love must be costly and sacrificial, if only in terms of mental pain."[71] Both testaments speak of God's love in this way (Isa. 63:9f.; 65:1–2; Hos. 11:8.f; Rom. 5:6–8; 1 John 4:9f.). When God's destructive wrath against sin was accepted by Jesus on the cross, it was thus not a father offering his son as a human sacrifice, as some have caricatured it, but God's own self-sacrifice. As Ronald Goetz has written, "But in nature, history and Scripture the 'love' of God is expressed in terrifying terms—a universe born in explosion, evolution lubricated by the blood of every creature, a history that is inevitably conflictual and tragic, and a love for sinners that requires the death of God's innocent son."[72] When he asks, "Is there a wrenching within the very Godhead over the ruthlessness of the divine means—inevitable violence, sin, suffering and death—and the love, self-sacrifice and mercy of God's redemptive ends?" our studies in this chapter seem to require us to offer a cautious yes. The yes is possible because our work supports Goetz's own conclusion: "For me it is only by God suffering with us, suffering at our hands as we suffer at God's own hands, that God can establish the credentials of a lover" (277).

Long ago, however, the prophets of Israel insisted God's intention for his world is a completely tension-free and painless life: peace on earth. Zechariah's vision of the new Jerusalem saw a place where

> [o]ld men and old women shall again sit in the streets of Jerusalem, each with staff in hand because of their great age. And the streets of the city shall be full of boys and girls playing in its streets. . . . For there shall be a sowing of peace; the vine shall yield its fruit, the ground shall give its produce, and the skies shall give their dew; and I will cause the remnant of this people to possess all these things. (Zech. 8:4f., 12)

The third Isaiah foresaw a new Jerusalem in which there would be no more weeping, no sound of distress, where dying before one reached a hundred years would be considered premature (note that he sees no need for death itself to be done away with), and where "they shall not hurt or destroy" (Isa. 65:17–25).[73] Israel was so convinced that this was God's real intention for his world that they projected the same ideas back to the beginning, saying God created a world that was "very good" (Gen. 1:31). The reflections in this section are not intended to deny the truth of that, but they may call for a redefinition of what God means by "good."

They lead us to ask whether human dreams of bliss, even those reinforced by prophetic visions, may be conducive to harmful fantasies; harmful because they make us less able to deal constructively with the pain that is an inescapable, and it seems essential, part of life.[74] Scripture says a world without tears is also God's dream for us (Rev. 21:4); theodicy keeps asking, Why not now? The only answer seems to be that a world without tears would really be a new heaven and new earth, as Isaiah 65 and Revelation 21 say, a world not at all like this world. They say it is coming; our reflections remind us that the new creation will involve still more pain for God, so that presumably when one day there are creatures without pain, they will be less like God than we are. As we look back at the texts from Paul discussed earlier, it seems that the incarnation and the cross were already understood by the early church to be the first stages of that new creation (2 Cor. 5:17; Rom. 8:18–25), and the suffering of Christians was understood to be participation in the divine pain of that new creation (2 Cor. 4:10f.; Rom. 8:17; Phil. 1:29f.; 1 Peter 4:13). Scripture provides no philosophically rigorous answer to theodicy's question, Why not now? It does have a great deal to say in answer to the existential question, In the meantime, how then can we live?

The notion that in some way God suffers is a disturbing one to many, for they cannot believe that suffering is anything other than the result of weakness. Even some of the theologians who now support the belief in a suffering God accept that as a corollary, and think they need also to justify belief in a weak God. I claim that scripture speaks of a God who suffers pain, which is not an indication of weakness, but of his vitality. God's pain is evidence that he is fully alive, creative, and involved in real, intimate relationships with the living things he has made. He is active killing and bringing to life, not in any heaven of our imagination—all sweetness and light—but filled with what must remain to us a highly disturbing vigor in which creating includes destroying and loving includes weeping. No "bliss" there, so it should be no shock to us that bliss also eludes us. And yet the New Testament speaks of the intense *joy* those first Christians experienced, and the worship language of the Old Testament is filled with rejoicing. Have I missed something? No, I have just delayed it until now. Bliss won't do; even happiness may be too much to expect. As Robert Frost said, "Happiness makes up in height for what it lacks in length."[75] Let me try another word, and suggest that Christians experience something like "glee" when we discover that we can put our pain to work and make something of it (as God does), and thereby become "more than conquerors."

This, it will be recognized, is no attempt to construct a theodicy. Excessive pain is another subject, related, but involving materials that have not been a part of our work in this chapter. The effort throughout this rather long discussion has been only to understand some of the disturbing things the Bible says about God, in order to decide whether they represent only "primitive" notions, or whether we may in fact discover that they are accurate reflections of the full spectrum of the Christian's experience of the love of God in Jesus Christ.

CHAPTER 7

GOD OF GRACE AND GOD OF GLORY

Exodus 15b—31; 35—40

As Israel remembered the exodus and its consequences, they associated two very different kinds of activities with God in Egypt and with God in their early days in the wilderness. God does nothing destructive in chapters 15b through 31. There are some warnings and threats concerning the future, but the only violent activity recorded takes place entirely at the human level, when the Israelites under the leadership of Joshua and Moses beat off an attack by the Amalekites (Ex. 17:8–13). The strongest verb used with God as subject in the pre-Sinai wilderness materials is "test" (*nissah*), and that in fact may be a key word for this section. No test results in punishment, however, for even though the theme of "murmuring in the wilderness" is introduced immediately, God's reaction to it is to hear (16:7, 8, 9, 12) and to help, without any mention of impatience or judgment, such as we encounter in the murmuring stories in Numbers. The wilderness materials in Exodus introduce us at length to the God of grace. He is also the God of glory, for the priestly parts use that word as their way of speaking about the immediate presence of God in the midst of his people, beginning with 16:10 and continued in the tabernacle materials (chapters 25—31, 35—40).

This is a long and complex section of Exodus, but I am dealing with it in a single chapter because it presents a uniform picture of Israel's memory that God graciously willed to establish an intimate relationship with them at the beginning of their existence as a people; indeed, they insist, it was that relationship that made them a people. As the book is now structured, God is said to have had a close relationship with Moses (and Aaron, for P) since chapter 3, but as yet there is no such relationship with Israel. He acts on their behalf for the sake of his promise to their ancestors (Ex. 2:24; 6:8), and they come to know of his will for them through the messages brought by Moses. Finally they are brought to believe in him (and Moses) by what they see done to the Egyptians at the Sea (14:31). As the book describes the period in Egypt, it depicts God as working for Israel from something of a distance (Exodus 3—14), and that continues through the early wilderness traditions (Exodus 15—18), with God bringing about a significant change at Sinai. The divine self-affirmations addressed to the Israelites in this section reveal this movement toward them: "I am Yahweh who heals you" (15:26); "Then you shall know that I am Yahweh your God" (16:12); "I am Yahweh your God, who brought you out of the land of Egypt" (20:2); "I, Yahweh your God, am a jealous God" (20:5); "I am compassionate" (22:27); "I will dwell among the Israelites, and I will be their God" (Ex. 29:45).

The relationship God established at Sinai was disrupted immediately by the scandal of the golden calf (Exodus 32—34), and that will in fact make a permanent change in it, but the Priestly redactor deliberately placed the materials concerning the building of the tabernacle, concluding with the appearance of the glory of God, after that event (chapters 35—40), insisting that God still intends to be with his people. The subject matter of chapters 32—34 is in a class by itself, and will be dealt with in the final chapter of this book. Taking the activity of God as our guiding principle, we can divide the materials in Exodus 15:22–31:18 and chapters 35—40 into four parts, each of which emphasizes one feature that reflects God's movement toward Israel. They may be given the alliterative titles "Care" (chapters 15—18), "Covenant" (chapters 19 and 24), "Commandment" (chapters 20—23), and "Communion" (chapters 25—31, 35—40).

No part of the Bible contains as many literary and historical problems as this section of Exodus. It is impossible to write the history of the wilderness or Sinai experiences, and no one has offered a satisfactory explanation of the puzzling structure of chapters 19—24. Fortunately, these problems are not critical for our subject—Israel's conception of the nature of God—but the difficulties will be noted where necessary. There are other much-discussed subjects in these chapters which belong in a full-scale biblical theology, but which will not be developed here, because of the defined purpose of this book, with its focus on the concept of God. Left to one side, then, will be the office of Moses, some aspects of Israel's role as chosen people, the ethical and social significance of the Commandments, and all the details of Israel's worship.

Israel alluded to an intimate relationship with God early in its recital of the exodus story, when Moses was told to say to Pharaoh, "Thus says the LORD: Israel is my firstborn son" (Ex. 4:22). We have seen why the concept of "firstborn" was introduced so early; it was in anticipation of the tenth plague. Nothing more is made of that kind of relationship, however, until God addresses Israel at Mount Sinai (19:4–6). The intervening chapters describe first what God did *to* Egypt on Israel's behalf, then, in the wilderness, what he did to Israel, for their benefit, and at Sinai, what he did *with* Israel, in terms of covenant, commandment, and communion. As an example of this change in emphasis, in the tenth plague, the word used in connection with God's action is *mash-ḥith,* "destroyer" or "destruction," and it is active with reference to the Egyptians, passive with reference to Israel (Ex. 12:23). The first wilderness story, concerning the bitter water at Marah, speaks of God as the *rophe',* the healer active on behalf of Israel (15:26). But the Song of Moses (15:1–18) acts as a transitional passage between these two parts of the book. Most of it looks back at the Wonder at the Sea, but the latter part looks forward to celebrate God's positive work on Israel's behalf:

> In your steadfast love you led the people whom you redeemed;
>   you guided them by your strength to your holy abode.
> . . . .
> You brought them in and planted them on the mountain of your
>   own possession. (Ex. 15:13, 17a)

"Steadfast love" (*ḥesed*) will be a very important word later in the book; but this is the first time it has occurred in Exodus. The intervening verses, 14–16, speak of the terror and dread that afflict Philistia, Edom, Moab, and Canaan as the Israelites make their triumphal progress to the mountain of God, so the song properly belongs with the first part of the book of Exodus, but it does anticipate what is coming, and we shall see another kind of transition being made at this point in the book as we compare the structure of the "murmuring" stories with chapter 14.

Care: Exodus 15:22–18:27

From God's perspective, the theme of these stories is not "murmuring in the wilderness" but "care in the wilderness." There is a significant difference between the way Israel's need for water, bread, and meat is told in Exodus and in the parallel passages in Numbers, where God's anger bursts out against them, and they are sometimes severely punished (Numbers 11; 20). There can be little doubt that the final authors selected the differing versions of these stories so as to locate all stories that spoke of judgment after the incident of the golden calf. In Exodus, God's activity is all positive. He hears, gives, instructs, commands, and promises healing. The testing (15:25; 16:4) has an ominous ring, because we know what is coming, but it produces no negative effects as yet. There are no sin words in chapters 15—18. The account of the visit of Jethro in chapter 18 is a special case, for although God is referred to frequently, he neither speaks nor acts. There is a very prominent emphasis on God's deliverance of Israel from Egypt (*natsal*: 18:4, 8, 9, 10; *yatsa'*: 18:1; *'asah*: 18:1, 8, 9), but this is not a new subject, so we need not focus on this chapter. God figures in the battle against the Amalekites only in the sequel, in which he threatens eventually to blot out the remembrance of Amalek (17:8–16). This is one of several references to God's future judgmental activity, which we shall consider in due time. The other wilderness stories follow a standard pattern, and that pattern plus other features that will be noted reveals that Israel retold them frequently enough that there came into existence the genre: wilderness story.

It was mentioned above that chapter 14 should be compared with the "murmuring stories," and at this point it will be helpful to lay out the pattern that appears there, in the three comparable stories in chapters 15—17, and also in Num. 20:1–13, which is the closest in structure to the Exodus material. The principal parts are as follows:[1]

> *A note concerning movement:* 14:1–2; 15:22b–23; 15:27–16:1; 17:1a; Num. 20:1.
>
> *Description of the problem:* 14:3–10a; 15:22b–23; 16 (missing; appears within the complaint); 17:1b; Num. 20:2a.
>
> *People complain:* 14:10b–12; 15:24; 16:2–3; 17:2–3; Num. 20:2b–5.
>
> *Moses cries to the Lord:* 14:13–14; 15:25a; 16 (missing); 17:4; Num. 20:6.
>
> *The Lord responds:* 14:15–18, 26; 15:25b; 16:4–5; 17:5–6a; Num. 20:7–8.
>
> *Moses obeys:* 14:21a, 27a; 15:25b; 16:6–12; 17:6b; Num. 20:9–11a.
>
> *Results:* 14:19–20, 21a–26, 27b–31a; 15:25c; 16:13–21; 17 (missing); Num. 20:11b.

Each story has a conclusion, but they vary considerably: 14:31b; 15:25d–26; 16:22–30; 17:7; Num. 20:12–13.

The outline shows clearly that there was a standard way to structure such a story, and this is supported by the fact that, with one exception, the verb we have traditionally translated "murmur" (*lun,* "complain" in NRSV) appears only in the wilderness stories.[2] In Exodus, unlike Numbers, it is taken to express a legitimate life-or-death need in desert conditions, and God responds immediately to their complaints with help.[3] At the very beginning of their story Israel expressed their belief in a God who provides for his people by telling how he made it possible even for a band of complete novices to survive in the desert. They made other uses of the wilderness traditions as well, emphasizing their rebelliousness, but we shall come to that later.

The account of the Wonder at the Sea in chapter 14 is an exact fit to the pattern, although the verb *lun* is not used, and it has sometimes been called a part of the wilderness tradition, rather than part of the exodus tradition proper.[4] The significant difference for our purposes is the kind of divine action recorded, as noted above, and so it seems that the author has used the Song of Moses to set off chapter 14 from the wilderness material. With the brief account of the problem of bitter water at Marah, he introduces a new section of the book, in which God immediately begins to establish his relationship with Israel by showing them the kind of God he intends to be to them. These final verses of chapter 15 seem fragmentary, and that may be because the author has overloaded this first wilderness story with indications of what is to come. Let us try to interpret 15:22–26 in that way.

Life in the desert is hard, and the Israelites were well aware of that, so every wilderness story they told dealt with a critical problem of some kind. It was surely appropriate that the need for water was put first in the sequence. Immediately the author introduces the verb *lun,* "murmur" or "complain." He did not use it in chapter 14, perhaps because it functions to hold together the wilderness traditions in Exodus and Numbers as a discrete group. God's provision for sweetening the water is described very briefly, and then are added some comments that have puzzled commentators. "There the LORD made for them a statute and an ordinance and there he put them to the test" (15:25b). It is unlikely that this was part of the original Marah tradition, but it now has an important function as an introduction to the rest of the book of Exodus. We are not told what the statute and ordinance may have been, and are given no explanation how the bitter water was understood as a test, but looking ahead, both statements make sense.

Every relationship requires some mutually accepted ground rules, if it is to succeed, and every relationship involves some testing at first, as the participants learn what to expect of one another. At Sinai God will establish the ground rules, but the author thinks it is appropriate to introduce the subject here, since the establishment of the relationship is already under way. He adds an explanation of their value: "If you will listen carefully to the voice of the LORD your God, and do what is right in his sight, and give heed to his commandments and keep all his statutes, I will not bring upon you any of the diseases that I brought upon the Egyptians; for I am the LORD who heals you" (15:26). God's character has been demonstrated by the caring act of providing sweet water, and at the end of the pericope his character is summed up by a title: Healer (cf. Ex. 23:25). The Old Testament does not develop that aspect of God's work at length, although sickness and healing are connected with his saving activity in the psalms of lament, and some eschatological passages include the promise of healing in the last days (Isa. 29:18; 33:23–24; 35:5–6; 42:7, 16; Jer. 31:8; Micah 6:7; Zeph. 3:19).[5] It will become a very important part of the New Testament message, but it is striking that the author has chosen to introduce it here.

The theme of testing runs through this section of Exodus, for the verb *nissah* occurs with both God and the people as subject. Prior to this, it has appeared only once, when God is said to have tested Abraham by telling him to take his only son, Isaac, and offer him up as a burnt offering (Gen. 22:1). That is by far the most troublesome use of the word, and we must not be diverted into a discussion of that passage here. Elsewhere, when God is the subject, the verb refers to an aspect of human freedom. It is used in cases where people clearly know what is right, but the question is whether they will do the right thing or not. In Ex. 16:4 God gives the Israelites instructions on what to do with the manna, then adds, "In that way I will test them, whether they will follow my instruction or not." When the people are terrified at the awesome display on Mount Sinai, Moses explains, "Do not be afraid, for God has come only to test you and to put the fear of him upon you so that you do not sin" (Ex. 20:20). Elsewhere it is associated with the wilderness experiences in general (Deut. 8:2, 16), with the temptations to follow the ways of the Canaanites rather than God's ways (Judg. 2:22; 3:1, 4), and with Hezekiah's freedom to decide what to do about envoys from Babylon (2 Chron. 32:31). Early in the story of the establishment of the relationship, then, we see that it is being made with a partner who is free to obey or disobey.

The use of this verb is anticipatory both of the giving of the law and of Israel's failure to obey it, for it is used four times in this section, and twice it is Israel who tests God. At Rephidim there was no water to drink, and Moses accused them of testing God, perhaps because by that time they should have seen abundant evidence that he was caring for them (Ex. 17:2). At the end of the story, the place is given two names, Massah, which is derived from the verb we have been studying, and Meribah, derived from a verb meaning "contend," and the explanation is added, "because the Israelites quarreled and tested the LORD, saying, 'Is the LORD among us or not?' " (17:7). That question also anticipates what is coming, for eventually the Priestly writer will give the resounding answer: "I will dwell among the Israelites, and I will be their God" (Ex. 29:45). When we know what is coming, this fourfold use of "test" has an almost ironic ring to it, because with the golden calf Israel failed Yahweh's test, and from the calf incident on, Israel will test Yahweh beyond any right. So I have identified it as a key word because it is an intimation of how the rest of the wilderness sojourn will go. It becomes a part of the tradition of "rebellion in the wilderness," recurring in Num. 14:22; Deut. 6:16; 33:8; Pss. 78:18, 41, 56; 95:9; and 106:14.

There is at least one more anticipation of what is to come, in this section, and that refers to the Priestly writer's use of "glory" to denote God's visible presence in the midst of his people. Eventually that will be connected with the tabernacle, but the story of the giving of the manna is given a special prominence by the appearance of the glory of the Lord before meat and bread is promised (Ex. 16:7, 10). As we shall see later, Israel's most prominent memory of the wilderness period was that it was a time of great danger in which they inevitably failed the test, a time when God punished them for their rebelliousness, and yet did not give up on them. God's patience will become a major theme. That makes it all the more remarkable that the wilderness stories selected for this position in Exodus emphasize so strongly God's gracious care for his chosen people and the potential that once lay before them for a better relationship than in fact they had ever been able to enjoy.

Covenant: Exodus 19 and 24

It seems safe to say that the structure of Exodus 19—24 presents more unanswerable questions than any other part of the Old Testament. At the most elementary level, it is not even possible to be certain how many times Moses is supposed to have ascended and descended Mount Sinai.[6] The Decalogue interrupts the context in a highly puzzling way. An innocent, first reader would not know what was inscribed on the stone tablets until Ex. 34:28 says it was the Ten Commandments (Ex. 34:28).

These are examples of the problems that have led scholars to try elaborate analyses into sources, complicated proposals of a series of redactions, and radical reconstructions of the supposed actual history lying behind the Sinai experience. No one can be said to have succeeded.[7] My very tentative suggestion is that these are materials most of which have been preserved in the liturgy, hence in a context of worship rather than a historical context. Important aspects of the Sinai experience were probably celebrated regularly and were thus well known, but we find no evidence that Israel had preserved a coherent memory of how the theophany at the mountain in the desert (even the name is uncertain: Sinai or Horeb?) led to the sealing of a covenant relationship between themselves and Yahweh, accompanied by the necessary qualifications of that relationship. The final author of Exodus seems to have combined those liturgical fragments as best he could, without having access to a tradition that told him how they belonged together. Sinai may have been from the beginning, then, less a part of history and more a part of worship than the other traditional materials used in the Pentateuch.[8]

The most radical approaches to the Sinai materials will claim the whole thing is the construction of a late author, and given the scarcity of references to covenant making at Sinai in the rest of the Old Testament, one cannot show that to be obviously wrong.[9] The uniqueness of the material and its lasting impact on late Israel and early Judaism, however, raise serious questions about whether it can simply be explained as a work of a creative theologian of the exilic or postexilic period. Whether the idea of the covenant is to be dated very early, such as at the time of the exodus, or as late as the book of Deuteronomy (eighth or seventh century) is at present an unsettled question.[10] Even the widely accepted belief that the covenant was the basis for law in Israel has been challenged, and defended.[11] In 1972 Dennis McCarthy wrote that we do not yet have anything like an adequate theology of the covenant.[12] It seems there has been little effort to remedy that in the past twenty years, and furthermore we must add there is nothing like an adequate history of the covenant. Fortunately, the historical questions just noted need not be solved in order to understand what Israel testified concerning the nature of its God, since there is consistency on that subject between these otherwise confusing traditions and the rest of the Old Testament.[13]

The word "covenant" is actually not very common in Exodus, and it is completely missing from large portions of the Old Testament, so I propose to look at the various kinds of evidence for the nature of God's relationship with Israel, using covenant, where it appears, as only one part of that evidence. Exodus begins with references to the covenant with the ancestors, as God remembers his promises to Abraham, Isaac, and Jacob (2:24; 6:4–5). That led, as we have seen, to God's intervention in history in order to establish an exclusive relationship with their descendants. "Israel is my firstborn son," is God's claim (Ex. 4:22), and that accompanies the refrain "my people," which occurs fifteen times in chapters

3—10 (plus "your people" in 5:23; 15:16). This is clearly one of the major themes of Exodus, since "my people" occurs only one other time in the Pentateuch (Lev. 26:12). At Sinai, God moves to make the exclusive relationship an intimate one. We have seen that essentially God had worked on their behalf from afar, until they reached the wilderness, but now the word "covenant" will be used at key points (and only there) to denote the relationship. It brackets the covenant-making scene (19:5; 24:7–8) and God's act of covenant remaking (34:10, 27–28). It does not define the relationship, the nature of which is worked out in detail in chapters 19—24, but only denotes it. Elsewhere we find the word "covenant" only in one reference to the Sabbath (presumably meaning it is to be observed as a sign of the Sinai covenant) and in warnings not to make covenants with the Canaanites (23:32; 34:12, 15), a new consequence of God's exclusive claim on Israel.

The nature of the relationship is expressed succinctly in the classic text 19:4–6. It has a few parallels with other passages, but contains some highly distinctive expressions. James Muilenberg has made a strong case for its unity, based on his rhetorical analysis,[14] but others less sensitive to its artistry continue to dissect it. Muilenberg also believed it to be archaic, and that is more difficult to establish. General opinion currently associates it either with a Deuteronomistic[15] or a priestly[16] redaction, but some of the ideas it contains are hard to explain as having originated in either milieu, and the possibility that it is an archaic liturgical fragment should not be dismissed out of hand. Whatever its date, it now serves to explain what is to come in succeeding chapters and to connect that with the exodus.

Since the speech is not easily compared with any other text, we may be justified in resorting to an analogy suggested earlier in Exodus as a way of relating it to other parts of the Old Testament. The use of the expression "firstborn" in Ex. 4:22 suggests using the imagery of adoption as a means of access to the ideas present here. This speech does not use parent-child language explicitly, but that analogy is commonly used in the Old Testament with reference to the relationship between God and Israel (cf. Deut. 32:6, 18; Isa. 50:1; 63:16; 64:8; Ezek. 16:1–7; Hos. 11:1–9).[17] R. J. Sklba may have gone a bit further than the evidence will support in claiming that the covenant is entirely based on the idea of kinship between Yahweh and Israel, but he calls our attention to significant aspects of the covenantal language.[18] Some of the language in 19:4–6 is not far removed from the imagery used of parent and child elsewhere. "I bore you on eagles' wings" is reminiscent of Deut. 32:11, which speaks of the eagle's care of its young. "Brought you to myself" and "treasured possession" allude to Yahweh's choice of Israel, and the verb *baḥar,* "choose," is used in direct connection with *segullah,* "treasured possession," in Deut. 7:6; 14:2; and Ps. 135:4. In Mal. 3:17 the treasured possession is explicitly compared with a child. Finally, obedience is the primary responsibility of the child in an Israelite family (Prov. 4:1–4; Deut. 21:18–21). The parent-child relationship will provide a useful analogy for understanding the first part of the Sinai experience, but like every analogy, it must not be pushed too far, and there will come a point where it clearly breaks down, and that in itself will be instructive.

"You have seen what I did to the Egyptians" (19:4a): This was an act of God's free initiative, and in fact God's motive for it remains unknown. The author of Deuteronomy puzzles over it and can attribute it only to love (Deut. 7:7–8), a feature that strongly suggests Deuteronomy is later than this, for in Exodus the question of motive does not come up. In adoption, the initiative is entirely that of the parents, and it is entirely a matter of free choice, unlike the birth of one's biological offspring, which may happen for a variety of reasons. Here also, Deuteronomy has recognized the implications of an idea that is not developed in Exodus, for it introduces the verb *bahar,* "choose," which is not used in Exodus. God, like adoptive parents, decided for reasons entirely his own, to take a child to whom he owed nothing, and to bring that child to himself.

The new relationship is thus a gift, and many interpreters of the Sinai covenant have emphasized that. In the act of deliverance from Egypt, God had already cared for Israel before he asked any response from them. He had begun to nurture them in the wilderness, and now he shows the strong desire to establish a closer relationship with them. As noted earlier, every good relationship requires mutual understanding of what the partners can expect of one another, and in the parent-child relationship, the child can expect love, protection, and nurture; the parent can expect love and obedience. So the next clause must be, "Now therefore, if you obey my voice and keep my covenant . . ." (19:5a). Note that covenant is not necessarily the key word in the passage; it just alludes to the relationship already established and to the conditions necessary to maintain it in harmony. More will be said about obedience in the section on commandment, and in the final chapter of the book, when God must decide how to deal with disobedience.

The adopted child who accepts an obedient role will truly become a full member of the family, belonging in every sense, and it is right that God emphasizes that more strongly than anything else, using three images: "you shall be my treasured possession out of all the peoples. Indeed, the whole earth is mine, but you shall be for me a priestly kingdom and a holy nation" (19:5b–6). The *segullah* is not a common term in the Old Testament, but its meaning is clear. It is used of physical treasure twice (1 Chron. 29:3; Eccl. 2:8), once of those in the postexilic community whom Malachi judges to be fearers of Yahweh (Mal. 3:17), using the parent-child analogy, and five times of Israel's special status, as God's treasure, as holy (Ex. 19:6; Deut. 7:6; 14:2), and as chosen by him (Deut. 7:6; 14:2; Ps. 135:4).

Only here in the Old Testament is Israel (or any group) called a "holy nation." Elsewhere the expression "holy people" does occur. Since we are moving at this point in Exodus from Yahweh's exclusive claim to Israel to his establishment of an intimate relationship, the term "holy" is most likely used here in its basic sense, meaning "set apart for God," rather than referring to the character of the people themselves. The latter would be an entirely new subject for this passage. "Treasured possession" and "oly nation" thus seem to be synonymous parallels. "Kingdom of priests" or "priestly kingdom" is a unique expression, without even a remote parallel elsewhere, and so it has been interpreted as: (1) Israel's consecration to God; (2) Israel as mediator among the nations; (3) Israel as ruled by priests; and (4) Israel both consecrated to God and ruled by priests.[19] The second option has appealed to many interpreters, since it fits nicely with theology that can be developed from other parts of both Testaments, but Exodus offers not a hint that any such idea should be associated with Sinai. I doubt that the two Hebrew words can support the idea that priestly rule is implied. Parallelism suggests the meaning ought to be similar to "holy nation," and since priests were "sanctified" to their office, set apart by an act of consecration for God's service, the simplest reading of the text would be to take the words as meaning "a kingdom of those set apart" (like priests) for God, and thus an exact parallel to the other two terms.[20]

Is this entirely election for privilege, then? We cannot say it is not, at this point, for nothing is said in Exodus about what God intends to do with these chosen people, except bless them (cf. Deut. 26:19). The prophets will have something more to say about that.

When we come to the people's response, in 19:8 (also 24:3), we have gone as far as the adoption analogy can properly take us. God has done it all, taking a helpless child and making it his own, and there is only one thing Israel has to contribute to the relationship: "Everything that the LORD has spoken we will do." At two points, with reference to the treasured possession and to the kind of obedience God requires, the analogy of adoption must be abandoned, for God "owns" Israel in a way no parent should claim, and God requires a measure of obedience no parent has a right to expect. That becomes clear as we see what the Commandments say about the relationship.

Israel's enthusiasm does not last long, as we know, and with that in mind we need to ask what the covenant-ratification section of Exodus may say about a possible abrogation of this relationship. With the covenant curses of Leviticus 26 and Deuteronomy 28 and the judgment messages of the prophets in mind, it may be surprising to find that no provision is made in Exodus 19—31 for dealing with a human refusal of God's offer. The if-clauses have only one part, the positive side. Yes, there are some warnings, and we need to look at them. The Decalogue speaks of punishing children for the iniquity of parents (Ex. 20:5) but not of bringing the relationship with Israel to an end. It warns that the Lord will not acquit anyone who misuses his name (20:7), but that is also an individual punishment. The most severe warning comes in the Book of the Covenant, connected with God's concern for the widow and orphan: "If you do abuse them, when they cry out to me, I will surely heed their cry; my wrath will burn, and I will kill you with the sword, and your wives shall become widows and your children orphans" (Ex. 22:23–24). Once again, this is individual, but it makes a strong point about God's character, as shown in his care for the oppressed, which we will come back to in the next section. Finally, Israel is warned not to make a covenant with the Canaanites and their gods, when they come into the land, for obvious reasons, but the threat attached to it is remarkably mild, "for if you worship their gods, it will surely be a snare to you" (23:33).

The final author of Exodus thus seems to have chosen his material very carefully, for he certainly knew of the kind of covenant threats that appear in Deuteronomy, and he will soon deal with the issue of disobedience in the classic passage concerning the golden calf. His refusal to include the possible negative effects of disobedience on Israel's part in this section must surely also reflect Israel's ongoing belief in the character of their God, who is slow to anger and abounding in steadfast love and faithfulness (Ex. 34:6), and their belief that this relationship depends primarily and ultimately upon the will of their God.

Why would the final author of Exodus have included in the same text these two statements: "You cannot see my face; for no one shall see me and live" (Ex. 33:20), and "they saw the God of Israel . . . God did not lay his hand on the chief men of the people of Israel; also they beheld God, and they ate and drank" (Ex. 24:10a, 11)? The former statement was the common wisdom in Israel; the latter preserves the record of an incident entirely unparalleled in the rest of scripture. It is true that in a few other passages someone speaks of "seeing" God, but they are all accounts of visions, and what is actually "seen" is very carefully qualified (1 Kings 22:19; Isa. 6:1, 5: Ezek. 1:26–28). Could this have been a vision experienced at one time by seventy-four people? Of course that is a question we cannot answer. The passage (24:9–11) is clearly a fragment, apparently separated from its original introduction in 24:1–2, and having no evident relationship with what now precedes and follows it. It is probably very old, since it corresponds to nothing in mainstream Israelite theology, but the principal theological question is why something so different would have been preserved in this prominent location. I suggest that for the compiler of these "Sinai fragments" it served a useful purpose, in keeping with what was said early in this section. It is one of the most striking ways of setting off Sinai from all the rest of Israel's experiences, as one that was completely unique. All the commentators properly observe that even here, what the seventy-four may actually have seen is carefully qualified, for nothing is described but the pavement under God's feet, but the passage still dares to say "they saw the God of Israel." This remained one of Israel's ways of insisting that at one time in their past there was a nearly indescribable and completely unrepeatable encounter with a God who from that time on defined who they were.[21]

Commandment: Exodus 20—23

God might have created humans as highly intelligent creatures of instinct, like the dolphins or elephants, and left us to enjoy ourselves in the world, presumably providing a good deal of enjoyment for him also. Or he might have experimented with giving us a will and freedom to use it; then having found that we used it too frequently to do great harm to ourselves and the rest of creation, he might either have seen to it that we became extinct or left us in the mess we had made. Or, loving us in spite of ourselves, he might have intervened (like the overprotective parent) to clean up every mess we made, continually restarting us on the right track.

Instead he gave us commandments. His love for us led him to give us the knowledge that he is our creator, and led him to make us more than "creatures," for how could mere creatures be partners in a relationship with the Holy One, and even be given some choice in the matter? But this is what Israel claimed was happening in their history. To let them know where they stood, once they had achieved self-awareness through evolution and then an awareness of God through revelation (as we would put it), God gave them commandments. The commandments made it clear that this is not a relationship between equals, and they offered direction for the human will, which is supported at the human level neither by adequate wisdom nor by adequate goodness to keep them from making terrible mistakes.

I have written this introduction in terms of humanity in general because that is the way Israel began to talk about commandments. In the priestly account of creation, humans get a blessing and a command: "God blessed them, and God said to them, 'Be fruitful and multiply, and fill the earth and subdue it; and have dominion over the fish of the sea and over the birds of the air and over every living thing that moves upon the earth" (Gen. 1:28). In the Yahwistic account, God's first word to the human is a prohibition: "You may freely eat of every tree of the garden; but of the tree of the knowledge of good and evil you shall not eat, for in the day that you eat of it you shall die" (Gen. 2:16b–17). God's blessing of Noah, after the flood, also included a prohibition: "You shall not eat flesh with its life, that is, its blood. For your own lifeblood I will surely require a reckoning: from every animal I will require it and from human beings, each for the blood of another, I will require a reckoning for human life" (Gen. 9:4–5). Israel, like other societies, assumed that life required boundaries, and believed that God had provided them from the beginning.

But by the time the earliest parts of the Old Testament were written, Israel's thinking had moved beyond the level of taboos, found in primitive cultures (although we think we can see echoes of that earlier level in places), and had rejected the mythical justification of laws and customs used by their neighbors, in which stories were told tracing them back to the primordial time. Except for a few scattered commandments such as those mentioned above, and the rules for circumcision in Genesis 17 and for the observance of the Passover in Exodus 12—13, Israel claimed that their whole law was given at a moment in time after a quite considerable amount of history had elapsed. This would seem far from satisfactory to later Jews. The author of the *Jubilees* projects all the most important commandments back into Genesis, and the rabbis were certain that the law had been created in heaven before the world was made (*Gen. Rab.* 1.4). But early Israel resisted that tendency, and Sinai remained a moment in history. They also resisted the power that kings exercised everywhere else, claiming the right to be lawgivers, or transmitters of divinely ordained law (as in the preface to the Code of Hammurabi). There can be no doubt that the kings of Israel and Judah did promulgate laws, but the writers of the Old Testament have suppressed all that. All law, according to the theory, came directly from God through Moses at Mount Sinai. That theory was held in spite of the fact that the Pentateuch contains distinct compilations of laws that often differ from one another: what we call the Book of the Covenant in Exodus 21—23; the legal material in Deuteronomy, and the priestly collection of laws in Leviticus and Numbers. No matter what the actual origins of the various commandments and codes may have been, Israel made a profound statement about them by claiming that at Sinai they were God's gift, which set Israel apart as his people (19:5).

The law was later given an extended theological explanation in Judaism, and the beginnings of that are to be found in Deuteronomy, as we shall see in a later section of this chapter. The Holiness Code (Leviticus 19—26) offers a rationale for all of law, "You shall be holy, for I the LORD your God am holy" (Lev. 19:2, etc.), insisting that the people of God must reflect the character of God himself. The earlier material in Exodus contains only a few indications of that kind of reflection, however, and it is the location of the commandments within the narrative of covenant making that offers the first indication of their theological significance. There are certain commandments that point directly to Israel's understanding of the nature of God, however, and this section will focus on them.

God's exclusive claim to these people returns with prominence in the Decalogue. Previously it had been a claim addressed to the pharaoh; now it is addressed to Israel. "I am Yahweh your God, who brought you out of the land of Egypt, out of the house of slavery; you shall have no other gods before me" (20:2f.).[22] As has often been noted, the First Commandment does not deny the existence of other gods, but the question of their existence is irrelevant to God's claim, for as far as Israel is concerned, it makes no difference whether there are other gods or not. A similar commandment in the Book of the Covenant makes this a matter of life or death for the individual: "Whoever sacrifices to any god, other than the LORD alone, shall be devoted to destruction" (Ex. 22:20).

The Second Commandment begins, "You shall not make for yourself an idol," according to NRSV, which thus presumes the answer to a debated question. Was the "graven image" of the Hebrew text understood to be a statue of a foreign god—an idol—or a representation of Yahweh? Either is possible, as the commandment is worded.[23] The worship of other gods was a continual temptation for the Israelites in Canaan, and that issue reappears more frequently than any other in this section (cf. 22:20; 23:24, 32f.). But to think that Yahweh could be represented by any part of creation would lead to a complete misunderstanding of who

Yahweh was, and that may also have been the concern of this commandment. Walter Harrelson offers a valuable interpretation of this commandment, based on the priestly theology found in Genesis 1, where it is said humans have been created in the image of God (Gen. 1:26f.). This positive use of the idea of "image" (not the same Hebrew words) at a much later time than the formulation of the Second Commandment helps us to appreciate the implications of the original prohibition. As Harrelson says, for the priestly tradition, "No cultic representation can do justice to the living God; only human beings can be a kind of representation of God on earth, and they must be such a representation not at the cult center where their representation is set up, but in daily life, demonstrating faithfulness to the commandments of the God who created them."[24]

The prohibition of images has been expanded with the partial citation of "creedal" material that appears in full in Ex. 34:6–7: "[F]or I the LORD your God am a jealous God, punishing children for the iniquity of parents, to the third and the fourth generation of those who reject me, but showing steadfast love to the thousandth generation of those who love me and keep my commandments" (20:5b–6). Since chapters 32—34 seem to provide the most useful context for interpreting the significance of that often quoted material, the full discussion of it will be provided when they are dealt with. The two parts of the creed appear in the opposite order in these two Exodus passages, however, and that is probably because Exodus 34 is essentially a forgiveness text, whereas in the Decalogue the creedal statement is introduced by "I the LORD am a jealous God" (20:5). That led to putting the statement about punishment of sin first.

That God is "jealous" or "zealous" for his people (the root *qanah* can be translated either way) is another way of describing that exclusive claim we have been tracing throughout the book of Exodus. Like "fear of the Lord," jealousy is another biblical term that doesn't quite ring true in English, but the problem is with the English idiom, not with the original sense of the Hebrew. At the human level, jealousy is never justified, for it makes a claim on another person which violates the person's own integrity. Both Testaments speak of jealousy as a sin, but the Old Testament uses the same root to denote a fully appropriate attribute of God, and the New Testament speaks at least three times of divine jealousy (1 Cor. 10:22; 2 Cor. 11:2; James 4:5; cf. Heb. 10:27). The difference is that human jealousy is unrightful possessiveness, but God has every right to make an absolute claim upon those he has created. The word occurs in two Exodus passages, each time with special prominence. It has become part of the Decalogue in chapter 20, and in 34:14 it is a part of the divine name itself: "[Y]ou shall worship no other god, for Yahweh *Qannah* is his name; a jealous God is he" (author's translation). The word represents God's zeal for this relationship; it is no sideline for him. It is thus associated both with his anger and with his love, as Bernard Renaud has shown in his study.[25] Israel is always the point of reference for God's jealousy, and it may lead to his wrath against them when they rebel against him, as in Deut. 6:15; Ezek. 5:13, and elsewhere, or to his wrath against Israel's enemies, when they have caused his people undue suffering, as in Joel 2:18; Zech. 8:2, and so on. Renaud is led to use the same imagery we used in the interpretation of Ex. 19:4–6, saying that it is love that excites Yahweh against Israel's enemies (Isa. 26:11; 59:17; 63:15), and even when his jealousy is aroused against Israel, it is motivated by the love of a father (Deut. 32:16, 21; Ps. 78:58) or a husband (Ezek. 16:38, 42; 23:25).[26] The word is thus a fully appropriate one to describe the kind of relationship we have found Yahweh establishing with Israel, beginning with his claim, "my people."

The Third Commandment, "You shall not make wrongful use of the name of the LORD your God, for the LORD will not acquit anyone who misuses his name," is also concerned with the nature of God, but since a previous chapter of this book has dealt with the name of God at length, no additional discussion of that seems to be called for here.

Unlike the covenants with Noah (Genesis 9), Abraham (Genesis 15; 17), and David (2 Samuel 7; Psalms 89; 132), which David Noel Freedman has aptly described as covenants of "divine commitment,"[27] in which God makes a promise but does not specify a set of obligations that the recipients are required to observe, the Sinai covenant is one of "human obligation." The introduction to Sinai, we have noticed, includes an if-clause: "Now therefore, if you obey my voice and keep my covenant . . ." (19:5a). The if-clause was already anticipated in 15:26, with another general statement about listening to the voice of God, doing what is right in his sight, giving heed to his commandments, and keeping all his statutes. One other if-clause occurs in this section, and it is more specific: "But if you listen attentively to his [the angel's] voice and do all that I say, then I will be an enemy to your enemies and a foe to your foes" (Ex. 23:22). These clauses show that the Sinai covenant is not simply imposed upon Israel. Noah, Abraham, and David had nothing to do with establishing the covenants God gave them, but Israel is given the opportunity to make a choice. We have seen that in this section they make an enthusiastic response ("All that the LORD has spoken we will do, and we will be obedient," 24:7b; cf. 19:8). Like the other covenants, the initiative is entirely with God, but God does not want to deal with robots or pets. He seeks a relationship entered into freely.

The use of the apodictic form in many of the commandments makes it clear that this is a personal relationship, and not just an abstract code of laws. The Book of the Covenant does contain a good many laws formulated in the third person. Everything from 21:1 through 22:17 either takes the casuistic form ("If, or when, something happens, then such-and-such shall be done") or the form beginning with a participle in Hebrew and usually with "whoever" in English. But the Decalogue, Ex. 20:22–26, and much of 22:18–23:33 are in the second person, God speaking to the people. And most of the second-person verbs are in the singular, so in the law individuals are addressed. This offers an answer to a question raised by what the Bible has said of the divine relationship with humans thus far: Is it solely with the community? So far we have heard of the people, with only Moses and Aaron apparently having a special, personal relationship with God. Ludwig Köhler, for example, claims the Old Testament concept of covenant has no reference to individual piety, for the people continue no matter what happens to individuals.[28] But if law is an essential part of the relationship between God and Israel, the fact that it is addressed to individuals shows that only their personal responses can maintain the health of the community. The sense of individual responsibility that is present in very early wisdom and legal material helps to explain how a deep sense of personal relationship with God appeared in Israel,[29] even though the "official statements" such as we have in the Pentateuch speak of the community as a whole.

Communion: Exodus 25—31, 35—40

Despite several problems of continuity in Exodus 19—24, the logic of the structure seems fairly clear until we reach the middle of chapter 24. The people have been prepared, God has addressed them with the Decalogue, then Moses approached God (20:21) and was given the instructions we now call the Book of the Covenant. He reported them to the people (24:3) and wrote them in a book (24:4) as part of the ceremony of sealing the covenant by sacrifice and the sprinkling of blood. Then he and a select group ascended the mountain where they ate and drank in God's presence. One would think that should have completed matters, but next God instructs Moses to come up the mountain again, to receive tablets of stone with the law and the commandment (24:12–18), and Moses remains there forty days. This surprising turn in the narrative is accompanied by a clear change in vocabulary and interest, corresponding to the materials called the Priestly source. The key word in this passage is "glory," a term that will appear at climactic points in chapters 25—31 and 35—40. Glory is here associated with God's presence on Mount Sinai, but from here on it will have a new location, the tabernacle, to be built by the Israelites and to occupy the center of their camp. This Priestly source already shifts interest away from Mount Sinai to the movable camp of the Israelites in the wilderness, and intends to show that God will be present in the very midst of his people at all times. Because of the holiness of God, the most careful preparations must be made in order for that to be possible, and the priests believed they understood exactly what was required. So we read in these chapters detailed instructions on how to build the tabernacle, how to outfit and ordain a priesthood, and how to carry out appropriate worship. Except for chapters 32—34, which clearly interrupt the continuity of the tabernacle material, we find ourselves in quite a different world from the one we have encountered in the rest of Exodus.

One of the trends in contemporary biblical scholarship is the discovery of polarism of one kind or another in the literature, which is taken to reflect social, political, and theological polarities in ancient Israel. Expounding the contrast between a prophetic and a priestly outlook, already proposed in the nineteenth century, is still popular. That may be associated with supposed differences between the theologies of the Northern and Southern Kingdoms,[30] with the difference between "name" theology and "glory" theology,[31] or with the supposed conflict in the postexilic period between apocalyptic ideas and establishment thinking.[32] Polarization between the theology of the tribes during the early period of the settlement and the theology of the monarchy is a more distinctively modern theory.[33] I read every interpretation of this kind with reservations, because one always discovers that the author approves of one side of the polarity and is highly judgmental of the other. The dichotomy that has been discovered in scripture becomes the means of showing that the "valid" part of scripture supports one's own theology. The fact that everyone knows this is what Julius Wellhausen was doing in his negative evaluations of the law and of priesthood in the postexilic period has not, I fear, cast a sufficient pall of disapproval over the continuance of the same practice, with contemporary modifications. This is a preface to the consideration of material that most of us do not find very interesting. It is clear to all except a few who insist on a single author for the whole book that chapters 25—31 and 35—40 belong to a distinctive source, whose interests are appropriately called "priestly," and at least since Wellhausen, priestly has regularly been taken to mean "mistaken"—holding some wrong priorities. The prophets' criticism of the cult was originally appealed to in justification of that. Although careful studies have clarified the prophets' relationship with the cult, other reasons have been found for discounting priestly theology.[34] Now, as a Presbyterian, I have no great interest in the priesthood, and as a low-church Presbyterian, no great interest in ritual. But that leads me to approach the Old Testament not with the intent of pointing out what was wrong with the priestly understanding of the way humans should respond to God, but rather with the attitude that here is the opportunity for me to learn from those who have experienced the same God in different ways. I am not likely to be converted to their ways, but I expect to be enriched by them.

The variety in scripture strongly suggests this is the way it ought to be. Whether or not there existed any of these postulated polarizations in Israelite society, the time came when the believing community agreed that all these points of view belonged together. So we do not find a single source being used for the Sinai tradition, nor a homogenized version produced by the supposed majority party, but a composite that obviously was prized because each part contributed something the community could recognize as an authentic testimony to the God they knew.

The priestly mind-set was greatly concerned for order, for the structuring of life in accordance with the will of God, with stability, and thus with security. That could be obtained, they believed, by organizing the community's life in such a way that God could choose to dwell in their very midst. It led them to say more about the structure than about God, but they made their theology explicit enough that we do not have to intuit it. In this section we shall focus on those few explicit passages dealing with the presence of God and with his manifestation in "glory."

There is general agreement that two different tent traditions may be found in the Old Testament, located in the wilderness period and with a very sketchy history thereafter. They may conveniently be distinguished by using the terms "tent of meeting" of the older tradition and "tabernacle" of the tradition typical of the Priestly source, although it should be noted that the latter source has identified its tabernacle with the tent of meeting (cf. 40:34). The principal text that has led to the conclusion there was an early "tent of meeting" distinct in several ways from the tabernacle is Ex. 33:7–11, and it is appropriate to deal with that here rather than in the next chapter. Other evidence for this tradition has been detected in Num. 11:16f., 24–30; 12:1–16; and Deut. 31:14f. Trygve Mettinger's list of distinguishing features represents a widely accepted point of view: The tent of meeting (*'ohel mo'ed*) is associated with the verb "meet" (*no'ad*) as the way of referring to the divine presence, with the cloud as the medium of presence, and with the door of the tent as the site of the theophany. The tabernacle (*mishkan*), however, is associated with the verb "dwell" (*shakan*), with glory as the medium of presence, and with the "mercy seat" (*kapporet*) on the ark of the covenant as the site of the theophany.[35] There is less agreement over whether the two traditions represent different concepts of the divine presence, what Mettinger calls a "rendezvous theology" for the tent, versus the idea of the tabernacle as a permanent dwelling. But there is little evidence for a sacrificial cult having been associated with the tent of meeting, and the evidence that remains for it suggests a practice of seeking divine guidance through oracles, received at a tent located at the edge of the community. The Priestly source has not allowed the sacrificial ritual to overwhelm the idea that the worship center was a place of instruction, however, for the purpose of the ark is described as follows: "There I will meet with you, and from above the mercy seat, from between the two cherubim that are on the ark of the covenant, I will deliver to you all my commands for the Israelites" (Ex. 25:22).

It is significant that the priestly tradition clearly intends to transfer to the tabernacle what the older traditions said about God's presence on Mount Sinai.[36] The introduction to Moses' forty days on the mountain speaks of the glory of the Lord dwelling there and of the cloud covering it, and the glory is described as appearing like a devouring fire to the people below (Ex. 24:16f.). "Glory" is a favorite Priestly way to denote the visible signs of the presence of God; prior to this it has been used in Exodus only in 16:7, 10, where the people see it in the cloud, and subsequent to this it will be found in 29:43; 40:34f.; and in a passage that may not be from the Priestly source, 33:18, 22. The occurrences in chapters 29 and 40 mark the two most important comments made by the Priestly authors concerning their belief in the immediate presence of God in the midst of his people. The instructions for the daily burnt offering say it is to take place:

> at the entrance of the tent of meeting before the LORD, where I will meet with you, to speak to you there. I will meet with the Israelites there, and it shall be sanctified by my glory; I will consecrate the tent of meeting and the altar; Aaron also and his sons I will consecrate, to serve me as priests. I will dwell among the Israelites, and

I will be their God. And they shall know that I am the LORD their God, who brought
them out of the land of Egypt that I might dwell among them; I am the LORD their
God. (29:42b–46)

Some of the most important themes of Exodus are brought together here in a
new context, the expected ongoing life of a faithful worshiping community that
would be blessed by God's presence in their midst. Deliverance from Egypt is
here; the divine self-introduction, "I am Yahweh their God"; the recognition
formula, "and they shall know that I am Yahweh their God"; half of the so-called
covenant formulary, "I will be their God"; and now, a moveable place where the
glory of the Lord may be encountered, no matter where the Israelites go.

If the Priestly source was completed in the Babylonian exile, as seems very
likely, then this stress on a moveable sanctuary may be a major key to that
theology. At that time the Temple in Jerusalem had been destroyed, and for many
of the exiles, the attitude was "How could we sing the LORD's song in a foreign
land?" (Ps. 137:4) and "Our bones are dried up, and our hope is lost; we are cut off
completely" (Ezek. 37:11). Many believe that the idea of the tabernacle is a
response to such attitudes, taking what had been said about God's presence on
Mount Sinai and on Mount Zion, and now asserting that in a "wilderness" a
disciplined people could once again find the presence of God in their midst.[37] If
so, then it is highly significant that the golden calf episode, with the critical
questions it raises about whether there can be any future with God for a rebellious
people, has been inserted between the instructions for building the tabernacle and
its actual construction. The conclusion of the book, describing the appearance of
the cloud over the tabernacle, with the glory filling it (40:34–38), would represent
the priestly group's insistence that all was not yet lost, in spite of the apostasy that
led to the destruction of the temple and loss of the Promised Land.[38]

THE OLD TESTAMENT

Letting the book of Exodus set the theological agenda has led me to think
about Sinai in the broad terms of relationship between Yahweh and Israel that
have been used in the preceding sections, and to let the traditional key words come
in where they seemed appropriate. After all, words such as "covenant" and the
various terms for law are used only a few times in those chapters. The survey of
what the rest of the Old Testament has to say about this relationship will also
avoid the traditional rubrics. Exodus has guided me to think in terms of five
aspects of the relationship, and this survey will offer a selection of examples of
how they are used in other parts of the Old Testament and of how they changed.
Here also, the key words such as "covenant" will be dealt with where they appear,
rather than taking the word-study approach.

In Exodus we have found a regular insistence on (1) the divine initiative. God
intervened in Egypt in his own good time; all was done according to his agenda

and for reasons he said little about. This can be a very uncomfortable truth to learn about God, but the Old Testament insists on it. (2) The divine choice was not merely to deliver Israel from bondage in Egypt, but to take Israel to himself in an intimate relationship that completely excluded allegiance to anyone else. (3) Israel was not only to belong to Yahweh, but would be cared for by him and have him near them always. (4) God desired not just a one-way relationship, and Israel's appropriate response was obedience. (5) To be God's people thus meant to develop a character reflecting the character of God himself, becoming an "image of God" on earth.

Since the comparisons between the Old Testament and ancient Near Eastern treaties began to be made, the book of Deuteronomy has been recognized as being more distinctly a "covenant document" than any other part of the Old Testament. It was also accurately described long ago by von Rad as "the law preached." It is thus not surprising, but still gratifying, to find a little sermon in Deut. 10:12–22 which expounds the essence of the relationship between Yahweh and Israel in very much the same way as I have just described it, although its style is far superior to mine:

> So now, O Israel, what does the LORD your God require of you? Only to fear the LORD your God, to walk in all his ways, to love him, to serve the LORD your God with all your heart and with all your soul, [13]and to keep the commandments of the LORD your God and his decrees that I am commanding you today, for your own well-being. [14]Although heaven and the heaven of heavens belong to the LORD your God, the earth with all that is in it, [15]yet the LORD set his heart in love on your ancestors alone and chose you, their descendants after them, out of all the peoples, as it is today. [16]Circumcise, then, the foreskin of your heart, and do not be stubborn any longer. [17]For the LORD your God is God of gods and LORD of lords, the great God, mighty and awesome, who is not partial and takes no bribe, [18]who executes justice for the orphan and the widow, and who loves the strangers, providing them food and clothing. [19]You shall also love the stranger, for you were strangers in the land of Egypt. [20]You shall fear the LORD your God; him alone you shall worship; to him you shall hold fast, and by his name you shall swear. [21]He is your praise; he is your God, who has done for you these great and awesome things that your own eyes have seen. [22]Your ancestors went down to Egypt seventy persons; and now the LORD your God has made you as numerous as the stars in heaven.

The Deuteronomist has developed, here and elsewhere, the theology that was stated only briefly and to some extent even remained implicit in Exodus. Verses 14–15 speak of the divine initiative: the God of the whole universe has chosen Abraham, Isaac, Jacob, and their descendants, and Deuteronomy offers a reason that is lacking in Exodus: He set his heart in love upon them. Verses 12b and 20 speak of the exclusiveness of the relationship, although not at the length that is common in Deuteronomy, since warnings against idolatry are not included here. They are to serve God with all their heart and all their soul, to hold fast to him, for he is their God. Verses 13b and 20–22 speak of the intimacy of the relationship, which involves God's continual care and presence. The commandments are not for God's arbitrary reasons, but for their own well-being, and they are reminded of all that he has done for them in the past. Verses 12–13 and 16 speak of the response that is necessary, for the sermon begins with "What does the LORD require of you?" The human response is one that has to be freely given, so the relationship has to be preached: "Circumcise, then, the foreskin of your heart, and do not be stubborn any longer." And the people of God must behave as God behaves (vv. 17–19). He loves the stranger (the resident alien, immigrant); they also must love the stranger.

Deuteronomy has thus expounded the theology of Sinai, developing far more than Exodus has done the implications of the events recorded in Exodus for Israel's understanding of the nature of God. Chapter 4 is another good example of the way the meaning of Sinai was preached in Israel. It pushes the exclusiveness of the relationship beyond what we found in the Decalogue, now claiming there exists only one God: "there is no other besides him" (v. 35, cf. v. 39). And it thinks of Israel as a witness to the nations of the greatness of God, something completely missing from Exodus: "You must observe them diligently, for this will show your wisdom and discernment to the peoples, who, when they hear all these statutes, will say, 'Surely this great nation is a wise and discerning people!' For what other great nation has a god so near to it as the LORD our God is whenever we call to him?" (Deut. 4:6–7). But this is not exclusively Deuteronomic theology, as the following examples of each of the five aspects, drawn from various parts of the Old Testament, will show.

Divine Initiative

Even Genesis speaks of God's freedom to choose without regard to human judgments as to what is proper.[39] He offered his promise to Abraham and Sarah, two elderly people without children, even though it was a promise that would be nonsense to people who could expect to have no descendants (Gen. 11:30; 12:1–3; 15:1–6). He preferred Abel's offering to Cain's for reasons the author of Genesis sees no reason to disclose (Gen. 4:1–7). And for reasons of his own he chose the second born, Jacob, rather than the firstborn, Esau, to become the father of the chosen people (Gen. 25:23).

God intervened in the settled order of things, even to bring to an end a hereditary line of priests. In the story of the rise of Samuel, God judges the family of Eli, and chooses the young Samuel, who is not a member of a priestly family, not even from the tribe of Levi, to serve him as priest, prophet, and judge (1 Sam. 3:11–14, 19–21). The account of the rise of kingship in Israel also insists on God's freedom, even though the "anti-kingship" sections claim God only agreed to give them a king because of their insistence on it (1 Sam. 8:22). He chose Saul (1 Sam. 9:15–17), even though he is depicted as being a rather shy, country boy

(10:20–24), but then we are told God was free to change his mind about his selection (15:10f., 23).

The verb *baḥar,* "choose," is a favorite of the Deuteronomist and the Deuteronomistic writers, but it also occurs with some prominence in the Psalms and in Second Isaiah. One occurrence in Deuteronomy should be noted, since it takes up the question of God's motive:

> For you are a people holy to the LORD your God; the LORD your God has chosen you to be a people for his own possession, out of all the peoples on earth to be his people, his chosen possession. It was not because you were more numerous than any other people that the LORD set his heart on you and chose you—for you were the fewest of all peoples. It was because the LORD loved you and kept the oath that he swore to your ancestors. (Deut. 7:6–8)

This theme entered into Israel's language of praise, as in Ps. 33:12: "Happy is the nation whose God is the LORD, the people whom he has chosen as his heritage" (cf. Pss. 105:6, 43; 106:5; 135:4). It became one of the bases for the exilic prophet's message of hope for restoration:

> But you, Israel, my servant,
>   Jacob, whom I have chosen,
>   the offspring of Abraham, my friend;
> you whom I took from the ends of the earth,
>   and called from its farthest corners,
> saying to you, "You are my servant,
>   I have chosen you and not cast you off";
> do not fear, for I am with you,
>   do not be afraid, for I am your God. (Isa. 41:8–10a)

Second Isaiah could make a new use of Israel's hymnic language, seeing a better future as imminent for the exiles, but long before that, Israel's recognition that they have a God who chooses freely and is not bound by human customs, institutions, or reasoning appears in more disturbing contexts. Amos was not using the election tradition in a completely new way when he declared this word from God: "You only have I known of all the families of the earth; therefore I will punish you for all your iniquities" (Amos 3:2). He did carry it to a conclusion for which none of his contemporaries was prepared, however, asserting that what was coming was not only punishment but the end of Israel as the people of God (Amos 8:2).

An Exclusive Relationship

It has long been noted that one of the most significant differences between the religion of the patriarchs in Genesis and the religion of Sinai is that the former shows no exclusivism. They have differences with the people of Canaan over water rights and other matters (e.g., Gen. 26:17–33), but nowhere are they depicted as devotees of a "jealous God," whose cult and ethic are radically different from those of the gods of Canaan. Given the intensity of the opposition to the gods of Canaan found in the rest of the Old Testament, these must be old traditions, preserved in spite of their different religious outlook. They, plus all the information we now have concerning the polytheistic religions of the ancient Near East, emphasize by contrast the unique character of the God who was said to have revealed himself to Israel at Sinai. One way to denote the relationship established there was with the simple expression, "I will be your God, and you shall be my people." It occurs only in Priestly material in Exodus (6:7; 29:45; cf. Lev. 26:12), but must have been used much earlier than the exilic period, for it is one of Israel's beliefs that is negated by Hosea's experiences as a prophet: "And the LORD said, 'Call his name Not my people, for you are not my people and I am not your God' " (Hos. 1:9). It became a favorite expression in the promises of restoration in the books of Jeremiah and Ezekiel (Jer. 24:7; 30:22; 31:1, 33; 32:38; Ezek. 11:20; 14:11; 34:30; 36:28; 37:23, 27). Those reciprocal possessives "your God/my people" would at that time have been assurances that the unique relationship once established and then broken, could be hoped for once again.

We recall again Amos 3:2, with a different emphasis, "You *only* have I known of all the families of the earth." Shortly after the time of Amos, Hosea used the marriage relationship, with its expectations (demands) of faithfulness, as the imagery for the kind of relationship that should exist between God and Israel (Hosea 2). It had already been broken, by Israel, Hosea claimed, because of their readiness to worship other gods (Hos. 4:12–19, etc.). Later, Jeremiah used the same imagery, insisting on the same exclusive demand of God (3:1–10). Ezekiel made their ingratitude to God for his choice of them seem all the worse by using both adoption and marriage imagery. He depicted Jerusalem as a foundling child, rescued, cared for, and brought up by God (Ezek. 16:1–7). When she reaches marriageable age he takes her as his wife, and then the adultery story is told again.

The theme is as prominent in Deuteronomy and the Deuteronomistic Historical Work as it is in the prophets. God's thoroughgoing demand for Israel's loyalty could lead to the ferocity shown toward the Canaanites and all their ways in Deut. 7:1–6. Warnings appear throughout the book, and since it is now dated in the eighth or seventh century, it is clear that they are so frequent, and sometimes so violent, because the author is looking back at what has already happened. "If you do forget the LORD your God and follow other gods to serve and worship them, I solemnly warn you today that you shall surely perish" (Deut. 8:19; cf. 4:20, 24). The Deuteronomist found that the traditions preserved from the period of the Judges contained evidence that thoroughgoing syncretism was the normal way of life for early Israel, and he used those stories as horrible examples of failure to worship Yahweh alone (e.g., Judg. 2:11–15; 3:7f.; etc.). He told most of the history of the monarchy in the same way (cf. 2 Kings 17:7f.; 33—40).

The Deuteronomist's depiction of Israelite syncretism, corroborated by the prophetic books, reveals that for the preexilic period probably most Israelites had no more than the vaguest notion that Yahweh expected them to worship him alone.[40] The idea seems to have been characteristic of Yahwism as far back as we can trace it, but it was evidently too radical for popular religion to accept for a long time. The classic example of this is the contest with the prophets of Baal staged on Mount Carmel by Elijah. Elijah insists the Israelites make a choice: "If Yahweh is God, follow him; but if Baal, then follow him" (1 Kings 18:21). But the people do not answer, and I think it is because they do not understand what Elijah's problem is. Elijah came originally from the Transjordan region, and it may be that in that marginal area a stricter form of Yahwism had been preserved. At any rate, this story is the first in the history of Israel's life in Canaan to raise this issue. Elijah won on that day (1 Kings 18:39), but the history and the prophetic books show us that this exclusive aspect of the relationship did not take full effect in popular religion until the exilic period.

Only the "saints and scholars" of preexilic Israel seem to have understood the absolute demand Yahwism made on the people, but the other side of it, the easy part, was affirmed very readily. That is, Yahweh had a special commitment to Israel. This raises the question of his relationship to other peoples. No doubt, most Israelites throughout the preexilic period thought of him as a national God, like the gods of the other nations, and thus their peculiar property in that respect. But once someone like the Deuteronomist can say there is only one God that exists, and he is Yahweh, then the relationship of the other nations to him will inevitably be seen in a different light. The various attitudes expressed toward the nations in the Old Testament cannot be dealt with here, but the subject needs to be noted because of its importance later for Judaism and Christianity.[41]

Intimacy—God's Care and Presence

"For what other nation has a god so near to it as the LORD our God is whenever we call to him?" (Deut. 4:7). The sermons in Deuteronomy use the wilderness period as their classic example of God's nearness and care. "The clothes on your back did not wear out and your feet did not swell these forty years" (Deut. 8:4; cf. vv. 2–4, 15–16). Added to that was thanksgiving for the gift of the land of Canaan, with cisterns they did not dig and vineyards they did not plant (Deut. 6:10f.; 8:7–10; 26:8–10). Their God responded to cries for help, for even in the time of the judges, with all its perversions, "Whenever the LORD raised up judges for them, the LORD was with the judge, and he delivered them from the hand of their enemies all the days of the judge; for the LORD would be moved to pity by their groaning because of those who persecuted and oppressed them" (Judg. 2:18). God's nearness and his care for Israel form the subject matter of all the hymns of praise in the psalter, taking an especially moving form in Second Isaiah's reassurances offered to the exiles:

But Zion said, "The LORD has forsaken me,
    my LORD has forgotten me."
Can a woman forget her nursing child,
    or show no compassion for the child of her womb?
Even these may forget, yet I will not forget you.
See, I have inscribed you on the palms of my hands;
    your walls are continually before me. (Isa. 49:14–16)

The second-person-singular form of most of the laws in Exodus led us to think in a preliminary way about how individuals understood themselves to be related to God. It is evident that they made an instinctive transfer of the promises addressed to the nation, which they heard in the cult, to themselves personally. As a matter of course, David expresses his faith that God will help him in his battle with Goliath, saying, "The LORD who saved me from the paw of the lion and from the paw of the bear, will save me from the hand of this Philistine" (1 Sam. 17:37). Mention of some of the psalms of confidence should be an ample reminder at this point of the Israelites' personal sense of the nearness and care of God (e.g., Psalms 23, 34, 73, 139). This is a theme that could be illustrated from every book of the Old Testament, so only a few examples have been offered here. It will take on some distinctive forms in Judaism and Christianity, however, which are only loosely related to the Old Testament, and they will be discussed in more detail.

The Need for Response

One part of the response God required was loyalty to him alone, with the rejection of allegiance to any other god, as we have seen earlier. We now look at the other side of the response, obedience to those laws of God which concerned the kind of life Israel was to lead. As they recalled the covenant-making ceremony at Sinai, they understood it to be something not imposed upon them by God, but requiring their free decision to accept it. The response is described in the same way in the covenant-renewal ceremony in Joshua 24. Joshua calls upon the people at Shechem to "revere the LORD, and serve him in sincerity and in faithfulness" (24:14), but there is another option: "Now if you are unwilling to serve the LORD, choose this day whom you will serve, whether the gods your ancestors served in the region beyond the River or the gods of the Amorites in whose land you are living; but as for me and my household, we will serve the LORD" (24:15; cf. Judg. 10:14; Ps. 16:4). If there had been no human contribution necessary, there would have been no need to preach the covenant, as Deuteronomy does (cf. 4:37–40; 6:4–25). And yet we found little evidence in Exodus of the possibility that God might abrogate the covenant if Israel refused to live up to its part. Two later documents that reworked the law for their own time added something that is missing from Exodus, a series of curses that will befall Israel if they refuse to live by the commandments they accepted at Sinai (Leviticus 26; Deuteronomy 28). It is difficult to find any evidence as to how early a series of curses such as these may have been used in Israel. Both passages now show that they were put into their present form during the exile, for they know vividly the experience of defeat and are concerned about prospects for Israel beyond exile (Lev. 26:27–45; Deut. 28:64–68). There is little to indicate whether anything like this was used before the experience of exile demonstrated that the prophets had been right when they said God had no obligation to continue the relationship since the people continually refused to respond to him in obedience.

The prophets say the law, which should have been a part of their daily life, had been perennially neglected. "My people are destroyed for lack of knowledge; because you have rejected knowledge, I reject you from being a priest to me. And since you have forgotten the law of your God, I also will forget your children" (Hos. 4:6). Micah has God figuratively call Israel into court, and the Lord's case is based on the facts that he chose them to deliver them from slavery in Egypt and has been their savior. What he requires of them is to do justice, and to love kindness, and to walk humbly with their God (Micah 6:1–8). Isaiah's book begins with a divine lament: "Ah, sinful nation, people laden with iniquity, offspring who do evil, children who deal corruptly, who have forsaken the LORD, who have despised the Holy One of Israel, who are utterly estranged!" (Isa. 1:4). Ezekiel retold the classic history of salvation as a history of continual rebellion (Ezek. 20:5–31).

At some point in Israel's history there came enough awareness of their responsibility that it found a place in worship. The wilderness theme was then reused as a basis for confession. In Ps. 106:6–33 the worshipers admit that as their ancestors in the wilderness had continually provoked God's patience, so also they have sinned and need forgiveness. The conclusion of this psalm shows that it was formulated in exile and thus came from people who accepted the truth of the prophetic message (v. 47). Psalm 78:17–55 uses the wilderness tradition to exalt God's patience and forgiveness: "Yet he, being compassionate, forgave their iniquity, and did not destroy them; often he restrained his anger, and did not stir up his wrath" (Ps. 78:38).

The exile taught those who remained alive after the futile war with Babylonia that the prophets had been right after all, in their interpretation of the true nature of their relationship with Yahweh. It was not a divine guarantee without conditions, as many had wanted to think (cf. Amos 5:14f.). And the postexilic Jewish community understood that to be a Yahwist was to be defined by willingness to devote oneself wholeheartedly to the keeping of the law. "Their delight is in the law of the LORD, and on his law they meditate day and night" the first psalm says, and the longest of the psalms develops that theme for 176 verses (Psalm 119). Repentance, as we shall see, becomes a major theme in rabbinic theology.

The prophets Jeremiah and Ezekiel, living at the time of the fall of Jerusalem and looking back at what had brought their people to this state, came to the conclusion that the will of their people was not really free to choose to obey. Rebelliousness had become a part of their very nature, according to Jeremiah:

"Can Ethiopians change their skin or leopards their spots? Then also you can do good who are accustomed to do evil" (Jer. 13:23). The relationship that had been one-sided until God finally decided to bring it to an end and start over will require an anthropological change if it is to work in the future, according to these two prophets. So Jeremiah speaks of a new covenant:

> The days are surely coming, says the LORD, when I will make a new covenant with the house of Israel and the house of Judah. It will not be like the covenant that I made with their ancestors when I took them by the hand to bring them out of the land of Egypt—a covenant that they broke, though I was their husband, says the LORD. But this is the covenant that I will make with the house of Israel after those days, says the LORD: I will put my law within them, and I will write it on their hearts; and I will be their God, and they shall be my people. (Jer. 31:31–33)

He does not claim there was anything wrong with the covenant made at Sinai. But there was something wrong with the people who were its recipients. The new covenant will thus be new because the recipients will be changed. No longer will the law stand over against them, but it will be internalized, so that obedience will be possible. Ezekiel says the same thing in slightly different words, promising that God will provide a new heart and a new spirit so that then they will be able to obey (Ezek. 36:25–27).

Although other authors assume that people can obey God if they really want to (cf. Deut. 30:11–14), and there is no doctrine of total depravity in the Old Testament except for these few verses in Jeremiah and Ezekiel, the human side of the relationship with God remains a troubled one. It requires warnings, instruction, admonitions, and promises, and eventually it will lead to a new beginning; what Ezekiel interpreted as a death and resurrection of his people (Ezek. 37:1–14).

Reflection of the Character of God

Although the Old Testament does not have a conception of Israel comparable to the Christian imagery of the church as the body of Christ, later materials offer some indication that the law of God was intended to do more than establish the boundaries of behavior permitted to God's people. We saw at the beginning of this section that Deuteronomy based its admonition to love the stranger on the fact that God loves strangers, as they learned from the way he dealt with them in Egypt (10:18–19). The law concerning release of Hebrew slaves when they had served for six years, which appears in its earliest form in Ex. 21:2–11, is expanded in Deuteronomy by several motive clauses. One of them emphasizes that Israelites should behave as Yahweh behaves: "Remember that you were a slave in the land of Egypt, and the LORD your God redeemed you; for this reason I lay this command upon you today" (Deut. 15:15). This parallel is direct; release of slaves is involved in both cases. The principle could be used in a broader way, as in Deut. 24:17–18, taking what God did for Israel in Egypt as evidence of his concern for anyone in danger of being oppressed: "You shall not deprive a resident alien or an orphan of justice; you shall not take a widow's garment in pledge. Remember that you were a slave in Egypt and the LORD your God redeemed you from there; therefore I command you to do this."

Leviticus uses "holy" in its developed sense, meaning more than the fundamental idea of belonging to, being set apart for God, when it says, "You shall be holy, for I the LORD your God am holy" (Lev. 19:2). The affirmation introduces a sequence of commandments that includes several of those in the Decalogue, in addition to the far-reaching ideals "you shall love your neighbor as yourself" and "you shall love the alien as yourself, for you were aliens in the land of Egypt" (19:18b, 34b). Holiness has here absorbed the fullness of God's character, and this priestly collection of laws claims that God's character ought to be shared by Israel.

Earlier we noticed in Deuteronomy the beginnings of a concern that the nations might see in Israel's way of life evidence of the nature of the true God (Deut. 4:6). That is not developed very far in the Old Testament, as it is later in Judaism and Christianity, but there are a few other indications of it. Ezekiel speaks of the nations as witnesses to Israel's scandalous behavior throughout his book (e.g., 5:5–6; 36:16–20). So their disobedience is seen by him as a negative witness: "But when they came to the nations, wherever they came, they profaned my holy name, in that it was said of them, 'These are the people of the LORD, and yet they had to go out of his land' " (Ezek. 36:20). He does not expect the exiles to be able to do anything to remedy that, but promises God will take action to cleanse and redeem them, making it possible for them to be obedient, and his action will lead the nations to know that he is Yahweh (cf. 36:36; 39:21–24).

Second Isaiah's notion of Israel as the servant of the LORD makes the responsibility of the exilic community much clearer. The term "servant" could be used of powerful people as well as those doing menial labor. The servant of a king, for example, might be a general or a vizier, somewhat as we speak of politicians today as "public servants." What the general and the field hand had in common was that they were carrying out the will of someone else. If Israel could be called the servant of the Lord, then it would mean that with their freedom of the will they had fully accepted the lordship of God's will. We need not go into the problem of the identity of the servant, who sometimes is clearly identified as Israel (e.g., Isa. 41:8; 44:1) and at other times seems to be one individual (as in Isa. 52:13–53:12). Our interest here is in the references to Israel as servant, thus presumably a people whose lives now carry out the will of God. For example:

> Let all the nations gather together,
>   and let the peoples assemble.
> Who among them declared this,
>   and foretold to us the former things?
> Let them bring their witnesses to justify them,
>   and let them hear and say, "It is true."

You are my witnesses, says the LORD,
     and my servant whom I have chosen,
so that you may know and believe me
     and understand that I am he. (Isa. 43:9–10)

This sketch of the elements of the relationship between God and Israel omits a great deal, but to tell the full story would be a book in itself. At this point, it is important, however, to consider what Exodus omitted, before we turn to the developments of these ideas in Judaism and Christianity. We found that it said little about God's own motives for drawing a group of human beings so close to himself. That was probably wise, for who can know the mind of God? Deuteronomy took a safe move, attributing it to divine love, and more will be made of that in later literature. But the mystery will remain, and will create some serious problems in the formulation of the Christian doctrine of election. Deuteronomy also asked a question that Exodus ignored, and that is, Why Israel? Judaism will have more to say about that later. But the more serious implications of that question have to do with those not chosen. What sort of relationship do or can non-Jews have with the God of Israel? Christianity will have a new answer to that question. But except for these areas, the five aspects discussed in this section will be developed subsequently in a fairly straightforward way.

JUDAISM AND CHRISTIANITY

Judaism

The precarious state of Jewish existence during much of the Hellenistic and Roman periods did not make the Old Testament insistence on God's freedom of choice an attractive one, except in this form: In spite of everything, God did choose us. Since the covenant with Abraham was an unconditional one, God's free choice of him was often appealed to as reassurance that God had in fact committed himself to the welfare and future of the Jews. This use of the Abrahamic covenant appeared as early as the exilic or early postexilic period. In exile the provisions of the Sinai covenant offered little comfort, for it clearly was no longer in effect. The covenant curses in Leviticus 26, for example, referred to things that had actually happened. But at the end of the series of curses, the author speaks of the possibility of restoration, based on God's faithfulness to his covenant with Abraham, Isaac, and Jacob (vv. 40–42), and the repentance of the exiles. Then he seems to hope for a renewal of the Sinai covenant (vv. 44–45).

In a similar way, later Jewish literature emphasized God's love for and choice of Abraham and the everlasting covenant made with him, but this did not mean they de-emphasized Sinai. Since they had become convinced that the Torah was God's gift to them identifying them as his chosen people, Moses, Sinai, and the Torah are subjects that appear with great frequency. We shall follow the same order of topics as in the preceding Old Testament section, although many of the quotations used as examples will fit in two or more places.

The wilderness experiences were of course the subject of exegetical work (e.g., *Exod. Rab.* and *b. Yoma* 75–76 on the manna), but little theological use was made of them. Torah as God's gift and Israel's responsibility, and the presence of God with his people are the two subjects from this part of Exodus that reappear most frequently. A passage from Sirac (17:12–24) summarizes all the points dealt with in the previous section, although the need to reflect the character of God in their behavior remains implicit. He begins with a reference to Sinai, mentioning covenant, law, and God's immediate presence with the people:

> He established with them an eternal covenant,
>   and revealed to them his decrees.
> Their eyes saw his glorious majesty,
>   and their ears heard the glory of his voice.

The necessary response of obedience to God's commandment logically follows next:

> He said to them, "Beware of all evil."
>   And he gave commandment to each of them
>   concerning his neighbor.
> Their ways are always known to him;
>   they will not be hid from his eyes.

The exclusiveness of the relationship is not omitted:

> He appointed a ruler for every nation,
>   but Israel is the Lord's own portion.

The importance of the response leads Sirac to expand on that subject:

> All their works are as clear as the sun before him,
>   and his eyes are ever upon their ways.
> Their iniquities are not hidden from him,
>   and all their sins are before the Lord.
> One's almsgiving is like a signet-ring with the Lord,
>   and he will keep a person's kindness like the apple of his eye.
> Afterward he will rise up and repay them,
>   and he will bring their recompense on their heads.

But God is gracious, willing to forgive and present to help when needed.

> Yet to those who repent he grants a return,
>   and he encourages those who are losing hope.

There is no hint in this that postexilic Judaism had replaced a personal relationship to God with a sense of duty to obey an abstract law, as Christian critics have so often claimed.[42] Nor is there good evidence for the claim that the law and the sacrificial cult served to distance God from the individual, for our examples will show a contrary development.

The divine initiative in freely choosing Israel to be God's own is wondered at, but there is no mystery about the motive, for the Jews had learned from Deuteronomy that it was love. The adoption motif, which I brought in as a way of interpreting Ex. 19:4–6, appears in this parable, which compares God to a loving, adoptive father:

> Another explanation of *'But now, O Lord, Thou art our father.'* The Holy One, blessed be He, said: 'You have ignored your own fathers, Abraham, Isaac and Jacob, and Me do you call father?' To which they replied, 'Thee do we recognise as our Father.' It can be compared to an orphan who was brought up with a guardian that was a good and trustworthy man, and brought her up and looked after her most carefully. Later he wished to marry her, and when the scribe came to write the marriage document he asked her: 'What is your name?' to which she replied: 'So-and-so'; but when he asked her: 'What is the name of your father?' she was silent. Whereupon her guardian said to her: 'Why are you silent?' and she replied: 'Because I know of no other father save you, for he that brings up a child is called a father, and not he that gives birth.' . . . Similarly, the orphan is Israel, as it says, *We are become orphans and fatherless* (Lam. V,3). The good and faithful guardian is the Holy One, blessed be He, whom Israel began to call 'Our father,' as it says, *'But now, O Lord, Thou art our father'* (Isa. LXIV, 7). (*Exod. Rab.,* Ki Tissa, XLVI, 5)[43]

This loving decision of God was an act of pure grace. The rabbis' comment on Hos. 14:5 ("I will love them freely") was: "My soul volunteered to love them, though they are not worthy of it" (*Midrash Tanhuma* 5:9a).[44]

It was not only Paul who emphasized that the covenant relationship began with Abraham, long before Sinai and the giving of the law (Romans 4), for this was important to Judaism as a whole. Here are two examples of the role played by Abraham in the Jewish understanding of their relationship to God:

> And when they [human beings] were committing iniquity in your sight, you chose for yourself one of them, whose name was Abraham; you loved him, and to him alone you revealed the end of the times, secretly by night. You made an everlasting covenant with him, and promised him that you would never forsake his descendants; and you gave him Isaac, and to Isaac you gave Jacob and Esau. You set apart Jacob for yourself, but Esau you rejected; and Jacob became a great multitude. (2 Esd. 3:13–16; cf. 5:23–27)

Note that God's freedom to chose Jacob instead of Esau is not overlooked here. God's fatherly love for Abraham's descendants, the Jews, is emphasized in the *Psalms of Solomon* (18:3–4a):

> Your compassionate judgments [are] over the whole world,
>   and your love is for the descendants of Abraham, an Israelite.
> Your discipline for us [is] as [for] a firstborn son, an only child,
>   to divert the perceptive person from unintentional sins.

These statements about God's love as the motive for his free choice of Israel remind us of the intimacy of the relationship God intended to establish at Sinai and show that Jewish legalism had done nothing to diminish that. These quotations come from a variety of sources, dating from the early second century B.C.E. well into the Common Era, and including wisdom literature, a hymn, an apocalyptic book, and rabbinic literature.

The exclusive nature of the relationship on God's side is reflected every time the literature uses the word "chosen," and Israel's requirement to be loyal to the Lord alone is reflected throughout the literature. The stories of faithfulness under persecution in 1 and 2 Maccabees, and the elaboration of the deaths of martyrs in 4 Maccabees plus the legend about the salvation of intended martyrs in 3 Maccabees, provide one type of example. The stories of Judith and Tobit are intended to glorify those who take great risks to be faithful to God alone. And idolatry came to represent the sin that somehow comprehended all sins. In a statement that should not be taken literally, the rabbis said that those who deny idolatry profess the whole Torah, while those who worship idols have broken the whole law (*Sifre on Num.* 15:22; cf. *Midrash on Psalms* 15:7).

The sense of having an exclusive relationship with God did not mean Jews thought God was unconcerned with the rest of the world. One of the best statements of the belief that God cares for everything he has made appears in the Wisdom of Solomon:

> For you love all things that exist,
>   and detest none of the things that you have made,
> for you would not have made anything if you had hated it.
> How would anything have endured if you had not willed it?
>   Or how would anything not called forth by you have been preserved?
> You spare all things, for they are yours, O LORD, you who
>   love the living. (Wisd. Sol. 11:24–26; cf. 12:13)

The same thought reappears in the *Mekilta*: "It is the Holy One, blessed be He, who gives to every one his wants and to everybody according to his needs. And not to good people alone, but also to wicked people and even to people who are worshipping idols" (II, 178). But universal outlooks of this kind raised a question about God's fairness in giving the Torah only to Israel. The question was answered by claiming that he had in fact offered it to all the nations, but only Israel accepted it (*Mekilta* II, 234f.; cf. *Pesiq. Rab. Kah.* II, 17a; *Sifre Deut.,* Berakah, sec. 343, 142b).

The intimacy of the relationship was expressed in two new ways in post–Old Testament Jewish literature. First, "Wisdom" was exalted as the way by which God makes his presence known in the world. In Wisdom of Solomon, divine Wisdom is said to function much the same as the Holy Spirit in Christian teaching:

> Although she is but one, she can do all things,
> and while remaining in herself, she renews all things;
> in every generation she passes into holy souls

and makes them friends of God, and prophets;
for God loves nothing so much as the person who lives with wisdom. (Wisd. Sol.
    7:27f.)

For Sirach, Wisdom "came forth from the mouth of the Most High, and covered the earth like a mist" (Sirach 24:3), but by the command of God took up residence in Israel: "Make your dwelling in Jacob, and in Israel receive your inheritance" (24:8b). The imagery of the tabernacle, in which God became present to Israel in the wilderness, is now used to describe the presence of divine wisdom: "In the holy tent I ministered before him, and so I was established in Zion" (24:10). Finally, Sirach drops imagery and identifies Wisdom directly with the Torah: "All this is the book of the covenant of the Most High God, the law that Moses commanded us as an inheritance for the congregations of Jacob" (24:23). At that point, the understanding of Wisdom thus seems to have been narrowed, in Sirach's desire to emphasize that Israel has direct access to knowledge of the will of God, losing some of the broader functions it possesses when described as the ever-present, divine spirit.

The second way of speaking of God's presence appears first in the Targums and is used regularly thereafter. The noun *Shekinah* was derived from the root *shakan*, "dwell," from which the word we translate "tabernacle" was also derived. It thus meant "the act of dwelling," and was used in the Targums whenever the presence of God was perceived by humans.[45] For example, *Targum Onkelos* reads Ex. 29:45: "And I will cause My Shekinah to dwell in the midst of the sons of Israel, and I will be their God."[46] This term, derived from the tabernacle sections of Exodus, was used to speak of God's continuing presence with Israel. "R. Hananiah b. Teradion said: If two sit together and no words of the Law [are spoken] between them, there is the seat of the scornful, as it is written, *Nor sitteth in the seat of the scornful.* But if two sit together, and words of the Law [are spoken] between them, the Divine Presence [Shekinah] rests between them" (*'Abot* 3.2). Israel's continuing, unresolved problem, from 70 C.E. onward—the exile—could be dealt with by affirming that the Shekinah accompanied them wherever they went (*b. Megillah* 29a).[47] Without using the term itself, God's presence with his people wherever they might be was asserted in this striking way:

Another exposition of the text, *'My beloved is like a gazelle'* is that as the gazelle leaps from place to place, from fence to fence, from tree to tree, and from booth to booth, so the Holy One, blessed be He, travels by leaps and bounds from one congregation to another. Why all this alacrity? So that He may bless Israel; according to the text, *In every place where I cause My name to be mentioned I will come unto thee and bless thee* (Ex. XX, 21).[48]

Israel had learned well the lesson taught by the experience of exile, that God's gracious offer of the Torah required a faithful response:

'Why is Israel called God's people?' 'Because of the Torah.' R. Jose b. Simon says: Ere you stood at Sinai and accepted my Torah, you were called 'Israel,' just as other nations, e.g., Sabtekhah and Raamah, are called by simple names, without addition. But after you accepted the Torah at Sinai, you were called 'My People,' as it says, 'Hearken, O my people, and I will speak' (Ps. L, 7). (*Tanhuma*, Wa'era, 9a)[49]

So it was Israel's acceptance of Torah that made it possible for them to continue to be called God's people, even though it was all God's initiative at the beginning. That was so great a privilege that they ought to die for it, if need be: "Fight to the death for truth, and the LORD God will fight for you" (Sirach 4:28). The need did arise, with the persecutions of Antiochus Epiphanes (167–165 B.C.E.), and Mattathias's exhortation became the watchword of the Maccabean revolt: "Now, my children, show zeal for the law, and give your lives for the covenant of our ancestors" (1 Macc. 2:50).

This responsibility was not considered by the rabbis to be a burden, however, except in this sense: "He that takes upon himself the yoke of the Law, from him shall be taken away the yoke of the kingdom and the yoke of worldly care; but he that throws off the yoke of the Law, upon him shall be laid the yoke of the kingdom and the yoke of worldly care" (*'Abot* III.5). On the one hand, "the wicked caused the *Shechinah* to depart from the earth, but the righteous have caused the *Shechinah* to dwell on the earth" (*Num. Rab.* XIII.2),[50] emphasizing the necessity of obedience, but on the other hand, Israel was not to think they were earning God's blessings: "All those miracles and mighty deeds which I have wrought for you were not done so that you should recompense Me, but merely that you should honour Me as children and call Me your father" (*Exod. Rab.* XXXII.5).[51]

Finally, obeying the Torah would make Israel a true testimony to the character of God himself. "O be like Him! Just as He is gracious and merciful, so be thou also gracious and merciful."[52] Solomon Schechter notes that this God-likeness to which the Jew ought to aspire was confined to God's mercy and righteousness, and it was taught that one should not imitate God in four things which he alone can use as instruments: jealousy (Deut. 6:5), revenge (Ps. 94:1), exaltation (Ex. 15:21; Ps. 93:1), and acting in devious ways.[53] Schechter did not offer an example of the fourth, but we may think the rabbis had in mind passages such as God's commission of a lying spirit to lead Ahab to his death (1 Kings 22:19–23).

For the rabbis, the necessity of reflecting God's character in the lives of Jews could sometimes be expressed in stronger terms than those of testimony. The life of the Jew could advance or hold back God's work on earth:

R. Judah b. R. Simon in the name of R. Levi b. R. Tarfon said, "When the Israelites carry out the will of the Holy One, blessed be He, they add strength to the strength of heaven: 'And now, I pray you, let the power of the Lord be great' (Num. 14:17). But when they do not, they weaken the power of the One who is above and they too 'fled without strength before the pursuer.' " [citing Lam. 1:6][54]

> *Therefore ye are My witnesses, saith the Lord, and I am God* (Isa. 43:12)—that is
> "When ye are My witnesses, I am God, and when ye are not My witnesses, I am not
> God."[55]

Certainly there is some homiletical overemphasis in these two passages, and
they should not be taken too literally. Another passage, which cites Lev. 26:3 and
Hag. 1:10, should probably be taken as a more straightforward expression of
Judaism's acceptance of responsibility to be manifestations of God's righteousness in the world:

> Thus it is on your account that the Gentiles suffer. Joshua b. Levi said: If the
> Gentiles only knew that they would suffer through Israel's sin, they would establish
> two armies so as to guard every Israelite from wrong-doing. Yet it is not enough that
> the Gentiles do not guard Israel, but they even induce them to abandon the
> commandments. But if Israel sin not, the whole world is blessed (Gen. XXVI, 4).
> (*Tanhuma*, Behukkotai, 55a)[56]

These citations show that the five aspects of the relationship between God and
Israel which we identified as characteristic of the Sinai material in Exodus were
reaffirmed and developed in distinctive ways in various types of Jewish literature
produced during the Intertestamental period, and that these developments continued in rabbinic Judaism into the Middle Ages.

The New Testament

The five aspects of the relationship with Israel initiated by God in Egypt and
brought to fulfillment at Sinai are elaborated to such an extent in the New
Testament that they could almost be the basis for a complete theology of that part
of the canon. The main New Testament emphasis that is missing from the Sinai
material discussed thus far is the need for God to deal with sin, and that appears in
Exodus in chapters 32—34. We can do little more within these limits than present
a sketch of some of the principal New Testament materials that fall under each of
the five aspects, with the principal contribution being observations on the
relationships between the New Testament and the ideas in Exodus with which our
study began. Many of these subjects have produced a tremendous body of
scholarly literature, and there is too much of that to be surveyed here. In most
cases, consulting the major commentaries on the passages cited here will be the
logical first step for one who wishes to follow these discussions.

The authors of the New Testament books make their primary message the
declaration that as God had, by his own initiative, intervened in human history in
the past, he has taken the initiative once again, in a dramatically new way (cf. Heb.
1:1–4). That the coming of Jesus Christ was entirely God's own unmerited gift to
humanity is expressed in a striking way that is quite different from Old Testament
language, in Rom. 5:6–10:

For while we were still weak, at the right time Christ died for the ungodly. Indeed, rarely will anyone die for a righteous person—though perhaps for a good person someone might actually dare to die. But God proves his love for us in that while we still were sinners Christ died for us. Much more surely then, now that we have been justified by his blood, will we be saved through him from the wrath of God. For if while we were enemies, we were reconciled to God through the death of his Son, much more surely, having been reconciled, will we be saved by his life.

Paul begins with an assumed situation of enmity between God and humans, while the Old Testament message concerning what God did for Abraham and for the slaves in Egypt began from a "neutral" situation. From the perspective of the book of Exodus, we may say Paul's is the post–golden-calf outlook. He also speaks in individualistic terms, rather than of God's free choice of a people. The latter concept has not been lost from the New Testament, for the understanding of the church as the people of God is developed elsewhere, but the problem of the individual's relationship with God, which seemed to be secondary in the Old Testament perspective, has become primary in Paul's thinking.

This means that some new concepts have been added to the traditional language that Paul still finds useful. He speaks of peace with God (Rom. 5:1), and *shalom* was one of the gifts of God about which the Old Testament speaks frequently (e.g., Num. 6:24–26; Isa. 54:10), although peace *with God* is a New Testament idea. It also is a result of the conviction that humanity's original status is one of enmity. But the work of Christ means that another traditional term, the "glory of God," can be spoken of in a new way, as something believers can hope to share in (5:2). The love of God, which we did not find emphasized in Exodus, but which appeared in Deuteronomy and elsewhere as a partial explanation of God's motive for intervening in history, has become for Paul the source of the power that changes human beings (5:3–5, cf. v. 8). Because of his emphasis on the estrangement of individuals from God, concepts that are not at all well-represented in the Old Testament appear: justification and reconciliation (5:1, 9–11). And the discovery that Christ's sufferings had redemptive value meant that Paul could speak of the sufferings of his followers in a significantly new way (5:3–5). This single text shows us that as we trace the Sinai themes into the New Testament, we are going to encounter amid the continuity more important new elements than we have found in our earlier studies.

In fact, the very name chosen by Christians to denote the books they added to the canon alludes to Sinai, and to something different from Sinai, for they called these books the "New Covenant" (or "Testament"). The term "new covenant" occurs in the Hebrew Bible only in Jer. 31:31, and we have seen that the reference there was clearly to the Sinai covenant, since it speaks of bringing Israel out of Egypt, and of the law. The Christian observance of the Lord's Supper included the claim that something like the Sinai event had occurred again with the death of Jesus. Each account of the Last Supper alludes to his blood, and the Sinai covenant was the only one sealed with blood (Ex. 24:6–8). Moses' words, "See the blood of the covenant that the LORD has made with you" (Ex. 24:8b), are echoed in various ways: "This is my blood of the covenant" (Matt. 26:28; Mark 14:24), "This cup is the new covenant in my blood" (1 Cor. 11:25; cf. Luke 22:20). Although Matthew and Mark do not use the expression "new covenant," Matthew does allude to Jer. 31:34 by adding, "which is poured out for many for the forgiveness of sins." We saw that what was new about the covenant promised by Jeremiah was not the content of what had been offered at Sinai, but a change in the recipients, the law to be written on their hearts, internalized, we would say, so that obedience would become possible. The Jeremiah text thus already points toward the concern for the individual's relationship with God which we found developed so extensively in Rom. 5:1–11. The church remembered Jesus' words at the Last Supper as his promise that somehow his death would put that covenant, with the reality of forgiveness and a newly obedient life, into effect.

The church insisted also that Jesus' death was a matter of his own initiative, and not in truth the result of human decisions (cf. Matt. 26:24). There are debates about the authenticity of Jesus' predictions of his own death, but for the church these traditions were important testimonies that in his death the will of God was being carried out (e.g., Matt. 16:21–23). Jesus' prayer in Gethsemane on the night before his death was transmitted as evidence that his will and the divine will were in fact one, although he in no way behaved as an automaton (Matt. 26:36–45, par.). John's statement that "God so loved the world that he gave his only Son" (John 3:16) was thus by no means to be taken as a claim God offered up a human sacrifice, as some later interpreters have misunderstood it, for Jesus' free acceptance of God's will as his own choice is emphasized by John (cf. John 4:34; 5:30; 6:35–40). God's initiative is identified by the New Testament writers with the initiative of a human being who not only carries out God's will, like a new Moses, but is somehow the divine will himself. The divine eagerness to come close to human beings which we have seen evidence for in the Old Testament is now emphasized beyond anything those older writers could say, with the claim that Jesus and God were somehow one: what will soon become the doctrine of the incarnation.

Covenant language is not used extensively in the New Testament, except in Hebrews, where the superiority of the new covenant to the old is emphasized at length as a way of explaining the benefits of the death of Christ (Heb. 7:22; 8:6–13; 9:15–20; etc.). Paul's use of the term "new covenant" in 2 Cor. 3:1–18 is relevant to our focus on the divine initiative, for he attributes even his competence to be a minister of the new covenant entirely to the gift of God (2 Cor. 3:5f.).

The language of election, which is associated with the covenants in the Old Testament, appears in prominent ways in the New Testament, however. Although the Gentile church was a newly created organization made up of individuals who had chosen a new faith and way of life, the New Testament writers did not think of it in that way. They made use of the Old Testament concept of "people of God," and the church as a whole was thought of as God's chosen, as Israel had spoken of itself. First Peter 2:10 uses Hos. 1:9 and 2:23 in a new way to refer to this appearance of the church on earth: "Once you were not a people; but now you are God's people." So, even though individual decisions were essential to the formation of the church, unlike Judaism, the conviction that this was all the work of God, through Christ, led Christians to continue the Old Testament emphasis on divine choice. The introduction to the letter to the Ephesians, for example, includes this: ". . . just as he chose us in Christ before the foundation of the world to be holy and blameless before him in love. He destined us for adoption as his children through Jesus Christ, according to the good pleasure of his will, to the praise of his glorious grace that he freely bestowed on us in the Beloved" (Eph 1:4–6). Note, within these few words, the appearance of "choice," "adoption," "grace," and the "good pleasure of his will." Similar statements about the church appear in Col. 1:27; 3:12; 1 Thess. 1:4; 2 Thess. 2:13; 1 Peter 1:2 and 2:9. The last of these calls for special attention, since it quotes Ex. 19:6: "But you are a chosen race, a royal priesthood, a holy nation, God's own people, in order that you may proclaim the mighty acts of him who called you out of darkness into his marvelous light."

These Christian writers thus dared to claim that God's election of Israel to become his chosen people had now been extended to include all who come to him via faith in Jesus Christ as his Son who had died for them. This obviously raises questions about the second aspect of the God of Sinai, the exclusiveness of his relationship with Israel, but Peter's words have already offered a Christian answer to one of the questions we asked about God's choice of Israel; namely, for what purpose was it? Peter's answer is apparently that the royal priesthood are to be "evangelists," testifying to the world, by word and deed (cf. 1 Peter 2:11–15), concerning the truth about the one God.

We have seen that the exclusiveness of the relationship established by God with Israel required them to acknowledge and serve him alone (Deut. 6:4–15). That had become so central to Judaism that it was simply accepted by the church without discussion, and the traditional attacks on idolatry were resumed when necessary as the church expanded into the Gentile world (1 Cor. 12:2; 1 Peter 4:3; 1 John 5:21). But the other side of the matter, that Israel's relationship with God was different from that of any other people, would raise serious issues when the Christian movement began to separate itself from Judaism, and those issues remain with us to this day.

Jesus seems to have understood himself to have been sent by God to minister to Israel (Matt. 15:24; 10:5f.), and the record of his own activities shows him extending the limits of the chosen people only by his work of healing and forgiving Jews whose lives had disqualified them, whether by deliberate action or otherwise (e.g., Luke 7:36–50; 8:26–36, 43–48; 19:1–10). However, Matthew claims that after the resurrection Jesus sent his disciples to "make disciples of all nations, baptizing them in the name of the Father and of the Son and of the Holy Spirit, and teaching them to obey everything that I have commanded you" (Matt.

28:19–20). That this is not entirely a projection of later Christian ideas back upon Jesus is strongly suggested by the fact that the preaching of Jesus as Messiah to any and all who would hear began very soon after his resurrection, and apparently without any great discussion as to whether that was appropriate (Acts 8:4; 10:1–48; 11:19f.). Indeed, it was very soon taken to be necessary. The only debate was over the conditions for acceptance of Gentiles into full fellowship with Jewish believers (Acts 11:1–18; 15:1–29; Gal. 2:1–14). But the leadership of Paul, and to a more limited extent Peter, in accepting Gentiles into the "chosen people" via faith in Jesus Christ, without requiring the response of obedience to the Torah, led to the separation of church from synagogue before the end of the first century C.E.

There were now two groups claiming to be God's chosen people. The apostles' claim, "There is salvation in no one else, for there is no other name under heaven given among mortals by which we must be saved" (Acts 4:12), which in the early days may have been homiletical enthusiasm rather than exclusivist doctrine, did become the basis for saying that Jews who did not accept Jesus as Messiah could not be saved. Within Paul's own lifetime, it had become evident that the church was becoming mostly Gentile, and he devoted three chapters of his letter to the Romans to his struggles with the theological implications of that. The most important point to note, in our rapid survey of the New Testament, is that, unlike the later church, Paul did *not* conclude in Romans 9—11 that the church had replaced Judaism as God's chosen people.[57]

In one sense, then, Christianity broke away from the traditional Jewish sense of peoplehood, based as it was on God's choice of Abraham and the definition of what it meant to be God's people offered at Sinai. In the church a new people was being created, drawn from "every nation and tongue," and that people, like the Jews, was set apart from the rest of humanity by its loyalty to one God and by its way of life. But the rise of a concern about "salvation" after death, a subject scarcely to be found in the Old Testament, led to a new kind of exclusivism within the church. That was the idea that only those who had confessed their faith in Jesus Christ could be saved from punishment after death. Salvation in the Old Testament, and still to a considerable extent in Judaism, was God's gift for this life. That remains true for much of New Testament thought, as well, and it is obvious that in this life those who do not believe in Jesus Christ do not have their lives changed for the better by him. In that sense, the salvation that we experience in this life comes through "no other name." It is the unknown world of life after death that has produced the endless discussions of whether the church alone possesses the gift of salvation, and those concerns do already appear in the New Testament (cf. Matt. 8:11f.; 25:31–46; Rom. 2:5–10).[58]

At the conclusion of the Gospel according to Matthew, the risen Christ promises his disciples, "And remember, I am with you always, to the end of the age" (Matt. 28:20b), and the intimacy of the relationship Christians have with God has been emphasized in this way and in many others. The Old Testament concept of the Spirit of God, which was bestowed on those whom God had chosen for special tasks (e.g., Ex. 31:3; Num. 11:17; Judg. 6:34; 1 Sam. 11:6; 16:13), had been elaborated in Judaism, as wisdom was identified with the divine spirit, and in Christianity it was democratized, with the claim that God came near to every individual believer via his gift of the Holy Spirit (Acts 2:1–21; 10:44–48). The experience of the presence of the risen Christ in the church was accounted for by equating the Spirit of Christ with the Spirit of God, as Paul does in Rom. 8:9–11. Indeed, the Christian understanding of the Spirit claims that God is not only *near* to the believer, but actually is *within,* so that God by his Spirit actually helps us to pray to him (Rom. 8:14–16, 26–27). Elsewhere Paul emphasizes this access to God via his Spirit by making a curious sort of contrast between Christians and the people at Sinai, who were not allowed to see the glory of Moses' face, taken to be a reflection of God's glory (2 Cor. 3:7–18; Ex. 34:29–35). He says, "And all of us, with unveiled faces, seeing the glory of the Lord as though reflected in a mirror, are being transformed into the same image from one degree of glory to another; for this comes from the Lord, the Spirit" (2 Cor. 3:18). He protects himself from seeming to say they can see something physical called the glory of the Lord, while insisting they have a new access to glory via the Spirit.

The tabernacle, which in Exodus became the focus of the priestly understanding of God's presence in the midst of his people, provided terminology that some New Testament authors used in order to speak of the incarnation. The choice of words in the prologue to the Gospel according to John is recognized to have been influenced by the tabernacle tradition. With verses 14–18 of John 1, reflections of the Sinai material clearly appear. "And the Word became flesh and lived among us" uses the word *eskenosen*, which literally means "tabernacled," and which was certainly chosen because of the use of the same Greek verb in the Septuagint.[59] "We have seen his glory" also reminds us of the wilderness passages in Exodus, and the qualification "[no] one has ever seen God" echoes Ex. 33:20. The parallel clauses in 1:17, "The law indeed was given through Moses; grace and truth came through Jesus Christ," might be taken as antitheses, but the words "grace and truth" may very well be the Greek equivalents of *ḥesed* and *'emeth* in Ex. 34:6, which are usually translated as "steadfast love and faithfulness" in English. John may thus be claiming that all that was promised at Sinai had come into their very presence in the person of Jesus (cf. 1 John 1:1–3). The letter to the Hebrews uses the whole complex of tabernacle material, including the instructions concerning the priesthood and sacrifices, in order to explain the person and work of Christ. The aim of the book is to show that Christ completed perfectly what the older cult could only offer imperfectly, and the note in Exodus that Moses was to build the tabernacle according to the pattern that God showed him on the mountain (Ex. 25:40) was taken as evidence that the "true" tabernacle is located in heaven and is the locus of Christ's atoning work (Heb. 8:1–6, etc.).[60] Once again we see New Testament writers claiming that what God had begun to do at Sinai has been completed in Jesus Christ.

The Exodus material concerning the wilderness experiences was sometimes used in the New Testament to speak of God's care for his people, in continuity with the emphasis we found in Ex. 15:22–17:16. The first four verses of Paul's application of the wilderness experience to the Christian life, in 1 Cor. 10:1–13, remind them of God's care; then he turns to Exodus 32 and materials from Numbers in order to draw a warning lesson against putting Christ to the test.[61] Hebrews also uses the wilderness material as the basis for a warning, in 3:7–4:13, but makes the positive comparison as well: "the good news came to us just as to them" (4:2). The assurances of God's loving care for his people, which Christianity inherited from Judaism, were elaborated in various ways by the New Testament authors. Jesus expounded it in an unparalled way in the Sermon on the Mount: "Do not worry about your life. . . . Consider the lilies of the field. . . . But strive first for the kingdom of God and his righteousness, and all these things will be given to you as well" (Matt. 6:25–33). Every book contains such assurances, but the most impressive of them, apart from Jesus' own words, is to be found in Romans 8, with its conclusion, "I am convinced that neither death, nor life, nor angels, nor rulers, nor things present, nor things to come, nor powers, nor height, nor depth, nor anything else in all creation, will be able to separate us from the love of God in Christ Jesus our Lord" (vv. 38f.).

As some of the Old Testament writers became convinced from their sense of nearness to God that even death could not change that (Pss. 49:15; 73:23–26; 139:7–12), so also Christians believed their communion with God in this life would continue after death (2 Cor. 5:1–8), and their belief in the resurrection of Christ gave them a piece of evidence for life after death which no others had (1 Cor. 15:3–9, 50–57).

The need for a response to God's gracious offer was not diminished by Jesus' teaching, but was insisted upon in more forceful ways by his demand for personal loyalty. He called upon people to forsake everything they had dedicated their lives to in order to follow him. Luke recounts a sequence of three such incidents in 9:57–62. In Mark 10:17–22, Jesus reaffirms the Decalogue as the summary of what God requires, but then adds two more requirements: "Go, sell what you own, and give the money to the poor, and you will have treasure in heaven; then come, follow me" (Mark 10:21).[62] He claimed a loyalty that in Judaism was rightly owed to God alone: "Whoever loves father or mother more than me is not worthy of me; and whoever loves son or daughter more than me is not worthy of me; and whoever does not take up the cross and follow me is not worthy of me" (Matt. 10:37f.). It is no surprise, then, that such claims were resisted on the ground of piety. When Jesus offered forgiveness to the paralyzed man, the response of the scribes who were there was perfectly normal: "Why does this fellow speak in this way? It is blasphemy! Who can forgive sins but God alone?" (Mark 2:7). But Jesus claimed that divine power had been given him both to forgive and to heal (Mark 2:9–11; cf. Luke 7:50; 8:48).

The sense among Jesus' followers that they had in fact been healed and forgiven by his power led to their faith that he was indeed the presence of God in their midst, meaning that all God's promised blessings could be received through him. That is one way of introducing Paul's insistence on salvation by grace alone, through faith in Jesus Christ. The questions this has raised about the place of the Torah as the response God expects from those he has chosen are among the most troublesome to be found in inner Christian history, as well as in the attitude taken by Christians toward Judaism. Recent studies of the Pauline literature have brought forth persuasive evidence that much of what he says about the law is best understood as part of his defense of the Gentile mission and of his attack on Gentile misunderstandings of the gospel, rather than as an attack on traditional Judaism.[63] But there can be no question that "faith" as the primary response expected from humans took on a prominence in the New Testament which it does not have in the Old.[64]

Faith as mere intellectual assent was by no means a sufficient response, as some misunderstood the Christian message, however. The warning of James, "So faith by itself, if it has no works, is dead. . . . You believe that God is one; you do well. Even the demons believe—and shudder" (James 2:17, 19), does not differ in essence from Paul's teaching about the need for the person who believes in Christ to live in accordance with that belief. "Should we continue in sin in order that grace may abound? By no means!" (Rom. 6:1b-2a). The ethical life, what the New Testament calls the life of holiness, should be the outcome of the forgiving and transforming work of Christ within the believer, and so the New Testament does not do away with ethical instruction. Both Jesus, who claimed to be greater than the law (Mark 2:23–27), and Paul, who claimed that the law does not have the power to save (Romans 2—3), also expected the highest of ethical behavior from those who believed in Christ. But the law was not a "means of grace," as in Judaism; it was properly to be understood as instruction in the ways the loving person normally behaves, as guidance for those who in gratitude to God try to serve him faithfully as a result of, not in order to gain, their salvation (cf. Romans 12).

Christianity's emphasis on divine election and on salvation by grace alone did not reflect a different concept of God from that found in the Old Testament. It was not a more one-sided relationship, with less expected from the human side, as the New Testament statements about the Christian life as the reflection of the character of God reveal. Ephesians exhorts Christians to be "imitators of God" (Eph. 5:1). The Holiness Code's slogan, "You shall be holy, for I the LORD your God am holy" (Lev. 19:2), is echoed twice. Jesus' formulation of it, in the Sermon on the Mount, is "Be perfect, therefore, as your heavenly Father is perfect" (Matt. 5:48). In 1 Peter it is quoted more directly: "Instead, as he who called you is holy, be holy yourselves in all your conduct; for it is written, 'You shall be holy, for I am holy' " (1 Peter 1:15–16). Holiness had become a term that summed up the entire character of God, so this was no small expectation of the Christian life. As God had become personally present on earth in a new way, in the life of Jesus, the church came to see its own life as a continuing manifestation of his presence, speaking of itself as the "body of Christ." This is another of the New Testament developments that go beyond anything we have found in the Old Testament. The physical body of the Christian is a part of Christ, according to 1 Cor. 6:15, but more often it is the corporate church that is thought of as his physical body, present and active on earth, as in 1 Cor. 12:12–17 and especially in Eph. 1:23; 2:16; 4:4, 12, 16.

Earlier we noticed that in 1 Peter the aim of God in choosing a people for himself was made explicit. In 1 Peter 2:9 it was "in order that you may proclaim the mighty acts of him who called you out of darkness into his marvelous light." Nowhere is this need to reflect God's own character associated with proving anything to oneself or to God. It is neither self-fulfillment nor works salvation. Peter connects his ethical teachings explicitly with the need to show the Gentile world by the Christian life what the true character of God is. So, the Gentiles must not see anything in the life of a Christian that would lead them to think less of God (2:11–4:19).

This includes a willingness to suffer unjustly, if need be. This new understanding of suffering was also a result of the awareness that Christians should try to become like the God who chose them, for Christ's goodness led not to rewards but to suffering and a death that he accepted in order to become the redeemer of humanity. The good news was that the sufferings of his followers need not be meaningless, but could be added to Christ's sufferings, if endured for his sake, thus to become a part of his redemptive work. So Peter can even say, "But rejoice insofar as you are sharing Christ's sufferings, so that you may also be glad and shout for joy when his glory is revealed" (1 Peter 4:13). Paul understood that death as well as life could reflect the character of God as revealed in Jesus Christ: "I want to know Christ and the power of his resurrection and the sharing of his sufferings by becoming like him in his death, if somehow I may attain the resurrection from the dead" (Phil. 3:10–11). Elsewhere he described the ability to triumph over the tribulations of this life as the result of this sharing: ". . . always carrying in the body the death of Jesus, so that the life of Jesus may also be made visible in our bodies. For while we live, we are always being given up to death for Jesus' sake, so that the life of Jesus may be made visible in our mortal flesh" (2 Cor. 4:10–11).

The Christian message that the one God revealed in the Old Testament had chosen to come into the lives of all who would accept him in a very personal way, by coming into the world in the person of Jesus, and then by the indwelling of the Holy Spirit within the believer, was taken to be great good news by many. But there was much in it that was hard to understand, and unfortunately the good news produced not only transformed lives but also much controversy, as the concluding section of this chapter will show.

Christianity

The aspects of God's nature which we encountered in the Sinai materials of the book of Exodus made such a profound effect on Christian theology that a rather full history of doctrine could be written on these topics. In this context no more can be done than note some of the most distinctly Christian developments, and to observe the variety of Christian experiences of God which led to controversy over how these aspects of the nature of God should properly be expressed.

The freedom of God was celebrated in Christianity, especially with regard to his saving grace, but in practice Christians have often found ways to limit it, without admitting that is what they are doing. Dostoyevsky's chapter "The Grand Inquisitor" in *The Brothers Karamazov* accuses the church of usurping the way to salvation and of claiming to make Christ no longer necessary. Less dramatic and thus less extreme is the section in J. B. Phillips's book *Your God Is Too Small* called "God-in-a-Box," in which he points out how denominations and sects have tended to insist God must fit their definition, and theirs alone.[65] These are two analyses of the truth that sometimes Christians have fallen prey to the natural human desire to get God under control, in spite of scripture's insistence that that cannot be done.

One of the most far-reaching and influential ways of trying to maintain an insistence on the freedom of God, with respect to the Bible's message that it is God who takes all the initiative in making our salvation possible, is the doctrine of election, and the ideas about predestination that accompanied it. As developed by Augustine and those such as Luther and Calvin who were strongly influenced by him, the doctrine of humanity (the Fall, original sin, total depravity, etc.) played a large role in what was said about election, in that this meant human beings had no chance of saving themselves. But that view of fallen humanity was set over against the concept of a sovereign God, whose gracious decree determined the salvation of those whom he chose. By contrast, Augustine's rival, Pelagius, had an optimistic view of human potential and this influenced his view of the grace of God, which was useful but not necessary for salvation. The materials we have surveyed in scripture show that the Christian doctrine of election was soundly based on the testimony that it is God who takes the initiative in establishing the relationship with humanity. The logical development of the doctrine, which led to "double predestination," the idea that God's choice of some for salvation means he has in effect chosen not to save the rest, has probably gone beyond anything the writers of scripture intended, however. In a way, it limits God by claiming to know more than humans can know about God's decision concerning those who show no signs of faith in him, in this life. The Second Helvetic Confession, having affirmed double predestination, adds the wise counsel, in the effort to avoid the problems that creates, that "we must hope well of all, and not rashly judge any man to be a reprobate" (Chap. X, Of the Predestination of God and the Election of the Saints). The truth of the doctrine of election can probably be best explained in terms of the experience of many Christians, who realize on careful examination of their lives, that the good they have done has not fully been of their own doing, that some power greater than themselves has kept them from many a sin they really wanted to commit, and that they have a profound sense of being loved by God before they came to love him (cf. 1 John 4:19).

The problem with any idea of election is that it is conducive to feelings of superiority over those believed to be the reprobate. We have just noted the concern over that problem expressed in the Second Helvetic Confession, but it exists in a variety of forms among Christians, many of whom have no patience with double predestination. It appeared first in the controversy between church and synagogue, as soon as Christianity became a movement that was obviously distinct from Judaism. As Christian apologists in the second century undertook to defend the truth of their way over against both paganism and Judaism, they seemed to find it necessary to depict Judaism not as the rightful parent from whom they had sprung but as a religion of error. Hence the appalling history of Christian anti-Semitism began with the claim that the exclusive relationship God established with humanity included Christians but excluded Jews. We have already seen from our brief look at Romans 9—11, the most important passage in the New Testament dealing with this subject, that this traditional Christian claim is not necessarily well-grounded in scripture. Only late in the twentieth century, however, have many Christians begun to recognize that their exclusive claim upon the God of Abraham may contain a serious theological error, in addition to the ethical error of committing crimes against the Jewish people with that as an excuse.

Passages such as "there is no other name under heaven given among mortals by which we must be saved" (Acts 4:12b) have led to claims, expressed in various ways, that there is no salvation outside the church. In a sense this is an ironic turn, for one of the ways Christianity has differed historically from Judaism has been its missionary zeal, its eagerness to bring in converts, no matter who they may be. It offers an exclusive relationship with God, since it is possible only through faith in Jesus Christ, but it is exclusive in no other sense. Early in the fourth century, for example, Eusebius contrasted old and new covenants in this way: "And I have shown that the ideal of the new covenant must be helpful to the life of all nations: the members of its kingdom are to be restricted in no way whatever. Considerations of country, race or locality, or anything else are not to affect them in any way at all."[66] But as the idea of salvation in Christianity tended to focus on life after death, rather than on this life, no salvation outside the church presumably meant that everyone who did not express faith in Jesus Christ was damned to hell. And what of those who had never heard of him? That raised serious questions about the love and grace of God, and about his freedom, as well, leading (sometimes) to careful qualifications of the exclusive claim. In the Roman Catholic church, the concept of "baptism of desire" allowed God the freedom to save those who had never heard of Christ, but who would have believed in him if they had been given the opportunity. In Reformed Christianity we may quote the Second Helvetic

Confession, once again; for having asserted, "Outside the Church of God There Is No Salvation," it goes on to make allowances for those unable to partake in the sacraments, those in whom faith fails, or in whom imperfections or errors due to weakness are found, adding the interesting comment, "For we know that God had some friends in the world outside the commonwealth of Israel." It also finds it necessary to point out that not all who are in the church are of the church, and concludes with the caution not to judge rashly or prematurely, which might lead to rejection of those whom the Lord does not want rejected (Chapter XVIII, Of The Catholic and Holy Church of God, and of The One Only Head of The Church). The tension created by the conviction that God loves and desires the salvation of all humanity, and the insistence that salvation is possible only through confession of faith in Jesus Christ has remained a troublesome one for the church.

During the past two centuries, liberal theology has moved in the direction of universal salvation. This has often involved the doctrine of humanity as well as the doctrine of God, since liberal theology has been marked by a tendency not to take sin as seriously as orthodox Christianity has done. On God's side, it claims that the love of God could not permit him to condemn anyone to hell. Even though liberal theology for the most part has no great interest in heaven and hell, universalism may reveal the influence of the traditional overemphasis on salvation as the fate of the dead. The idea of universal salvation clearly fails when we take seriously God's intention to save us in this life, for it is obvious that millions of people do not experience salvation in this life, physically, mentally, or spiritually. When that tragedy is confronted, it becomes less important whether they can obtain it without faith in Christ, and more important that faith in Christ does make it possible.

The intimate presence of God with his people, which played an important role in Israel's concept of the covenant relationship, and which was experienced in new ways in Judaism, was emphasized all the more strongly in Christianity, with its development of ideas concerning the continuing presence of the risen Christ with the church, and of the work of the Holy Spirit in the world and within the believer. The doctrine of the Trinity was thus a necessary result of Christian experience, and not the product of exegesis or doctrinal speculation. Converts to Christianity found that their lives were radically changed by a power that seemed to come from outside themselves, a power that came to them as they heard about Jesus and came to believe that he had died and risen from the dead for their sakes. They associated that power with scripture's promise of the Holy Spirit. Eventually something had to be clarified about the relationship of that power with God and with Jesus, and the Nicene Creed (fourth century) defined it as follows: "And we believe in the Holy Spirit, the Lord and Giver of Life, who proceedeth from the Father and the Son, who with the Father and the Son together is worshipped and glorified, who spoke by the prophets." Another way to put it: Where the Holy Spirit was present, God the Father and the risen Christ were also experienced as present, and not as three beings, but as the One God revealed in the Old

Testament. Orthodox or mainstream Christianity was wise enough to recognize that this must remain a mystery, since every attempt to define exactly the inner nature of a Triune God produced results that were in conflict with scripture or with Christian experience.

As early Christians participated in the Lord's Supper, they took with the utmost seriousness the New Testament's statements indicating that the risen Christ was somehow present in a unique way in or with the bread and wine. Paul had written to the Corinthians, "The cup of blessing that we bless, is it not a sharing in the blood of Christ? The bread that we break, is it not a sharing in the body of Christ?" (1 Cor. 10:16), and Jesus' words as found in the Gospel according to John, "Those who eat my flesh and drink my blood have eternal life" (John 6:54) were taken to refer to the elements of the Lord's Supper. This eventually led to the doctrine of transubstantiation, which claimed that with the prayer of consecration, the Holy Spirit transformed the real essence of the elements into the flesh and blood of Christ. Transubstantiation became one of the issues of the Protestant Reformation, but most of the Reformers did not reject the belief in the real presence of Christ in the Supper. Having rejected transubstantiation, the Scots Confession (1560) insisted "that in the Supper rightly used, Christ Jesus is so joined with us that he becomes the very nourishment and food of our souls" (Chap. XXI, The Sacraments). But the way in which Christ is present in the sacrament not only divided Protestant from Catholic; it remained an irresolvable difference among Protestant groups as well, ranging from Zwingli's purely symbolic interpretation of the elements, through the Calvinist teaching concerning real spiritual presence, to Luther's more literal reading of Jesus' words: "This is my body, . . . this is my blood." By 1646 the Westminster Confession was reacting to both Catholic and Protestant views when it said:

> Worthy receivers, outwardly partaking of the visible elements in this sacrament, do then also inwardly by faith, really and indeed, yet not carnally and corporally, but spiritually, receive and feed upon Christ crucified, and all benefits of his death: the body and blood of Christ being then not corporally or carnally in, with, or under the bread and wine; yet, as really, but spiritually, present to the faith of believers in that ordinance as the elements themselves are to their outward senses. (Chap. XXIX, Of the Lord's Supper)

With respect to the Holy Spirit and to the real presence of Christ in the Lord's Supper, theology has thus showed itself unable thus far to account adequately for the range of Christian experiences of the near and caring presence of God, in keeping with the teachings of scripture. In various ways, Christian history also reveals threats to these experiences of God's nearness. The elaboration of liturgy and of the privileges of the priesthood in the Roman Catholic and Eastern Orthodox churches produced a formal separation of the laity from God, as corporate worship was practiced. Personal devotion was not necessarily affected by this, and the history of those churches shows how the instincts of believers found ways to resist the structure's distancing of God from them. In parts of Protestantism, purity of doctrine sometimes became dominant, so that intellectual assent to a given creed seemed to take the place of a personally close relationship with God. In the present century, secularization and life in a world dominated by technology appear to have produced a kind of numbing effect, raising questions about whether there is a God who can be known personally.

Some of the forms of resistance to these trends can only be listed at this point. Mysticism has always provided for some a more direct route to God than anything the church offered in its liturgy, its doctrine, or even its scriptures.[67] In the Protestant churches, pietism arose as a reaction to the overemphasis on intellectual assent to doctrine, and this infused new life into the movement, and has remained an important influence from the seventeenth century to the present.[68] The Society of Friends (Quakers) are one of the most influential movements claiming that direct access to God via the Holy Spirit is possible, without the necessity of any other aid. Other emphases on the presence of God within the believer are to be found in the various charismatic movements, with their focus on the "gifts of the Spirit." In spite of various kinds of threats to scripture's promise that God's intention is to come near to his people with his blessings, history shows that Christians' experiences of the truth of that have resisted them all.

The kind of response that God expects from human beings has been debated without end by Christians. The issue arises first because of what the Gospels and Paul say about law. Faith in Jesus Christ rather than obedience to the Torah was declared to be the primary response people should offer to God's willingness to enter into fellowship with them. That, however, left many unanswered questions, which Paul attempted to deal with (e.g., Romans 6), but which have left Christians with ambivalent attitudes toward the law of God. We note here only some of the extreme positions. Antinomianism claims that since we are saved by the grace of God alone, with faith the only requirement put upon us, then God has given us complete freedom to do as we like, and if that does involve anything that might still be called sin, God freely forgives. Paul encountered those ideas, either as misunderstandings or misrepresentations of his teachings, but they reappeared with some prominence in some of the most extreme reactions to Roman Catholicism during the time of the Reformation.

A much more common tendency in the history of Christianity, however, has been legalism of one sort or another. The fact that the Old Testament is Christian scripture and contains repeated insistences that God expects his law to be obeyed has led many Christians to uncertainty about what to do with the Old Testament's legal material. The most common tendency has been to try to separate the moral from the cultic, then to say God expects obedience to the former, while the latter has been abrogated. The New Testament never provides any such explicit guidance as that, however, since it speaks of law as a whole. Even the Ten Commandments include two cultic provisions; the commandments concerning images and the Sabbath. Given the extensive ethical sections in the Gospels and letters of the New Testament, it is clear that God expects an obedient life as a part of the response of those who believe in him, but the difference from true legalism is to be found in the insistence that it is not the obedient life that *establishes* the relationship. We do not and cannot prove anything to God by our "goodness," and obedience to his law in no way obligates him to us. In fact, from the Christian perspective, "law" is an incorrect term, and the original sense of the Hebrew word *Torah,* "instruction" (that is, guidance as to how the loving person normally behaves), fits the role played by the ethical materials in the New Testament. That behavior is thus subsequent to the knowledge that we have been saved by grace, and is motivated by gratitude. But that explanation of God's intended relationship with us has been difficult to understand for many who consider themselves to be Christians.

Finally, the idea that God wants his true character to be reflected to the world in the lives of those he has chosen to be his people has had an important influence on many of the most devout Christians, although it remains too high an ideal for others.[69] Examples need not be given here, but one of the New Testament's most important contributions to this insight, which had already been developed in Judaism, was its equation of God with love (e.g., 1 John 4:7–21), and its exaltation of Lev. 19:18 as the second great commandment (Matt. 22:39, par.; note that Jesus adds it to his citation of commandments from the Decalogue in Matt. 19:19). If Christians were supposed to reflect the true character of God in their own lives, that meant they, like God, ought to love the sinner and to love their enemies (Matt. 5:43–48), too high an ethic for many human beings to achieve, but one that continues to challenge those who take their faith most seriously. They recognize that to love one's enemy may result in suffering or death, but the new understanding of suffering for Christ as suffering with him, noted in the New Testament section, has been answer enough for those who have provided for us the most persuasive testimonies that God indeed is love.

CHAPTER 8

THE DISTANCING OF GOD

Exodus 32—34

I was ready to be sought out by those who did not ask,
to be found by those who did not seek me.
—Isaiah 65:1a

Mercy triumphs over judgment.
—James 2:13b

Throughout scripture and throughout the history of Judaism and Christianity, God has been praised for his merciful nature, for his willingness to forgive the sins of those who ask it. We have praised him for it far more often than we have considered what it costs him. Christianity seems to have emphasized that more than Judaism, because of the cross. It seems easier for God to forgive in the Old Testament than in the New.

He does not retain his anger forever,
because he delights in showing clemency [*ḥesed*]. (Micah 7:18b)

Or as the rabbis said later, "It is only becoming for the great God that he should forgive the great sins."[1] But there is at least one place in the Old Testament where the turmoil brought about on earth by human sin seems to produce a turmoil in God himself. It is the point in the Pentateuch where the subject of sin and forgiveness is first brought up in a serious way, the story of the golden calf. In Exodus 32—34 we are thus introduced to aspects of the character of God about which the Bible has largely been silent so far, and in the lengthy dialogue between God and Moses in these chapters we may be brought as close to God as it is possible for scripture to take us.[2]

These chapters made the bridge between past and present for Israel; in effect they make the rest of the Old Testament possible. There was a terrible irony in their preservation of the words, "Everything that the LORD has spoken we will do" (Ex. 19:8; 24:7), for each time they were repeated they must have grated against the rest of Israel's story.

Both we and our ancestors have sinned;
  we have committed iniquity, have done wickedly. (Ps. 106:6)

Their history, as they remembered it, was as often the story of curses as of
blessings, and prayers of confession such as Psalm 106 show that Israel realized
they deserved it. Yet they could not give up the conviction that God still intended
them for his chosen people. As individuals, they experienced guilt, repentance,
confession, and forgiveness in their relationships with God, and they attributed to
him the same ways of dealing with their nation. The book of Exodus thus reaches
its theological conclusion with chapters 32—34, for they explain how it can be
that the covenant relationship continues in spite of perennial sinfulness.

Although the chapters reach their climax with the renewal of the covenant,
based on the fact that God is "merciful and gracious, slow to anger, and abounding
in steadfast love and faithfulness," I have borrowed the title "The Distancing of
God" from a book on another subject, in order to call attention to the way these
chapters reflect real life. On the one hand, Moses and the people show their
awareness that the presence of God in their midst is absolutely essential if they are
to have any future, but on the other hand, that stands in tension with God's
knowledge that to be present in the midst of sinful people puts them in terrible
danger. The choices throughout these chapters seem at first to be only two: dying
in their sins, if God visits them, or, if God distances himself, existing in their sins,
without hope for anything good to come. Moses desperately tries to break through
that impasse, to establish another option, as he pleads with God for forgiveness,
and eventually God will reestablish a relationship by grace alone, but he has a lot
of things to work through with these people, first.[3] These chapters thus became
one of Israel's classic statements of their awareness that to continue as the people
of God, with all their imperfections, involved a terrible tension, within themselves, and within God. It was a tension that could be eliminated only by
appealing to some kind of "cheap grace," and no justification for that can be found
here.

Our focus on the nature of God as revealed in Exodus will allow us to bypass many
of the widely discussed topics connected with these chapters. We can leave to one side
questions about the calf, whether it was supposed to represent Yahweh or another god,
supposed to replace Yahweh or Moses, and how it is related to Jeroboam's golden
calves (1 Kings 12:28). Only the seriousness of the sin, since it is taken to mean a
complete rupture of the covenant relationship, will be important for us. The roles of
Aaron, Joshua, and the Levites in the story represent other interesting traditions that do
not contribute to our work, and even Moses' shining face will not occupy our attention
for long. The literary and historical questions concerning the relationship between the
covenant sealed in chapter 24 and the one given Israel in chapter 34 are of significance
for our purposes only in that as these materials were combined to form the present book
of Exodus, chapter 34 represents the renewal of a broken covenant. Whether these may
originally have been two versions of the same covenant ceremony remains a debated

subject, but in chapters 32—34 as they now exist all the theology associated with them makes sense only with reference to a rupture and efforts to bring about healing. Once these subjects have been bracketed, it becomes clear that most of the theology in this section is contained in a long dialogue between God and Moses, which extends from 32:7 through 34:10 (from there on it is monologue), and we shall concentrate on that.

Exodus 32—34

The tensions within this passage are represented vividly by the first and last speeches of the Lord. God begins with "Let me alone, so that my wrath may burn hot against them and I may consume them" (32:10), but concludes with "Yahweh, Yahweh, a God merciful and gracious, slow to anger, and abounding in steadfast love and faithfulness" (34:6). Moses' own behavior reflects the two sides of God. He intercedes on behalf of Israel, in 32:11–13, but it is he who breaks the tablets and who carries out judgment, sorting out the righteous from the wicked as he calls out, "Who is on the LORD's side?" (32:26). The tension established in chapter 32 is increased, not relieved, as we move through the three chapters.

We do not know how much of that is deliberate, a reflection of Israel's awareness of the mystery of God, and how much may be simply the result of the effort to combine, as best they could, old traditions that did not fit together very well. There are so many apparent discontinuities within chapters 32—34 that even the commentators you might expect to try rearranging things in order to make it read more smoothly have given up, and they just try to make as much sense of it as they can in the present order. There is general agreement that we have here a collection of various traditions concerning the presence of Yahweh with Israel in the wilderness, some of which (especially the verses about the tent of meeting, 33:7–11) don't fit very well together, but serious efforts have been made to determine what the final editor had in mind, as he put them together in this order. I shall offer you one reading of it, with comments on how others have done it, but first let us see just how difficult it is.

The people committed a terrible sin against the very essence of the covenant relationship (32:1–6), God decided to be done with them as hopeless cases and to start over with Moses, but Moses manages to avert that plan (32:7–14). That does not mean the wicked will not be judged, however, and in fact it is Moses who begins the judgment (32:15–29). But now, having destroyed the apostates via the swords of the Levites (we thought), he offers to go up to the Lord to try to make atonement for the people's sin (32:30–34). So whom did the Levites kill? In verse 30 and for the rest of the passage all the people seem to be considered guilty. Here is the first discontinuity.

The Lord won't talk about forgiveness at all, at this point, but does say that Moses should lead these people to the Promised Land. And judgment lies somewhere ahead (32:33–34). Then we are told of a plague, sent directly by the Lord, in punishment for the golden calf. Is that the judgment just mentioned?

Next comes a repetition and elaboration of the command to leave Mount Sinai (33:1–3), an apparent doublet of 32:34. No one can explain why it should have been said twice. The word that Yahweh will not go with them leads to mourning on the part of the people, and that leads the Lord to repeat and reinforce his reason for it: that to be in their midst would mean their destruction (33:5). Then we are told that the people stripped themselves of their ornaments from that time on, without ever being told exactly what that means. The flow of verses 1–6 is not at all smooth, but with careful reading we may come to the conclusion that it is just the author's style, and that we can follow the progression of thought adequately. I shall try to show that later.

The narrative about the tent of meeting (33:7–11) is perfectly straightforward, in contrast to the rest of the chapter, but there is still a problem with it, and that is how to understand what it means in this context. I shall not spend much time with that section, since we are focusing on the dialogue between Moses and God, but the best explanation seems to be that the author is here recalling the means by which Moses encountered God before they came to Mount Sinai. All the dialogue in these chapters seems to take place on the mountain, but because of the amount of dialogue it may have seemed appropriate to include this record of earlier encounters in order to include the line, "Thus the LORD used to speak to Moses face to face, as a man speaks to his friend" (v. 11).

Moses appeals to God, asking that he go with them on the journey, basing the appeal now on his own personal relationship with God (33:12f.), and God seems to relent, but with conditions (33:17–23). God then offers a new covenant (34:1–7), but Moses' response to that is to express anxiety that God might not go with them (34:9). At every point there is danger associated with the presence of God, but God's presence is also essential, and so Moses dares to approach and to ask. God's speech in which he reestablishes the broken covenant begins with a gracious promise (34:10), but that promise includes the words, "for it is an awesome thing that I will do with you."

Interpreters have tried to relieve the tensions in this passage in one of two ways. The older source analysis, which took the obvious discontinuities that appear as we move from one paragraph to another as evidence for different writers, could conclude that we simply have different, conflicting theologies, and would not try to make anything of the passage as a whole. An even older solution was simply to emphasize the parts that appealed to the interpreter and then ignore or explain away the rest. But the current generation of scholars insists on trying to read these three chapters as a whole. They acknowledge that individual paragraphs may have a prior history, which we cannot reconstruct, but believe that the way the parts have been put together is meaningful.[4] These authors believe, as I do, that the tensions are essential, for both themes are part of authentic experiences of God in the lives of believers. Indeed, the crucial problems of this passage are not literary or historical, they are theological. The starkness of the way these tensions are represented here brings us very close to the true God, as scripture reveals him.

A few words must be said about the enormity of the sin, as described in Exodus and as understood by all later interpreters, for this provides the essential context for the dialogue between Moses and God.[5] The golden calf is seen by Moses and by the author of the passage as a direct violation of the first two commandments, and those commandments have always been understood by Jews to contain the essence of God's requirements of them: No other God but Yahweh, and no physical representations of anything claimed to be god.[6] But forty days later the covenant relationship has already been broken, and when one breaks a relationship that was supposed to be exclusive, as this was, the effects will be severe. As Amos put it, "You only have I known of all the families of the earth; therefore I will punish you for all your iniquities" (3:2). Terence Fretheim appropriately compares the relationship to marriage, as the Old Testament already does, and the golden calf incident to the pain of divorce.[7] The rabbis, given their commitment to one God who could not be represented by anything in heaven or on earth, considered the golden calf to be the worst sin ever committed by Israel. *Exodus Rabbah* says, "Had Israel waited for Moses and not perpetrated that act, there would have been no exile, neither would the Angel of Death have had any power over them" (XXXII:1; cf. XLIII.2). It is thus as close as Judaism gets to a concept of original sin, and so Fretheim speaks of this as Judaism's "fall story."[8]

Potentially, then, the first six verses of chapter 32 might have led to the appearance of one of scripture's repeated themes: "starting over." That is in fact what God proposes to do, in verse 10: "Now let me alone, so that my wrath may burn hot against them and I may consume them; and of you I will make a great nation." Starting over is an important biblical theme, but not the dominant one. It first appears in scripture in the Flood story. At the end, the author has to admit the Flood really served no purpose, and was thus not to be understood as revealing God's way of bringing about the cure for human sin. God had wiped out the wicked and was about to start over with one righteous man and his family, but then he must admit, "I will never again curse the ground because of humankind, for the inclination of the human heart is evil from youth; nor will I ever again destroy every living creature as I have done" (Gen. 8:21). And the drunkenness of Noah, in the next chapter, is the first example of the truth that the inclination is evil from youth and that sin will have to be dealt with in some other way. The theme of starting over does reappear, however; most prominently in the message of the prophets, who interpreted the exile as the death of old Israel and then promised that God would start over with resurrection in the form of a new, forgiven people (Ezek. 37:1–14). And the later apocalyptic writers also thought of God one day carrying out a dramatic wiping out of all evil, to replace it with a new creation. But throughout scripture that theme stands in tension with the other one, represented by the working out of the promise to Abraham, and this latter one tends to dominate, as the wording of God's reflection on the Flood already predicts (Gen. 8:21–22 and 9:8–17). Moses will dare to challenge God's inclination to start over with him by reminding him of what he had promised to the descendants of Abraham, and so that slow and difficult process which is the basic Old Testament story will continue.

God initiates the dialogue while Moses is still on the mountain, with the shocking words that the whole plan has already failed (32:7–10).[9] In the first exchange (32:7–14) we shall concentrate on two words: *hanniḥah*, "let (me) alone," in verse 10, and *hinnaḥem*, "repent" (better, with NRSV: "change your mind") in verse 12. This is one of the most striking passages in the whole Bible concerning what may be called the "vulnerability" of God. Having said that, I must immediately emphasize that in this passage God's vulnerability is set alongside strong statements concerning his sovereignty. God appears in verses 7–10 as the judge who pronounces Israel guilty, worthy of annihilation. It is in these chapters that the freedom of God is declared in the classic statement, "I will be gracious to whom I will be gracious, and will show mercy on whom I will show mercy" (33:19). And the covenant eventually is renewed without any request by Moses or the people, by the initiative of God alone. Yet this sovereign God, who is fully in charge, according to most of the verses in these chapters, not only listens to the appeals of Moses and grants them—albeit in accordance with his own freedom to modify them—but is also represented as a God who will change his plans as a result of human intervention, and more than that; he indicates that he has subjected himself to some extent to the will of Moses. There has been a good deal of discussion over the centuries of the attribution of "repentance" to God, and I will come to that shortly, but not so much has been done with the "let me alone" of verse 10, very likely because it doesn't fit most people's theology very well. I intend to take both words seriously.

Moses has been on the mountain forty days and the people have given up on him. "As for this Moses, the man who brought us up out of the land of Egypt, we do not know what has become of him" (32:1b). But they have really given up on Yahweh, as God sees it. Having made them his people forty days earlier, Yahweh now will not call them "my people." They are "your people" in verse 7 and "this people" in verse 9. They have turned aside quickly from the way God commanded them, and they have corrupted themselves (NRSV: "acted perversely"). The root is the same one used in the prelude to the Flood story: "And God saw that the earth was corrupt; for all flesh had corrupted its ways upon the earth" (Gen. 6:12). In the next verse the narrator uses the same root to describe what God will do with the Flood, here translated "now I am going to destroy them along with the earth." The root seems to describe something like a physical corruption, such as rot, which destroys the thing corrupted. But at Sinai the people have insisted on it: "I have seen this people, how stiff-necked they are" (32:9). There is judgment even in the choice of the common word "see," at this point. Exodus speaks rarely about what God has seen. In 2:25; 3:7; 4:31 he saw the misery of Israel in Egypt, and that led to his determination to save them. He saw Moses approach the burning bush (3:4), and he saw the blood on the doorposts on the Passover night (12:13). Seeing is a part of the gracious, saving acts of God, until chapter 32, but now he sees this is a stiff-necked people he has chosen. Seeing already involves a decision. The decision corresponds to justice. In their preference for the golden calf, they have rejected the way of life, so they should die. That need not mean God has failed, for he is free to chose whom he will, and he means to choose Moses, just as long before he had chosen to start over with one righteous man, Noah, and just as he had freely chosen Abraham and Sarah to be the recipients of his gracious promise. Indeed, the offer to Moses is a clear reflection of the promise to Abraham, "and of you I will make a great nation" (32:10b; cf. Gen. 12:2).

There is something new in this passage, however. Noah and Abraham had no choice in the matter, but Moses does. God has to get Moses' permission, believe it or not. Moses hasn't said anything yet, is still on the mountain and knew nothing of what was going on down below until God tells him about it, but God strangely does not feel free to act without consulting Moses. "Now therefore let me alone [*hannihah*], so that my wrath may burn hot against them and I may consume them; and of you I will make a great nation." What shall we make of this?

The word is a hifil imperative of the root *nuªh*, which means to let something lie in a place, to leave behind, to let something remain, to allow something to happen, or, in five occurrences, all in the imperative, to let someone alone. The blind Samson says to the guard who is holding him, "let me alone that I may feel the pillars supporting the house" (Judg. 16:26). David says to those who would kill Shimei for cursing him, "let him alone and let him curse" (2 Sam. 16:11). Josiah uses the expression of the remains of a prophet whose tomb is found at Bethel, "let him alone, let no one move his bones" (2 Kings 23:18). And God says through Hosea, "Like a stubborn heifer, Israel is stubborn; can the LORD now feed them like a lamb in a broad pasture? Ephraim is joined to idols—let him alone" (Hos. 4:16–17). These are the other occurrences. In each case someone who has the power to do something to another is asked to refrain. Only once, in the Bible, is God the one affected, as he asks of a human being, "Let me alone, that. . . ."[10] Who would dare to write such a thing?

As you might expect, interpreters have either glossed over the expression, saying nothing about it, or have said this is an example of God accommodating himself to our human inability to understand him in his fullness, or have said it is actually God's invitation to Moses to intercede. But for the time being, at least, let us stay with the plain meaning of the words in verse 10, and allow that God is, for some reason, unwilling to act without Moses' "permission." Having been told to let God alone, however, Moses disobeys. He will not let God alone. George Coats discusses this passage as one of the striking examples of how faithfulness sometimes must be expressed by challenging God, rather than meekly obeying. But how, he asks, does one know what distinguishes an accusation addressed to

God as an act of loyal trust and faith from one that can only be taken as rebellion or apostasy? His conclusion, which is supported by this passage, and others such as the first chapter of Habakkuk, is that to contend with God is the mark of an obedient servant when it is based on the conviction that God will live up to his reputation and will keep his promises.[11] We shall see that Moses does begin with reputation, but that his clinching argument has to do with God's faithfulness to his promise.

Moses has three points that have been neatly labeled by Fretheim as reasonableness (v. 11), reputation (v. 12), and promise (v. 13).[12] The first two begin with a familiar word from the laments, "Why?" and we recognize from this and other features that Moses does in fact use elements of Israel's traditional language of prayer.[13] "O LORD, why does thy wrath burn hot against thy people, whom thou hast brought forth out of the land of Egypt with great power and with a mighty hand?" (32:11). God has gone to considerable trouble to get them this far. They didn't really want to come, in the first place, and once they hit the wilderness they wanted to go back. Pharaoh took even more persuading than the Israelites, and the plagues and crossing of the Sea showed that even the cosmos itself had to be disrupted in order to bring this about. Certainly the golden calf is far worse than the earlier incidents of "murmuring in the wilderness," but shouldn't God reconsider this new plan? Isn't he overreacting? Be reasonable, Moses dares to say to God.

Next he asks God to consider what the neighbors will say: "Why should the Egyptians say, 'It was with evil intent that he brought them out to kill them in the mountains, and to consume them from the face of the earth'?" It makes a difference, in Israel, what the nations think of their God. Deuteronomy's version of Moses' plea introduces yet another insult that might come from Egypt, no doubt based on what foreigners who had defeated Israel actually did say, in later times: ". . . otherwise the land from which you have brought us might say, 'Because the LORD was not able to bring them into the land that he promised them' " (Deut. 9:28).

Then come four potent verbs, as Moses moves to his third argument. Turn (*shuv*), the common verb used of human repentance; repent (the niphal of *nhm*), better translated with the NRSV "change your mind"; remember (*zkr*), and swear (the niphal of *shv'*). Let us take them in reverse order, understanding "turn" and "repent" to be synonymous here. As we have seen, biblical Hebrew has no word that literally means "promise," but the Old Testament is full of promises, nevertheless. The most potent word in the language associated with the idea of promising is "to swear, to take a solemn oath." Moses' quotation of the divine promise is not an exact citation of anything in Genesis, but most of what he says may be found by combining Gen. 22:16–17 with 12:7 or 15:18. He appeals to God's solemn oath, as the clinching argument that he should not give up on Israel. Yes, he has the right and the power to start over, but that is not the way he has been working with the descendants of Abraham. But in a way, this is a very weak argument, for God has offered to start over with Moses, who is a descendant of Abraham, Isaac, and Jacob, and who could keep the line intact. So maybe the key word in the sentence is "remember."

"Remember" is used in a special way with God as subject. It is not as if they thought God's memory was faulty when they call upon him to remember, or God is said to have remembered. One of the uses of *zkr* in Hebrew has to do with the decision to take action, and they typically use it of God in that way. God is the subject of the verb only three times in Exodus. We found it associated with three other potent verbs in 2:24–25: "And God *heard* their groaning, and God *remembered* his covenant with Abraham, with Isaac, and with Jacob. And God *saw* the people of Israel, and God *knew* their condition."

We have already observed the contrasting uses of "see" in chapters 2 and 32. "Know" is also a common word, but is used with God as subject in only a few significant places in Exodus. And "remember" occurs only with reference to the covenant with the patriarchs. The other passage is 6:5: "I have also heard the groaning of the Israelites whom the Egyptians are holding as slaves and I have remembered my covenant." The occurrences in chapters 2 and 6 mark God's decision to begin the exodus, the first step toward fulfilling his promise to Abraham, Isaac, and Jacob, which the oppression in Egypt seemed to have made a thing of the past. It had begun; Moses appeals to God to let it continue somehow. He cannot defend Israel; they are guilty and do not deserve to go on. If the justice of God were the subject there could be no argument; the matter is clear. Moses can appeal to no ground for continuance in Israel, but he believes there is a ground in the character of Yahweh himself. And that allows him to ask God to change his mind.

The so-called repentance of God first occurs in Gen. 6:6, the prelude to the Flood story.[14] The KJV translated that verse, "and it repented the LORD that he had made man on the earth, and it grieved him at his heart," trying to find a passive sense for the niphal stem of the root *nḥm*. Now we recognize that the niphal of that root is active, so the RSV, the NRSV, and other modern versions translate, "and the LORD was sorry." Elsewhere, however, the RSV frequently used "repent," in the active voice, but occasionally chose "relent," or "change his mind." The NRSV has now appropriately abandoned "repent," when God is the subject, as he usually is, for the English word carries undesirable connotations. We ordinarily use it to speak of repenting of sin, and it is never said that God sins or needs to repent of sin. There are two other English words beginning with *re-* that convey the appropriate connotations: regret, and relent.[15]

The statistics on the use of this term are important. It occurs thirty-six times. Thirty times God is the subject; humans are the subject six times. Twice the human subject repents of sin (Jer. 8:6; 31:19); the other references speak of change of mind or regret, like those in which God is subject.[16] This is one of the more unusual ways of speaking of God's mercy. Of the thirty occurrences with God as subject, twenty-four of them speak of him changing his mind, and in nineteen of those he changes his mind away from an intended or actual judgment of sinful people. Among the other five uses, only one is from mercy to judgment. Jeremiah proposes a hypothetical case, claiming that if a nation does evil, God will change his mind about his intended blessings (Jer. 18:10). In two passages the word is used twice each to speak of God's regret that something intended for good has not worked out: the creation of human beings (Gen. 6:6, 7) and the selection of Saul to be king (1 Sam. 15:11, 35).

The other six occurrences speak of God not changing his mind. Jeremiah and Ezekiel claim that the imminent judgment they proclaim cannot be averted (Jer. 4:28; 20:16; Ezek. 24:14), and Zechariah refers back to that judgment (8:14). In Ps. 110:4 God affirms that he will never change his mind about his oath to the house of David: "You are a priest forever according to the order of Melchizedek." This leaves the most puzzling of such statements, for it is very general and it occurs in 1 Samuel 15, right in the midst of the story in which it is said twice that God did change his mind about Saul. Samuel is relentless, in spite of Saul's confession of sin and appeal for forgiveness; God has rejected him. And the finality of that is sealed by this theological statement: "Moreover the Glory of Israel will not recant or change his mind; for he is not a mortal, that he should change his mind" (v. 29, NRSV).

Does the chapter contradict itself? Fretheim claims it does not.[17] He sees this as a classic example of our inability ever to express the full truth about God in human language. Whereas Calvin approached the matter from the divine direction, speaking of God's accommodation of his speech to our meagre capacities of understanding, the modern way is to approach it from the human direction, via linguistic studies of the uses of metaphor. The ideas of regretting or changing one's mind come from human experience; they can be no more than imperfect metaphors for what God is really like, but they do convey a measure of truth. So Fretheim says the two apparently contrary uses of *hinnahem* are evidence of the discontinuity between human metaphors and divine reality. In 1 Sam. 15:29 and again in Num. 23:19 it is said that God does not change his mind, because he is not a human being. But in Hosea 11, when God does change his mind, saying "I will not execute my fierce anger; I will not again destroy Ephraim," the reason given is the same one we have just found in 1 Samuel and Numbers for not changing his mind: "For I am God and no mortal, the Holy One in your midst" (v. 9). Earlier I emphasized the tensions in the way God is represented in chapters 32—34, and insisted we should live with them, for they are likely to get us closer to the true God than any simple, easily understood picture. Here is another example of those tensions. But the burden of the evidence is that God's consistency is in his intention to save, so that he may decide to avert an act of judgment for any reason at all, and sometimes for no reason that we can see.

Moses' insistence that God change was clearly based on his conviction as to what is unchangeable in God, namely his unwavering intention to save. And according to the author of the story, Moses was not wrong. "The LORD changed his mind about the disaster that he planned to bring on his people" (32:14).

Moses, however, seems to have undergone a dramatic change of mind, once he saw what the people had done, for a terrible scene of violence follows (32:15–29). Seeing the calf and the orgy surrounding it, Moses smashed the tablets, which were the visible symbol of the covenant relationship. He burnt and ground the calf into dust, put it into water, and forced the people to drink it. We are not told what the results of that may have been, unless it produced the plague that God is said to have sent, in verse 35. He then made a division between those on Yahweh's side—who seem to be only his own tribe, the tribe of Levi—and the others, and ordered the members of his tribe to slaughter "every man his brother, and every man his companion, and every man his neighbor." Since God had agreed not to give up on Israel entirely, one would think this would settle the matter; it sounds as though the apostates have all been killed. But the next day dawns, and it seems nothing has been settled. We hear of no distinctions between faithful and apostate from here on out; they are just "the people," and the word "sin" appears in connection with them seven times in the next four verses. What Moses accomplished the first time on the mountain, and what he had done in the camp are now completely ignored, and he attempts to make atonement by confessing their sin (v. 31) and by appealing for forgiveness. As in verses 7–14, however, Moses refuses to set himself apart from them. If God will not forgive them, presumably meaning death for them all, Moses wants to die with them (v. 32). Here is a case where many (not all) Christian interpreters have read vicarious atonement into a passage where it does not properly belong. Martin Noth, for example, says Moses attempts to atone by offering himself as a vicarious sacrifice,[18] but the text does not say that, and it is more appropriate to understand him saying if Israel must die, he wants to die with them.[19]

Moses has asked two things, so far: forgiveness for the people, and if not, death for himself along with them. God's answer, "Whoever has sinned against me I will blot out of my book" (32:33), has been taken in two ways. Some take it as an answer to the forgiveness question, an unqualified reaffirmation of strict retribution, apparently ruling out forgiveness on any grounds. It seems to me more fitting to take it as an answer to Moses' second request, as other interpreters do. Sinners will be blotted out of God's book, yes, but not Moses. And with that blunt statement, God moves quickly to a new subject, the journey that should now begin from Mount Sinai to the Promised Land. The one sentence (v. 34) contains a command, a promise, and a threat. The promise seems here to be a repeat of one made earlier, in 23:20–24, of an "angel," called here and in 23:23 "my angel," who will go before the people to lead them to the land. Usually the word *mal'ak* should be translated "messenger," for that is what they ordinarily do, but this figure is a guide and a guardian, not a messenger. As a messenger, the *mal'ak* speaks God's word, in the first person, and this guide and guardian is also closely identified with God in Ex. 23:21, when God says, "my name is in him." The modern translations still use "angel," and so do many of the commentators, but I suggest that more appropriate renderings are "representative" or "agent." As your agent represents your will in a matter, just as if you were there, speaking for you and acting for you, even signing for you if the agent has power of attorney, so the *mal'ak* functions for God in the Old Testament. So far, then, this looks like a promise; it will be different when the word reappears in 33:2, however, and we shall have to think about it again.

The threat in verse 34 is singularly menacing, for it specifies no time or place or form of punishment: "Nevertheless, in the day when I visit, I will visit their sin upon them" (RSV). The word "visit" (*paqad*), which can mean to visit in order to bless or visit in order to punish, has been used in the favorable sense up to now (Ex. 3:16; 4:31; 13:19), but the next visit is marked as a time for judgment. It is not likely that as Israel remembered this threat, they took the next verse, concerning the plague, to be the end of the matter. Given their awareness of the seriousness of the sin with the golden calf, they probably saw this as a threat under which they lived from that time on, ready to fall upon them at any time they committed such a sin again.

As we turn to Ex. 33:1–3, we cannot explain why command, promise, and threat should be repeated immediately. It is likely that these were originally parts of two separate traditions, but why would the author have included them both, and why separate them by the reference to the plague? The command and the promise are both elaborated in a way that has been familiar since God first spoke to Moses at the burning bush, with reference to the promise to the ancestors and to the expulsion of the inhabitants of the land, but the threat is different. God now introduces the theme of distancing. "I will not go up among you, lest I consume you in the way, for you are a stiff-necked people" (v. 3). The withdrawal of the promise of his presence coordinates with a missing pronoun; in 32:34 it was "my agent" that would go before them, but now it is just "an agent." Commentators struggle mightily to try to understand what the difference might be. It is assumed that the promise of the agent in chapter 23 is a promise that God's presence will be with them, but now somehow his presence is distinguished from that of the agent. Several have tried to imagine two different kinds of angels, but there is no textual support for that. Using my word, "agent," may help us to get an appropriate feeling for the reason these words are called "evil tidings" (RSV; "harsh words," NRSV) in the next verse. Ordinarily, your agent serves you very well, carrying out your business just as if you were there, and your business associates feel no problem in dealing with the agent instead of personally with you. But now your wedding is approaching and you inform your intended spouse that your agent will be there to take the vows for you (we won't carry the analogy any further), then your mother dies, and you send your agent to the funeral with instructions to show appropriate grief. There are certain things the agent could do, but it isn't appropriate to do them that way, and those things are one's personal relationships, which are, after all, the most important things in life. Something like this may be happening in verse 3: God will fulfill his promise to Israel; Moses had convinced him that was the right thing to do back in the previous chapter. They will get the Promised Land, but that is all. Verse 4 tells us the people knew that was not enough.

They mourned. Some take this, along with verse 6, to indicate sincere and lasting repentance, but it has been pointed out that the typical word for repent (*shuv*) is not used, and that mourning can simply express regret.[20] But we know Israel is well aware that they have lost something essential. Whether that has produced any real change in them is not so clear. It would help if we knew what the ornaments meant. Some connect them with the loot they got from the Egyptians, and say they have given that up. Most think of them as finery worn during times of worship, which they no longer wear since they were signs of their redeemed state. One other possibility is that the ornaments were symbols of pagan cults, which they now give up.

God's next word to Moses repeats the warning: "If for a single moment [a wink of the eye, in Hebrew], I should go up among you, I would consume you" (v. 5). Although the people mourn it, God's distancing is actually protective. The threat of 32:34, "in the day when I visit, I will visit their sin upon them," is mitigated somewhat by God's decision to distance himself from these people, whom he knows to be still "stiff-necked." The author dares here to show us God struggling with his options. He will not just override the rebellious human spirit; since Eden God has not worked with us that way, but has allowed us our free will. Neither does God make a quick fix by sorting out righteous from wicked, and wiping out the latter. The Flood story already tells us that is not his chosen way, and Paul eventually realized that if God did, there would be no one left. We know that God will choose the way of forgiveness, but the righteous God will not just say to the murderer, the torturer, the tormenter, "That's all right; it doesn't really matter." It matters a great deal, and the way the Old Testament speaks of how much it matters is in terms of burning wrath, and in terms of physical distance. God is said to hide his face, or his presence, and that leaves us in mourning, but at least it leaves the future open. Israel understood the way to forgiveness is no easy one, for how can forgiveness avoid condoning evil? God is depicted here as struggling within himself: "Put off your ornaments from you, that I may know what to do with you," but at least that means all is not yet lost for Israel.

We come now to the most difficult part of the passage, verses 12–17. Moses asks two lengthy questions, to which God gives two brief answers, but the thought does not move smoothly or clearly. Moses seems very cautious at this point, compared with his boldness in chapter 32, and a major part of what he has to say concerns his own status with God. The people come in almost as afterthoughts, and nothing at all is said about their sinfulness in these verses. Perhaps they are not afterthoughts at all, however, but are brought in by Moses very carefully, after he tries to lay some groundwork based on God's choice of him to carry out the task of bringing these people to Sinai in the first place. The journey from Sinai to the Promised Land, which God has ordered Moses to begin, is the issue now, along with the question of who will accompany him and these people.

Moses' two speeches follow the same pattern. Each begins on a negative note, in each case apparently contradicting something God has said:

> [Verse 12] See, you have said to me, "Bring up this people"; but you have not let me know whom you will send with me. [Verse 15, *Just after God has said, "My presence will go"*] If your presence will not go, do not carry us up from here.

Moses apparently is not at all sure what is supposed to happen next. Is he completely on his own from here on, as leader of these people? The distinction between God's presence and the agent's presence, which God made in verses 2–3, was apparently no clearer to Moses than it is to us.[21] Moses' own status is evidently in question, for the question does not concern God's sending the agent before the people, but whom God will send with *him*.

Moses' special status before God thus becomes the thread that runs through this passage, and also through the next section, verses 18–23. Note how it dominates each of the four speeches:

> MOSES: Yet you have said, "I know you by name and you have also found favor in my sight." Now, if I have found favor in your sight . . . [then comes his first request]. (vv. 12b-13)
>
> GOD: I will give you rest. (v. 14b)
>
> MOSES: For how shall it be known that I have found favor in your sight, I and your people? (v. 16a)
>
> GOD: For you have found favor in my sight, and I know you by name. (v. 17b, no reference to the people)

Now it so happens that nowhere earlier in Exodus can we find God saying to Moses, "I know you by name and you also have found favor in my sight," so we have no basis in our text for knowing why Moses says this. God does not contradict it, however, but affirms it in the same words in verse 17. These are two potent expressions. Earlier, we considered at length the significance of one's name; that to know one's name is thus to have intimate knowledge of a person. One might then think it could be said God knows everyone's name, and in a sense that fits Hebrew thought, but the expression can be used in a special way to indicate divine favor. For example:

> Do not fear, for I have redeemed you;
> I have called you by name, you are mine. (Isa. 43:1b)

Moses is in fact the only person in the Bible of whom it is said, God *knew* him by name. Furthermore, there are only two people who are said to have "found favor in God's sight," and they are Noah and Moses. Moses says God had assured him earlier that he held this favored status, but his insecurity comes out in the request that follows: "*If* I have found favor in your sight, show me your ways, that

I may know you *and* find favor in your sight" (33:12). God knows Moses, but Moses is not at all sure he can claim to know God. Outwitting and defeating the Egyptians in order to get a people who could be Yahweh's own he could understand; finding ways to deal with the people's undisciplined nature in the wilderness he could understand; making a covenant with them which involved responsibility on their part he could understand; but now that they had demonstrated how stiff-necked they were and God had said to go ahead and lead them toward the Promised Land anyway, Moses does not understand. If his favored status is really to continue, he must know more than this. Then, with caution, he adds to his personal request, "Consider too that this nation is your people."

Moses' caution kept him from asking God's presence to go with them; he has only alluded to his uncertainty about who will accompany him. God brings in that subject, and a new one, so he does not respond directly to Moses' request to know his way or to consider that this nation is his people. His answer, in Hebrew, is simply, "My presence will go." Translators have added "with you," making the response less vague than it really is. God is not committing himself to very much, at this time. His new subject is the promise of rest for Moses: nothing specific except, as most commentators take it, reassurance of eventual relief from this present anxiety, and perhaps that is what does come in the next chapter, although the author never alludes to it again.

God's answer to Moses has been positive, but vague, and Moses is still not sure about this journey they have been commanded to undertake. His second speech begins in a negative way, as the previous one did. "If your presence will not go [no "with me" in the Hebrew here, either], do not carry us up from here" (33:15). Then he moves to his personal status again, but getting much bolder, reminding God that his original intention was for these people also to have a special status in his sight. He alludes to that exclusive relationship we traced in the previous chapter of this book: "You shall be my treasured possession out of all the peoples" (19:5). Now Moses says, "For how shall it be known that I have found favor in your sight, I *and your people?*" On that basis, appealing to God's covenant promise, Moses asks him to reconsider his decision not to go with them: "In this way, [then the reference to chapter 19:] we shall be distinct, I and your people, from every people on the face of the earth" (33:16).

That tension between God and Moses concerning these people, which appeared in chapter 32, reappears here. God is still very reticent about being able to make anything of such people, but Moses will not give up on them. Saying it that way seems to put God in a bad light, but maybe God's reticence is well-grounded; maybe he understands the problem better than Moses does. But once again, as in chapter 32, God does not stand aloof, making royal decisions without getting involved with the people concerned. God listens to Moses, and Moses' commitment to these people makes a difference. I do not read passages such as these as evidence humans have to try to persuade, somehow, a reluctant God to do what is right. The picture of God presented to us throughout the Old

Testament is that of a God who has chosen to work *with*, rather than just *upon* human beings, so that humans (in this case Moses) are given the chance, if they will accept that responsibility, to contribute to a future that will be different from what it would have been, had they remained passive.

That is what God seems to be saying to Moses, at any rate, in verse 17. The answer is not specific, but it is direct and not vague: "I will do the very thing that you have asked," and he will do that because of who Moses is: "for you have found favor in my sight, and I know you by name."

Moses' response reveals that even this answer is not enough for him, for next he will ask to see God's glory, not just to know his ways.

It is his briefest speech, four words in Hebrew, "Please show me your glory" (33:18). I am going to offer an explanation of this which differs from every commentator I have consulted so far. This is regularly taken to be a request for a direct vision of God himself, surpassing even the "face-to-face" conversations. We can see why interpreters have taken it that way; it is because God's answer reminds Moses that humans cannot see God and live. But, having understood the reference to "glory" as a request for a direct vision, they then are puzzled over the apparent discontinuity with what had just ensued. The subject had been Moses' request that God's presence accompany them through the wilderness, and God had just granted that request, in verse 17. Why would Moses now be asking for something like a personal, mystical experience for himself? It seemed so inappropriate to Calvin that he commented, "Thus far the desires of Moses had been confined within the limits of moderation and sobriety, but now he is carried beyond due bounds, and longs for more than is lawful or expedient; for it is plain from his repulse that he had inconsiderately proceeded further than he should." Note that he based that reading on the way God responded, as all other interpreters do, but it may be helpful to recall that in every case throughout this dialogue, except for verse 17, which speaks only in general terms, God's responses to Moses are never direct answers to what Moses has been saying. We shall see that continues to be true in the final exchange, 34:9–10. So maybe in 33:19–23, as elsewhere, God is introducing his own subject matter.

My reason for suggesting that comes from a study of the ways "glory" is used elsewhere, especially in Exodus itself. It occurs in only six passages in this book, and three of them are instructive for us. In chapter 16, in connection with the gift of the manna, the people are told, "in the morning you shall see the glory of the LORD" (v. 7), and they do: "they looked toward the wilderness, and the glory of the LORD appeared in the cloud" (v. 10). Note that glory and the cloud are associated, and that in 34:5 the Lord will descend in the cloud. In 24:16–17, "The glory of the LORD settled on Mount Sinai, and the cloud covered it for six days; on the seventh day he called to Moses out of the cloud. Now the appearance of the glory of the LORD was like a devouring fire on the top of the mountain in the sight of the people of Israel." Once again, glory and cloud are together, and the people see the glory. The same thing is said in connection with the tabernacle, in chapter

40: "Then the cloud covered the tent of meeting, and the glory of the LORD filled the tabernacle. . . . For the cloud of the LORD was on the tabernacle by day, and fire was in the cloud by night, before the eyes of all the house of Israel at each stage of their journey" (vv. 34, 38). Elsewhere in Exodus we find that the glory is what *can* be seen of God's presence, so what's the problem when Moses asks to see God's glory here? I suggest there is no problem, either of Moses asking more than he should have, or of an apparent change of subject over against verses 12–17. The cloud, within which the glory of the Lord could be seen, had accompanied Israel out of Egypt and had led them to Mount Sinai. God had ordered Moses now to leave Sinai and proceed to the Promised Land, but with only an agent to guide them. Moses and the people are alarmed at this, and he appeals to God for his presence to go with them, an appeal that God has finally granted in verse 17. Now Moses' request to see God's glory would seem to be the expected next step, for elsewhere in Exodus it represents God's guiding presence with the people.

Reading verse 18 that way makes it a natural consequence of the dialogue in verses 12–17. God's answer is closely related to what follows in 34:1–10, however. There is an impressive sequence of relationships showing that 34:5–8 are the fulfillment of what God promised to do in 33:19–23. (1) In tracing the use of "glory" in Exodus we saw that it is associated with the cloud. Moses' request to see the glory is paralleled by 34:5: "And the LORD descended in the cloud." (2) God says, "[T]here is a place by me where you shall stand," in 33:21, and in 34:5 we are told the Lord "stood with him there." (3) God tells Moses, "I will make all my goodness pass before you," and "while my glory passes by" (33:19, 21), and in 34:6, "The LORD passed before him." (4) God promised to pronounce before Moses his name, Yahweh (33:19), and in 34:6, he passed before Moses and proclaimed, "Yahweh, Yahweh. . . ." (5) In 33:19 he offers a preliminary definition of his name, "I will be gracious to whom I will be gracious, and will show mercy on whom I will show mercy," and in 34:6–7 comes the full definition, using the same two words: "Yahweh, Yahweh, a God merciful and gracious." Many, though not all, commentators thus agree that the verses 33:19–23 are the introduction to 34:5–8, and that verses 34:1–4 are the preparations for the fulfillment of what God had just promised.

Some further comments on 33:19–23 are called for. I have suggested that Moses' request to see God's glory has not been an impertinence, and that the ensuing verses are no rebuke of him.[22] God's response in fact does more than Moses asks here, and picks up his earlier request that God show him his way, that he might know Yahweh. But, as always, God sets his own agenda, for God knows what we need better than we do. Moses asked to see, but here he is told that it is not by seeing that God is best known. Desiring to see the glory of the Lord is not desiring enough, for revelation comes by hearing, not by seeing, according to scripture.[23] God promises that his "goodness" will pass before Moses and offers to proclaim before him the divine name. Yes, he will also be given something that can be seen, but that must be very limited, and we are not told of anything that

Moses learned from that. The vision cannot amount to very much, but the words that accompany it are astonishing.

Since Moses asked to see God's glory and God responded by saying he would make his goodness pass before him, some take the word *tuv* to mean "beauty," as it does in some occurrences. Others, myself included, think that this is a divine correction of Moses' request, replacing something that can be seen with a revelation of God's attributes, so that the goodness that will pass before him is the statement "merciful and gracious, slow to anger. . . ."[24] If so, it is easier to understand the next part of the sentence, "and I will be gracious to whom I will be gracious, and will show mercy on whom I will show mercy." That is part of the goodness, the revelation of God's way Moses asked for earlier. The structure of that sentence is very interesting, since it follows a reference to the proclamation of the name Yahweh, and it echoes what God said when he first revealed his name to Moses: *'ehyeh 'asher 'ehyeh*, "I am who I am." We have seen that can be taken to be an affirmation of God's freedom, or as a promise of God's presence. So also, two different emphases have been found in verse 19b. Many see this as God's insistence on his freedom to choose those to whom he will be gracious and merciful. Calvin found that to be an important text, and he devotes two and one-half pages of his commentary to this defense of God's freedom. Others, however, see this kind of expression to be one of the ways the Hebrew language used for emphasis, so it might be translated, "I will have mercy . . . yes indeed I will have mercy," but they do not deny that God's freedom is also a part of it. Here God begins to speak of his essential character, which Moses certainly has been depending on all along, or he never could have dared approach God the way he has, but which Moses himself has never mentioned. Note that his intercessions in chapter 32 say nothing of grace and mercy. As the story is told, the author is building toward this and makes the message about grace and mercy come from God alone. That message would be worth nothing if it could be thought to have originated in Moses' or Israel's wishful thinking; if there is anything to it at all it must come straight from God.

Those words were in anticipation of the revelation that comes in chapter 34, but before that happens God says something about the ontological difference between the divine and the human. Hebrew puts it rather bluntly: "No one shall see me and live." As we have seen in the chapter on the numinous, in Israel that absolute difference was partly understood in a physical way, as energy that would consume anything not holy that came too near it. Often the physical analogy was fire, as we have seen in connection with the efforts to describe the glory of God. It is a purely physical sense of God's holiness that appears here, probably more physical, in its use of parts of the human body—face, back, and hand—than any other passage in scripture. The author is trying to describe some sort of unique experience Moses had of God's presence, but since God is wholly other, really does not have language to do that. So he speaks of God protecting Moses from his presence, covering him with his hand—so presumably it is not the nearness itself but what Moses might see that is dangerous—and then does allow him to see something more than other mortals have done. Various futile attempts have been made to explain the use of "back" here. Some early Christian authors (e.g., Tertullian) took it to mean "what comes after," namely Christ. Calvin rejected that as "altogether wide of the genuine meaning," and took it to be a similitude drawn from our experience of only partially recognizing someone whose face is turned away. Others have tried to make it temporal in the sense of what comes after, meaning that Moses will see the results of God's work in history, but that seems farfetched. Calvin was probably on the right track. Since the word "face" was used in Hebrew to mean in front of or in the presence of, our author more or less in desperation used the opposite of face, namely back, in an effort to say that although God was near to Moses in a way none of us has ever experienced, Moses did not really "see" God. The experiences of both Moses and Elijah on this mountain should be compared (1 Kings 19:9–18).

If we read chapter 34 as the immediate consequence of 33:19–23, as many interpreters do, then verses 1–4 represent the preparations for God to "pass by" while Moses is hidden in the rock. As usual, God is full of surprises, however, for a great deal more is going to happen than verses 19–23 have prepared us for. There is a self-introduction of God, which reminds us in some ways of Exodus 3, and then God announces that he is making a covenant, followed by the stipulations of that covenant, which have their parallels in Exodus 21—23. This time, however, there are no provisions for acceptance by the people nor any ceremony for sealing the covenant. This may be an early parallel to the covenant-making materials in chapters 19—24, but as noted at the beginning of the chapter, the problems of the prior history of these traditions remain unsolved. For our purposes it is best simply to take them as now presented, as a restoration of the original covenant, made possible because of the character of God which is now made explicit in 34:6–7.

This list of divine attributes is one of the most remarkable passages in the Old Testament, and the way it has been treated by commentators is also remarkable. It is impressively formulated, a true creedal statement, as we understand creeds, and it obviously meant a great deal to ancient Israel, since there are quotations of it or echoes of it in at least twenty-five other passages, including law, historical narrative, prayers, and prophetic texts. In spite of that, many commentaries say very little about it. Noth says only, "we have here an addition which is made up of customary, stereotyped phrases." Childs, whose commentary is more than twice as long, says, "The frequent use through the rest of the Old Testament of the formula in v. 6 . . . is an eloquent testimony to the centrality of this understanding of God's person" but does not offer any discussion of the words themselves. Durham provides one paragraph, and Fretheim one page, but for any detailed discussion of these important words one must search for articles on the passage.[25]

It is an impressive statement. The creed even uses specially formulated words, as another way of insisting that we are not dealing with anything that can be adequately spoken or understood by human beings, but can be represented only imperfectly by analogies. The words translated "merciful and gracious" are forms of well-known roots, *rḥm* and *ḥnn,* but they are special forms, used only of God. One of the words derived from the root *rḥm* is *reḥem,* "womb," and a good deal has been made of that recently, as an indication of feminine qualities in God. I think it is more important to recognize that this form is a unique word that is used only of God, neither masculine nor feminine, if we hope to avoid resexualizing the God that Israel struggled so hard to desexualize. Words derived from *rḥm* that are used of human relationships speak of compassion or pity; hence the usual translation here, "merciful," perhaps needs to be given a stronger emotional quality than the word "mercy" usually has. In chapters 32—34, God's compassion has been kept fairly well hidden until now, but the fact that it is the first word to be used in his self-description may thus be very important in revealing something of the struggle that has been going on within the deity himself.

Ḥannun, "gracious," is a special form derived from the root that means "to condescend, to show favor," thus "to act graciously" toward someone. The two words appear together eleven times in the Old Testament as unique designations of the character of God. The same Israelites who spoke of the wrath of God which is aroused by human sin confessed their faith beginning with the words "compassionate and gracious." They knew of a God who feels the effects of their sin and feels it all the more severely because his essential will for them is that they have what is good. We who are parents know very much what that feeling is like, although again we must remind ourselves we are dealing only with analogies. We have desired only what is good for our children, and when their misdeeds bring suffering upon them we know compassion; we share their pain. But sometimes our emotional reaction to their foolishness may be anger, and at the least we will do some yelling. The creed knows what to do with that analogy, for what comes next, "slow to anger," defines the difference between us and God.[26]

Associated with slow to anger is "abounding with steadfast love and faithfulness." Here we encounter that important word *ḥesed,* which cannot be adequately translated by anything short of a paragraph. "Steadfast love" is probably the best we can do, but there are places where it is better translated as grace or mercy or kindness or loyalty.[27] In the light of our studies of the covenant making in Exodus 19—24, Zimmerli's comment is valuable: "*Ḥesed* always contains an element of spontaneous freedom in the demonstration of goodness or in kindly conduct, and it cannot be reduced to what is owed or to a duty."[28]

"Faithfulness" is an accurate translation of *'emeth,* the root from which the word "amen" is derived. Another word derived from this root is the one used by Habakkuk in that verse which has become so famous because it is quoted by Paul: "The just will live by his faithfulness" (Hab. 2:4). It carries the sense of firmness, thus certainty and truth and faithfulness. When used of God, the meanings of truth and certainty and faithfulness are all appropriate, and here they serve to emphasize doubly what *ḥesed* already said.

The rest of the creed sets up an essential contrast: forgiveness on the one hand, but "visiting the iniquity" on the other. Two verbs are used in each part and they take two contrasting objects:

> keeping steadfast love . . . . but not acquitting
> forgiving . . . . but visiting the iniquity

Steadfast love is for thousands, and all understand that to mean thousands of generations. Iniquity is to be visited upon four generations, and more needs to be said about that shortly. The object of God's forgiveness is the whole repertoire: iniquity and transgression and sin. What may not be acquitted are the guilty, and obviously that contrast calls for some understanding.

This is an essential contrast, because as Fretheim says, it defines the difference between mercy and indulgence,[29] and as Freedman says, God does not declare the guilty innocent or the innocent guilty, or say it really doesn't matter.[30] There is no such thing as mercy unless right is still right and wrong is still wrong. This brings us squarely up against the mystery of forgiveness, but it is a mystery—how God can be just and still forgive sin—and scripture does the best it can with the formulation we have before us. As a God of justice, Yahweh maintains standards that are never compromised. Guilt is guilt, without apology, and guilt of the kind we have encountered in this passage, rejection of the source of life himself, leads to death. That defines the nature of genuine mercy. Mercy is not indulgence, saying, well, you really shouldn't do that but if you do I probably won't do anything about it. Mercy is not something that can be claimed, as if the standards were faulty or impossibly high, and God really owes us leniency. Mercy finds us condemned, and then for some reason we do not know, set free. That is what has happened in this passage. Moses has just been trying to save his people's skins, and then to get some help to get through the wilderness. But now comes a new covenant, after the first had been, to all appearances, nullified. That happens entirely by the initiative of a God of compassion and mercy.

Even though the contrast is made between God's steadfast love for thousands of generations and his visiting the iniquity of parents on only the three following generations, the latter seems unfair to our individualistic mind-sets, so let me offer one interpretation of that which may help. This is clearly an example of the sense of corporate responsibility that appears so prominently in the Old Testament. The good that a person does brings good to the whole family, or tribe or nation, and the evil a person does likewise brings suffering. Some families today may have five generations alive at the same time, but it is not very likely that in ancient Israel, when the average life span was probably about forty years, there were ever more than four generations contemporary with one another, and usually it was probably only three. That may explain the reference to third and fourth generation. It may be a limiting factor, hence also to be associated with God's grace, saying that indeed the sins of one family member will bring suffering on the whole family, all the generations now alive (we know that is true), but that person's iniquity will not be visited on an unlimited number of generations.[31]

One more comment on iniquity: When God is said to forgive iniquity and transgression and sin, the verb used is the familiar *nasa'*, which has the literal meanings "to lift up, to bear, to carry." Very likely it came to be used as a word for forgiveness because of the sense of having something lifted from one, but commentators cannot resist considering whether Israel also thought of God "bearing" the sin that had been lifted from the sinner. That may be introducing some New Testament theology, but there are at least two places in the Old Testament where a human being is said to bear the sins of his people, and I think we are not mistaken in seeing those two men as pointers toward God's intention to bear our sins on the cross. The first is one of the symbolic acts of Ezekiel, in which he is ordered to lie on his left side for 390 days, saying, "you shall bear their iniquity for the number of days that you lie there" (Ezek. 4:4). The second is better known; the same verb is used of the Suffering Servant in Isa. 53:4, "Surely he has borne [*nasa'*] our infirmities and carried our diseases," and in the next verse, "But he was wounded for our transgressions, crushed for our iniquities." Hebrew contains several other words used of forgiveness, and Moses will use a different one in verse 9, so it seems not insignificant that *nasa'* is used here, in association with God's compassion and patience.

The provisions of the covenant that God makes with Israel in 34:10–26, and the aftermath with its description of Moses' shining face, do not contribute anything significantly new to our study, which means that 34:9–10 serve as the conclusion of our work on Exodus. Verse 10 is of course the introduction to the whole covenant-making passage, but it can also serve us as an appropriate conclusion.

Moses brings together the main themes of the three chapters in a single sentence (34:9). We are reminded of the golden calf by the fourth reference to Israel as a stiff-necked people. The theme of God's presence and absence appears in the renewed request that he go in their midst. Moses' unique role as mediator, as the only one who might be an intercessor because of his special relationship with God, reappears. And having had his request for forgiveness of Israel refused early in the story (32:32), Moses finally dares to ask it again, for it seems that God has now indicated he is ready to forgive. Fretheim devotes comparatively much space to this single verse in his commentary, for he sees it as a major turning point in the Old Testament story.[32] This is where forgiveness first appears as the way God deals with human sin. In Genesis the only use of the idea of forgiveness is on the human level; Joseph's brothers ask him to forgive what they did to him (50:17). In Exodus, Pharaoh once asks Moses and Aaron to forgive him, after the plague of locusts (10:17), and in 23:21 Israel is warned about that divine agent that God proposes to send before them: "Be attentive to him and listen to his voice; do not rebel against him, for he will not pardon your transgression; for my name is in him." When we look for forgiveness language in the Old Testament, then, and discover that it does not appear in any significant way until Exodus 32—34, we can see a reason for agreeing with Fretheim's earlier statement that the golden calf serves as a kind of Fall story for Israel.[33] The honeymoon is over; their optimistic affirmation, "All that the LORD has spoken we will do," has been cast in doubt forever by their quickness to turn aside from the way the Lord commanded them (32:8), and if they are to have any future with God, it will have to depend on patience and forgiveness. So the basic pattern of scripture's story is presented for the first time here.[34]

As usual God does not give Moses a direct answer. As with Moses' request in 33:18, he gives a better answer than what Moses had asked. The divine reluctance has all disappeared, replaced by a divine enthusiasm for resuming the work of salvation which had got off to such a poor start. No use asking Israel for participation; he knows they will fail. It is simply done, with four Hebrew words: "Behold, I make a covenant." They and the surrounding peoples had seen marvels already, but now, "Before all your people I will do marvels, such as have not been performed in all the earth or in any nation; and all the people among whom you live shall see the work of the LORD; for it is an awesome thing that I will do with you." The word "marvels" is the word used earlier of the plagues and the crossing of the Sea, but here an astonishing word is introduced in connection with them. They are marvels such as have not been "created" in all the earth. Another of the special words that is used only with God in the Old Testament appears: *bara'*, "to create." They have crossed so massive a watershed that what God is now about to undertake can appropriately be called "creation." (As we turn to the other, related Old Testament materials, we shall see that forgiveness itself begins to be seen as an eschatological event, a new creation.) There will be witnesses of this great event, for eventually God will be known by the nations as well. This also reminds us of the role of the nations in the eschatological parts of the Old Testament. And what it all means is finally summed up with the word "terrible," in the RSV, which is softened to "awesome" in NRSV and REB. The NEB was very literal in choosing "fearful," for the word is derived from the root meaning "to be afraid."

We have seen that the expression "fear of the Lord," which is so difficult for our contemporaries to understand, actually means "piety," in the good sense that the word formerly was used, or "devout obedience," since obedience is clearly part of it (Gen. 22:12), but it is obedience to the God of whom one stands in awe. The RSV's "terrible" is definitely misleading, as none of the ways we use that word is appropriate, but "fearful" would be all right if we realize that it refers again to our earlier subject, the holiness of God, God's otherness, the danger God's energy and urgency and purity represent to faulty human beings, the mystery, the incomprehensibility of the ways of One who is both just and merciful. Our text has not explained how that can be, but our text celebrates it. It is not easy to celebrate without beginning to feel satisfied with ourselves, but true celebration of this mystery cannot involve any self-congratulation, as Moses and Paul well understood, and this final word, "it is a fearsome thing that I will do with you," reminds us that proper celebration of the mercy and compassion of God must involve some trembling.

THE OLD TESTAMENT

Having emphasized God's initiative throughout the Exodus story, we have now encountered a significant human exercise of initiative, directed toward God, in Moses' intercessions on behalf of a guilty people. Israel believed that the sovereign of all the earth did really listen to human prayers and was willing to be affected by them. Intercession, though a human activity, makes sense only if God has a certain character, and so it is appropriate for us to consider some additional examples of such prayers for what they teach us about Israel's understanding of God's responsiveness to human petitions. The qualities in God that make him responsive are of course those expressed in the classic formulation of Exodus 32—34, so it will be helpful to look at restatements of that "creed." This will lead us to other forgiveness passages and finally to a consideration of whether the Old Testament maintains that sense of tension between a God willing to forgive and a people unable to give up sinning that we found expressed so powerfully in Exodus 32—34.

When Israel confessed their sins in worship, associating themselves with their ancestors' rebelliousness in the wilderness (Ps. 106:6–33), they remembered the power of one man, Moses, whose prayers God answered:

> Therefore he said he would destroy them—
>   had not Moses, his chosen one,
> stood in the breach before him,
>   to turn away his wrath from destroying them. (Ps. 106:23)

One other man in the Old Testament is said to have averted God's intention to destroy his people, and that is Amos. He saw a vision of locusts devouring the second growth of hay and, understanding it to be a message of Israel's coming destruction, prayed, "O LORD God, forgive, I beg you! How can Jacob stand? He is so small!" (Amos 7:2). Then he reports another vision, of fire devouring the deep and the land, and cried out the same prayer, using the verb "cease" this time, instead of "forgive" (7:4). He reports the same response to both prayers: "The LORD relented concerning this; 'It shall not be,' said the LORD" (7:3, 6). God "relents" (*hinnahem*) here, as in Ex. 32:7–14, and the word used for "forgive" (*salach*) is the one Moses used in Ex. 34:9. In the book of Amos, however, two more such visions are recorded (7:7–9; 8:1–3), with neither intercessory prayer nor promise that God will relent. We shall have to return to the subject of nonforgiveness shortly.

Moses interceded on behalf of a rebellious people again, in Num. 14:11–23, and both sides of the dialogue show close relationships with Exodus 32—34.[35] Abraham's appeal on behalf of the innocent who might be found in Sodom also depends on his convictions about the merciful nature of God (Gen. 18:22–33).[36]

Great men such as Moses and Abraham were not the only ones to address God with prayers of this kind,[37] for the same kinds of reasoning with God, in effect challenging him to live up to his reputation, appear frequently in the psalms of lament, the language of worship of the people. This teaches us something important about the nature of God, as Israel understood him, which has not appeared until now in our study of Exodus. In the human world, when dealing with someone very powerful, protocol is very important, and people have always tended to project that onto their relations with God. When a private addresses a general, he had better show proper respect and watch his language. When a peasant addressed a king, in the past, he had to be very careful not to say anything to offend, and generally the more flattering he could be, the better. But the Old Testament writers believed their God was far greater than any king or general. They dared to conceive of a God who is so great his feelings cannot be hurt by anything a human being might say. And so, despite the violence of some of the prayers in the Old Testament, we never find God saying, in effect, "How dare you speak to me that way!" Israel had the remarkable capacity for being able to pour out all their doubts and anger before God in the presence of the worshiping congregation, as the laments show us (e.g., Pss. 69:3; 88:8, 14, 18; 102:9f., 23f.). When we think about the destructive effects such public language would be likely to have on a contemporary worshiping congregation, it becomes evident that the Israelite congregations could handle this only because the people as a whole were convinced they had a God who allowed it.[38]

Two other occurrences of the "creed" show how Ex. 34:6f. was used in creative ways by Israelite writers. In Joel 2:12–14 it becomes part of a call to repentance:

> Yet even now, says the LORD,
>   return to me with all your heart,
> with fasting, with weeping, and with mourning;
>   rend your hearts and not your clothing.
> Return to the LORD, your God,
>   for he is gracious and merciful,
> slow to anger, and abounding in steadfast love,
>   and relents from punishing.
> Who knows whether he will not turn and relent,
>   and leave a blessing behind him . . . ?

The passage appears in abbreviated form with all the judgmental parts omitted, so as to offer the most encouragement possible to those being exhorted to change their ways. Furthermore, a clause is added ("and relents from punishing," NRSV;

"and repents of evil," RSV), introducing into the creedal formulation the verb that played such an important part in Moses' dialogue with God in Exodus 32 (*hinnaḥem*). But forgiveness is no more an easy or automatic matter in Joel's time than it was in the wilderness, for the prophet's promise is carefully worded: "Who knows whether. . . ?" It is all a matter of grace, and grace cannot be presupposed.

Jonah uses the same wording of the creed, but in a highly ironic way, as the basis for a complaint rather than as an assurance.[39] Having been literally forced by God to announce to Nineveh its coming destruction in forty days, he was then made a false prophet when God changed his mind as a result of the Ninevites' repentance (and note the king's "Who knows? God may relent . . ."). In his anger that God had thus ruined his reputation, Jonah protested that the reason he did not want to announce judgment in the first place was: "I knew that you are a gracious God and merciful, slow to anger, and abounding in steadfast love, and ready to relent from punishing" (Jonah 4:2). Repentance and forgiveness are thus a possibility for the nations, as well as for Israel, in this book, but the author makes the king of Nineveh a good theologian by making him acknowledge that it all ultimately depends on the will of God.

God's forgiving nature was celebrated with an extended vocabulary, sometimes alluding to Ex. 34:6f., as in Ps. 103:8, but adding references to healing (103:3) and comparing God's compassion to that of a loving father who knows how frail we are (103:13f.). Once in the Old Testament, God's redeeming activity, which elsewhere always refers to deliverance from physical distress, is applied to forgiveness of sin (Ps. 130:8; cf. vv. 3–4). The book of Micah concludes with a hymn to the compassionate, forgiving God which does not cite Ex. 34:6–7, but which of course uses some of the same vocabulary, and may refer to that passage in the last verse (Micah 7:18–20):

> Who is a God like you, pardoning [*nose'*] iniquity
>   and passing over the transgression of the remnant of your possession?
> He does not retain his anger forever,
>   because he delights in showing clemency [*ḥesed*].
> He will again have compassion [*raḥam*] upon us;
>   he will tread our iniquities under foot.
> You will cast all our sins into the depth of the sea.
> You will show faithfulness ['*emeth*] to Jacob
>   and unswerving loyalty [*ḥesed*] to Abraham,
> as you have sworn to our ancestors from the days of old.

These are a few of the more impressive examples of Israel's ongoing belief that they could depend on a compassionate God who would enable them to remain in harmony with them in spite of their repeated failings.[40] Ordinarily, it was taught that humans had the responsibility and the ability to repent, to desire truly to change their ways and to appeal sincerely to God for forgiveness (Deut. 30:1–10; Ezek. 18:21–32), but near the end of the monarchy, even that possibility was questioned by Jeremiah (Jer. 8:5; 13:23), and he and Ezekiel speak of an eschatological forgiveness that produces repentance, rather than being God's response to anything humans can do (Jer. 24:4–7; 29:10–12; Ezek. 16:49–63; 20:43; 36:31; 39:25–27; cf. Isa. 44:22). This reminds us that the forgiveness Moses asked for and received on behalf of his people also did not involve any sincere repentance on their part (Exodus 32—34; Numbers 14).[41] The Old Testament thus contains more about "salvation by grace alone" than many readers have noticed. The eschatological forgiveness that the prophets hoped would accompany and make possible the restoration of the people from exile (e.g., Jer. 33:7–9) would require a new creation, an inner transformation that would make full obedience possible (Jer. 31:31–34; Ezek. 36:24–27; 37:23), and that should have resulted in a people who would no longer sin, as Jeremiah promises in 50:20.[42] The actual effect of the restoration, during the sixth century B.C.E. and after, however, was an increased emphasis on repentance and reaffirmations of God's willingness to forgive, as we shall see in the next section.

Although the assurances of God's compassion which were repeated in Israel's language of worship led individuals to feel the distance between themselves and God had been bridged by him (cf. the psalms of confidence, e.g., Pss. 4:8; 16:7–11; 23:4–6), the prophets of the preexilic period had an intense feeling of estrangement between God and Israel, and could at best look forward to God's eventual fulfillment of the covenant promise: "They shall be my people and I will be their God" (e.g., Ezek. 37:23). The increased confidence of the postexilic prophets in the possibility of an ongoing harmonious relationship between God and his people, based on his mercy, was not free from tension, and the awareness of a certain distance that they expected to be fully overcome only in that new creation appears here and there in their writings. Second Isaiah speaks of a time when the nations will confess, "God is with you alone, and there is no other; there is no god besides him," then immediately adds, "Truly, you are a God who hides himself, O God of Israel, the Savior" (Isa. 45:14b–15).

JUDAISM AND CHRISTIANITY

Judaism

The mercy (*eleos*) of God is referred to frequently in the Apocryphal books, but that is usually equivalent to God's loving care for his people, and prayers for mercy are normally offered by the righteous asking his help in times of distress. God's willingness to respond to the prayers of the righteous is a favorite theme of postbiblical Jewish literature, but references to intercessory prayer tend to focus on those biblical characters, such as Moses, who were thought to possess that special kind of access to God. Examples of Moses as intercessor will be provided later in this section. We do find a continuation of the Old Testament idea that God will change his intention to punish the wicked. Sirach, especially, has a good deal to say about forgiveness: "Have you sinned, my child? Do so no more, but ask forgiveness for your past sins" (Sirach 21:1). True repentance is essential, however:

> Forgive your neighbor the wrong he has done,
>   and then your sins will be pardoned when you pray.
> Does anyone harbor anger against another,
>   and expect healing from the Lord?
> If one has no mercy toward another like himself,
>   can he then seek pardon for his own sins? (Sirach 28:2–4)

Here is another example of the need to reflect God's character in one's own.

The language of Baruch contains strong echoes of several parts of the Old Testament, including the prayers of confession in Nehemiah 9 and Daniel 9. On the one hand, the sins of the exiles in Babylonia are confessed, and God's mercy is appealed to, as in 2:11–15: "Hear, O Lord, our prayer and our supplication, and for your own sake deliver us, and grant us favor in the sight of those who have carried us into exile; so that all the earth may know that you are the Lord our God, for Israel and his descendants are called by your name" (vv. 14–15). We hear a bit of Ezekiel's theology in the single motive for forgiveness: "for your own sake," and also in the desire that the nations may achieve some knowledge of the Lord from what he does for Israel. Later, God's mercy is appealed to in the proper sense of the word "mercy," when there is nothing the petitioner has to offer. This case has to do with the continuing effects of the sins of their ancestors, which had been responsible for exile. Having confessed their own sins (Bar. 3:2), the exiles pray:

> O Lord Almighty, God of Israel, hear now the prayer of the people of Israel, the children of those who sinned before you, who did not heed the voice of the Lord their God, so that calamities have clung to us. Do not remember the iniquities of our ancestors, but in this crisis remember your power and your name. (3:4–5)

Note that they have nothing to claim in their own right, but appeal to God's power and name as a trustworthy basis for mercy, so that the idea of God's freedom to forgive when and as he wills is continued.

The rabbis' discussions of the golden calf incident tended to find ways of mitigating the seriousness of the sin.[43] They claimed, for example, that it was the "mixed multititude" (Ex. 12:38) alone who were reponsible for it. Elsewhere, Moses as intercessor argues on Israel's behalf, unlike the way the story was originally told in Exodus. We find nothing in Ex. 32:7–14 like *Exodus Rabbah* XLII.1: "I have some things to say in their favour, O Lord of the Universe." Moses' boldness in attempting to change God's mind is discussed at length in this midrash. The usual way of explaining God's words "Now let me alone" (Ex. 32:10), to which we devoted a good deal of attention, was to say that God was in fact inviting Moses to intercede (XLII.9).

Another comment on the same passage emphasizes God's freedom to change from judgment to mercy:

'God is not a man that He should lie, or a mortal that He should repent' (Num. XXIII,19). Samuel son of Nahmani said: When God promises good, He does not change His promise, come what may, unlike a mortal king who may withhold a promised gift to his son, if the son provokes him. God keeps His promise in spite of man's sin. In Ps. CV,44 it says: 'He gave them lands of nations that they might keep His statutes.' They did not keep His statutes, but He gave them the land. After the Golden Calf, God said to Moses, 'I am not a man to make a promise and retract.' But when God swore in His wrath, He did retract, for He swore to punish. For God said: 'I am not a mortal man to swear to punish and to exult in doing so.' (*Tanhuma,* Wayera, sec. 13, f. 36a fin.-36b init.)[44]

We see, then, that the mystery of God's willingness to change on behalf of mercy remained a part of ongoing Jewish theology.

The so-called "creed" in Ex. 34:6f. is not repeated in the later literature the way it is in the Old Testament, but fainter echoes of it appear here and there. The clearest one is probably Sirach's reassurance:

Consider the generations of old and see:
    has anyone trusted in the Lord and been disappointed?
Or has anyone persevered in the fear of the Lord and been forsaken?
    Or has anyone called upon him and been neglected?
For the Lord is compassionate and merciful;
    he forgives sins and saves in time of distress. (Sirach 2:10f.)

God's compassion for human beings because of his knowledge of their frailty is emphasized in Sirach 18:7–14. Wisdom of Solomon has much less to say about forgiveness than Sirach, but one passage does contain a possible echo of Ex. 34:6f., alongside a theology of sanctification that is quite different from what we have found in the Old Testament:

But you, our God, are kind and true,
    patient, and ruling all things in mercy.
For even if we sin we are yours,
    knowing your power;
but we will not sin, because we know that you acknowledge us as yours.
For to know you is complete righteousness,
    and to know your power is the root of immortality.
                                                    (Wisd. Sol. 15:1–3)

Since the only subject of the Prayer of Manasseh is sin, repentance, and forgiveness, we should expect to find language concerning God's mercy, and verse 7a does have a familiar ring: "For you are the Lord Most High, of great compassion, long-suffering, and very merciful, and you relent at human suffering." In the *Letter of Aristeas,* the king of Egypt is advised by one of the Jewish scholars who are banqueting with him that the best way to maintain his kingship to the end is to emulate the character of God as we have been tracing it in this chapter: "You would administer it best by imitating the eternal goodness of God. By using longsuffering and treatment of those who merit (punishment) more leniently than they deserve, you will convert them from evil and bring them to repentance" (*Ep. Arist.* 188).

The rabbis found a definition of the meaning of God's name in Ex. 34:6f.:

> R. Abba b. Mammel said: God said to Moses, 'Thou wishest to know My name. Well, I am called according to My work; sometimes I am called "Almighty God," "Lord of Hosts," "God," "Lord." When I am judging created beings, I am called "God," and when I am waging war against the wicked, I am called "Lord of Hosts." When I suspend judgment for a man's sins, I am called "*El Shaddai*" (God Almighty) and when I am merciful towards My world, I am called "*Adonai*" [i.e., the Tetragrammaton], for "*Adonai*" refers to the Attribute of Mercy, as it is said, *The Lord, the Lord* (Adonai, Adonai) *God merciful and gracious* (Exod. xxxiv,6). (*Exod. Rab.*, Shemot, III,6)

They also derived God's thirteen attributes of mercy from this passage, so it is clear that it continued to sum up much of what Jews believed about God, as it had done earlier for Israel.[45]

That forgiveness is impossible apart from the grace of God, meaning there is nothing like a contractual relationship to which humans can appeal, is emphasized more in the rabbinic literature than in earlier Jewish writings. Sirach warns the sinner that mercy cannot be assumed, but uses that as the basis for a call to repentance:

> Do not say, "I sinned, yet what has happened to me?"
>   for the Lord is slow to anger.
> Do not be so confident of forgiveness
>   that you add sin to sin.
> Do not say, "His mercy is great,
>   he will forgive the multitude of my sins,
> for both mercy and wrath are with him,
>   and his anger will rest on sinners.
> Do not delay to turn back to the Lord,
>   and do not postpone it from day to day;
> for suddenly the wrath of the Lord will come upon you,
>   and at the time of punishment you will perish. (Sirach 5:4–8)

The part of Exodus we have been considering seems often to have led the rabbis to consider their dependence on the free grace of God. Rabbi Johanan found ten words for prayer in scripture, then said:

> And of all those designations of prayer Moses made use only of *tahanunim* [associated with *ḥen* "grace"]. R. Johanan said: Hence you learn that no creature has any claim on his Creator, because Moses, the teacher of all the prophets, made use only of *tahanunim*. . . . The Holy One, blessed be He, spake to Moses thus: *And I will*

be gracious to whom I will be gracious (Ex. XXXIII, 19). God said to Moses: 'To him who has any claim upon Me, *I will show mercy,* that is, I will deal with him according to My Attribute of Mercy; and as for him who has no claim upon Me *"I will be gracious,"* that is, I will grant [his prayer] as an act of grace.' (*Deut. Rab.,* Wa'ethanan, II,1)[46]

To Christians unacquainted with the rabbinic literature, this sounds like a doctrine of God they have claimed for themselves, over against their conception of "Jewish legalism," so some additional examples need to be provided, in order to show this is not a peculiar case.

Israel's dependence on grace at Mount Sinai is emphasized in this interesting account of part of the dialogue between God and Moses:

And Moses made haste, and bowed his head toward the earth, and worshipped [Ex. 34:8]. What did Moses see?—R. Hanina b. Gamala said: He saw *long-suffering* [as one of His attributes]. The Rabbis say: He saw [His attribute of] *truth.* It has been taught in agreement with the one who holds that 'he saw *long-suffering,*' viz., When Moses ascended on high, he found the Holy One, blessed be He, sitting and writing *'long-suffering.'* Said he to Him, 'Sovereign of the Universe! Long-suffering to the righteous?' He replied, 'Even to the wicked.' He urged, 'Let the wicked perish!' 'See now what thou desirest,' was His answer. 'When Israel sinned,' He said to him, 'didst thou not urge Me, [Let thy] long-suffering be for the righteous [only]?' 'Sovereign of the Universe!' said he, 'but didst Thou not assure me, Even to the wicked!' (*b. Sanh.* 111a, b)[47]

A comment on Ps. 119:123f. acknowledges that good works are inadequate without God's mercy (*ḥesed*):

We have neither merit nor good works. But deal Thou mercifully with us, as it is said *Deal with Thy servant according unto Thy mercy* (Ps. 119:124). The men of old whom Thou didst redeem, Thou didst not redeem because of their works. Thou didst deal mercifully with them and thus didst Thou redeem them. . . . Even as Thou didst deal with the men of old, deal Thou with us." (*Midrash on Psalms,* 119:123)[48]

And the grace of God may even operate where there is no repentance, contrary to the usual teaching, but in accord with some of the Old Testament texts we have noted:

There is no creature that is not indebted to God, but being gracious and merciful, He forgives all former misdeeds, as it is said, *'Remember not against us the iniquities of our forefathers'* (Ps. LXXIX, 8). It can be compared to one who had borrowed from a money-lender, and forgot about it. After a time, he appeared before his creditor and said, 'I know I am your debtor.' The other replied: 'Why do you remind me of the first debt; I have long since completely dismissed it from my mind?' So is the Sovereign of the Universe. Men sin before Him; and He, seeing that they do not repent, forgives them sin after sin, and when they come and remind Him of the debt they contracted previously, He says to them, 'Do not remind yourselves of the former sins.' (*Exod. Rab.*, Mishpatim, XXXI, 1; cf. *Pesiq. R.* 184a)

Of course, such a passage must be set alongside other warnings not to presume that one can sin and expect forgiveness from an indulgent God. Ramban makes an interesting comment on the verb *nasa'* in Ex. 34:7, which basically means "lift up, bear," and which is used of lifting up guilt or forgiving sin several times in the Old Testament, as we noted earlier. But here, he takes it in the sense of "bear," saying that Moses does not ask the forgiveness of "transgressions," since these are sins of a rebellious nature which God can only bear and by so doing not destroy the people. One can go too far, however, and this is as close as the rabbis get to the idea of "unforgivable sin":

> If the godless, for whose repentance God waits, do not do so, then even when they do think of it later on, He distracts their hearts from being penitent. . . . Though they wish later to return to God and to pray unto Him, they are no longer able, because He has bound them and barred the way before them. (*Exod. Rab.*, Wa'era, XI, 1)

Did there remain any sense of distance from God that could not be overcome in this life, in spite of God's grace? On the one hand, they affirmed their belief God would bridge the distance they could not overcome:

> Consider the parable of a prince who was far away from his father—a hundred days' journey away. His friends said to him: "Return to your father." He replied: "I cannot: I have not the strength." Thereupon his father sent word, saying to him: "Come back as far as you can according to your strength, and I will go the rest of the way to meet you." So the Holy One, blessed be He, says to Israel: *Return unto Me, and I will return unto you* (Mal. 3:7).[49]

They felt the presence of God with them in worship: "God said: 'Has anyone ever come to the synagogue and not found My Glory therein?' Rabbi Aibu said: 'And what is more, when you stand in the synagogue, God stands by your side' " (*Deut. Rab.*, Ki Tabo VII,2). But on the other hand, the sense of individual guilt, and the sufferings of the Jewish people as a whole meant that distance continued to be a problem, and the way they sometimes connected that to the incident of the golden calf is of interest here. *Exodus Rabbah* says, "Had Israel waited for Moses and not perpetrated that act, there would have been no exile, neither would the Angel of Death have had any power over them" (XXXII.1). Later it repeats a statement that appears also in the Talmud (*b. Sanh.* 102) and in the commentaries on Exodus by Rashi and Ramban: "There is no generation, said R. Assi, that does not receive a particle [of punishment] for the sin of the calf-worship" (*Exod. Rab.* XLIII.2).

Judgment and mercy were thus held in tension in Jewish teaching, much as in the Old Testament, but with perhaps a stronger emphasis overall on the mercy of God, in spite of all the suffering, which might have produced a much harsher view.

The New Testament

The New Testament contains few echoes of Ex. 34:6f. The closest is James 5:11, "you have seen the purpose of the Lord, how the Lord is compassionate and merciful." It has a vocabulary of Greek words which corresponds more or less to the attributes of God proclaimed in Exodus, however. "Mercy" (*eleos*) and "compassion" (*splangnon*) tend to be typical of the Gospels' description of Jesus' attitude toward the needy, and "grace" (*charis*) became the key word for Paul and the other writers of New Testament letters as they interpreted what God had done in Christ.

Jesus taught extensively on prayer, and emphasized God's readiness to respond to prayer in two striking parables recorded by Luke. In each of them, he takes the risk of comparing God with an uncaring human being, since the point is not that God cares (he and his listeners apparently are to presuppose that), but that persistence in prayer is called for. This may in fact be an aspect of that distance we found in Exodus 32—34, which will reappear in the New Testament in spite of the good news of reconciliation.

> "Suppose one of you has a friend, and you go to him at midnight and say to him, 'Friend, lend me three loaves of bread; for a friend of mine has arrived, and I have nothing to set before him.' And he answers from within, 'Do not bother me; the door has already been locked, and my children are with me in bed; I cannot get up and give you anything.' I tell you, even though he will not get up and give him anything because he is his friend, at least because of his persistence he will get up and give him whatever he needs. So I say to you, Ask, and it will be given you; search, and you will find; knock, and the door will be opened for you." (Luke 11:5–9, cf. vv. 10–12)

His parable of the unjust judge, in Luke 18:1–8, has the same essential point, concluding with, "And will not God grant justice to his chosen ones who cry to him day and night? Will he delay long in helping them? I tell you he will quickly grant justice to them" (vv. 7f.).

Intercessory prayer appears with prominence in the New Testament, showing that the early church believed prayer could influence God not only on one's own behalf but also on behalf of others. That included prayer for the forgiveness of those who so far showed no repentance, which would be puzzling had we not found evidence in the Old Testment of the idea that repentance may be the result of God's redemptive work, rather than the reverse. Jesus set the classic example, with his cry from the cross, "Father, forgive them; for they do not know what they are doing" (Luke 23:34). The first Christian martyr, Stephen, followed suit when he prayed at his death, "Lord, do not hold this sin against them" (Acts 7:60). These were extreme examples of Jesus' most difficult teaching about prayer: "Love your enemies and pray for those who persecute you, so that you may be children of your Father in heaven; for he makes his sun rise on the evil and on the good, and sends rain on the righteous and on the unrighteous" (Matt. 5:44f.; cf. Luke 6:27f.). Since God does not bless only those who deserve it, neither should Christians intercede only for those who deserve it. It is not surprising, then, that references to praying for their fellow Christians abound in the New Testament letters (2 Cor. 9:14; 13:7; 2 Thes. 1:11; 3:1; Heb. 13:18; James 5:14).

In spite of Jesus' saying, "Whatever you ask for in prayer with faith, you will receive" (Matt. 21:22), there is no guarantee that God will be bound by the prayers of humans, however, any more than in the Old Testament. Jesus' own experience in Gethsemane provides the classic example of the tension between God's willingness to hear and to answer our petitions and intercessions and the freedom of his will. Jesus' prayer, "My Father, if it is possible, let this cup pass from me; yet not what I want but what you want" (Matt. 26:39), could not be answered as Jesus wished.

Forgiveness and repentance tend to be emphasized in the Gospels, as in Judaism, but a different vocabulary appears in the Pauline letters, with the terms "justification" and "faith" tending to dominate. God's mercy for those who do not deserve it, except for their repentant spirit, was emphasized in Jesus' parable of the Pharisee and the tax collector (Luke 18:9–14). Luke says it was addressed to "some who trusted in themselves that they were righteous." Jesus said that after the tax collector's prayer, "God, be merciful to me, a sinner!" the tax collector went home justified rather than the Pharisee. The most distinctive characteristic of Jesus' ministry was that he reached out to the undeserving, extending to them the love of God. He often healed and offered forgiveness before being asked, in continuity with the Old Testament discovery that God must first do something about people before they can do anything to help themselves (e.g., Matt. 9:2–6; Mark 5:2–13; Luke 7:37–50; John 9:1–38). Of course, on many other occasions, he was asked both for healing and forgiveness (e.g., Luke 18:35–19:10).

Paul's emphasis on the divine initiative has already been dealt with to a limited extent in the previous chapter, but since his formulation of what God has done for humanity in Jesus Christ is "saved by grace through faith," a few other aspects of what he says about the grace of God should be noted here. The classic statement of his position comes just after he has shown what both Gentile and Jew have been missing apart from faith in Christ:

> But now, apart from law, the righteousness of God has been disclosed, and is attested by the law and the prophets, the righteousness of God through faith in Jesus Christ for all who believe. For there is no distinction, since all have sinned and fall short of the glory of God; they are now justified by his grace as a gift, through the redemption that is in Christ Jesus, whom God put forward as a sacrifice of atonement by his blood, effective through faith. (Rom. 3:21–25a)

His insistence that the righteousness of God was revealed in Jesus Christ, so that all who lived before then presumably could not possibly have had faith in him, has created problems for later theologians, but he passed over that problem rather quickly with a statement that reminds us of one of the rabbinic sayings (quoted in the previous section) about God's willingness to forget old sins: "He did this to show his righteousness, because in his divine forbearance he had passed over the sins previously committed" (Rom. 3:25b; cf. 2:4).

Paul does not explain how he worked out this theology of the cross, but we can see the roots of it in the Old Testament passages about God's freedom to forgive whomever he wills and about the triumph of mercy over justice within the divine will. Of course that means there is no contractual arrangement between God and humanity, and Paul quotes Ex. 33:19, "I will have mercy on whom I have mercy, and I will have compassion on whom I have compassion" as part of his argument justifying God's right to chose some and reject others. He has not overlooked the emphasis on mercy, rather than rejection, in the original context, however, for immediately after the quotation he says, "So it depends not on human will or exertion, but on God who shows mercy" (Rom. 9:16). Later in the section he draws a conclusion we would never expect to find in the Old Testament, but we can understand how he derived it from his scriptures: "For God has imprisoned all in disobedience so that he may be merciful to all" (Rom. 11:32). Since Paul did not work out an actual theology of atonement based on the death of Jesus, the mystery of how the God of justice can forgive sin remains as deep as it was before. Essentially the New Testament writers proclaim its truth and celebrate its reality in their own experiences.

This abundant grace and mercy that they celebrated was not to be mistaken for indulgence, however. We have already considered God's refusal to change his will that Jesus must die. Jesus himself showed reluctance to respond to the Canaanite woman who asked him to heal her daughter, another of the New Testament's puzzling texts. He does not say why, but I suggest it may have been because he assumed that as a Gentile she did not have any background for a proper understanding of his power. She might have seen him simply as a wonder-worker and have never progressed beyond superstition. Her persistence, like the people in Jesus' parables, persuaded him that she had progressed beyond superstition to faith, but the story depicts Jesus exercising that same freedom from human compulsion that is attributed to God (Matt. 15:21–31). Even an apostle had no special claim on God, as Paul learned when he prayed three times to be healed of his "thorn in the flesh." The answer, which he eventually understood to be answer enough, was, "My grace is sufficient for you, for power is made perfect in weakness" (2 Cor. 12:9).

One of the most troublesome passages in the Bible concerns the subject of forgiveness, and that passage is Jesus' saying about the "unforgivable sin." It occurs in each of the Synoptic Gospels; Matthew's formulation is: "Therefore I tell you, people will be forgiven for every sin and blasphemy, but blasphemy against the Spirit will not be forgiven. Whoever speaks a word against the Son of man will be forgiven, but whoever speaks against the Holy Spirit will not be forgiven, either in this age or in the age to come" (Matt. 12:31f.). We are reminded of the rabbinic saying to the effect that the person who perennially refuses to repent will eventually find that even the effort to repent will not be accepted by God. Something like that idea may lie behind the expression "blasphemy against the Spirit," but the Gospels provide no further clues as to what these sentences mean. At any rate, each of the two religions did think about the possibility that even the compassionate and merciful God might determine that there are certain human beings for whom forgiveness would be of no avail.

The character of God formulated in Ex. 34:6f. influenced the Christian message so profoundly that "grace, mercy, and peace" (and variants thereof) became a standard greeting, as many of the New Testament letters show. Even amid the great enthusiasm that gripped the first-century church, with its assumption that they were living in the last days and would soon witness the consummation of God's redeeming work, there is evidence that they were aware of a certain distance remaining between them and their Lord. Paul claimed to have access to the will of God on many matters (1 Cor. 7:10, 12), yet he admitted, "Now we see in a mirror, dimly, but then we will see face to face" (1 Cor. 13:12). And although he spoke of the presence of the risen Christ with his church, as we noted in the previous chapter, at least once he could admit the feeling that in this life he was in some sense "away from the Lord" (2 Cor. 5:1–10). So, at the same time, Christians could have confidence that in spite of their failings, God had graciously accepted them through their faith in Jesus Christ, but could also be painfully aware that their failings were a disgrace to the name of the God who loved them. They took seriously Jesus' promise that God hears and responds to every prayer offered in faith, but found that God often answered their prayers in surprising ways. But those who did not lose their faith because it was too hard to live with a God who is free found that his grace was sufficient.

CHRISTIANITY

One of the popular Christian hymns proclaims: "There's a wideness in God's mercy, Like the wideness of the sea; There's a kindness in his justice, Which is more than liberty."[50] Although not every Christian in history has been that generous with God's mercy, the hymn does remind us of a central feature of the religion. One difference between Christianity as a religion and Judaism is that in addition to preserving the message of the grace of God, as Judaism did, Christianity took up with enthusiasm the responsibility of proclaiming it to the nations. In its development of philosophically based theologies, however, Christianity once again encountered aspects of the mystery of God which led to controversy. The Greek concept of an impassible god, which we encountered earlier, also included the insistence on an immutable god, and that has been accepted and the biblical material adjusted to fit it through most of Christian history. And the need to explain how the death of Christ brought about forgiveness of sins for all humanity led to a series of conflicting doctrines of the atonement.

We have dealt with the apparent willingness of God to change in response to prayer, as that issue was raised for us by Exodus 32, and in this section will note only two of the contributions to the immense literature on prayer which Christianity has produced, selecting them because they take seriously the implications of what the Old Testament says about prayer and its effect on God. One probably would not expect Calvin to be one of those chosen, but his comments on God's words "Let me alone" (Ex. 32:10) are of special interest, since his wisdom and his Christian experience did not permit the logic of his doctrine of predestination to deny the real effectiveness of prayer. His discussion of God's "repenting" (Ex. 32:12, 14) makes use of his principle of accommodation: God's use of human language, despite its inadequacy to describe him, in order to explain to us as much about himself as it is possible for human minds to grasp. Using that principle, he can hold to the traditional doctrine of God's immutability. But when he comments on Ex. 32:10 he is led to make a valuable comment about prayer:

> Hence we gather that His secret judgments are a great deep; whilst, at the same time, His will is declared to us in His word as far as suffices for our edification in faith and piety. And this is more clearly expressed by the context; for He asks of Moses to let Him alone. Now, what does this mean? Is it not that, unless He should obtain a truce from a human being, He will not be able freely to execute His vengeance?— adopting, that is to say, by this mode of expression the character of another, He declares His high estimation of His servant, to whose prayers He pays such deference as to say that they are a hinderance to Him. Thus it is said in Psalm cvi.23, that Moses "stood in the breach, to turn away the wrath" of God. Hence do we plainly perceive the wonderful goodness of God, who not only hears the prayers of His people when they humbly call upon Him, but suffers them to be in a manner intercessors with Him.[51]

Calvin is speaking of accommodation here, without using the word, so he, like others before and after him, would not say God changed his mind as a result of Moses' prayer. The traditional explanation of such passages said that God's unchangeable will decreed judgment for sinners, but forgiveness for those who turned from evil ways, and in fact might also say that God knew from all eternity who would do that and when.[52] What he says about prayer, however, corresponds to the Christian insistence that petitions and intercessions do mean something, whether or not the idea fits the rest of our theology.

As twentieth-century theology has been willing to take the passages that speak of the suffering of God more literally than before, so also the idea of a God who changes and who thus truly does respond to prayer has brought theology a little closer to what Christians have believed about their prayer life all along. For surely the conviction, often poorly integrated with the rest of our theology, that God really does respond to us, which means God is willing to change, is the essential foundation for the belief that prayers of petition and intercession are possible. Otherwise, they are monologues, or nothing more than efforts to get our wills in tune with God's unchangeable will. Certainly the latter is an important part of prayer, but it scarcely fits all that is said of prayer in the Bible.

My second example, then, comes from the twentieth century. Karl Barth said about the changeability of God:

> It would be most unwise, then, to try to understand what the Bible says about God's repentance as if it were merely figurative. For what truth is denoted by the "figure" if we are not to deny that there is an underlying truth? . . . Of course, in so far as this relationship rests on an attitude of God's, it is immutable in the sense that it is always and everywhere God's relationship to man, the being and essence of the One who loves in freedom. Yet it would not be a glorifying, but a blaspheming and finally a denial of God, to conceive of the being and essence of this self-consistent God as one which is, so to speak, self-limited to an inflexible immobility, thus depriving God of the capacity to alter His actions and attitudes as they are manifested in His revelation in concurrence or in sequence.[53]

That outlook enabled him to say the following about prayer:

> The will of God is not to preserve and accompany and rule the world and the course of the world as world-occurrence in such a way that He is not affected and moved by it, that He does not allow Himself to converse with it, that He does not listen to what it says, that as he conditions all things He does not allow Himself to be determined by them. God is not free and immutable in the sense that He is the prisoner of His own resolve and will and action, that He must always be alone as the Lord of all things and of all occurrence. . . . He is free and immutable as the living God, as the God who wills to converse with the creature, and to allow Himself to be determined by it in this relationship.[54]

Barth has been chosen as a representative of twentieth-century thought, rather than a process theologian, for whom God's changeability is a major point, because Barth's work shows how a new look at scripture has influenced even more traditional approaches to theology, making them correspond more adequately, where prayer is concerned, to the realities of Christian experience than the older theologies have done.

This is not the place to offer a review of the various theories of the atonement in Christianity.[55] Evidence for the inadequacy of each of them is provided by the number that have been proposed. The best theories would seem to be those that best preserve the mystery of the process of forgiveness in God. Beliefs and practices related to forgiveness were affected by the increasing emphasis in Christian history on what happens to people after they die. Whereas the Old Testament speaks of divine forgiveness primarily as the way God maintains the covenant relationship in spite of sin, Christian teaching tended to emphasize forgiveness of sin in order that the believer might be freed from eternal punishment. The sacrament of baptism took on the form of an institutionalization of the process of forgiveness, as the belief developed that all prior sins could be forgiven when that sacrament was administered. In early Christian history that led to the delay of baptism as long as possible, on the part of converts; an unfortunate misunderstanding of the sacrament coupled with an apparent unawareness of the call to the Christian life that should go with conversion. The sacrament of confession and penance provided a further institutionalization of forgiveness, as the church came to believe God granted the power of absolution to his priests.

The Protestant Reformers rejected this as a claim to the kind of contractual relationship with God which scripture does not authorize. But in all parts of Christendom, tensions associated with the freedom of God to act with mercy remain. At one extreme, the legalist tends not to need grace, thinking the good life obligates God's acceptance. At the other extreme lies what Bonhoeffer called "cheap grace," and although he was describing the German church as he saw it in the 1930s, that remains a serious danger for much of Christendom:

> The essence of grace, we suppose, is that the account has been paid in advance; and, because it has been paid, everything can be had for nothing. . . . Cheap grace is the preaching of forgiveness without requiring repentance, baptism without church discipline, Communion without confession, absolution without personal confession. Cheap grace is grace without discipleship, grace without the cross, grace without Jesus Christ, living and incarnate.[56]

Bonhoeffer's emphasis on the "cost of discipleship" to the believer introduces a new subject, but the cost of grace to God has been a major theme introduced to us by the book of Exodus. The difficulty we have in comprehending grace, and in accepting it without distorting it, suggests it is one of the essential differences between God and humanity.

As to the question whether the distance between God and his people of which Exodus 32—34 speaks, a distance bridgeable only by God's grace, remains in the experiences of Christians, it seems we have returned to the beginning, and the reader may, if necessary, consult again some of the comments made in the Introduction and chapter 1 of this book.

ABBREVIATIONS

AB	*The Anchor Bible*
AnBib	Analecta biblica
ANET	*Ancient Near Eastern Texts,* ed. J. B. Pritchard
AUSS	*Andrews University Seminary Studies*
BETL	Bibliotheca ephemeridum theologicarum lovaniensium
BIOSCS	*Bulletin of the International Organization for Septuagint Studies*
BJRL	*Bulletin of the John Rylands Library*
BKAT	Biblischer Kommentar: Altes Testament
BT	*The Bible Translator*
BZAW	Beihefte zur *ZAW*
CBQ	*Catholic Biblical Quarterly*
CBQMS	Catholic Biblical Quarterly—Monograph Series
ConBOT	Coniectanea biblica, Old Testament
ExpTim	*Expository Times*
HBT	*Horizons in Biblical Theology*
HSM	Harvard Semitic Monographs
HTR	*Harvard Theological Review*
HUCA	*Hebrew Union College Annual*
IBC	Interpretation: A Bible Commentary for Teaching and Preaching
IDB	*Interpreter's Dictionary of the Bible*
Int	*Interpretation*
ITC	International Theological Commentary
JAAR	*Journal of the American Academy of Religion*
JBL	*Journal of Biblical Literature*
JETS	*Journal of the Evangelical Theological Society*
JR	*Journal of Religion*
JSOT	*Journal for the Study of the Old Testament*
JSOTSup	Journal for the Study of the Old Testament—Supplement Series
JTS	*Journal of Theological Studies*
JTSA	*Journal of Theology for Southern Africa*
KJV	King James Version of the Bible
LXX	Septuagint Version of the Old Testament
NEB	New English Bible
NIV	New International Version of the Bible
NRSV	New Revised Standard Version of the Bible

NTS	*New Testament Studies*
OTL	Old Testament Library
OTP	*The Old Testament Pseudepigrapha*, ed. James Charlesworth
PTMS	Pittsburgh Theological Monograph Series
REB	Revised English Bible
RefRev	*Reformed Review*
RR	*Review of Religion*
RSV	Revised Standard Version of the Bible
RTP	*Revue de théologie et de philosophie*
SBLMS	Society of Biblical Literature Monograph Series
SBT	Studies in Biblical Theology
SJT	*Scottish Journal of Theology*
TDNT	*Theological Dictionary of the New Testament*, ed. G. Kittel and G. Friedrich
TDOT	*Theological Dictionary of the Old Testament*, ed. G. J. Botterwick and R. Ringgren
ThStud	*Theologische Studiën*
TLZ	*Theologische Literaturzeitung*
TToday	*Theology Today*
UUA	Uppsala Universitetsarsskrift
VT	*Vetus Testamentum*
VTSup	Vetus Testamentum, Supplements
WMANT	Wissenschaftliche Monographien zum Alten und Neuen Testament
ZAW	*Zeitschrift für die Alttestamentliche Wissenschaft*

RABBINIC LITERATURE

The Babylonian Talmud

b. Ber.	Tractate *Berakot*
b. Ketub.	Tractate *Ketubim*
b. Meg.	Tractate *Megillah*
b. Sanh.	Tractate *Sanhedrin*
b. Sukk.	Tractate *Sukka*
b. Yoma	Tractate *Yoma*

Midrash Rabbah

Gen. Rab.	*Genesis Rabbah*
Exod. Rab.	*Exodus Rabbah*
Lev. Rab.	*Leviticus Rabbah*
Num. Rab.	*Numbers Rabbah*
Deut. Rab.	*Deuteronomy Rabbah*

Other Rabbinic Works

Mek.	*Mekilta*
Pesiq. R.	*Pesiqta Rabbati*
Pesiq. Rab Kah.	*Pesiqta de Rab Kahana*

NOTES

INTRODUCTION

1. For recent surveys, see Gerhard F. Hasel, *Old Testament Theology: Basic Issues in the Current Debate*, 4th ed. (Grand Rapids: Wm. B. Eerdmans Publishing Co., 1991); Henning Graf Reventlow, *Problems of Old Testament Theology in the Twentieth Century* (Philadelphia: Fortress Press, 1985); idem, *Problems of Biblical Theology in the Twentieth Century* (Philadelphia: Fortress Press, 1986).

2. Readers will at first think this sounds like the kind of work Brevard S. Childs did in his *The Book of Exodus: A Critical, Theological Commentary* (Philadelphia: Westminster Press, 1974). Certainly, his approach to commentary writing has parallels with my approach to writing biblical theology, and I have been encouraged by his work to deal with scripture as I have done, but the two books will be found to be very different in content.

3. D. H. Kelsey, in *The Uses of Scripture in Recent Theology* (Philadelphia: Fortress Press, 1975), 98–101, shows that for recent theologians, "canon" is some aspect or pattern in scripture which they take to be determinative. So they do not appeal to scripture as such to authorize their proposals, but to that aspect or pattern. It is my hope that beginning by asking what Exodus says about God and attempting to take it all seriously (i.e., without deciding on our own grounds whether parts of it are superior to or more likely to be true than other parts), we may be able to make a different sort of use of scripture from those Kelsey has described.

4. Brevard S. Childs, *Old Testament Theology in a Canonical Context* (Philadelphia: Fortress Press, 1986), 12.

5. Harry Y. Gamble, *The New Testament Canon: Its Making and Meaning* (Philadelphia: Fortress Press, 1985), 75.

6. Hartmut Gese, "Tradition and Biblical Theology," in *Tradition and Theology in the Old Testament,* ed. Douglas A. Knight (Philadelphia: Fortress Press, 1977), 314.

7. My method differs from the strictly canonical approaches in taking seriously the real historical continuity between the Testaments. To many, this is alarming, as it seems to put all kinds of material on the same level with the canon of scripture. I have no intention of denying the idea of canon, however, putting all religious thought on the same level, for the history of tradition itself argues against that. The Intertestamental literature used the books we now call the Hebrew scriptures *as* scripture, although there was no canon as yet, and they took the central ideas of those books as the revelation of the will of God. It is even more obvious that post–New Testament literature does the

same for the Old and New Testaments. So our use of them points us toward the books that were their scripture, and are also our scripture.

I am writing something different from propositional theology, which probably needs clear-cut statements of truth from divinely inspired books, which must be qualitatively different from all other books. It is true that there are no books comparable to Exodus or Matthew, but comparison does not show what the qualitative difference may be between Proverbs and Sirac, or Esther and Tobit. For a theology based on the testimony of the people of God, the history of the canon shows that this is not a serious problem, however.

I do not hold to some sort of pre–Vatican II equation of scripture and tradition; neither do I find the solution of some Protestants, of a canon within the canon, acceptable. The history of the canon suggests another term: "essential canon." It is drawn from the terms used by the early church as they discussed the varying collections being used throughout Christendom: "books accepted by all," "books accepted by some, rejected by some," and "books rejected by all." The books accepted by all were what I call the essential canon. They have always been, as far back as we can trace it, definitive of the nature of the Jewish and Christian communities. They include most of the books of both Testaments. The middle group includes canonical works such as Song of Songs, Esther, and Ecclesiastes, in the Old Testament, and Revelation and Jude in the New Testament. It also includes the books Protestants call the Apocrypha. There is no significant difference in quality or orthodoxy to explain why some ended up inside the canon and some outside. But that doesn't really matter, since none of these books is or would be decisive in determining the nature of the believing community. The line could be moved one way or another and make no real difference, as long as it does not touch the essential canon. Theology is and always has been based on it, but all the other books, inside or outside, are useful, and so they should not be ignored.

8. Dietrich Ritschl, *The Logic of Theology* (Philadelphia: Fortress Press, 1987), 42.

9. Compare Gese's "Tradition and Biblical Theology" in *Tradition and Theology*, ed. Knight, 301–26, and "The Biblical View of Scripture," in idem, *Essays on Biblical Theology* (Minneapolis: Augsburg Publishing House, 1981), 9–33. I have a quite different understanding of the canon from that advocated by Gese. For evaluation, see Reventlow, *Problems of Biblical Theology,* 148–54; Gerhard F. Hasel, "Major Recent Issues in Old Testament Theology 1978–1983," *JSOT* 31 (1985): 32f.

10. First in his *Biblical Theology in Crisis* (Philadelphia: Westminster Press, 1970), and in his later works.

11. Compare James Barr, "Le Judaïsme postbiblique et la théologie de l'Ancien Testament," *RTP* 18 (1968): 209–17.

12. That is, since J. P. Gabler described biblical theology as making the distinction between historical particularity and universal propositions: John H. Sandys-Wunsch and Laurence Eldrege, "J. P. Gabler and the Distinction between Biblical and Dogmatic Theology: Translation, Commentary, and Discussion of His Originality," *SJT* 33 (1980): 133–58. Ben C. Ollenburger offers a helpful discussion of Gabler in "Biblical Theology: Situating the Discipline," in *Understand the Word: Essays in Honor of Bernhard W. Anderson*, ed. J. T. Butler et al., JSOTSup 37 (Sheffield: JSOT Press, 1985), 37–62. The expression "what it meant/what it means" has been widely

used since Krister Stendahl defined biblical theology as a purely descriptive discipline in "Biblical Theology, Contemporary," *IDB* 1:481–532, and "Method in the Study of Biblical Theology," in *The Bible in Modern Scholarship*, ed. J. Philip Hyatt (Nashville: Abingdon Press, 1965), 196–209.

13. Ben Ollenburger, "What Stendahl Meant," *HBT* 8 (1986): 73.

14. What I offer here may or may not satisfy James Barr's definition of what is properly theological, but it takes his strictures seriously: "Theology could never be simply an organization of the biblical material, in whatever mode or on whatever level, but must be the construction, criticism, and refining of *our* concepts of God in Christ and in the church." Barr, "The Theological Case against Biblical Theology," in *Canon, Theology, and Old Testament Interpretation,* ed. Gene M. Tucker, D. L. Peterson, and R. R. Wilson (Philadelphia: Fortress Press, 1988), 9.

15. Robert Morgan with John Barton, *Biblical Interpretation,* The Oxford Bible Series (Oxford: Oxford University Press, 1988), 257.

16. Compare Childs: "Biblical Theology seeks not only to pursue the nature of the one divine reality among the various biblical voices, it also wrestles theologically with the relation between the reality testified to in the Bible and that living reality known and experienced as the exalted Christ through the Holy Spirit within the present community of faith." B. S. Childs, *Biblical Theology of the Old and New Testaments* (Minneapolis: Fortress Press, 1993), 86.

17. Gerd Theissen, *A Critical Faith: A Case for Religion* (Philadelphia: Fortress Press, 1979), 82.

18. For the claim that the cultural differences are insuperable, see Dennis Nineham, *The Use and Abuse of the Bible: A Study of the Bible in an Age of Rapid Cultural Change* (London: George Allen & Unwin, 1976). For a response to a similar claim, based on the linguistic theories of Derrida and followers, see Michael LaFarge, "Are Texts Determinate? Derrida, Barth, and the Role of the Biblical Scholar," *HTR* 81 (1988): 341–57.

19. A.K.A. Adam, "Biblical Theology and the Problem of Modernity: *Von Wredestrasse zu Sackgasse,*" *HBT* 12.1 (1990): 8. For a similar point of view, see Karlfried Froehlich, "Biblical Hermeneutics on the Move," *Ex Auditu* 1 (1985): 12.

20. Compare Rolf Rendtorff, "Toward a Common Jewish-Christian Reading of the Hebrew Bible," in *Hebrew Bible or Old Testament? Studying the Bible in Judaism and Christianity,* Christianity and Judaism in Antiquity, 5, ed. R. Brooks and J. J. Collins (Notre Dame, Ind.: Notre Dame University Press, 1990), 89–108.

21. Gerhard Ebeling, *The Word of God and Tradition: Historical Studies Interpreting the Divisions of Christianity* (Philadelphia: Fortress Press, 1968), 29.

22. Wilfred Cantwell Smith, "The Study of Religion and the Study of the Bible," *JAAR* 39 (1971): 139f.

23. Compare Ebeling's daunting insistence in *Word of God and Tradition:* "The exegete must not only know the history of interpretation, but must also realize to the full what the systematic theologian's task involves in the exposition of the text, namely the encounter of theology in its totality with human existential totality. Similarly, the systematic theologian can only fulfil his task when he has mastered exegesis and Church history in the broadest sense, that is, when he has really taken the historical nature of existence seriously" (14).

CHAPTER 1: THE ABSENCE OF GOD

1. John I. Durham, *Exodus,* Word Bible commentary, 3 (Waco, Tex.: Word Books, 1987), 17; Terence E. Fretheim, *Exodus,* IBC (Louisville, Ky.: Westminster/John Knox Press, 1991), 38.

2. A classic example of this is Plastaras, who understands 2:23–25 better than any other commentator and may even overemphasize the absence of any consciousness of God among the Israelites. In spite of this, he claims, "In reading through Exodus 1:1–2:22, one can recognize the hand of God in every event narrated." James Plastaras, *The God of Exodus: The Theology of the Exodus Narratives* (Milwaukee: Bruce Publishing Co., 1966), 26f., 41.

3. For "outcry" as a key to Korean *minjung* theology, see Ee Kon Kim, " 'Outcry': Its Context in Biblical Theology," *Int* 42 (1988): 229–39.

4. Plastaras, *God of Exodus,* 49–59. Noted briefly by Werner H. Schmidt, *Exodus,* BKAT, 2 (Neukirchen-Vluyn: Neukirchener Verlag, 1977), 96.

5. Samuel Balentine, *The Hidden God: The Hiding of the Face of God in the Old Testament* (Oxford: Oxford University Press, 1983).

6. Willy Schottroff, *'Gedenken' im Alten Orient und im Alten Testament: Die Wurzel Zakar im semitischen Sprachkreis,* WMANT, 15 (Neukirchen-Vluyn: Neukirchener Verlag, 1964), 201. See pp. 202–11 for the verb with "covenant," as in Ex. 2:24.

7. The only places where some attempt is found to ascribe idolatry to the slaves in Egypt are Josh. 24:14 and Ezek. 20:7–8.

8. Samuel Terrien, *The Elusive Presence: The Heart of Biblical Theology* (San Francisco: Harper & Row, 1978), 29.

9. James L. Crenshaw, *A Whirlpool of Torment: Israelite Traditions of God as an Oppressive Presence,* Overtures to Biblical Theology (Philadelphia: Fortress Press, 1984), 122.

10. Balentine, *Hidden God.* Earlier studies: H. Schrade, *Der verborgene Gott: Gottesbild und Gottesvorstellung in Israel und im alten Orient* (Stuttgart: Kohlhammer, 1949); L. Perlitt, "Die Verborgenheit Gottes," in *Probleme biblischer Theologie: Festschrift Gerhard von Rad,* ed. H. W. Wolff (Munich: Chr. Kaiser Verlag, 1971), 367–82.

11. W. E. Oates and C. E. Oates, *People in Pain: Guidelines for Pastoral Care* (Philadelphia: Westminster Press, 1985), 121: "A vicious cycle of abandonment, creating more abandonment, intensifies the temptation to isolation, forsakenness, and self-pity. Subtly the integrity of the patient is eroded." For more on sickness in the laments, see my "Salvation as Healing," *Ex Auditu* 5 (1989): 4–9.

12. Balentine, *Hidden God,* 50–56, 66–68, 166.

13. English translations of 64:5b suggest the same idea, but the meaning of the Hebrew is uncertain.

14. The prophetic interpretation of Israel's history is summed up neatly, with emphasis on the hiddenness of God, in Deut. 31:16–18.

15. Martin Buber, *The Prophetic Faith* (New York: Macmillan Co., 1949), 188–97.

16. Terrien, *Elusive Presence,* 362.

17. André Neher, *The Exile of the Word: From the Silence of the Bible to the Silence of Auschwitz* (Philadelphia: Jewish Publication Society of America, 1981), 27.

18. Dale Patrick, "Job's Address of God," *ZAW* 91 (1979): 268–82.

19. Crenshaw, *Whirlpool of Torment*, chap. 4: "The Silence of Eternity: Ecclesiastes"; B. Hessler, "Koheleth: The Veiled God," *The Bridge* 1 (1955): 191–203.

20. Hans-Peter Müller, "Wie sprach Qohälät von Gott?" *VT* 18 (1968): 507–21.

21. Perlitt, "Die Verborgenheit Gottes," 382.

22. Balentine, *Hidden God*, 172.

23. Balentine's survey of uses of "hide the face" shows that it is a distinctively biblical expression, seldom appearing in later literature, although it is found in prayers in Tobit 3:6 and 3 Macc. 6:15. *Hidden God*, 113f.

24. The Thanksgiving scroll from Qumran also speaks of God's absence because of sin: "And I said, It is because of my sins that I am abandoned far from Thy Covenant. But when I remembered the might of Thy hand together with the greatness of Thy mercy I rose up and stood, and my spirit stood upright in the face of the blows" (*Hodayoth*, col. 4, l. 35). A. Dupont-Sommer, *The Essene Writings from Qumran* (Cleveland: World Publishing Co., 1961), 214.

25. *B. Ber.* 32b.

26. Ibid.

27. Jacob Neusner, *Lamentations Rabbah: An Analytical Translation* (Atlanta: Scholars Press, 1989), 355.

28. Jürgen Moltmann, *The Crucified God: The Cross of Christ as the Foundation and Criticism of Christian Theology* (New York: Harper & Row, 1974), 146.

29. David H. C. Read, "The Cry of Dereliction," *ExpTim* 68 (1957): 261.

30. Ibid., 262.

31. Karl Barth, *Church Dogmatics*, Vol. IV: *The Doctrine of Reconciliation* (Edinburgh: T. & T. Clark, 1956), 1.185.

32. Moltmann, *Crucified God*, 202, 203.

33. Ibid., 246.

34. Martin E. Marty, *A Cry of Absence: Reflections for the Winter of the Heart* (San Francisco: Harper & Row, 1983), 136, 139.

35. Evelyn Underhill, *Mysticism: A Study in the Nature and Development of Man's Spiritual Consciousness* (New York: Noonday Press, 1955), 382.

36. Ibid., 389.

37. St. John of the Cross, "The Dark Night" II.3.3, *Selected Writings* (New York: Paulist Press, 1987), 199.

38. Underhill, *Mysticism*, 383.

39. St. John of the Cross, "The Dark Night," II.9.1, p. 204.

40. Jürgen Moltmann, *Theology of Hope: On the Ground and the Implications of a Christian Eschatology* (New York: Harper & Row, 1967), 210f.; discussed at greater length and qualified in his *Crucified God*, 200–207.

41. "[R]egardless of whether he [God] is or not, his reality, as the Christian tradition has presented it, has become culturally irrelevant: God is *de trop*, as Sartre would say." Gabriel Vahanian, *Wait without Idols* (New York: George Braziller, 1964), 32.

42. In the Old Testament "hiding the face" usually meant the same thing as "forsaking," for example, so absence, hiddenness, inactivity, and inaccessibility have

been used synonymously up until now. In Christian theology, however, "hiddenness" may also be used to refer to God's incomprehensibility. [Discussed thoroughly in John Dillenberger, *God Hidden and Revealed* (Philadelphia: Muhlenberg Press, 1953).] Karl Barth devotes a twenty-five-page section of his *Church Dogmatics* to the hiddenness of God, as a part of the chapter on the limits of the knowledge of God, but this section never takes up the issues we have been tracing. *Church Dogmatics*, Vol. II: *The Doctrine of God,* 1.179–204. The mystery or incomprehensibility of God is also an Old Testament theme, appearing especially in the wisdom literature (e.g., Prov. 20:24; Job 28:20–28; Eccl. 3:11), but we shall continue to leave that to one side in order to focus on the questions about whether there is a God who does anything.

43. William Hamilton, "The Death of God Theology," *The Christian Scholar* 48 (1965): 31.

44. Karl Rahner, S.J., *Encounters with Silence* (Paramus, N.J.: Newman Press, 1960), 19f., and see p. 56.

45. Peter C. Hodgson, *Jesus—Word and Presence: An Essay in Christology* (Philadelphia: Fortress Press, 1971), 4f.

46. Neher, *Exile of the Word.*

47. Ibid., 236.

48. Emil L. Fackenheim, *God's Presence in History: Jewish Affirmations and Philosophical Reflections* (New York: Harper & Row, 1970), 78f.

49. Ibid., 84.

50. Ibid., 95–97.

51. Marty, *Cry of Absence*, 49.

CHAPTER 2: THE NUMINOUS

1. Examples of presuppositions: (1) Every word of scripture is inerrant: therefore this happened exactly as described, and presumably the burning bush and the voice of God could have been videotaped. (2) The laws of science do not permit such things to happen: therefore this was an entirely inner experience of Moses. (3) The Old Testament contains no reliable historical information: therefore this is to be understood as a work of fiction.

2. Norman Snaith, *The Distinctive Ideas of the Old Testament* (London: Epworth Press, 1944), 21–50; Helmer Ringgren, *The Prophetical Conception of Holiness,* UUA 1948:12 (Uppsala: A.-B. Lundequistska Bokhandeln, 1948) 7f.

3. Rudolf Otto, *The Idea of the Holy: An Inquiry into the Non-rational Factor in the Idea of the Divine and Its Relation to the Rational,* trans. John W. Harvey (1917; reprint, New York: Oxford University Press, 1958). Compare Edmond Jacob, *Theology of the Old Testament* (New York: Harper & Row, 1958), 88: "[N]owhere do the essential characteristics of holiness present themselves to us with such precision as in the scene of the burning bush, where both name and holiness are the most adequate expressions for the divine life."

4. Available in English in two editions: Pelican Books, 1959, and Oxford University Press, 1958. All citations will be from the latter.

5. Useful studies of Otto's description of the numinous: Stephen Beasley-Murray, *Towards a Metaphysics of the Sacred* (Macon, Ga: Mercer University Press, 1982);

Robert F. Davidson, *Rudolf Otto's Interpretation of Religion* (Princeton, N.J.: Princeton University Press, 1949); Dillenberger, *God Hidden and Revealed,* chap. 3: "God Revealed as the Wholly Other"; John M. Moore, *Theories of Religious Experience with Special Reference to James, Otto, and Bergson* (New York: Round Table Press, 1938); Harold Turner, *The Idea of the Holy: A Commentary* (Aberdeen: People's Press, 1974). I think the reason for most of the misunderstandings was already anticipated by Otto when he wrote, "The reader is invited to direct his mind to a moment of deeply-felt religious experience, as little as possible qualified by other forms of consciousness. Whoever cannot do this, whoever knows no such moments in his experience, is requested to read no farther; for it is not easy to discuss questions of religious psychology with one who can recollect the emotions of his adolescence, the discomforts of indigestion, or, say, social feelings, but cannot recall any intrinsically religious feelings." Otto, *Idea of the Holy,* 8.

6. Mircea Eliade, *The Sacred and the Profane: The Nature of Religion,* trans. Willard R. Trask (New York: Harper & Brothers, 1961), 8–10.

7. Walther Eichrodt, *Theology of the Old Testament,* OTL (Philadelphia: Westminster Press, 1961), 1:270–82.

8. Among the commentators, only Durham takes this route: "[T]here is not the slightest reason to imagine some unusual thunderstorm or to look for an extinct volcano as a means of locating Sinai. . . . The storm and fire imagery of vv. 16–19a is one part of an attempt to describe the indescribable experience of the coming of Yahweh." Durham, *Exodus,* 270.

9. Othmar Keel-Leu, *The Symbolism of the Biblical World: Ancient Near Eastern Iconography and the Book of Psalms* (New York: Seabury Press, 1978), 214–17.

10. Jörg Jeremias, *Theophanie: Die Geschichte einer Alttestamentliche Gattung,* WMANT 10 (Neukirchen-Vluyn: Neukirchener Verlag, 1965).

11. For the theology of the book of Habakkuk, see Donald E. Gowan, *The Triumph of Faith in Habakkuk* (Atlanta: John Knox Press, 1976).

12. J. H. Eaton, "The Origin and Meaning of Habakkuk 3," *ZAW* 76 (1964): 144–71.

13. Otto, *Idea of the Holy,* "Foreword by the Author to the First English Edition," and pp. 1–4. See also the translator's preface, pp. ix–xix.

14. Ibid., 25–30.

15. He includes two more chapters on the early and crude forms of apprehension of the numinous (ibid., 117–35), and does not expand his original, ten-page description of the *fascinans* in a comparable way.

16. B. J. Bamberger, "Fear and Love of God in the Old Testament," *HUCA* 6 (1929): 39–53; Geo Nagel, "Crainte et amour de Dieu dans l'Ancien Testament," *RTP* 33 (1945): 175–86; Mayer I. Gruber, "Fear, Anxiety, and Reverence in Akkadian, Biblical Hebrew, and Other North-West Semitic Languages," *VT* 40 (1990): 411–22.

17. Martin Noth, *Exodus,* OTL (Philadelphia: Westminster Press, 1962), 50.

18. Brevard S. Childs, *The Book of Exodus,* OTL (Philadelphia: Westminster Press, 1974), 104.

19. Rabbi Abraham Ben Isaiah and Rabbi Benjamin Sharfman, *The Pentateuch and Rashi's Commentary: A Linear Translation into English: Exodus* (New York: S. S. & R. Publishing Co., 1949), 37f. For a helpful survey of the early interpretations: Geza Vermes, *Scripture and Tradition in Judaism* (Leiden: E. J. Brill, 1973), chap. 7: "Circumcision and Exodus IV 24–26: Prelude to the Theology of Baptism," 178–92.

20. "[T]hese [Ex. 4:24–26 and Gen 32:24–32] are accidental survivals from the dark childhood of the race, preserved usually for some incidental reason that has nothing to do with theology." Robert C. Dentan, *The Knowledge of God in Ancient Israel* (New York: Seabury Press, 1968), 156.

21. Paul Volz, *Das Dämonische in Jahwe* (Tübingen: J.C.B. Mohr, 1924); Martin Buber, *Moses: The Revelation and the Covenant* (New York: Harper & Row, 1958), pp. 56–59 ("Divine Demonism").

22. Volz, *Dämonische*, 31.

23. Volz, *Dämonische*, 40 (my free translation).

24. Schmidt, *Exodus*, 232–34 (my translation).

25. Otto, *Idea of the Holy*, 11, 113, 136–42.

26. Waldo Jewell-Lapan, "A Naturalistic View of 'Numinous' Experience," *RR* 2 (1937): 25–32; John Oman, "The Idea of the Holy," *JTS* 25 (1924): 275–86. The latter's point of view is to be taken more seriously than the former. Others have offered approaches attempting to correct the weakness of this assumption, e.g., Beasley-Murray, *Metaphysics of the Sacred;* John Morrison Moore, *Theories of Religious Experience: With Special Reference to James, Otto, and Bergson* (New York: Round Table Press, 1938), 92–112.

27. "Rudolf Otto's 'Idea of the Holy,' whatever it may be, is at all events not to be regarded as the Word of God, for the simple and patent reason that it is the numinous, and that the numinous is the irrational, and the irrational something no longer distinguishable from an absolutised power of Nature. Upon this very distinction everything depends, if we are to understand the concept of the Word of God." Barth, *Church Dogmatics*, Vol. I: *The Doctrine of the Word of God*, 1.153.

28. Eliade regularly discusses the features that distinguish the Old Testament and the religions descended from it from all other religions. See *The Sacred and the Profane,* passim.

29. A purely numinous experience, without any regard for morality, was available in the Greco-Roman world, in the cult of Dionysus. Harold R. Willoughby, *Pagan Regeneration: A Study of Mystery Initiations in the Graeco-Roman World* (Chicago: University of Chicago Press, 1929), 68–89.

30. D. S. Russell, *The Method and Message of Jewish Apocalyptic: 200 BC–AD 100,* OTL (Philadelphia: Westminster Press, 1964), 140–57.

31. William James, *The Varieties of Religious Experience: A Study in Human Nature*, Introduction by Reinhold Neibuhr (New York: Collier Books, 1961), 59–77, 299–336; Johannes Lindblom, *Prophecy in Ancient Israel* (Philadelphia: Fortress Press, 1962), 13–26.

32. Burton M. Leiser, "The Sanctity of the Profane: A Pharisaic Critique of Rudolf Otto," *Judaism* (Winter, 1971): 87–92.

33. Lawrence A. Hoffman, *Beyond the Text: A Holistic Approach to Liturgy* (Bloomington: Indiana University Press, 1989), 151–63.

34. Jacob Neusner, *The Incarnation of God: The Character of Divinity in Formative Judaism* (Philadelphia: Fortress Press, 1988), 165–230.

35. Sentences in quotation marks are from Neusner's translation in *Incarnation of God,* 228f.

36. The traditional Passover prayer that begins "The breath of every living thing" strikes me as one of the most impressive examples of numinous prayer language. *The*

Passover Haggadah, ed. Nahum N. Glatzer, rev. ed. (New York: Schocken Books, 1969), 79–83.

37. Compare also the reactions of the Roman, Cornelius, to his vision and subsequent encounter with Peter, in Acts 10:3–4, 25.

38. Jan Milic Lochman, *The Lord's Prayer* (Grand Rapids: Wm. B. Eerdmans Publishing Co., 1990); quoting J. Carmignac, *Recherches sur le "notre Père"* (Paris: Letouzey, 1969), 237f.

39. J. Schniewind, *Das Evangelium nach Mattäus,* 11th ed. (Göttingen: Vandenhoeck & Ruprecht, 1964), 88.

40. Otto, *Idea of the Holy,* 99f. The reader may be referred to chapter 12 and appendix 6 in *The Idea of the Holy* for Otto's discussions of the numinous in Luther.

41. The following quotations are from *Augustine: Confessions and Enchiridion,* trans. and ed. by Albert C. Outler, Library of Christian Classics, 7 (Philadelphia: Westminster Press, 1955), 33, 34, 251.

42. Robert F. Davidson, *Rudolf Otto's Interpretation of Religion* (Princeton, N.J.: Princeton University Press, 1947), 64.

43. Peter L. Berger, *A Rumor of Angels: Modern Society and the Rediscovery of the Supernatural,* exp. ed. (New York: Doubleday, 1990), 6.

44. Eliade, *Sacred and Profane,* 202f.

45. Mircea Eliade, *Myth and Reality* (New York: Harper & Row, 1963), chap. 9: "Survivals and Camouflages of Myths," 169–93.

46. Berger, *Rumor of Angels,* 55–85.

47. Harold K. Schilling, *The New Consciousness in Science and Religion* (Philadelphia: Pilgrim Press, 1973), 30. See also the appendix: "On the Meaning of 'Mystery,' " pp. 267–76. He refers to Otto only once in the book, but the parallels to Otto's work, drawn from a completely different area of life, are striking.

48. Ibid., parts 1 and 2.

49. Theissen, *Critical Faith,* 34, and see 12–15.

50. John Bowker, *The Sense of God: Sociological, Anthropological, and Psychological Approaches to the Origin of the Sense of God* (Oxford: Clarendon Press, 1973), and *The Religious Imagination and the Sense of God* (Oxford: Clarendon Press, 1978). From the former: "But the question, nevertheless, would then become whether the sense of God is simply built up from an extensive patterning of stable, consensual cues which then receive (but do not actually demand) theistic interpretation, or whether some of the cues, so to speak, arrive from that reality in existence to which a term such as 'god' is appropriately applied, so that those cues arriving from the external universe demand (but do not always receive) a response of faith?" (157). He concludes that recent advances in various disciplines are not "dissolving the possible reality of reference in the term 'God'—they actually seem to demand a return to that possibility if sense is to be made of their own evidence" (181). I raised this issue earlier in this section, but have not pursued it further, since as mentioned there, it moves beyond anything that could be called biblical theology.

51. Arthur Cohen entitled his book on the Holocaust *The Tremendum* (New York: Crossroad, 1988).

52. Edith Barfoot, *The Witness of Edith Barfoot: The Joyful Vocation to Suffering* (Oxford: Basil Blackwell Publisher, 1977), 7f.

CHAPTER 3: "I WILL BE WITH YOU"

1. There are no feminine objects of the preposition. There are differences of opinion over the inclusion of sentences in the form "I am with God," rather than "God is with me." That form does not occur very often in the OT, and it seems to have the same meaning, so I have included them, contrary to other studies.

2. I am using 104 verses, in some of which the formula occurs twice. The only verb in these occurrences is "to be," expressed or understood. This means that I have excluded some texts found in other studies. For example, "walk with God" (as in Micah 6:8) means something distinctly different, focusing on obedience, as do the related expressions "walk before God" and "walk after God," so they belong with a different study.

3. Here are the best examples I have found of a commentator calling attention to the formula. From Brueggemann: "The introduction of this formula dare not be treated like a cliché. It is the amazing new disclosure of Jacob's God, one who is willing to cast his lot with this man, to stand with him in places of threat." But no more is said about Gen 28:15. Walter Brueggemann, *Genesis,* IBC (Atlanta: John Knox Press, 1982), 245. From Knight: ". . . the most important affirmation about himself that any of the OT writers has been able to record. God now, v. 12, makes a declaration to Moses in three simple Hebrew words: 'That, I-will-be, with-thee.' " And Knight does devote a page to the explanation of the three words in Ex. 3:12. George A. F. Knight, *Theology as Narration: A Commentary on the Book of Exodus* (Grand Rapids: Wm. B. Eerdmans Publishing Co., 1976), 21f.

4. He deals with Ex. 3:12, but without calling special attention to "I shall be" as it occurs anywhere else. Terrien, *Elusive Presence,* 113.

5. These studies will be of interest to us later, in connection with the tabernacle material. That material will also call our attention to two other expressions, which might be thought synonymous to "with": *b^{e}qerev* and *b^{e}thok,* both of which mean "in the midst of." In a few passages they are used in a way similar to "with" (e.g., Num. 14:42–43; Hag. 2:4–5), but it will be shown later that they typically have overtones missing from "God is with us."

6. The NEB and NRSV omit "but," taking the conjunction *ki* to be just the indication of a direct quote to follow. In this context, however, it seems more likely that the asseverative sense of the word is present, as noted by Knight, *Theology as Narration,* 21, and acknowledged in a footnote by James Muilenberg, "The Linguistic and Rhetorical Usages of the Particle *ki* in the Old Testament," *HUCA* 32 (1961): 144n.28.

7. F. J. Helfmeyer, s.v. *'oth, TDOT* (Grand Rapids: Wm B. Eerdmans Publishing Co., 1974), 1:181–85.

8. W. C. van Unnik, "*Dominus Vobiscum*: The Background of a Liturgical Formula," in *New Testament Essays: Studies in Memory of T. W. Manson*, ed. A.J.B. Higgins (Manchester: University Press, 1959), 270–305.

9. Horst Dietrich Preuss, ". . . ich will mit dir sein," *ZAW* 80 (1968): 158, 172.

10. Dieter Vetter, *Jahwes Mit-Sein—ein Ausdruck des Segens,* Arbeiten zur Theologie, 1, Reihe, Heft 45 (Stuttgart: Calwer Verlag, 1971), 3.

11. E. Kutsch, "Gideons Berufung und Altarbau, Jdc 6,11–24," *TLZ* 81 (1956): 75–84. Dealing with the Amos quote of the people's use of the formula, Neubauer

found enough evidence to persuade himself it was sometimes a cultic cry of confidence, but all subsequent studies have rejected the cultic connections. K. W. Neubauer, "Erwägungen zu Amos 5,4–15," *ZAW* 78 (1966): 292–316.

12. Preuss's work was dominated by the fact that he began with the Genesis occurrences, assuming they represented the original *Sitz-im-Leben*, and considered the patriarchs to have been a "nomadic" people. Thus he was led to emphasize God's "going with" his people and can bring in every reference to "way" in the Old Testament, and every kind of journey as somehow related to this formula. Some of Vetter's emphases are different, but he did accept Preuss's theory of nomadic origin. But anthropological studies have shown that the very use of the word "nomad" with reference to the Old Testament is dubious. See J. W. Rogerson, *Anthropology and the Old Testament* (Atlanta: John Knox Press, 1978), 41–45. And the kind of life-style described for the patriarchs is in fact far different from Preuss's wanderers, who understand their God primarily as the one who guides them on their way. Vetter's emphasis on blessing is less misleading than Preuss's journey theory (which dominates his whole presentation), but it is weakened by the fact that there are only three texts that closely associate *'eth* or *'im* with blessing: Gen. 26:24; 26:28–29; Deut. 2:7. The two are adjacent to each other also in Num. 23:20, 21 and Ruth 2:4. Both ignore other possible contexts that are more likely, both on literary and historical grounds, especially holy war and kingship ideology.

13. Gen. 21:20, 22; 26:3, 24, 28; 28:15, 20; 31:3, 5; 35:3; 39:2, 3, 21, 23; 48:21; Josh. 14:12; Job 29:5.

14. 1 Sam. 10:7; 16:18; 17:37; 18:12, 14, 28; 20:13; 2 Sam. 5:10; 7:3, 9; 14:17; 1 Kings 1:37; 11:38; 18:7; 1 Chron. 11:9; 17:2, 8; 22:11, 16; 28:20; 2 Chron. 1:1; 13:12; 15:2, 9; 17:3; 19:6; 35:21; Hag. 2:4.

15. Deut. 31:8, 23; Josh. 1:5, 9, 17; 3:7; 6:27; Judg. 2:18; 6:12, 13, 16; 2 Chron. 32:7–8.

16. Ex. 3:12; 4:12, 15; 10:10; 18:19; Josh. 1:5; 1 Sam. 3:19.

17. Gen. 21:20; 39:2, 3, 21, 23; Josh. 6:27; 1 Sam. 3:19; 18:12, 14, 28; 2 Sam. 5:10; 2 Kings 18:7; 1 Chron. 9:20; 11:9; 2 Chron. 1:1; 15:9; 17:3.

18. Gen. 21:22; 26:28; 48:21; Ex. 10:10; 18:19; Deut. 31:8; 1 Sam. 10:7; 2 Sam. 7:3; 1 Chron. 22:18; 28:20; 2 Chron. 13:12; 15:2; 19:6; 20:17; 25:7; 32:7–8; Isa. 7:14 (if the child "God with us" is the sign given to Ahaz). Note that the expression became a favorite part of the Chronicler's speech-writing style.

19. *yare'* with *'al*: Gen. 21:17 and 20; 26:24; Deut. 20:3–4; 1 Chron. 22:11 and 13; 28:20; 2 Chron. 20:15 and 17; 32:7; Isa. 41:10; 43:1 and 2, 5; Jer. 1:8; 30:10–11; 42:11; 46:28; Hag. 2:5. *yare'* with *lo'*, apodictic or affirmative: Deut. 20:1; 32:8; Pss. 23:4; 46:2 and 7. *'arats* with *'al*: Josh. 1:9. *hathath* with *'al*: Jer. 1:17 and 19. Fear is associated in other ways in Gen. 28:15–20; Ex. 3:6 and 12; 1 Sam. 18:12; 28–29.

20. E.g., Neubauer, "Erwägungen zu Amos 5,4–15," 298–300.

21. Walter Grundmann, "*sun—meta* with the Genitive," *TDNT* 7 (Grand Rapids: Wm. B. Eerdmans Publishing Co., 1971), 775, 774.

22. Van Unnik, "*Dominus Vobiscum,*" 284.

23. Norman Habel, "The Form and Significance of the Call Narratives," *ZAW* 77 (1965): 297–323.

24. Kutsch, "Gideons Berufung," 78–82.

25. Van Unnik, *"Dominus Vobiscum,"* 282.

26. Brunet points out that except for the eschatological name predicted by Jeremiah—*Yahweh Tsidkenu,* "The Lord is our Righteousness"—this is the only name in the Bible that has a plural suffix. He proposes to take the "El" in the name not as the common abbreviation of Elohim, the God of Israel, but as the Canaanite god El, thus making Isaiah's statement derisive and hostile, a reference to those in Israel who still worship El. But this overlooks the frequency of use of "El" as an abbreviation for the God of Israel in other proper names, and also does not take into consideration the special characteristics of the formula we have been studying, in which Yahweh and Elohim are readily interchanged. Gilbert Brunet, *Essai sur l'Isaïe de l'histoire: Étude de quelques textes notamment dans Isa. 7, 8, and 22* (Paris: Éditions A. & J. Picard, 1975), 18–25.

27. Ibid., 31–34.

28. Van Unnik, *"Dominus Vobiscum,"* 273, 293.

29. Ibid., 280–81.

30. A. Cowley, *Aramaic Papyri of the Fifth Century B.C.*, edited with translation and notes (Oxford: Clarendon Press, 1923), No. 22, col. 6, l.105; p. 70.

31. This is the RSV translation, following uncials B and A; NRSV follows Sinaiticus, which omits everything after "the dead."

32. For studies of this subject in the New Testament, see H. Frankemölle, *Jahwebund und Kirche Christi: Studien zur Form- und Traditionsgeschichte des Evangeliums nach Matthäus* (Münster: Aschendorff, 1974); Grundmann, *"sun—meta* with the Genitive"; van Unnik, *"Dominus Vobiscum."*

33. The same preposition, *meta,* is used in all the New Testament passages.

34. The fullest development of this aspect of Matthew's theology may be found in Frankemölle, *Jahwebund und Kirche Christi,* 1–83. Thanks to my former colleague Ulrich Mauser for this reference. Unfortunately Frankemölle concludes that this is a covenant formula in the Old Testament, to be associated with "I will be your God and you shall be my people," and our studies have not found support for that.

35. Frankemölle, *Jahwebund und Kirche Christi,* 79.

36. Jesus used the preposition "with" once in a negative sense, in a lament that refers specifically to his earthly ministry (Matt. 17:17), and used it in an eschatological sense at the Last Supper (Matt. 26:29). Thus Matthew has used the phrase to speak of what the church would later call the incarnation in chaps. 1 and 17, of the continuing presence of the Risen Christ with the church in chap. 28, and of the hope for Christ's return in chap. 27, each time using the phrase "with you."

37. Grundmann, *"sun—meta* with the Genitive," 781–94.

38. Gregory Dix, ed., *The Treatise on the Apostolic Tradition of Saint Hippolytus of Rome* (London: SPCK, 1968), 7, 39, 50.

39. A detailed account of the history of the greeting may be found in the chapter by Kurt Frör, "Salutationen, Benediktionen, Amen," in *Leiturgia: Handbuch des evangelistischen Gottesdienst,* ed. K. F. Müller and W. Blankenburg (Kassell: J. Standia-Verlag, 1955), 2:570–81.

40. Van Unnik, *"Dominus Vobiscum,"* 298n.1.

41. Isa. 41:10; as paraphrased in the hymn "How Firm a Foundation."

42. Ruth Page, *Ambiguity and the Presence of God* (London: SCM Press, 1985), 141.

CHAPTER 4: THE NAME

1. Consider the two ways Ps. 139:7–12 is read. For some, "Where can I go from your spirit? Or where can I flee from your presence?" is comforting reassurance, for others it is a threat. It all depends on who the reader thinks God is. See Tryggve N. D. Mettinger, *In Search of God: The Meaning and Message of the Everlasting Names* (Philadelphia: Fortress Press, 1987), 23: "Everything depends on the identity of the one who stands behind the promise."

2. For examples of such explanations, see Mettinger, *In Search of God,* 1–13; Johannes Pedersen, *Israel: Its Life and Culture* (London: Oxford University Press, 1926), 1:245–59; Max Reisel, *Observations on 'ehyeh 'asher 'ehyeh (Ex. III.14), hu'h' (D.S.D. VIII.13) and shem hammephorash* (Assen, Netherlands: Van Gorcum, 1957), 1–4. For a reevaluation of the meaning of names, see James Barr, "The Symbolism of Names in the Old Testament," *BJRL* 52 (1969): 11–29.

3. Carl E. Braaten, ed., *Our Naming of God* (Minneapolis: Fortress Press, 1989), 1.

4. Dale Carnegie, *How to Win Friends and Influence People* (New York: Simon & Schuster, 1937), 113.

5. Paul Tournier, *The Naming of Persons* (New York: Harper & Row, 1975), 19.

6. Jean Shepherd, *In God We Trust: All Others Pay Cash* (New York: Bantam Books, 1967), 32. The quote has a special piquancy for those of us old enough to remember Pierre André as the announcer for "Radio's Orphan Annie."

7. E: vv. 1, 4b, 6, 9–15; J: vv. 2–4a, 5, 7, 8, 16–22. E is so fragmentary that I find myself among the minority of scholars who think it may never have been a separate, continuous source, but probably represents supplements to J.

8. Some of the useful surveys: Mettinger, *In Search of God,* 14–49; G. H. Parke-Taylor, *Yahweh: The Divine Name in the Bible* (Waterloo, Ont.: Wilfrid Laurier University Press, 1975); Reisel, *Observations on 'ehyeh 'asher 'ehyeh.*

9. Ramban (Nachmanides), *Commentary on the Torah: Exodus,* translated and annotated by Rabbi C. B. Chavel (New York: Shilo Publishing House, 1973), 33. Martin Buber continued the same kind of reasoning, claiming one never asks for a person's name in Hebrew with the interrogative *mah* (What?) but always with *mi* (Who?). *Moses, 48.* This is immediately disproved by Gen. 32:28, however. See also Childs, *Exodus,* 60–70, and Henri Cazelles, "Pour une exégèse de *Ex.* III 14," in his *Autour de l'Exode (Études)* (Paris: J. Gabalda, 1987), 27–44.

10. For a fuller discussion, see Reisel, *Observations on 'ehyeh 'asher 'ehyeh,* 12–20.

11. K.-H. Bernhardt, *"hayah," TDOT* 3 (Grand Rapids: Wm. B. Eerdmans Publishing Co., 1978), 369–81; Georg Fischer, *Jahwe unser Gott,* OBO 91 (Göttingen: Vandenhoeck & Ruprecht, 1989), 148–50. Both work with the same list, but find fewer texts that cannot be read as futures. Bernhardt, only Ruth 2:13; Fischer, Ruth 2:13 and 2 Sam. 15:34. De Vaux's objection, that this would mean the speaker did not yet exist, is beside the point if the meaning of the verb is not existence, and most scholars agree it is not. Roland de Vaux, "The Revelation of the Divine Name YHWH," in *Proclamation and Presence: Festschrift G. Henton Davies,* ed. J. I. Durham and J. R. Porter (Richmond: John Knox Press, 1970), 66f.

12. For a useful study of the root, see G. S. Ogden, "Time, and the Verb *hayah* in the Old Testament Prose," *VT* 21 (1971): 451–69.

13. Georges Auzou, *De la Servitude au Service: Étude du Livre de l'Exode* (Paris: Éditions de L'Orante, 1961), 119 (my translation).

14. J. R. Lundbom, "God's Use of the *idem per idem* to Terminate Debate," *HTR* 71 (1978): 193–201.

15. Other texts that have been cited as *idem per idem* express significantly different ideas and are not useful parallels: Gen. 43:14; Ex. 4:13; Esth. 4:16; Zech. 10:8.

16. The same conclusion is reached by Bernhardt ("*hayah,*" 381) and Terrien (*Elusive Presence,* 119).

17. Ludwig Köhler, *Old Testament Theology* (Philadelphia: Westminster Press, 1957), 40f., 43.

18. Walther Zimmerli, *Old Testament Theology in Outline* (Atlanta: John Knox Press, 1978), 20.

19. Walther Zimmerli, "I Am Yahweh," in his *I Am Yahweh* (Atlanta: John Knox Press, 1982), 1–28. Also relevant to this discussion is his "Knowledge of God according to the Book of Ezekiel," in the same volume, 29–98, since it deals with the "recognition formula": "Then you/they will know that I am Yahweh."

20. *ANET,* 450.

21. Zimmerli, *I Am Yahweh,* 13.

22. Mettinger, *In Search of God,* 65–74.

23. See Jon Levenson, *The Hebrew Bible, the Old Testament, and Historical Criticism* (Louisville, Ky.: Westminster/John Knox Press, 1992), 151–53. This is a revision of the original article by Levenson, "Exodus and Liberation," *HBT* 13 (1991): 160–62.

24. Noth, *Exodus,* 60.

25. Even NRSV still uses "angel" to represent *mal'ak.* That is misleading since the word literally means a "messenger," who can be either a human or a heavenly figure in the Old Testament. Since the *mal'ak* here and elsewhere sometimes does more than deliver a message, but has the power to carry out God's work, an appropriate modern translation would be "agent."

26. Auzou, *De la Servitude au Service,* 120.

27. Zimmerli, *Old Testament Theology,* 124; cf. Childs, *Book of Exodus,* 409–12.

28. Gottfried Quell, "The Old Testament Name for God," *TDNT* 3 (Grand Rapids: Wm. B. Eerdmans Publishing Co., 1965), 1070.

29. Hans Bietenhard says *shem* is "the side of Yahweh presented to man" (*TDNT* 5, 257). Cf. Dentan, *The Knowledge of God,* 190: "[I]t came to function rather as a concentrated expression and symbol of the mysterious essence of Yahweh's character."

30. Roland de Vaux, "Le lieu que Yahvé a choisi pour y établir son nom," in *Das Ferne und Nahe Wort: Festschrift Leonhard Rost,* BZAW 105 (Berlin: Alfred Töpelman, 1967), 219–28.

31. Good examples of these views, from the Greek world, are provided by Bietenhard, *TDNT* 5, 246–51.

32. Tournier, *Naming of Persons,* 78f., 84.

33. There are different interpretations of the tradition that the priests no longer pronounced the name after the death of the High Priest Simon the Just (early second century B.C.E.). See Samuel S. Cohon, "The Name of God, A Study in Rabbinic Theology," *HUCA* 23.1 (1951): 588, 591.

34. Bientenhard, *TDNT* 5, 269.

35. Translations of the three quotations are from *Philo*, English translation by F. H. Colson, Loeb Classical Library, vol. 7 (Cambridge: Harvard University Press, 1950).

36. Moses Maimonides, *The Guide for the Perplexed* (London: Routledge & Kegan Paul, 1904), 90, 95.

37. For a helpful exegesis of this petition, see Ernst Lohmeyer, *The Lord's Prayer* (London: Collins, 1965), 63–87.

38. Joseph A. Fitzmyer, S.J., "The Semitic Background of the New Testament *Kyrios*-Title," in *A Wandering Aramean: Collected Aramaic Essays,* SBLMS 25 (Missoula, Mont.: Scholars Press, 1979), 115–42; Patrick Skehan, "The Divine Name at Qumran, in the Masada Scroll and in the Septuagint," *BIOSCS* 13 (1980): 14–44; Joseph A. Fitzmyer, S.J., "New Testament Kyrios and Maranatha and Their Aramaic Background," in *To Advance the Gospel: New Testament Studies* (New York: Crossroad, 1981), 85–101; A. Pietersma, "Kyrios or Tetragram: A Renewed Request for the Original LXX," in *De Septuaginta: Studies in Honour of John William Wevers*, ed. A. Pietersma and C. Cox (Mississanga, Ont.: Benben Publications, 1984), 85–101.

39. Mettinger, *In Search of God,* 43–48.

40. Barth, *Church Dogmatics*, Vol. I: *Doctrine of the Word of God,* 1.366.

41. Contemporary discussion of the name of God tends to focus on "Father" and "Son" and the fact that they are masculine. See Braaten, *Our Naming of God,* and Robert P. Scharlemann, ed., *Naming God* (New York: Paragon House, 1985), which also deals more generally with theological language.

42. Lohmeyer, *Lord's Prayer,* 75, 76.

43. Paul Tillich, "The Divine Name," *Christianity and Crisis* 20 (1960–61): 55–58.

44. Barth, *Church Dogmatics,* Vol. I: *Doctrine of the Word of God,* 1.364–65. Cf. p. 400.

45. John Hick, *God Has Many Names* (Philadelphia: Westminster, 1982).

CHAPTER 5: PROMISE

1. Note the first definition of the noun in the *Oxford English Dictionary.* I shall have more to say about the positive use of the word shortly.

2. For a thorough treatment, see Claus Westermann, *The Promises to the Fathers: Studies on the Patriarchal Narratives* (Philadelphia: Fortress Press, 1980).

3. On the latter question, see Gerhard von Rad, *Old Testament Theology* (New York: Harper & Row, 1962), 1:133–35, 167–71.

4. Ronald E. Clements deals only with this understanding of promise in "The Old Testament as Promise," in *Old Testament Theology: A Fresh Approach* (London: Marshall, Morgan & Scott, 1978), 131–54. Walter Kaiser's *Toward an Old Testament Theology* (Grand Rapids: Zondervan Publishing House, 1978) is based entirely on this traditional pattern.

5. Various points of view on this are represented in *Essays on Old Testament Hermeneutics*, ed. Claus Westermann (Richmond: John Knox Press, 1963).

6. Does this account for the fact that few Old Testament theologies have a section on promise? Von Rad's history-of-tradition approach leads him to take it seriously, as

noted above. Clements deals with only one aspect, already noted. Childs is concerned only with eschatology in *Theology in a Canonical Context,* 236–47 ("Life under Promise"). Zimmerli does have a section called "Yahweh, God of the Fathers: The Promise" in his *Old Testament Theology in Outline,* 27–32.

7. For the exact meaning of "promise," as the philosophy of language analyzes it, see John R. Searle, *Speech Acts: An Essay in the Philosophy of Language* (Cambridge: At the University Press, 1969), 57–61.

8. Claus Westermann, "The Way of Promise through the Old Testament," in *The Old Testament and the Christian Faith: A Theological Discussion,* ed. B. W. Anderson (New York: Harper & Row, 1963), 200–224.

9. E.g., *ANET,* 449–51; Daniel D. Luckenbill, *Ancient Records of Assyria and Babylonia* (Chicago: University of Chicago Press, 1926–27), 2:238–41; Francois Martin, *Textes religioux assyrobabyloniens* (Paris: Letouzey et Ané, 1903), 89, 91.

10. Von Rad, *Old Testament Theology* 1:171.

11. Cf. Hans Walter Wolff, "The Kerygma of the Yahwist," *Int* 20 (1966): 131–58.

12. Bertil Albrektson compares this kind of Old Testament material with similar explanations of disasters in the other ancient Near Eastern cultures in *History and the Gods: An Essay on the Idea of Historical Events as Divine Manifestations in the Ancient Near East and in Israel,* ConBOT 1 (Lund: CWK Gleerup, 1967).

13. Compare Westermann, "Way of Promise," 214f.

14. Donald E. Gowan, *Eschatology in the Old Testament* (Philadelphia: Fortress Press, 1986), 1–3.

15. Approaching the subject in two different ways, my former colleague Marjorie Suchocki (a process theologian) and I define it the same way. See her *The End of Evil: Process Eschatology in Historical Context* (Albany: State University of New York Press, 1988).

16. Emphasized in the last chapter of my *Eschatology in the Old Testament,* 121–29.

17. Donald E. Gowan, "The Exile in Jewish Apocalyptic," in *Scripture in History and Theology: Essays in Honor of J. Coert Rylaarsdam,* PTMS 17, ed. A. L. Merrill and T. W. Overholt (Pittsburgh: Pickwick Press, 1977), 216–20.

18. Westermann ("Way of Promise," 220f.) seems too pessimistic in claiming "The history of the promise in the Old Testament cannot be continued through the postexilic period," since "From the Exile on clear phases, turning points, and modifications can no longer be established in the realm of promises," except in the development of apocalyptic. This seems to be only an expression of the typical and unfortunate attitude of many Christian scholars, that nothing interesting happened in postbiblical Judaism.

19. Solomon Schechter, *Aspects of Rabbinic Theology* (New York: Schocken Books, 1961), 293–343.

20. Glatzer, *The Passover Haggadah,* 31.

21. See, for example, Joseph Klausner, *The Messianic Idea in Israel* (New York: Macmillan Co., 1955), 388–517.

22. Readers may think immediately of Matthew's fondness for citing scripture as fulfilled prophecy, but one can see a difference between prophecy, as he and many

other writers used it, and the concept of promise. The promise was a personal offer made by God to his people. Matthew's use of the Old Testament as prophecy involved finding a correspondence between events in his time and a written testimony, and he can do that without ever speaking of a promise of God.

23. Niels Dahl, "Promise and Fulfillment," in idem, *Studies in Paul: Theology for the Early Christian Mission* (Minneapolis: Augsburg Publishing House, 1977), 128.

24. Gowan, *Eschatology in the Old Testament,* 32–42.

25. Sam K. Williams, *"Promise* in Galatians: A Reading of Paul's Reading of Scripture," *JBL* 107 (1988): 712.

26. In addition to the commentaries, see Dahl, "Promise and Fulfillment," 130–36; Williams, *"Promise* in Galatians," 709–20.

27. This reading follows that proposed by Williams in *"Promise* in Galatians," 709–16.

28. Cf. Werner Georg Kümmel, "Futuristische und Präsentische Eschatologie im ältesten Urchristentum," *NTS* 5 (1958/59): 113–26.

29. Ibid., 123.

30. This is what F. F. Bruce means by "Promise and Fulfillment in Paul's Presentation of Jesus," in *Promise and Fulfillment: Essays Presented to Professor S. H. Hooke,* ed. F. F. Bruce (Edinburgh: T. & T. Clark, 1963), 36–50.

31. The magnitude of a study of apocalyptic just during the Middle Ages is revealed by the bibliographic article by Bernard McGinn, "Apocalypticism in the Middle Ages: An Historiographical Sketch," *Mediaeval Studies* 37 (1975): 252–86.

32. James Preus, *From Shadow to Promise: Old Testament Interpretation from Augustine to the Young Luther* (Cambridge: Harvard University Press, 1969), 2; John Calvin, *Institutes of the Christian Religion* (Grand Rapids: Wm. B. Eerdmans Publishing Co., 1953), 1:494–98.

33. Preus, *From Shadow to Promise,* 1–6.

34. Christopher Morse, *The Logic of Promise in Moltmann's Theology* (Philadelphia: Fortress Press, 1979); Moltmann, *Theology of Hope,* esp. pp. 95–154. On the questions about eschatology and apocalyptic in twentieth-century theology and biblical scholarship, see Klaus Koch, *The Rediscovery of Apocalyptic,* SBT[2] 22 (London: SCM Press, 1970).

35. Wolfhart Pannenberg, "Dogmatic Theses on the Doctrine of Revelation," in *Revelation as History,* ed. W. Pannenberg et al. (London: Macmillan & Co., 1968), 123–58; for a brief evaluation, Allan D. Galloway, *Wolfhart Pannenberg* (London: George Allen & Unwin, 1973).

36. J. Severino Croatto, *Exodus: A Hermeneutic of Freedom* (Maryknoll, N.Y.: Orbis Books, 1981); George V. Pixley, *On Exodus: A Liberation Perspective* (Maryknoll, N.Y.: Orbis Books, 1987).

37. Jon D. Levenson, "Exodus and Liberation," *HBT* 13 (1991): 134–74.

38. Compare Zimmerli, "Promise and Fulfillment," in *Essays on Old Testament Hermeneutics,* ed. Claus Westerman. English tr. ed. James Luther Mays (Richmond: John Knox Press, 1993), 95.

39. See Rudolf Bultmann's "The New Testament and Mythology," in *Kerygma and Myth: A Theological Debate,* ed. H. W. Bartsch (London: SPCK, 1953), 1–44; compare with Koch's *Rediscovery of Apocalyptic,* 65–68.

CHAPTER 6: THE DIVINE DESTROYER

1. P. D. Miller, *The Divine Warrior in Early Israel* (Cambridge: Harvard University Press, 1973); Millard C. Lind, *Yahweh Is a Warrior: The Theology of Warfare in Ancient Israel* (Scottdale, Pa.: Herald Press, 1980).

2. Murdoch Dahl, *Daughter of Love* (Worthing, Sussex: Churchman Publishing Ltd., 1989); Johannes Fichtner, "The Wrath of Men and the Wrath of God in the Old Testament," *TDNT* 5 (1967): 392–409; Anthony Tyrrell Hanson, *The Wrath of the Lamb* (London: S.P.C.K., 1957).

3. In addition to the works cited in n. 2, see Abraham J. Heschel, *The Prophets* (New York: Harper & Row, 1955), chaps. 16–17, pp. 279–306; Walther Eichrodt, *Theology of the Old Testament,* 1:258–69; George A. F. Knight, *A Christian Theology of the Old Testament* (London: SCM Press, 1959), 131–45.

4. G. E. Mendenhall, *The Tenth Generation* (Baltimore: Johns Hopkins University Press, 1973), 76.

5. Lind, *Yahweh Is a Warrior,* 24–34, 46–64. On war in general, see Peter C. Craigie, *The Problem of War in the Old Testament* (Grand Rapids: Wm. B. Eerdmans Publishing Co., 1978).

6. The effort made by Schwager to account for the violence in the Old Testament in terms of René Girard's theories must be counted a failure at this time. Having counted about a thousand passages that speak of Yahweh's anger and punishment by death and destruction, etc., he then makes a move unsupported by the texts, in order to be able to use Girard's "scapegoat theory." Having claimed that the prophetic books "recount only how humans do violence to one another and kill one another" (p. 66), a statement negated by Isa. 63:1–6; Ezekiel 39, and many other texts, he then jumps to the conclusion, "Indeed it must become evident that whenever sacred violence is mentioned, it is always human beings attacking one another" (p. 67). He must ignore all of Exodus 5—15 and a great deal more of the Old Testament in order to make such a claim. Raymond Schwager, S.J., *Must There Be Scapegoats? Violence and Redemption in the Bible* (San Francisco: Harper & Row, 1987). Girard's theories are of interest in considering the origins of sacrifice, but they are a very poor fit to the general subject of violence in the Bible. René Girard, *Violence and the Sacred* (Baltimore: Johns Hopkins University Press, 1977); idem, *The Scapegoat* (Baltimore: Johns Hopkins University Press, 1986); idem, *Things Hidden from the Foundation of the World* (Stanford, Calif.: Stanford University Press, 1987). For an application to the New Testament, see Robert G. Hamerton-Kelly, *Sacred Violence: Paul's Hermeneutic of the Cross* (Minneapolis: Fortress Press, 1991). See also Robert North, "Violence and the Bible: The Girard Connection," *CBQ* 47 (1985): 1–27.

7. An exception: Karl Heim, *The World: Its Creation and Consummation* (Philadelphia: Fortress Press, 1962).

8. Helfmeyer, "'*oth*," *TDOT* 1: 167–88.

9. Childs is the only commentator to consider this at any length, and he comes to quite different conclusions. *Book of Exodus,* 142–49.

10. IV. 39, 42–43, 45–50, 96, *ANET,* 65–67.

11. The myth of Horus at Edfu also extends the contest, in which his kingship is at

issue, with a series of battles, in all of which Horus is victorious. H. W. Fairman, "The Myth of Horus at Edfu," *Journal of Egyptian Archaeology* 21 (1935): 26–36.

12. R. H. Charles, ed., *The Apocrypha and Pseudepigrapha of the Old Testament,* vol. 2: *Pseudepigrapha* (Oxford: Clarendon Press, 1913), 715–84.

13. For a survey, and an interpretation of their regularity, see my "Reading Job as a 'Wisdom Script,' " *JSOT* 55 (1992): 85–96.

14. Fretheim (*Exodus,* 154) comments on 14:1–18: "God's stated purpose is remarkable in that there is no mention of Israelite liberation. The focus is on what will happen to God and to the Egyptians' relationship to God."

15. Jon Levenson emphasizes, over against the claims of liberation theology, that the subject of these chapters is not freedom, but to which master will Israel belong. "Exodus and Liberation" 148–60.

16. Zimmerli, "Knowledge of God according to the Book of Ezekiel," in his *I Am Yahweh,* 29–98.

17. Compare Knight, *Theology as Narration,* 70; Lester Meyer, *The Message of Exodus* (Minneapolis: Augsburg Press, 1983), 77.

18. Childs, *Book of Exodus,* 170–75; Heikki Räisänen, *The Idea of Divine Hardening* (Helsinki: Publications of the Finnish Exegetical Society 25, 1972), 52–66; Robert R. Wilson, "The Hardening of Pharaoh's Heart," *CBQ* 41 (1979): 18–36. Recent articles emphasize sovereignty and knowledge, but from quite different perspectives: David M. Gunn, "The 'Hardening of Pharaoh's Heart': Plot, Character, and Theology in Exodus 1—14," in *Art and Meaning: Rhetoric in Biblical Literature,* ed. D.J.A. Clines, D. M. Gunn, and A. J. Hauser, JSOTSup 19 (Sheffield: JSOT Press, 1982), 72–96; Lyle Eslinger, "Freedom or Knowledge? Perspective and Purpose in the Exodus Narrative (Exodus 1—15)," *JSOT* 52 (1991): 43–60; J. Krašovec, "Unifying Themes in Ex. 7, 8–11, 10," in *Pentateuchal and Deuteronomistic Studies,* ed. C. Brekelmans and J. Lust, BETL 94 (Louvain: University Press, 1990), 47–66.

19. Fretheim, *Exodus,* 108; and see his article "The Plagues as Ecological Signs of Historical Disaster," *JBL* 110 (1991): 385–96.

20. Ibid., *Exodus,* 108–11.

21. For these interpretations, see my *From Eden to Babel: Genesis 1—11,* ITC (Grand Rapids: Wm. B. Eerdmans Publishing Co., 1988).

22. *ANET,* 93–95.

23. Brueggemann, *Genesis,* 167–76; Gerhard von Rad, *Genesis,* rev. ed., OTL (Philadelphia: Westminster Press, 1973), 211–15.

24. Compare Shalom M. Paul, *Amos,* Hermeneia (Minneapolis: Fortress Press, 1991), 153; Francis I. Andersen and David Noel Freedman, *Amos,* AB (New York: Doubleday, 1989), 445.

25. For this passage and the theme of pride in the Old Testament, see my *When Man Becomes God: Humanism and Hybris in the Old Testament,* PTMS 6 (Pittsburgh: Pickwick Press, 1975), 38–43.

26. Otto Kaiser, *Isaiah 13–39,* OTL (Philadelphia: Westminster Press, 1974), 173–79.

27. Ibid., 183.

28. Schwager, *Must There Be Scapegoats?* 43.

29. Walter Stuermann, *The Divine Destroyer: A Theology of Good and Evil* (Philadelphia: Westminster Press, 1967), 15–34, 115–40.

30. See Heschel's definition of "wrath" and defense of its use, *The Prophets,* chaps. 16–17, pp. 279–306.

31. See Morton Smith, "The Common Theology of the Ancient Near East," *JBL* 71 (1952): 35–47, and Walter Brueggemann's corrections in "A Shape for Old Testament Theology, I: Structure Legitimation," *CBQ* 47 (1985): 32.

32. It has been claimed that prehistoric societies that worshiped the mother goddess lived completely peaceful lives, but since we have no texts from those societies, that can never be proved. At any rate, the violence of nature itself can scarcely have been less evident to them than it is to us. Elinor W. Gadon, *The Once and Future Goddess: A Symbol for Our Time* (San Francisco: Harper & Row, 1989), 24.

33. Compare El in the Ugaritic texts, who is the high god, but doesn't do much of anything.

34. Compare Walter Brueggemann's use of this term to describe a different aspect of Old Testament theology in "Shape for Old Testament Theology, II," 395–99.

35. Compare *Apocalypse of Moses* 10–12. Theophilus of Antioch and Duns Scotus, among others, attributed the ferocity of animals to the Fall.

36. Philo, *De Vita Mosis I*, trans. F. H. Colson, Loeb Classical Library (Cambridge: Harvard University Press, 1950), 6:96.

37. *Mekilta de-Rabbi Ishmael*, trans. Jacob Z. Lauterbach (Philadelphia: Jewish Publication Society, 1976), II.13–19.

38. Glatzer, *Passover Haggadah,* 66f.

39. An allusion to Ezek. 18:23, 32.

40. *Mek.* 15.1, p. 5.

41. Anthony Tyrrell Hanson, *The Wrath of the Lamb* (London: SPCK, 1957), 178–80; Schwager, *Must There Be Scapegoats?* 214–81; Hamerton-Kelly, *Sacred Violence,* 101–3.

42. Gustav Stählin, "The Wrath of Man and the Wrath of God in the New Testament," *TDNT* 5 (1967): 423n.296: "There seems to me to be no doubt that in this logion Jesus has God in view, not the devil." Note the reference to destruction in the parable of the wicked tenants, Luke 20:16, 18.

43. C.E.B. Cranfield, *Romans: A Shorter Commentary* (Grand Rapids: Wm. B. Eerdmans Publishing Co., 1985), 32.

44. ". . . one of the most terrible insights of the Bible. Sin and unbelief, the two main causes of the *orge theou*, are also its effect." Stählin, "Wrath of Man," 443.

45. C. H. Dodd, *Romans,* The Moffatt Commentary (New York: Harper & Brothers, 1932), 29. For the debate whether wrath is personal or impersonal in Paul, compare Dodd (impersonal) with Cranfield, p. 29 (personal).

46. Dodd, *Romans,* 75.

47. C. K. Barrett, *A Commentary on the Second Epistle to the Corinthians,* Harper's New Testament Commentaries (New York: Harper & Row, 1973), 180.

48. Lactantius, *A Treatise on the Anger of God,* in *The Ante-Nicene Fathers,* vol. 7, ed. Alexander Roberts and James Donaldson (Grand Rapids: Wm. B. Eerdmans Publishing Co., 1975), 273.

49. L. R. Farnell, *The Attributes of God* (Oxford: Oxford University Press, 1925), 174; cited from Heschel, *The Prophets,* 304.

50. Dahl, *Daughter of Love,* 254–63.

51. "The God that holds you over the pit of hell, much as one holds a spider, or some loathsome insect, over the fire, abhors you, and is dreadfully provoked; his wrath towards you burns like fire; he looks upon you as worthy of nothing else, but to be cast into the fire; he is of purer eyes than to bear to have you in his sight; you are ten thousand times so abominable in his eyes, as the most hateful and venomous serpent is in ours." Jonathan Edwards, "Sinners in the Hands of an Angry God," in *The Works of President Edwards*, vol. 4, *Sermons on Various Important Subjects* (New York: Leavitt & Allen, 1843), 318.

52. A. R. Peacocke, *Creation and the World of Science* (Oxford: Clarendon Press, 1979), 329.

53. Heschel offers a compact survey of the history of the issue in *The Prophets*, chaps. 14–17, pp. 247–306.

54. Dodd, *Romans,* 21–29.

55. Heschel, *The Prophets,* 279–98; Dahl, *Daughter of Love.*

56. Ronald Goetz, "Karl Barth, Juergen Moltmann and the Theopaschite Revolution," in *Festschrift: A Tribute to Dr. William Hordern,* ed. Walter Freitag (Saskatoon: University of Saskatchewan, 1985), 17–28; Kazoh Kitamori, *Theology of the Pain of God* (Richmond: John Knox Press, 1965); Paul S. Fiddes, *The Creative Suffering of God* (Oxford: Clarendon Press, 1988); Joseph M. Hallmann, *The Descent of God: Divine Suffering in History and Theology* (Minneapolis: Fortress Press, 1991).

57. George Huntston Williams, "Christian Attitudes toward Nature," *Christian Scholar's Review* 2 (1971/2): 7–16.

58. Peacocke, *Creation and the World of Science,* 165. Compare Richard W. Knopf, *Evil and Evolution: A Theodicy* (Rutherford, N.J.: Fairleigh Dickinson University Press, 1984), 110–13.

59. My simple, working definition of "evil," which leaves many questions unanswered, is "that which God is against." S. E. Alsford begins her article with a similar approach, calling the "baseline definition" of evil: "that which is opposed to God and to God's nature and intentions, that which God does not wish, that which leads away from God." But she then wants to add "that which causes destruction, decay and suffering," the complication with which I intend to work in this section. "Evil in the Non-Human World," *Science and Christian Belief* 3 (1991): 120.

60. "We do not explain evil or the work of Chaos, nor do we escape it. We simply put up with it. The only authentic question relates to *how* we put up with it." Stuermann, *Divine Destroyer,* 140.

61. In H. G. Wells's rewriting of the book of Job (*The Undying Fire: A Contemporary Novel* [London: Cassell & Co., 1919]), he has his modern Job, who is suffering from a presumably cancerous tumor, say of his walk in the countryside, in which all he could see around him was cruelty and decay in nature: "Is there so much as one healthy living being in the world? I question it. . . . How can Man trust such a Maker to treat him fairly? . . . Either the world of life is the creation of a being inspired by a malignancy at once filthy, petty and enormous, or it displays a carelessness, an indifference, a disregard for justice" (104). Wells has God offer Job some healthy corrections to this view at the end, however.

62. G. Tom Milazzo has tried to develop a theology of "protest theism" because of his inability to accept death as a part of God's creation: *The Protest and the Silence: Suffering, Death, and Biblical Theology* (Minneapolis: Fortress Press, 1992).

63. "Each seeming advance—from plants to animals, from instinct to learning, from ganglia to brains, from sentience to self-awareness, from herbivores to carnivores—steps up the pain. We are not much troubled by seeds that fail, but it is difficult to avoid pity for nestling birds fallen to the ground." Holmes Rolston, III, "Does Nature Need to Be Redeemed?" *HBT* 14 (1992): 155.

64. Arnold Toynbee, "Traditional Attitudes towards Death," in *Man's Concern with Death*, by Arnold Toynbee et al. (London: Hodder & Stoughton, 1968), 62f.

65. Rolston, "Does Nature Need to Be Redeemed?" 153, 154f., 158. The surgeon Paul Brand expressed himself in much the same way, according to Philip Yancey in "God's Astounding Laws of Nature: An Interview with Paul Brand," *Christianity Today* 23 (Dec. 1, 1978): 287.

66. Paul Brand and Philip Yancey, *In His Image* (Grand Rapids: Zondervan Publishing House, 1984), 287.

67. Karl Barth will not even make that qualification: "The definition that we must use as a starting-point is that God's being is *life.* . . . This is no metaphor. Nor is it a mere description of God's relation to the world and to ourselves. But while it is that, it also describes God Himself as the One He is." *Church Dogmatics,* Vol. II: *Doctrine of God,* 1.263.

68. Peacocke, *Creation and the World of Science,* 166.

69. Rolston, "Does Nature Need to Be Redeemed?" 159, 160f.

70. Peacocke, *Creation and the World of Science,* 198.

71. Fiddes, *Creative Suffering of God,* 16.

72. Ronald Goetz, "Jesus Loves Everybody," *Christian Century* 109 (March 11, 1992): 275.

73. For a survey of hopes for an ideal future, from the Old Testament through the present, see my *Eschatology in the Old Testament.*

74. "The idea of a painless Utopia is quite meaningful to us and a delightful source of entertainment to the imagination. . . . But whether it can be the subject of a serious moral judgment is another issue." Allan D. Galloway, *The Cosmic Christ* (London: Nisbet & Co., 1951), 206.

75. The title of one of his poems. *The Poetry of Robert Frost,* ed. Edward Connery Lathem (New York: Holt, Rinehart & Winston, 1969), 333. Thanks to Bebb Wheeler Stone for this reference.

CHAPTER 7: GOD OF GRACE
AND GOD OF GLORY

1. This analysis is closer to that of Fretheim (*Exodus,* 173) than to that of Childs (*Book of Exodus,* 258), who believes there are two distinct patterns.

2. The verb occurs in Ex. 15:24; 16:2, 7, 8; 17:3 and nine times in the comparable stories in Numbers. The exception is Josh. 9:18, where the people murmur against their leaders for not attacking Gibeon. The word may also occur in Ps. 59:15, but the text is uncertain.

3. Shemaryahu Talmon offers a vivid description of what the wilderness is like, in "The 'Desert Motif' in the Bible and in Qumran Literature," in *Biblical Motifs—*

Origins and Transformations, ed. A. Altman (Cambridge: Harvard University Press, 1966), 42–44.

4. George W. Coats, "The Traditio-Historical Character of the Reed Sea Motif," *VT* 17 (1967): 253–65.

5. Ibid., "Healing and the Moses Traditions," in *Canon, Theology, and Old Testament Interpretation*, ed. Tucker et al., 131–46; Gowan, "Salvation as Healing," 1–19; J. Hempel, *Heilung als Symbol und Wirklichkeit in biblischen Schrifftum*, 2d ed. (Göttingen: Vandenhoeck and Ruprecht, 1965); A. Lods, "Les Idées des Israélites sur la maladie, ses causes et ses remédes," BZAW 41 (1925): 181–93; K. Seybold and U. B. Mueller, *Sickness and Healing* (Nashville: Abingdon Press, 1981).

6. For two different, recent estimates, see Daniel C. Arichea, Jr., "The Ups and Downs of Moses: Locating Moses in Exodus 19—33," *BT* 40 (1989): 244–46; and T. B. Dozeman, *God on the Mountain: A Study of Redaction, Theology, and Canon in Exodus 19—24*, SBLMS 37 (Decatur, Ga.: Scholars Press, 1989), 14.

7. "Though many helpful observations may be harvested from the critical work of more than a century, the sum total of that work is a clear assertion that no literary solution to this complex narrative has been found, with more than a hint that none is likely to be found." Durham, *Exodus,* 259.

8. Compare Edmond Jacob, *Theology of the Old Testament* (New York: Harper & Brothers, 1958), 213f.

9. For an array of opinions published during the 1980s, see Dozeman, *God on the Mountain*; Ernest W. Nicholson, *God and His People: Covenant and Theology in the Old Testament* (Oxford: Clarendon Press, 1986); A. Phillips, "A Fresh Look at the Sinai Pericope," *VT* 34 (1984): 282–94; John Van Seters, "Comparing Scripture with Scripture: Some Observations on the Sinai Pericope of Exodus 19—24," in *Canon, Theology, and Old Testament Interpretation*, ed. Tucker et al., 111–30.

10. For a full discussion, leading to an eighth- or seventh-century date, see Nicholson, *God and His People*. The reviews of his book show that this is by no means a consensus position.

11. Erhard Gerstenberger, "Covenant and Commandment," *JBL* 84 (1965): 38–51. This article challenged the idea that law was based on the covenant by comparing OT law with the stipulations in ancient Near Eastern vassal treaties, a comparison no longer considered to be very significant, but the recent claims for a very late date of the covenant idea raise questions about the possible priority of law to covenant.

12. D. J. McCarthy, *Old Testament Covenant: A Survey of Current Opinions* (Richmond: John Knox Press, 1972), 88.

13. I have serious questions about the methods being used in current studies, and those questions probably should be noted here as an explanation for my effort to find a way of dealing with the theology of the Sinai materials without becoming mired in the fruitless debates that presently occupy scholarship. One or more of the following four reservations about method are raised by virtually every work on the subject.

a. Overdependence on etymology. You will not find me discussing the various theories about the etymology of *berith,* "covenant," at all, for this is one of the classic examples of a word whose meaning is determined by context, not etymology. Yet, as Barr has pointed out, several influential recent works have tried to make more of etymology than can rightfully be made. James Barr, "Some Semantic Notes on the Covenant," in *Beiträge zur Alttestamentliche Theologie: Festschrift für Walther Zimmerli* (Göttingen: Vandenhoeck & Ruprecht, 1977), 23–38.

b. The assumption that an idea is present only where a specific word is present is known to be faulty method, but it appears in studies of the covenant.

c. Something like "pandeuteronomism" has appeared in recent works. That is, if a term occurs in Deuteronomy, then anywhere else that term may occur is thought to have been influenced by Deuteronomy. I have strong reservations about this, even though at present it seems to be a risky move for a scholar to suggest the influence might sometimes run the other way, or that influence may not be involved at all.

d. Redaction certainly took place in the creation of the Old Testament books, but there are too few objective criteria for determining what is redactorial, and the failure to find agreement on the composition of Exodus 19—24 is proof that most of the decisions being made are subjective. A good theory offers a simple explanation of the evidence, but biblical scholars, under the name of redaction criticism, are finding it all too easy to adjust the evidence to fit the theory. For example: one theory is that the covenant idea is no earlier than the seventh-century edition of Deuteronomy. But Hosea (eighth century) speaks of the covenant, so in order to maintain the theory, those references must be called later additions to Hosea.

14. James Muilenberg, "The Form and Structure of the Covenantal Formulations," *VT* 9 (1959): 347–65.

15. E.g., Childs, *Book of Exodus,* 360.

16. E.g., Roland James Faley, *The Kingdom of Priests* (Rome: Pontificium Athenaeum Internationale "Angelicum," 1960), 28–33; H. Cazelles, " 'Royaume de Pretres et Nation Consacrée' (Exode XIX,6)," in his *Autour de l'Exode (Études)* (Paris: J. Gabalda, 1987), 290.

17. Compare Knight, *Christian Theology of the Old Testament,* 169–74.

18. R. J. Sklba, "The Redeemer of Israel," *CBQ* 34 (1972): 10–16.

19. Faley, *Kingdom of Priests,* 15.

20. For a convenient summary of interpretations see Durham, *Exodus,* 263.

21. Note that another of the unrepeatable features in this section is the ceremony of sprinkling blood over the people, in 24:8.

22. Detailed exposition of these commandments, such as may be found in the commentaries on Exodus 20 and Deuteronomy 5, and in specialized works on the Decalogue, would expand the length of this work beyond reasonable limits. See, e.g., J. J. Stamm and M. E. Andrew, *The Ten Commandments in Recent Research,* SBT, n.s., 2 (London: SCM Press, 1970); Walter Harrelson, *The Ten Commandments and Human Rights* (Philadelphia: Fortress Press, 1980).

23. Durham, *Exodus,* 285f.; Fretheim, *Exodus,* 226.

24. Harrelson, *Ten Commandments and Human Rights,* 64.

25. Bernard Renaud, *Je Suis un Dieu Jaloux: Évolution sémantique et signification théologique de* qin'ah, Lectio Divina 36 (Paris: Les Éditions du Cerf, 1963), 137f.

26. Renaud, *Je Suis un Dieu Jaloux,* 143f.

27. David Noel Freedman, "Divine Commitment and Human Obligation: The Covenant Theme," *Int* 18 (1964): 419–31.

28. Ludwig Köhler, *Old Testament Theology* (Philadelphia: Westminster Press, 1957), 65, 69.

29. For example, Pss. 73:23–26; 139:1–18.

30. Murray L. Newman, Jr., *The People of the Covenant: A Study of Israel from Moses to the Monarchy* (Nashville: Abingdon Press, 1962).

31. Terrien, *Elusive Presence,* 161–213.

32. Paul D. Hanson, *The Dawn of Apocalyptic* (Philadelphia: Fortress Press, 1975).

33. Norman K. Gottwald, *The Tribes of Yahweh: A Sociology of the Religion of Liberated Israel, 1250–1050 B.C.E.* (Maryknoll, N.Y.: Orbis Books, 1979); Walter Brueggemann, *David's Truth in Israel's Imagination and Memory* (Philadelphia: Fortress Press, 1985), 19–39, 67–86.

34. Note esp. Terrien's evaluations of "name" and "glory" theology in *Elusive Presence,* 198–213.

35. Trygve N. D. Mettinger, *The Dethronement of Sabaoth: Studies in the Shem and Kabod Theologies,* ConBOT 18 (Lund, Sweden: CWK Gleerup, 1982), 83.

36. See Childs, *Book of Exodus,* 539f.; A. M. Rodriguez, "Sanctuary Theology in the Book of Exodus," *AUSS* 24 (1986): 131–37.

37. Rodriguez develops the idea that the priestly regulations were intended to protect the transcendence of God, while the emphasis on the glory was to be an assurance of his immanence. See his "Sanctuary Theology," 129–37.

38. See Mettinger, *Dethronement of Sabaoth,* 116–34; Childs, *Book of Exodus,* 543; Fretheim, *Exodus,* 313.

39. See Brueggemann's comments on these passages in his *Genesis.*

40. For the evidence for this evaluation of the preexilic religion of Israel, see my "Prophets, Deuteronomy, and the Syncretistic Cult in Israel," in *Transitions in Biblical Scholarship*, ed. J. Coert Rylaarsdam (Chicago: University of Chicago Press, 1968), 93–112.

41. For a survey, see my *Eschatology in the Old Testament,* 42–58.

42. E.g., "The gradual making absolute of 'the law' must be looked upon as a false track, which led to consequences which led right away from the authentic foundation of faith, which in the pre-exilic writings had formed the subject of the tradition, the ordinances, and the testimonies." Martin Noth, "The Laws in the Pentateuch: Their Assumptions and Meanings," in his *The Laws in the Pentateuch and Other Studies* (London: SCM Press, 1966), 106.

43. *Midrash Rabbah: Exodus,* trans. S. M. Lehrman (London: Soncino Press, 1939), 534.

44. Quoted from Schechter, *Aspects of Rabbinic Theology,* 61.

45. Raphael Patai, "The Shekhina," *JR* 44 (1964): 277.

46. Ramban offered a striking exposition of this text: "For in the plain sense of things it would appear that [the dwelling of] the Divine Glory in Israel was to fulfill a want below, but it is not so. It fulfilled a want above, being rather similar in thought to that which Scripture states, *Israel in whom I will be glorified* (Isa. 49:3)." *Commentary on the Torah: Exodus,* translated and annotated by Rabbi C. B. Chavel (New York: Shilo Publishing House, 1973), 506.

47. Patai, "The Shekhina," 280.

48. *Midrash Rabbah: Numbers,* trans. Judah J. Slotki (London: Soncino Press, 1939), I.414.

49. Quoted from C. G. Montefiore and H. Loewe, *A Rabbinic Anthology* (New York: Schocken Books, 1970) p. 81, #218.

50. *Midrash Rabbah: Numbers*, II.504.

51. *Midrash Rabbah: Exodus*, 409.

52. *Mekilta de-Rabbi Ishmael*, tr. Jacob Z. Lauterbach (Philadelphia: Jewish Publication Society of America, 1976), II.25.

53. Schechter, *Aspects of Rabbinic Theology*, 203f., citing his edition of *Midrash Hag-gadol*, Vol. I, Genesis (Cambridge: Cambridge University Press, 1902), 549.

54. Neusner, *Lamentations Rabbah*, 147.

55. *The Midrash on Psalms*, trans. William G. Braude (New Haven, Conn.: Yale University Press, 1959), II.303, on Ps. 123:2.

56. Cited from Montefiore and H. Loewe, *A Rabbinic Anthology*, p. 80, #215.

57. For recent discussions and bibliography, see R. David Kaylor, *Paul's Covenant Community: Jew and Gentile in Romans* (Atlanta: John Knox Press, 1988), 159–93; Cranfield, *Romans*, 214–90; and the articles in *Ex Auditu* 4 (1988): "The Church and Israel (Romans 9—11)."

58. Note the articles on salvation in *Ex Auditu* 5 (1989).

59. Craig R. Koester, *The Dwelling of God: The Tabernacle in the Old Testament, Intertestamental Jewish Literature, and the New Testament*, CBQMS 22 (Washington, D.C.: Catholic Biblical Association of America, 1989), 100–115.

60. Koester, *Dwelling of God*, 152–83; Childs, *Book of Exodus*, 544f., 551.

61. Ulrich Mauser, *Christ in the Wilderness: The Wilderness Theme in the Second Gospel and Its Basis in the Biblical Tradition*, SBT 39 (Naperville, Ill.: Alec R. Allenson, 1963), 63–74.

62. For the use of the Decalogue in the New Testament, see Reginald H. Fuller, "The Decalogue in the New Testament," *Int* 43 (1989): 243–55.

63. For a survey of the recent scholarly debate, see Stephen Westerholm, *Israel's Law and the Church's Faith: Paul and His Recent Interpreters* (Grand Rapids: Wm. B. Eerdmans Publishing Co., 1988).

64. A few texts have been much used, because there are so few: Gen. 15:6; Ex. 14:31; Isa. 7:9.

65. J. B. Phillips, *Your God Is Too Small* (New York: Macmillan Co., 1953), 37–41.

66. W. J. Ferrar, *The Proof of the Gospel: Being the Demonstratio Evangelica of Eusebius of Caesarea* (London: SPCK, 1920), Book I, chap. 5, p. 25.

67. For the classic study, see Underhill, *Mysticism*.

68. A. C. McGiffert, *Protestant Thought before Kant* (1911; reprint, New York: Harper & Brothers, 1961), 155–85.

69. Consider two influential works from two very different Christian sources: Thomas à Kempis, *The Imitation of Christ*, and Charles Sheldon, *In His Steps: What Would Jesus Do?* (New York: Grosset & Dunlap, 1935).

CHAPTER 8: THE DISTANCING OF GOD

1. *Lev. Rab.* 5.8, translation from Schechter, *Aspects of Rabbinic Theology*, 326.

2. "[T]he magnitude of his request drives Moses to probe into the very heart of God, as it were, to assure himself that God is in his deepest nature the kind of God who could 'pardon our iniquity and our sin and take us for [his] inheritance' (34:9de)."

John Piper, "Prolegomena to Understanding Romans 9:14–15: An Interpretation of Exodus 33:19," *JETS* 22 (1979): 207.

3. Brueggemann introduces an article on Ex. 33:12–23 in this way: "Thus the theological dialectic of *accessibility* and *freedom* for Yahweh is matched by Israel's experience of *assurance* and *precariousness*." Walter Brueggemann, "The Crisis and Promise of Presence in Israel," *HBT* 1 (1979): 47.

4. See the commentaries by Childs, Durham, and Fretheim, as well as R.W.L. Moberly, *At the Mountain of God: Story and Theology in Exodus 32—34,* JSOTSup 22 (Sheffield: JSOT Press, 1983); Brueggemann, "Crisis and Promise of Presence"; Terrien, *Elusive Presence,* 138–52.

5. See L. Smolar and M. Aberbach, "The Golden Calf Episode in Post-biblical Literature," *HUCA* 39 (1968): 91–116.

6. Compare Deuteronomy's interpretation of the two commandments in 6:4 and 4:15–16; and *Exod. Rab.* XLII.8.

7. Fretheim, *Exodus,* 284.

8. Ibid., 279.

9. Parts of this section on Ex. 32:7–14 also appear in my article "Changing God's Mind: Exodus 32:7–14," in *Biblical Texts for Preaching: Reflections on Biblical Texts by Jewish and Christian Scholars*, ed. Fredrick C. Holmgren and Herman E. Schaalman (forthcoming).

10. Deuteronomy does not soften it, as the story is retold in 9:8–21. A synonym, the hifil of *rph,* is used, and that term is also used of God only in this text.

11. George W. Coats, "The King's Loyal Opposition: Obedience and Authority in Exodus 32—34," in *Canon and Authority*, ed. George W. Coats and Burke O. Long (Philadelphia: Fortress Press, 1977), 91–109.

12. Fretheim, *Exodus,* 285.

13. For uses of the interrogative, see James Barr, "Why? in Biblical Hebrew," *JTS* 36 (1985): 1–33.

14. The best treatments of the subject are: Jörg Jeremias, *Die Reue Gottes, Aspecte der alttestamentliche Gottesvorstellung* (Neukirchen: Neukirchener Verlag, 1975); Terence Fretheim, "The Repentance of God: A Key to Evaluating Old Testament God-Talk," *HBT* 10.1 (1988): 47–70; Francis I. Andersen and David Noel Freedman, *Amos,* Anchor Bible (New York: Doubleday, 1989), 638–79: "Excursus: When God Repents."

15. An alternate proposal, that it means God "comforted himself" (taking niphal as reflexive and meaning the same as the hithpael of this root), has not been taken up by subsequent interpreters: Geo. B. Michell, "A Note on the Hebrew Root *nhm,*" *ExpTim* 44 (1932–33): 428. Parunak does take the basic meaning of the root to be "comfort, console" in all of its stems, but considers the niphal to have extended that meaning to describe "the release of emotional tension involved in performing a declared action (executing wrath), or retracting a declared action (such as sin, punishment, or blessing)." H. Van Dyke Parunak, "A Semantic Survey of NHM," *Biblica* 56 (1975): 512–32.

16. The normal word for human repentance is *shuv,* and that does appear in Ex. 32:12, in an unusual usage, with God as subject, as a synonym for *hinnahem.*

17. Fretheim, "Repentance," 52. For another explanation see Andersen and Freedman, *Amos,* 650–54.

18. Noth, *Exodus,* 251.

19. The idea of a heavenly list of names ("the book which you have written"), which is referred to a few times in both Testaments, may have originated with lists of the members of the community prepared during the exilic and postexilic period. Ezekiel says of those he considers to be false prophets, "They shall not be in the council of my people, nor be enrolled in the register of the house of Israel" (13:9). Later, Malachi speaks of the division between the faithful and the negligent in postexilic Jerusalem, and says, "Then those who feared the LORD spoke with one another; the LORD heeded and heard them, and a book of remembrance was written before him of those who feared the LORD and thought on his name" (3:16). It sounds like a list written and no doubt deposited in the Temple. Isaiah 4:3, ". . . every one who has been recorded for life in Jerusalem," may refer to a similar practice. In the Psalms (56:8; 69:29; 139:16), in Daniel (7:10; 12:1), and in Luke (10:20), Philippians (4:3), and Revelation (3:5; 20:12) we find references to a heavenly book, which is twice called the "book of life" (Phil. 4:3; Rev. 3:5).

20. For the former, Noth, *Exodus,* 254; for the latter, Moberly, *At the Mountain of God,* 60.

21. The word that is here translated "presence" reminds us how difficult it is to try to get into the minds of ancient Israelites in order to learn what kind of experience they were describing when they spoke of the presence of Yahweh. The word is *panim,* "face," which is used frequently to refer to the human visage, and very frequently in various idioms to mean "before, in front of, in the presence of." In chaps. 32:34 and 33:2 it is used of the agent going "before" them, and in 33:19 of God's goodness passing "before" Moses and of God proclaiming his name "before" Moses. In 33:16 it designates the "surface" of the earth. It denotes the closeness of Moses' relationship with Yahweh in 33:11, where they are said to talk "face to face." Those uses are straightforward, but then it gets trickier. Hebrew has no abstract noun corresponding to our word "presence," but uses *panim* metaphorically in that way, both of human beings and of God. So our translations speak of God's "presence" going with Moses in 33:14f., but when we come to his request to see God's glory, the same word is translated "face." "You cannot see my face; for man shall not see me and live" (v. 20). "You shall see my back; but my face shall not be seen" (v. 23)—as if God actually had a face and a back that could be seen! We can see why the translators render it literally, even though it cannot be understood that way. It is because of the use of the verb "see," for to see a presence is not good English, and also because of the puzzling use of the word "back," in contrast to *panim.* I have listed the uses of the word here as evidence that there are even linguistic difficulties that encumber getting started thinking about what is meant by the presence of God. See Aubrey R. Johnson, "Aspects of the Use of the Term PNYM in the Old Testament," in *Festschrift O. Eissfeldt,* ed. Johann Fück (Halle: Max Niemeyer, 1947), 155–59; J. Reindl, *Das Angesicht Gottes im Sprachgebrauch des Alten Testament, ThStud* 25 (Leipzig: St. Benno-Verlag, 1970).

22. Psalm 27 shows that similiar language was regularly used in worship: "One thing I asked of the LORD, that will I seek after: to live in the house of the LORD all the days of my life, to behold the beauty of the LORD, and to inquire in his temple" (v. 4). " 'Come,' my heart says, 'seek his face.' Your face, LORD, do I seek. Do not hide your face from me" (vv. 8f.). "I believe that I shall see the goodness of the LORD in the land of the living" (v. 13).

23. Compare Piper, "Understanding Romans 9:14–15," 213f.

24. Compare ibid., 211f.

25. The most useful are R. C. Dentan, "The Literary Affinities of Exodus xxxiv 6f.," *VT* 13 (1963): 34–51; David Noel Freedman, "God Compassionate and Gracious," *Western Watch* 6.1 (1955): 6–24; Thomas M. Raitt, "Why Does God Forgive?" *HBT* 13.1 (1991): 38–58. Compare J. Scharbert, "Formgeschichte und Exegese von Ex 34,6f und seiner Parallelen," *Biblica* 38 (1957): 130–50; G. Ernest Wright, "The Divine Name and the Divine Nature," *Perspective* 12 (1971): 177–85. One reason some scholars have tended to overlook this creed is that it does not at all fit the recent emphasis on Old Testament theology as the recital of the mighty redeeming acts of God. This makes Wright's article of some interest, since he was one of the early popularizers of this approach in America.

26. The theme of the patience of God is developed in a distinctive way, using the exodus and wilderness traditions, in Ezek. 20:1–31.

27. Full monographs on the word have been produced by Nelson Glueck, *Ḥesed in the Bible* (Cincinnati: Hebrew Union College, 1967); Katherine Doob Sakenfeld, *The Meaning of Ḥesed in the Hebrew Bible*, HSM 17 (Missoula, Mont.: Scholars Press, 1978).

28. Walter Zimmerli, *"Charis,"* TDNT 9:382.

29. Fretheim, *Exodus,* 306.

30. Freedman, "God Compassionate and Gracious," 14.

31. Compare ibid., 15.

32. Fretheim, *Exodus,* 303–7.

33. Ibid., 279.

34. There has been considerable discussion of the simple word *ki,* which introduces "it is a stiff-necked people," since that conjunction can mean "for/because" or "although" (as in RSV, NRSV, NIV) or "however much." An argument can be made for preferring "because" to "although," as putting the matter in the most serious possible way. What had been cited three times before as the reason for judgment is now be used by Moses as the reason why forgiveness is the people's only hope.

35. Katherine Doob Sakenfeld, "The Problem of Divine Forgiveness in Numbers 14," *CBQ* 37 (1975): 317–30.

36. Von Rad, *Genesis,* 210–15.

37. For additional insights into these prayers, see Samuel E. Balentine, "Prayers for Justice in the Old Testament: Theodicy and Theology," *CBQ* 51 (1989): 597–616, esp. 612ff.

38. Note the three helpful studies of these issues by Walter Brueggemann: "From Hurt to Joy, from Death to Life," *Int* 28 (1974): 3–19; "The Formfulness of Grief," *Int* 31 (1977): 263–75; "The Costly Loss of Lament," *JSOT* 36 (October, 1986): 57–71.

39. For a comparison of these two passages, see Thomas B. Dozeman, "Inner-Biblical Interpretation of Yahweh's Gracious and Compassionate Character," *JBL* (108): 207–23. For this interpretation of Jonah, see Elias Bickerman, *Four Strange Books of the Bible* (New York: Schocken Books, 1967); Jonathan Magonet, *Form and Meaning: Studies in Literary Techniques in the Book of Jonah,* Bible and Literature Series 8 (Sheffield: Almond Press, 1983).

40. Compare Eichrodt's discussion of the nature of forgiveness in his *Theology of the Old Testament,* 2:453–57.

41. Raitt notes two patterns: the commonplace sequence sin/chastisement/ repentance/forgiveness, which occurs throughout the Deuteronomistic literature and elsewhere, and the picture of the God who forgives and punishes, with those two attributes held in tension, found in Exodus 32—34; Num. 14:18f.; Ps. 99:8; Ex. 20:5f.; Deut. 5:9f.; 7:9f.; Jer. 32:18 and elsewhere in the prophets. Raitt, "Why Does God Forgive?" 47, 56.

42. For a survey of forgiveness in Old Testament eschatology, see my *Eschatology in the Old Testament,* 59–69.

43. Smolar and Aberbach, "Golden Calf Episode," 91–116.

44. Translation from Montefiore and Loewe, *Rabbinic Anthology,* p. 56, #152.

45. For a brief discussion of the attributes, see Montefiore and Loewe, *Rabbinic Anthology,* 43f.

46. *Midrash Rabbah: Deuteronomy,* trans. J. Rabbinowitz (London: Soncino Press, 1939), 30; compare Hans Bietenhard, *Midrash Tanhuma B,* Band 1, Judaica et Christiana 5 (Bern: Peter Lang, 1980), 413.

47. *The Talmud,* trans. H. Freedman (London: Soncino Press, 1935), Sanhedrin, 2:764.

48. *The Midrash on Psalms,* trans. William G. Braude (New Haven, Conn.: Yale University Press, 1959), 2.280.

49. *Pesikta Rabbati,* trans. William G. Braude (New Haven, Conn.: Yale University Press, 1968), 2.778.

50. By Frederick W. Faber, 1854.

51. John Calvin, *Commentaries on the Four Last Books of Moses Arranged in the Form of a Harmony* (Grand Rapids: Wm. B. Eerdmans Publishing Co., 1950) 3:341.

52. See the brief survey by Lester J. Kuyper, "The Repentance of God," *RefRev* 18.4 (1965): 3–16.

53. Barth, *Church Dogmatics,* Vol. II: *Doctrine of God,* 1.498. Also, "The special act of God in this new work [after the Fall] consists further in the fact that in these dealings God does not disdain to enter into a kind of partnership with man" (with reference to Genesis 18 and 32; Luke 18:1ff.). In the same work, 1.507.

54. Barth, *Church Dogmatics,* Vol. III: *Doctrine of Creation,* 3.285.

55. Cf. Gustaf Aulén, *Christus Victor: An Historical Study of the Three Main Types of the Idea of Atonement* (New York: Macmillan & Co., 1951); D. M. Baillie, *God Was in Christ: An Essay on Incarnation and Atonement* (New York: Charles Scribners' Sons, 1955).

56. Dietrich Bonhoeffer, *The Cost of Discipleship,* rev. and unabridged ed. (New York: Macmillan Co., 1963), 45, 47.

INDEX OF SCRIPTURE AND OTHER ANCIENT LITERATURE

INDEX OF AUTHORS